High White Notes

The Rise and Fall
of Gonzo Journalism

by David S. Wills

Beatdom Books

Also by the Author

About the Beat Generation
Scientologist! William S. Burroughs and the
'Weird Cult' (2013)
World Citizen: Allen Ginsberg as Traveller (2019)

Other Works
The Dog Farm (2011)
6 Stories (2014)
Crossing India the Hard Way (2018)
Grammar for IELTS Writing (2018)

Published by Beatdom Books

View the publisher's website:
www.beatdom.com

Printed in the United Kingdom
First Print Edition
ISBN 978-0-9934099-8-1

Contents

Introduction

Hunter S. Thompson was one of the most original writers of the twentieth century, producing several books and articles so shockingly different from anything that came before them that he came to inhabit his own literary genre: Gonzo. In an era of rampant experimentation, his innovations – including a deliberately disorienting fusion of fact and fiction – quickly became trademarks. In works like *Hell's Angels*, "The Kentucky Derby is Decadent and Depraved," *Fear and Loathing in Las Vegas*, and *Fear and Loathing on the Campaign Trail '72*, he introduced and honed a style so completely unique that anyone attempting to muscle in on it immediately looked like a thief.

But what made his work unique and, more to the point, what created a mind capable of inventing such groundbreaking stories? Many years ago, I noticed that you could pick almost any paragraph from anywhere in Thompson's career and immediately know it was written by him. Yes, there are the obvious elements—the truth/fiction conflation, uncommon word like "atavistic," odd capitalization, unrepentant drug use, over-blown descriptions, violent comedy—but this was all somewhat superficial, and early on in his career there were many more restrained articles, free of the "drugs and madness" that became his trademark with the publication of his most famous book, *Fear and Loathing in Las Vegas*. When the drugs and madness were scraped away, what remained was the work of a writer with an incredible grasp of language.

This was the genesis of *High White Notes*, a book that aims to explain the development of Hunter S. Thompson's literary style. The title, of course, comes from F. Scott Fitzgerald. Thompson was a lifelong fan and often referred to this quote. His interpretation of it was that "high white notes" are brief flashes of brilliance, usually sentences or paragraphs in a longer work that possess a peculiar and enchanting musicality. He sought these moments throughout his career and found them often during his most productive years. The famed "wave passage" from

Fear and Loathing in Las Vegas and the "Edge" section of *Hell's Angels* are prime examples.

This book will explore Thompson's life from his birth in Louisville in 1937 to his suicide in Woody Creek in 2005. It will chart the development of his writing style from his childhood, asking what could possibly have set a mischievous little boy on a course for global literary notoriety. It will look at his literary inspirations, from Jack London to Ernest Hemingway, from Joseph Conrad to John Dos Passos, from Samuel Taylor Coleridge to Norman Mailer, Tom Wolfe, and Ken Kesey. Of course, it will also explore his lifelong obsession with emulating Fitzgerald's American masterpiece, *The Great Gatsby*.

Yet this is no hagiography. My original aim may well have been answering the question, "Why was his writing so damned good?" but Thompson was, in life as in work, a complex, troubling, and enigmatic figure. He was a charmer and an abuser; motivated and lazy; an habitual liar in search of the truth. He labored over every word of some articles, yet phoned in subpar efforts for others. His work ranged in quality from among the finest in American literature to efforts so abysmal that it is hard to believe they were even written by a native speaker of the language, never mind a professional writer.

This inconsistency struck me as I re-read his oeuvre. How could the same man have written both *Fear and Loathing in Las Vegas* and *The Curse of Lono*? The latter sounds like a high school student's attempt at imitating the former. *Hell's Angels* is one of the finest non-fiction books of the twentieth century, yet *Kingdom of Fear* and *Hey Rube* are almost unreadably bad.

Thus, *High White Notes* will investigate how Thompson became such a brilliant writer and how he ended up writing utter drivel. This was a difficult task for me. Many years ago, Thompson's works inspired me to become a writer, and so it feels inherently wrong to devote almost half of this rather long book to essentially savaging his work. It was with a tremendous amount of guilt that I gave this book its subtitle: *The Rise and Fall of Gonzo Journalism*. Among Thompson fans, it is near heresy to acknowledge The Fall.

But this book is intended not to denigrate a wonderful writer whose contributions to literature, culture, and even politics were of undeniable importance. Rather, my hope is that this book will cast new light upon his work. For such a famous writer, there has been surprisingly little in the way of serious criticism. There are various biographies, but even the best of these dwell on the Thompson mythology. From his teenage years onwards, he consciously sought to perpetuate falsehoods around his life that built him into a literary legend. Whilst this was a great part of his literature, it ultimately made him into a cartoonish figure who is seldom taken seriously. It has made studying his life and work difficult, for getting at the truth is in some cases impossible. His interviews and letters, whilst endlessly entertaining, simply compound the problem by adding different versions of his innumerable falsehoods.

In this book, I have corrected a number of misconceptions about Thompson's life because in examining his work I had to dig up sources that others had missed. In looking at the interplay of fact and fiction within his work, I naturally uncovered a great many of his exaggerations and fabrications. Again, it is with a measure of guilt that I do this. Many classic stories from his life, which have even been reported as true in the best of his biographies, turned out to have been entirely made up. It is perhaps strange that a book of this nature would include so much biographical detail, but for Thompson life and literature overlapped. Amid the dizzying array of themes in his work, the focus was quite often himself. Even when looking elsewhere, he consciously embodied the things he was writing about in order to better examine them. Gonzo was a one-man genre largely because it always involved, to some extent, Hunter S. Thompson.

For Thompson, there were no clear lines between fiction and non-fiction, and there was no real delineation between his life and his work. It was all blurred and it was all unashamedly chaotic. To go along with his fabrications is fun but it does not allow us to adequately assess his work and whilst he did himself no favors by losing himself in the life of his alter ego, Raoul Duke, he always wished to be seen as a serious writer. It is my hope that by peeling back the layers of fiction and examining the truth, all the while looking at the mechanics of his work, this book will do just that.

It is high time that we put away the childish image of Hunter S. Thompson as the literary clown and acknowledge him as the exceptionally talented author he was, at least during the period up to 1972. Though no one has ever successfully emulated him, countless have tried. His work has been of incalculable significance in American culture and, to some extent, even politics. He was a comedic writer whose books portrayed the absurd so well that perhaps they did him a disservice, but Thompson wished to be viewed alongside other great satirists, including Mark Twain, and certainly should be.

This book, then, humbly aims to be the first to do justice to his work, exploring the entirety of his literary career in search of answers to the questions, "What made him so unique?" "What was Gonzo all about?" and "Why did he lose his literary powers?" It will explore his best-known works, but also a great many of the lesser-known pieces that have slipped between the cracks in Gonzo history, but which offer vital clues to the creation and meaning of Gonzo, and which help us to better understand this most misunderstood of writers. It will be an uncomfortable book for many. Thompson was an unsavory character in some ways. Whilst he often wrote about the idiocy of racism, his own work was guilty of the very thing he critiqued. Whilst he railed against injustice and bullying, he could be unspeakably vicious to the people who loved him. But this book will pull no punches, as they say. It is Hunter S. Thompson, warts and all. It is the both the Rise and the Fall and everything in between.

Acknowledgements

I owe a tremendous debt of gratitude to the biographers who have previously attempted to tackle the difficult subject of Hunter S. Thompson's life. Without these works, my own efforts would not have been possible. William McKeen, Peter Whitmer, Paul Perry, and E. Jean Carroll have made it possible for people like me to build on top of their research and they have my endless thanks. Though McKeen's is the most comprehensive and up to date of them all, each of these texts has a different focus and each has allowed me a better understanding of Thompson's life.

Jann Wenner and Paul Scanlon have also made an invaluable contribution by collecting an oral history of Thompson's life in *Gonzo*. Again, this text was hugely important in establishing certain biographical details. Doug Brinkley and Anita Thompson's efforts in editing collections of letters and interviews has also been of great help to me, for these are incredibly important sources of information.

I also owe a lot to Dr. Rory Patrick Feehan, who was not only helpful in answering questions about Hunter S. Thompson's life and work but is also responsible for running the Totally Gonzo website, which houses some important resources that were cited in this book. Wayne Ewing was also hugely important in answering questions about Thompson's later life and work habits. His documentaries, vlogs, and blogs were also useful in my research. A huge thanks also to Margaret Harrell for her suggestions and corrections, which greatly clarified the publishing process for *Hell's Angels*.

A Note on Sources

Much of Hunter S. Thompson's writing was published in newspapers or magazines first and then the best pieces were republished later in his various collections. He was often edited in order to remove his profanity or references to violence or drug use. Sometimes the editors took out his tangents or cut extraneous backstory. Later, when putting together his collected works, Thompson would often restore the deleted text. In researching this book, I have tried to acquire the original and collected versions of each piece of writing, but this has not always been possible. In most cases, however, I will refer to the text from his own collections because it is what the author intended and therefore more accurately reflects his style and ideas. However, sometimes it was appropriate or necessary to refer to the original published version. This will be noted in the text and also in the note section at the back of the book.

All typos, grammatical errors, and problems with punctuation in the quoted material are copied from the original source.

Part One
1937-1971

The Birth of a Writer

Turn back the pages of history and see the men who have shaped the destiny of the world. Security was never theirs [...] Where would the world be if all men had sought security and not taken risks or gambled with their lives on the chance that, if they won, life would be different and richer?

Hunter S. Thompson, age 17

In studying the work of a great writer, one often finds that even when their breakthrough came suddenly later in life much of what set them on this literary path can still be traced back to their childhood. Perhaps this is an obvious remark. We are all, essentially, products of our environment. Just as our parents' DNA shapes our faces, so too do experiences in our childhood often go a long way toward explaining what we do in our thirties and forties, long after those memories have faded away.

What, then, can be said about the creation of Gonzo journalism? What sort of childhood puts someone on the road to writing a book as hilariously twisted as *Fear and Loathing in Las Vegas*? What is it in the life of a little boy from Louisville that sets him on a course to becoming the countercultural hero of his day—an author better known for his debauched lifestyle than his innovative prose?

As absurd as it may seem, there is much in the childhood of Hunter S. Thompson that, in retrospect, set him on the path to being an outlaw journalist. It was in a quiet, middle-class neighborhood in the American South that a mischievous little boy with a forceful personality began to shape the worldview and personality that would one day propel him into the national consciousness as a

1

writer so unique that he inhabited a one-man literary genre, and whose bizarre imagination and penchant for excess had a profound impact upon American literature, journalism, and politics in the late twentieth century.

Hunter Stockton Thompson was born on July 18, 1937, to Jack and Virginia Thompson of Louisville, Kentucky. Though his hardworking parents were middle-class folk, Hunter came from a long line of rebels, misfits, and outsiders, with various members of his family named Lawless, including his uncle. He had outlaw blood and many of the characteristics that marked him as an adult were there from the very beginning. His first wife, reflecting on conversations with Virginia, once remarked that Hunter had "shot out of the womb angry." Indeed, he was not an easy baby. Young Hunter was rebellious from the get-go and made life difficult for his mother and most of the people around him. Even as a child, he was a nocturne with a resolute determination that the world around him would march to the beat of his drum, and not the other way around. His father, much older than his mother and embarking upon marriage and parenthood for the second time, had little patience for his crying. Virginia took care of him alone—a loving but exhausted mother alone with her irascible, obstinate child.

In interviews with his friends and family, it often seems that people are describing two Hunters. Almost everyone agrees that he was charming, handsome, and kind, but at the same time that he was violent, selfish, and petty. These threads ran through his personality from a very young age and marked him until his death in 2005. He was, in many ways, an enigma, a mess of contradictions. Anyone who knew him well enough and long enough to get past his grizzled exterior found the positives within him, but those were inseparable from the ferocious temper and inexcusable cruelty of which he could sometimes be capable.

Young Hunter was unusually charismatic. The other boys in his neighborhood flocked to him and followed him wherever he went, filled with admiration and a giddy sense of fear. He was handsome, too, with good manners, and so girls liked him. The only ones who did not, it seemed, were parents and teachers. Most of them could see that Hunter meant trouble and they warned their sons and daughters away from him. Still, he was such a magnetic force to these impressionable minds that they would continue to follow him around, and many were hurt as a result. Hunter would steal their toys, get them into trouble with teachers or parents, and was responsible for many a bloodied nose or blackened eye. In school, he barked questions at his teachers in a prematurely deep voice and may have been labeled "Little Hitler" by his principal.[1]

To his friends, Hunter was a barrel of laughs but being around him could also be stressful and exhausting, as his family well knew. He was frequently the center of attention and he commanded the respect and loyalty of his peers, requiring that his friends join in his escapades. These went a little beyond the purview of most pre-teen rebels because Hunter's imagination, even at this age, was bizarre. He loved thinking up wild pranks to pull, and the more complicated they were, the better. These would often involve meticulous planning and the concerted efforts of his loyal friends. His childhood sweetheart characterized him as both "excessive" and "highly experimental"—labels easily applied to much of his best writing as an adult.

Violence and chaos were also parts of his life from a young age. Hunter would stomp around his neighborhood, demanding to know if the other kids were Yankees or Confederates, and he would start fights with those who answered incorrectly. Friends recall him often turning to violence but seldom being caught because of his charm and loquacity. "Lying was the thing he did best," a childhood friend told one of Thompson's biographers. "He did it with total cool and total confidence." He also enjoyed staging battles in the nearby woods, throwing rocks at other children, and attempting to start race wars.

---

1   This quote is from *Kingdom of Fear* and is repeated in *Outlaw Journalist*. Thompson often made up stories that were not true, as we shall see many times throughout this book, and his own biographical accounts should be taken—in his own words—"with about nine grains of salt." [*Gonzo Tapes*] This one, like others, has been repeated often enough that it is taken as true, but may well have been just another attempt at humor, self-mythologizing, or both.

He would gather up his friends, rouse them into a frenzy, and then shoot BB guns and shout racial epithets at the local African American children. His lifelong passion for provoking chaos was very much in place.

At school, Hunter's behavior may have enraged his teachers but it brought him the sort of schoolyard infamy that ensured his popularity. Throughout much of his life, his eccentric attitude and actions set him apart and made him appear so outrageous that others were drawn to him. He was no class clown, but a mixture of bravado and humor made him popular. His former classmates recall him being hilariously funny without ever telling jokes. He was sarcastic and outrageous, and never worried about offending others or getting in trouble with parents and teachers.

For Hunter, the greatest form of entertainment was doing something shocking and watching people's reactions to it. It was even better if he could convince someone else to take all the risk while he just looked on. His lifelong obsession with bullwhips began early and one of his favorite pranks was chasing friends through public places and pretending to whip them half to death. While the very notion of this was amusing to him, it was the horrified faces of onlookers that made it all worthwhile. He also enjoyed forcing other boys to fake seizures in shops and he sometimes dressed up as an old lady just to see people's reaction when they figured out that it was actually him in a costume. In one legendary prank, he arranged a fake kidnapping that even made the newspapers.

When he was not staging elaborate pranks, Thompson was involved in acts of vandalism, some of which were also meticulously planned. One oft-cited example involved using clothespins, rubber bands, and matches to make little firebombs that he would shoot from his bicycle as he cycled around town in fall. He would aim these at the piles of leaves people swept up around their houses, so that they would smolder away for twenty minutes before catching fire, by which time Hunter was far enough away to avoid any blame. His vandalism went on for years, often bringing him in contact with the police. On one occasion, he even set fire to a restaurant called Joe's Diner.

Thompson was suspected of being behind a spate

of very serious incidents perpetrated by a group called "The Wreckers," who claimed responsibility for offenses including flooding churches, destroying athletic trophies, and cutting the sleeves off choir robes. Although Hunter and his friends were never formally charged with the damage, it was widely believed that they were responsible due to the incredibly bizarre nature of the vandalism. While Thompson enjoyed breaking things for the sake of breaking them, he was known for his creative capacity even in acts of destruction. Indeed, looking over the reports in hindsight, his guilt seems rather obvious. The vandals left messages scrawled in black crayon, claiming that they were "not thieves" and professing no reason for their crime other than "excitement," and then called in confessions in the wee hours. The caller, police reported, "did not sound like a juvenile at all." He had a "calm, cultured" and "cocksure" voice and sounded about twenty-five. At several vandalized locations, police found emptied fire extinguishers—another lifelong obsession for Hunter.

It is no surprise, then, that the young Hunter Thompson was often in trouble with the police. In *Kingdom of Fear*, he told the story of being confronted and nearly arrested by the FBI at age nine, after pushing a mailbox in front of a school bus. He claimed that, from this experience, he gained an attitude toward authority that served him well throughout his life—that he could do what he wanted and it was up to others to prove that he was guilty. Whilst possibly apocryphal, this story certainly captured his real attitude toward parents, teachers, and even the police.[2] However, it is not entirely out of the realm of possibility. After all, his first brush with the law had occurred at age eight, when he was taken to a police station after vandalizing a public toilet. In later years, he was arrested for drunk driving, drinking underage, and robbing a gas station.

Whilst Hunter was, by all accounts, a little hellraiser from his first years, it seems as though this rebellious tendency went into overdrive following his father's death. In 1952, when Hunter was just fourteen, his father passed away from a neuromuscular disease called myasthenia gravis, a painful illness that wore him down over several

---

2   The authenticity of this story is discussed in more detail in part two, chapter six.

months and left the family in ruins. Jack Thompson had been a quiet, passive parent who let his wife do most of the work raising their children, but he had exerted a strong influence over Hunter. Although he wasn't much involved in the boy's day-to-day life, he was a strict man and disciplined Hunter whenever necessary, whacking him with a razor strap when the boy got out of line. Hunter loved and respected his father and his troublemaking was somewhat tempered when he was around; however, with Jack gone, he spiraled out of control. His run-ins with the law became more frequent and more serious, his pranks became crueler and more complicated, and he began to terrify his family. According to his brother, he beat his mother and may even have pushed her down a flight of stairs.

By the time Jack Thompson passed away, Hunter had two younger brothers and this placed an incredible burden on Virginia, who was forced to take a job at the library to support the family. Exhausted, depressed, and stressed, she turned to alcohol to cope, and Hunter grew to loathe her for this. His behavior worsened partly as a protest against her absence and alcoholism.

So far, this portrait of the young Hunter Thompson perhaps gives the impression of him as being little more than a vicious child criminal; a reckless, anti-social thug. These certainly were elements of his personality, but he was no lost cause. Hunter was ferociously intelligent, as well as charming, witty, and loyal, and for those reasons many people saw past his bad behavior and felt there was something promising within him.

In addition to pranks, violence, and vandalism, Hunter and his friends were fascinated by literature. This was something his mother had encouraged since he was very young, and Douglas Brinkley, the editor of Thompson's letter collections, remarked that it was this intervention that prevented him from wasting his whole life:

> His mother stayed on top of Hunter and his brothers the best that she could, and it was her bringing books home from the library like *Huck Finn* and *White Fang* and

making her boys read that turned Hunter into a writer. Hunter had a criminal cast to his mind, and he would have become a criminal if not for the literature that his mother infused into their household.

Hunter and his friends would ride around town, starting fires, getting in fights, and raising hell, but then Hunter would say, "Let's go to the library," and his friends would, of course, all follow him. When they arrived at the library, they would quiet down immediately. For several hours, the hyped-up teens would sit and read, the very models of restraint, before heading back out to make more trouble.

At home, Hunter's room was packed with books. All around his bed were stacks of paperbacks two feet high. During elementary school, in addition to Twain and London, he was reading Thucydides for fun and later, after drinking all evening with friends, he would come home and read until three or four in the morning. A classmate who went on to Princeton remarked that Thompson was better read in high school than most people were when they graduated from Ivy League schools. Whether or not that remark was exaggerated, Hunter was undoubtedly a voracious reader with a keen intellect.

It was perhaps natural that his interest in reading morphed into something more. With his ego, his energy, and his wild imagination, it was no surprise that he quickly developed an interest in writing his own stories. At age ten, Hunter Thompson earned his first byline in *The Southern Star*—a mimeographed newspaper he produced with his friends. Although Walter Kaegi, one of his neighborhood buddies, edited the paper, Hunter wrote much of the copy, including a story about "Hunter's gang" provoking a fight with rivals called "The Voits" and an article about Walter's dog vomiting. Stories about the dog featured in subsequent issues of the newspaper, under the illuminating heading, "Dog News." The budding journalist and his friends wrote about their own lives, as well as whatever weird things took their fancy in local or national news, from dead snakes to baseball games to dying gorillas. The newspaper was illustrated with crude cartoons and cost a whopping three cents, with sixty-five to seventy copies printed and sold per issue. Local businesses even paid to advertise in it.

In January 1948, just a few months after *The Southern Star* was first printed, it was featured in the *Louisville Courier-Journal*—an early recognition of Hunter's journalistic and organizational talents. The writer begins:

> A dog gets sick, a little girl goes out on her first date, some kids find a live mouse and take it home in a tin can.
>
> All that is big news in The Southern Star, a newspaper published by a group of I.N. Bloom School pupils for residents of their neighborhood.

The article goes on to marvel over the newspaper's amusing sections devoted to fights and dogs, as well as their more conventional society column, real estate section, and financial pages. It was an incredible experience for the budding young writer.

Looking well into his future, Hunter decided that he wanted to join the elite Athenaeum Literary Association, which dated back to 1824 and was a veritable local institution. Primarily a social club for Louisville's upper-class citizens, it was also an intellectual outlet and published a journal that contained writing by its most talented members. Hunter realized that he must first gain the attention of the Athenaeum's feeder club, Castlewood Athletic, but he was too young, so he pushed to found his own society, The Hawks. His efforts impressed the people at Castlewood and he was extended an invitation in spite of his age. He was two years younger than his friends were when they were asked to join, testament to his charisma and perseverance.

From Castlewood, Hunter graduated to the Athenaeum in 1953 thanks to the recommendation of his English teacher, Harold Teague. In contrast to his struggling family, most of the members of the Athenaeum came from wealth. These people tended to like Hunter. They didn't know what to make of this bad boy from the other side of the tracks, but his outlandish antics lent him an outlaw allure. Every Saturday night, the members would gather in shirts and ties to sit and listen to or discuss works of literature. Each member was expected to produce something to read to the group and, when it was Hunter's turn, he impressed the others with well-written stories. They had viewed him as the "token anti-intellectual" whose presence was entertaining but who was not really one of them, but when he stood in front of them, reading aloud this raucous, impressive work, their opinions changed. It was different to what the other boys had produced but perhaps not surprising to people looking back on the development of Gonzo journalism, for Hunter just wrote about his own life and his antics with friends. It was funny but intelligent and kept his audience roaring with laughter for forty-five minutes.

Hunter's approach to writing at that time already showed some of the hallmarks of his later prose, and it was written in the same sort of late-night, last-minute frenzy. "He became extremely verbal after midnight," his friend, Ralston Steenrod, said. Working to meet a deadline for the Athenaeum journal, *The Spectator*, Hunter partied until the wee hours and then set about writing. He and Steenrod started work at 4:00 a.m., heads spinning from the beer they had consumed, and continued working until morning, producing not just their own work, but finishing other people's stories and editing the journal.

His writing for *The Spectator* articulated his philosophies on life at the time. In an essay called "Security," he rails against those who waste their lives doing what is expected of them rather than setting out on a course of reckless adventure:

> […] think of the tragedy of a man who has sacrificed his freedom on the altar of security, and wishes he could turn back the hands of time. A man is to be pitied who lacked the courage to accept the challenge of freedom and depart from the cushion of security and see life as it is instead of living it second-hand.

"Security" is a passionate argument for living life to its fullest and on one's own terms and argues for the merits of a life of action over one of academia. It is defiantly anti-conformity and likely inspired by Hunter's various outlaw interests at that time, which included Marlon Brando's character in *The Wild One*.[3] His language is grand yet derivative and clichéd, clearly inspired by his voluminous reading in those years.

In another piece of writing, "Open Letter to the Youth of Our Nation," Hunter begins to play with one of his favorite literary techniques: satire. Dripping in sarcasm, it is a preview of the barbed wit that he would hone in years to come:

> Young people of America, awake from your slumber of indolence and harken to the call of the future! Do you realize that you are rapidly becoming a doomed generation?

Not only does he use a word that would mark his future prose ("doomed"), but the very idea of writing a letter under a ludicrous pseudonym ("John J. Righteous-Hypocrite") was a never-ending source of amusement. It was something that he enjoyed as a teenager and an adult, and a device that he found incredibly useful for sending up foolish ideas.

While "Security" was essentially Hunter putting on his best literary voice in order to explain his rebellious attitude, "Open Letter" was closer to his true voice. He was filled with a bitter resentment at the world around him, and this manifested itself in his violent behavior and biting humor. Hunter's family was poor but everywhere he looked were rich people. His friends were rich, his neighbors were rich, the whole country seemed to be getting rich—and Hunter felt he had nothing. His father, inviting comparisons with Willy Loman, had pushed toward the American Dream by buying a modest house in a decent neighborhood, but he had never gotten rich and then he had died relatively young. Hunter began to look to outsiders and rebels as his heroes and, as one friend explained, he would "disparage anything that anyone thought was good." He enjoyed

---

3   Hunter was known by some as Marlon, a reference to his obsession with the actor.

breaking things, hurting people, and using his language to assault the ideas expressed by those around him. It seemed that literature offered him an outlet.

It was around this time that he read one of the books that marked him for life: F. Scott Fitzgerald's *The Great Gatsby*. Hunter loved it for many reasons and he would cite it decades later as his inspiration for *Fear and Loathing in Las Vegas*, but as a young man he no doubt observed the way that the narrator, Nick Carraway, felt living among the ultra-rich folk like Gatsby and the Buchanans. However, while Fitzgerald was content to portray and gently mock these people, Hunter wanted to tear them apart and attack everything that was important to them. Beyond that, he was drawn to Fitzgerald's prose. Among all the stories of Thompson's life, one of the most famous is that he would type out pages of Fitzgerald and Hemingway—something he began in high school.[4] "I just like to get the feel of how it is to write those words," he told Porter Bibb, another of his Louisville friends, when questioned about this odd habit.

Thompson was also reading Ayn Rand's *The Fountainhead* and J.D. Salinger's *The Catcher in the Rye* around this time. The former helped shape his interest in the notion of individuality as superior to collectivism and the latter pushed him further into rebelliousness, as he identified with the misanthropic Holden Caulfield. He found such books relatable as a disaffected and angry young man who felt that the whole world was out to get him, and he gradually began to see literature as a way of expressing his frustrations and the Athenaeum as the perfect vehicle for his fledgling talents. In school, his English teacher recognized his talents as well as his challenging attitudes, summing him up as "brilliant and unpredictable."

As well as writing, Hunter discovered a new method of expressing and recording his thoughts. In his final year of high school, he found a tape recorder at the home of Burton Shelley, another friend. He locked himself in a closet

---

4   This story appears in countless sources, including Thompson's own words. In some places, it is claimed that he typed out whole books, but he almost certainly just picked specific pages and typed these. This is strongly implied in several interviews.

with the machine and a bottle of booze, and talked into the microphone for hours. Rather than simply disappearing into the ether, his drunken wisdom was now recorded for future use. He would play the recording back to himself, then tape over sections, cutting ideas together until he had a bizarre and hilarious record of his wild imagination to play for friends. At five in the morning, he reappeared and people gathered around to listen to his manic outbursts. As with his readings at the Athenaeum, he was beginning to find his voice and a receptive audience.

Hunter was liked by many of the Athenaeum members for his near superhuman tolerance for alcohol. They called him "Dr. Hunto" because of his ability to lecture like an academic after dozens of drinks. His friends have commented that Thompson began drinking whiskey at around thirteen and that by the age of sixteen he was quite possibly an alcoholic, able to drink prodigiously without ever appearing drunk. The Athenaeum was not just a literary society; its members were expected to drink heavily and have fun, and these were things Hunter could do easily. He was accustomed to showing up in school on Monday wearing the same clothes he'd gone out in on Friday, having partied all weekend. Attempts to change his behavior were of course met with resistance. After being arrested one night with Gerald Tyrell, Hunter resolved to drink even more and embarked upon a marathon twenty-six-day binge.

Yet the Athenaeum was a place for young gentlemen, not winos. Hunter's antics were funny and he certainly had a number of followers among the club's ranks, but for many of them he was just too much to handle. His hazing routines for Hell Week were bizarre and often frightening. They showed the sort of ridiculously creative thinking that later marked his very best writing. His mind conjured up things that were so weird that they either shocked you into silence or sent you into raptures of laughter. In one instance, he forced a pledge to beat a rubber frog with a hammer in full view of their whole high school. Steenrod said that Hunter was always trying to "challenge your conventional ideas," and this was a theme that continued through his whole life. In his writing, and also in his daily life, he liked to shock people with ideas and images that they would never otherwise have imagined.

During his final year of school, there were clamors among the Athenaeum members to have Hunter either restrained or ejected from the group. He was bringing their good name into disrepute, leading members astray, and, according to the club president at the time, he had even started beating pledges. But his problems went far beyond being kicked out of a club. He was constantly in trouble with the police and was even arrested on several occasions. In one such instance, he was picked up for vandalism and sent to the Children's Center, where one biographer speculates that he may have witnessed children being sexually abused. In any case, he left with a healthy fear of jail and was determined never to return.

Alas, his lifestyle made this an inevitability. On May 11, 1955, at one o'clock in the morning, Hunter was driving around Cherokee Park with two friends, Samuel J. Stallings and Ralston W. Steenrod. They came upon a car parked near Hogan's Fountain, where Stallings got out and approached the parked vehicle. There were two young couples in the car, and Stallings asked them for a cigarette. He then robbed one of the boys of the eight dollars he was carrying, before grabbing the car keys and throwing them away.

A few hours later, Stallings was arrested for the robbery. He quickly gave up his friends, who were both immediately rounded up by police, and charges were filed. Stallings was eighteen and so he was sent to Domestic Relations Court while Steenrod and Thompson, who were still underage, were charged at Juvenile Court. Stallings was fined fifty dollars for disorderly conduct and armed robbery, as it was suggested that he may have had a gun. The light sentence was due to his father, a prominent local attorney, who theatrically retold the events of that fateful evening to make it seem like the victims were the criminals.

Thompson and Steenrod were charged in Juvenile Court on June 15, 1955. Steenrod was given probation because he had no criminal record, but Judge Jull knew Hunter well and immediately recommended jail. He explained to the defendant, whom the newspapers described as a "tearful high-school senior" that "I feel I've done you an injustice by waiting so long to take a positive step."

After what reporters called "long and emotional pleading by Thompson's mother," as well as calls for leniency from Stallings' father and Thompson's lawyer, the trial continued. Hunter had been arrested several times before and had appeared in court on numerous occasions, so Judge Jull did not want him to get off lightly again. He complained that Thompson always promised to change but never did. It was time to teach the boy a lesson. Stallings' father and the lawyer begged the judge to reconsider and suggested sending Hunter to the Air Force to "make a man out of him," but the judge said he would have to remain in jail until that could be arranged. The clamoring and pleading continued until the judge screamed, "What do you want me to give him, a medal?"

One of the girls from the car that had been robbed shouted from the public viewing area, "But he tried to help us!" Although Thompson was a teenage hell-raiser and had the capacity for bullying behavior, he still had a strong sense of morality. Both couples from the parked car at Hogan's Fountain came to court to argue with the judge over Thompson's sentence. One of the girls explained to a reporter that, after Stallings had approached the vehicle and "terrified" the occupants, Thompson walked over "and calmed things down." They had become friendly with him during the trial and did not want his life ruined by a stint in jail.[5]

It was testament to his charm that he had the victims of his supposed crime in the courtroom, calling for leniency, but it was not enough to dissuade the judge. He explained that the sentence handed down would not be the punishment meted out for one single incident, but instead it was retribution for years of criminal behavior. Thompson, who had long thought of himself as Louisville's own Billy

---

[5]   Interestingly, Thompson later claimed that he had participated in the robbery, often saying that he threatened to rape the two girls. This was most likely an attempt to build his own outlaw legend, and he made many other attempts to obfuscate his own true past. In 1968, he admitted to an editor his interest in such myth-making, telling her the story of his arrest and then writing, "I suggest you embellish the tale as best you can, and pass it along." [HA Letters, p.138]

the Kid, was finally about to face the consequences of his actions. He was sentenced to sixty days in Jefferson County Jail.[6]

Back at school, Stallings and Thompson were both given "indefinite suspension" by Principal Milburn because of their "cumulative records," but Steenrod was allowed to sit his final exam. Because of this, Thompson not only missed his graduation ceremony, but did not even graduate from high school at all. Of course, it is not certain that he would have graduated anyway. He was 241st out of 251 in his class at Male High School and, embarrassingly for a future journalist, he had nearly flunked typing. Perhaps even worse was the fact that he had been ignominiously kicked out of the Athenaeum.

This was hardly a surprise, as Thompson had been publicly berated by the group for his bad behavior, but it was nonetheless a cruel blow. While his friends celebrated one of the most important days of their lives, he languished in his cell, bemoaning the injustice that had brought him there (evidently forgetting the numerous legitimate arrests in his recent past and the fact that he had been on probation when arrested this time). He chastised himself for being so stupid and wrote letters of apology to his mother. In fact, he wrote vast amounts, feeling able to confess everything from behind bars. He was at an all-time low and so he could say anything to anyone without consequences.

He had felt for years that life was stacked against him and that injustice was rife, and here was proof. Stallings had robbed two couples—possibly at gunpoint—and Thompson had been sent to jail for it because he did not

---

6   In some biographies, this is adult jail and in others it is children's jail. This is a good example of Thompson's own mythologizing. In his interviews and writings, Thompson offers differing accounts of the event, his incarceration, and his release. Other sources are equally unreliable. The most authoritative source is William McKeen's biography, *Outlaw Journalist*. Here, he says that Thompson was sent to Jefferson County Jail for sixty days. Porter Bibb, a friend, claimed that he went to Louisville Children's Detention Center for a few days and that Thompson later made up the adult jail part. However, newspaper records suggest that McKeen's version was likely the truth.

have a wealthy, powerful lawyer for a father. Even though Mr. Stallings had defended Hunter, he felt the system was rigged and that he had never stood a chance. The judge's sentence made him extremely bitter and for the rest of his life he maintained a strong dislike for the law and for institutional power. Looking through Thompson's later career, it is not hard to see how his outlook on the world was shaped by that day in court.

By the time Hunter Thompson was sent to jail in 1955, he was seventeen years old and his childhood had come to a sudden but not unexpected end. As we will see in the next chapter, his conviction did not lead to a great repentance and sudden change in attitude. He would carry with him for the rest of his life those attitudes and lessons from his childhood: righteous anger, a strong sense of justice, a fierce intellect, a gift for words, a uniquely creative mind, and a wild sense of humor. These would shape the person he became and the things he wrote for the next fifty years. His rage, his determination to be an outlaw, and his use of writing to attack people and vent his own pent-up feelings were all characteristics that he developed in his first seventeen years and, although he was embarrassed by his jail time, he felt that it was a grave injustice against him rather than the law finally catching up with one of Louisville's most persistent child criminals. He had also picked up models for his personal and literary lives and, as evidenced by the fact that he already kept copies of most of his writing, he had determined that he was going to be a writer.

First, though, he had to contend with the fact that, while all his friends were going off to university to begin the next stage of their lives, he was in jail with no high school diploma and no prospects for a productive or happy future.

Becoming a Journalist

Airman Thompson has consistently written controversial material and leans so strongly to critical editorializing that it was necessary to require that all his writing be thoroughly edited before release.

Colonel William S. Evans

Life is not kind to those who flunk out of high school with long criminal records, and for those whose friends are privileged kids with rich parents and invitations to Ivy League schools, it is a tough pill to swallow to look at the future and see comparatively few options. Hunter Thompson experienced not just the anger of injustice and a sense of shame, but the awful sting of a caged animal. More than most, he was accustomed to freedom. He was obsessed by it. His wild behavior was an expression of this, but one needs only look back to his essay, "Security," from *The Spectator* and his infatuation with *The Fountainhead* to see that he firmly believed in every individual's absolute right to set his own course in life. Yet here he was in jail, told when to eat and when to sleep, locked in a six-by-ten-feet-wide cell. The sense of confinement must have been overwhelming.

Luckily, his sentence was commuted for good behavior. After serving just thirty of his sixty days, Thompson was remanded to the custody of a local businessman called Almond Cook, and soon after he signed up for the US Air Force. There are differing accounts of how this happened. Some biographers say that his early release from jail was conditional upon service to his country, and others suggest that he wrecked a truck after securing a delivery job, then absconded into the military as a way of avoiding retribution.[1] In any case, upon his release he headed to the home of a former teacher and threw bottles through his front windows in the middle of the night, indicating that not much had changed in his attitude. He went back the following evening and did it again. It looked like his life of crime might continue, but thankfully he was soon on a bus to Lackland Air Force Base, near San Antonio, Texas, for military training.

Airman Hunter Thompson arrived at Lackland in the summer of 1955. In an introduction that set the tone for his time in the military, he drunkenly vomited during roll call. Though he had been excited at the prospect of flying jet planes, the Air Force clearly saw that Thompson would not make a good pilot and decided to train him as an electrician—much to his chagrin, for he was afraid of electricity. From Lackland, he was sent to Scott Air Force Base in Illinois, where he spent six months enraging his superiors. At the Pine Top Inn, not far from Scott, he resumed the intensive letter writing that he had begun in jail. Sometimes he was apologetic and admitted to his mother that he had stepped out of line, and other times he wrote friendly, conversational letters about his life. He also vented at times, spewing his anger onto the pages he had laid out on the counter at Pine Top. He used very different styles of writing for these letters and it appears he viewed them as valuable writing practice, taking on the affectations of writers he was reading or had read in the past few years.

Thompson was drunk throughout most of his six months at Scott and sometimes drove down to Louisville to meet up with old friends and party. He was no model airman, but he was good at passing tests and managed to land a better position at Eglin Air Force Base, in Florida. In July 1956, the area around Eglin was vast and beautiful, not yet spoiled by sprawling hotels and condos. It was right on the Gulf, where white sand beaches stretched out east and west as far as the eye could see. It was still wild and pure, and the currents were dangerous. According to a former squadron commander, one or two airmen drowned

---

1   Thompson himself mostly promoted the latter story as it had more theatrical value but contemporary accounts are vague on the actual details.

each week in the deceptively pretty waters. Worse still, for Thompson at least, the nearest women were fifty miles away, in Pensacola.

He continued his correspondence from Florida, beginning to develop a style that would forever mark his writing. His letters are in turn hilarious and scathing, laced with sarcasm and oozing anger. His vocabulary now is more literary than later because he wants to sound like a writer, but throughout all of these letters is his own voice, albeit in an embryonic form. We can see him taking on quirks of style he found in Dos Passos and Fitzgerald, but also making his own weird innovations, with flights of fancy blurring his descriptions of real life. During this period, he began to write outrageous things as though they were true, like having been in a mental institution for five years or getting beaten half to death by a "pack of lesbians." These letters are clear evidence of Thompson working out elements of his writing style that would come to mark his most successful work a decade later. Indeed, in 1990 he claimed that it was in the Air Force that he learned "full-bore lying as a natural way of life," presumably a nod to his increasing tendency to exaggerate in writing.

Thompson's letters show a man regretful for his past failures and disgraces but eager to make himself a success. Much of his correspondence seems written for the purpose of impressing others, whether with his real accomplishments, his wit, his vocabulary, his ability to shock, or his madcap imagination. He lets others know that he is going to be a great writer someday—the "new F.S Fitzgerald"—but still he was embarrassed about his lack of education and signed up for night classes at Florida State University twice a week. He took literature and psychology courses and made the long drive to Tallahassee in the evenings. Here, Thompson also completed his high school credits and managed to obtain his diploma a year after all his Male classmates.

It was at the base education office, inquiring about courses, that Thompson fell upon one of the great strokes of luck in his life. While complaining about life at Eglin, he was interrupted by the education officer. "Know anything about sports?" the man asked. Thompson told the man that he knew plenty about sports. When the officer went on to say that there was a vacancy on the base newspaper, Thompson thought quickly and said he had been editor of his high school newspaper and had done some writing for *The Courier-Journal*. Thankfully, no one checked either of these claims because the last time Thompson's name had been in that newspaper it was for being thrown in jail.[2] Instead of being laughed at or questioned, he was given the position of sports editor at the Eglin base newspaper, *The Command Courier*.

It was hardly surprising that Thompson had not adapted well to military life. Throughout his teenage years, he had developed a fiercely independent worldview and was determined to lead life on his own terms. One friend had remarked that, "If he didn't want to do something, he simply would not, and no one was going to change his mind." In the military, he had to wake up early, follow orders, and generally submit to authority. Thompson claimed that he shirked orders and acted like a rebel, but Douglas Brinkley reckons that he did in fact obey orders most of the time. Still, he was relieved when he landed the position of sports editor. It bestowed upon him a massive amount of much-needed freedom. He was no longer required to get up at the same time as his fellow airmen and he was not required to follow many orders. He could make his own schedule and leave the base whenever he wanted. He told a friend that it was "the best deal I could possibly have in the Air Force" and he was absolutely right.

On August 30, 1956, he was appointed sports editor and a week later his first article appeared. After just one month at Eglin, the name "Hunter Thompson" was in the base newspaper.[3] He was nineteen years old and already a professional writer. Of course, Thompson knew little about editing or writing newspapers but, thanks to his voluminous reading as a child and teen, he had some skill with words. He had been raised on a diet of good books

---

2   He had also been the subject of a pair of stories in 1953, involving him losing and then finding a fifty-dollar bill.

3   Although Thompson used his full name with middle initial for almost all of his written work, the first seventeen instalments of his column were simply credited to "Thompson." After this, it was "Hunter Thompson." On page two, he was listed as "A 2/C Hunter Thompson… Sports Editor."

and thus had an ear for the rhythm of a piece of writing. Like his hero, F. Scott Fitzgerald, his grasp of punctuation was intuitive rather than formal, guiding the rhythm of his prose rather than logically demarcating clauses. He was able to hammer out articles and, over time, he worked out some of the flaws in his grammar and spelling.

Although he worked hard at his craft, producing prose that possessed a musical quality was something that came naturally to him. He did not necessarily know *why* a particular piece of writing sounded a certain way, but he wanted to know. Paul Scanlon, a managing editor at *Rolling Stone*, called Thompson an "ongoing student of correct grammar and syntax." Even in his final years he was still learning. His friend and editor, Shelby Sadler, taught him about scansion, which he intuitively understood despite any real education:

> He was so appreciative of learning all the little technical details. He knew how to write beautifully, but he didn't know why it was beautiful. He liked being taught the names of things—that this is an anapest, this is a spondee, this is a dactyl trisyllable. We worked on dactyl trisyllables for a week so he could learn what he was doing in his sentences to make them faster or slower, to put the poetry in and know what it was.

Thompson's first appearance in *The Command Courier* came on September 6. Every week for almost a year, he turned in various reports on sporting events in addition to a column that he titled "The Spectator," no doubt as a thumb in the eye of his old Atheneum friends. From the offset, both the reports and the column were intended to liven up the dull reality of sports reporting. Thompson threw in a wide array of creative and often violent verbs: "blasted," "walloped," "stomped," "exploded," "romped." His language was hilariously descriptive, claiming that some teams were "bent on revenge" and describing "the resounding thud of mammoth bodies colliding" during a description of a football game. He threw in plenty of adjectives and adverbs, calling people "speed merchants" and "bone-crushers," and in the first months seemed preoccupied with stuffing his articles with alliteration: "rock-ribbed," "perennially powerful," "Orgy of Oranges." In places, it is even amusingly sexual. One article about football features the words "orgy," "climaxed," "penetrated," and "thrust."

He covered various kinds of sports but football was clearly his favorite. His descriptions were intended to make every game seem like a battle to the death, and on several occasions informed his readers that even the wildest of Hollywood movies could not have matched the drama of the game he had watched. Still, he was perhaps at his best when deadpanning reports of wrestling professional wrestling matches. In one, he describes a man called "the Great Malenko" beating a referee. He "went berserk," Thompson writes. Malenko "ripped and slammed" the poor official until he had to be hospitalized. Throughout his year on the paper, he returned to pro wrestling in the same fashion, clearly reveling in the violence he otherwise had to insert into less exciting sports.

In the first weeks, Thompson's sports page changed a great deal. His column grew in length and the layout became far more complicated as he worked to arrange stories, scoreboards, photographs, headings, and cartoons. He also took the chance to insert more comedy into his writing, subtly slipping witticisms or imagined scenes into the text. Describing one team that had suffered a humiliating defeat, he says:

> It is rumored that several [of the players] have found it impossible to attend football games due to the fact that they have to be carried from the stadium, screaming deleriously [sic], when the score shows signs of becoming lop-sided.

In that same column, he claims that the Tennessee Volunteers would "literally eat Alabama alive." He could be incredibly sarcastic, too. In talking about the Oklahoma Sooners, who had been on a long winning streak, Thompson observed that the teams they had beaten had barely presented a challenge, writing "Let us doff our caps to the all-conquering Sooners of Oklahoma [whose previous opponents] would be hard-pressed to eke out a win over Paralysis U."

It was obvious that, in those first weeks and months, Thompson was gaining confidence in his abilities and pushing the limits of what he could get away with. At the end of one article, he appended a fake name and address – Lloyd Botch of North Dakota – to whom readers could send hate mail if they disagreed with his views. He was beginning to play with elements that would become part of his writing style in the future, including that fake name and even a fake editor's note that began one of his columns. He clearly inserted at least a few made-up quotes, including an obvious joke about golf that he passed off as a real news story. In one column, he interviewed his high school buddy, Porter Bibb, but failed to mention that they were friends or that Bibb came from Louisville. Bibb was presented as another sportswriter and used to make the case that Louisville's basketball team was one of the finest in the land. Indeed, many of Thompson's columns seemed preoccupied with presenting his hometown teams in an oddly favorable light.

His column was a place where he had relative freedom and could say what he wanted to his readers. However, by the end of October, he had gone a little too far. He took the opportunity to launch a scathing attack on the Air Force Personnel Service, but later was forced to issue an explanation that functioned as a half apology. This was notably his least coherent column, suggesting that he had done the bare minimum to make up for his earlier transgression, beginning an explanation of the difficulties faced by the Personnel Service but then not bothering to complete it. After that, his columns were more careful, with criticism lying between the lines.

Thompson once said that his column had "the most thought and literary polish" of anything in *The Courier* and that it was valuable practice in achieving his new goal of "becoming a successful young author." In its first months, he certainly seemed to be using "The Spectator" to flex his literary muscles. The writing here is playful and creative. There are early indications of the direction of his later writing style in columns titled "Voodoo In The Orange

Bowl" and even the occasional line that he has obviously labored over, such as this from his final column before the 1956 Christmas holidays: "with one last puzzled glance at our withered paper Christmas wreath, baking in the hot sun as it hangs lifelessly…" One can easily see here his interest in stuffing at many adjectives and adverbs into a sentence as possible, though with more restraint than his reports on football games.

If Thompson had known little about writing for newspapers, then he knew even less about editing them. To a friend, he wrote:

> Now you know, and I know, that it's ridiculous to even speak of any experience on my part, as far as layout or page arrangement goes. In short, we both know I'm no more qualified for a post like this than I am for the presidency of a theological seminary; but here is one major fact that makes it possible for me to hold this job: the people who hired me didn't bother to check any too closely on my journalistic background.

Eager not to let this opportunity pass, he borrowed a journalism textbook from the library and studied up on newspaper terminology. He told his aunt that he enjoyed the process of learning, even though it was obviously a lot of hard work. He was able to quickly learn enough that no one questioned his alleged editorial experience, and he invested enough time in writing and editing that there really wasn't much more anyone could have expected from him. On some days, he worked from 7:00 a.m. to 4:00 a.m. In addition to this, he pored over national newspapers and learned a great deal from them in terms of style and content. His cliché-ridden sentences began to evolve into tighter, straighter copy that read well and contained fewer errors.

At Eglin, he began reading Grantland Rice as an introduction to sports writing. Thompson admired Rice, whose genius, he believed, stemmed from the fact that he "carried a pocket thesaurus" to avoid repetition. This meant that his verbs and adjectives were descriptive, powerful, and original. A little over a decade later, Thompson looked back on this period and claimed that he could write like Rice, one of the great American sportswriters, and indeed his prose from Florida does seem a little derivative of Rice at times.

He was also reading H.L. Mencken, who had passed away earlier that year. Mencken's caustic attitude and satirical journalism greatly influenced Thompson, who said of his work on "the Spectator," "If H.L. Mencken could do it, then so can I." He certainly adopted a similar voice, slipping witty put-downs into his reporting and ridiculing his subjects.[4] Mencken was fearless in his writing and wielded his literary skill as a weapon. He once summed up his most cherished beliefs: "The two main ideas that run through all of my writing, whether it be literary criticism or political polemic are these: I am strongly in favor of liberty and I hate fraud." If the part about literary criticism were omitted, these could very well have been the words of Hunter Thompson. In a great many of his letters, he spoke passionately for the rights of the individual and against injustice.

It turned out that he had an eye for layout as well as words. In fact, decades later he claimed that his primary concern in regard to preparing his sports section was having everything look good on the page, with the right balance of words and pictures. "I was a layout freak for a long time," he said. This led him to purchase a camera and begin shooting his own photos for the paper, not so much to add to the story but to balance the text on the page. He became a talented photographer and was able to sell some of his photos alongside his articles during his early years as a journalist. Looking at his sports page over the first weeks and months of his time as editor, it is easy to see how quickly he learned as the page grew in complexity and sophistication.

---

4   One repeated victim of his editorializing was Elvis Presley, whom Thompson apparently loathed. Whilst discussing a football game, he pointed out that "if Elvis Presly can learn to make a fortune by yowling and bellowing into a microphone – then nothing is impossible." [*Command Courier*, October 25 1956, p.8]

Before he arrived at *The Command Courier*, the newspaper was about as interesting as one might have expected. Originally known as *The Eglin Eagle* (a name it returned to shortly after Airman Thompson left the Air Force), the headlines announced intolerably dull articles about safety and responsibility. A rare attempt at humor resulted in a story about a soldier named Wilfred J. Army, with the headline, "Army is Doing All Right in the Army Here." After Thompson's arrival, however, they just cried out to be read. One notable effort was the aforementioned "Voodoo In The Orange Bowl."[5] Accustomed to "just the facts" accounts of dull sporting contests, airmen on base were now subjected to an entertaining and fanciful form of prose:

> We can easily imagine the tearful scene which must have transpired at the fateful meeting of the Orange Bowl committee last Sunday. Vividly, we can see the members of the committee slumped in their chairs, expression of glazed agony on their chalk-white faces, listening to the chairman announcing to the press that Colorado will be invited to the Orange Bowl on New Year's Day.
>
> [...] At this point we can see one of the more high-strung members of the group leaping to his feet and, with a wild cry, jamming a huge pin through the midsection of one of a group of battered voodoo dolls lying in the middle of the table. The thoroughly pierced dolls, representing members of the ruling body of the Big Seven conference, had doubtlessly absorbed brutal torture up to that point, at the hands of the long-suffering Orange Bowl committee members.
>
> [...] And so, with a fearful look in the

---

5   Thompson referred to voodoo quite often in his writing, including a 1960 article called "A Louisvillian in Voodoo Country." He once—jokingly—wrote to a friend, saying, "I'm a well-known voodoo writer." [*Proud Highway*, p.218]

direction of Miami, the Big Seven broke the news that it would henceforth be impossible for the same team to represent the conference two years in a row. Then they huddled together and waited for the storm to break over their heads. And break it did – the Orange Bowl howled like a disinherited son; but to no avail.

Already, Thompson is inviting his readers to use their imaginations. He is presenting things that have not happened in any factual sense, but which he feels are representative of what happened. His readers encounter ideas that are engaging, shocking, and thought-provoking and come to an understanding of the real issue that is aligned with Thompson's own interpretations of it. This was an important discovery. Later, his writing would subtly prompt readers to join him on weird flights of fancy until finally he was famous enough that everyone knew it was heavily fictionalized, but that somehow it captured a sort of truth that might otherwise have been impossible to convey.

It was in these columns that Thompson first embarked upon the odd balancing act between truth and fiction that marked most of his work. Whilst he was happy to give articles exciting titles that promised "voodoo" and then amplify any sort of action to a fever pitch in order to satisfy his readers' thirst for bloody sports violence, he was also keen to bring truth to the masses—especially if that truth was meant to remain a secret. He was not afraid to attack the Air Force—or indeed even the newspaper staff—in his column, and this righteous anger translated quickly into a feeling of power:

> The *Courier* hit the streets early this morning, and all hell broke loose within an hour's time. The subject for all this angry yowling was a clever little column called "The Spectator"; composed each week by your friendly doctor [...] All day, I've been grinning at wild-eyed majors, captains, sergeants, lieutenants and last but not least,

several Colonels [...] From now on, when I
appear somewhere with a pencil in my hand
and a gleam in my eye, people will quiver
in their shoes and sweat freely. This is the
finest thing that could have happened. I
now have thousands of readers [...] crazed
with power and hell bent for the worst kind
of infamy.

In contrast with his later efforts in journalism,
Thompson's "Spectator" column saw him very much as
an observer rather than a participant in stories and, whilst
his ego was clearly on display from day one, it was not
as overwhelming as it would later become. He offered
opinions (particularly on sports betting) and made jokes,
but did not usually write about his own exploits. Indeed,
his byline started simply as "By Thompson" and later
morphed into "By Hunter Thompson." In the column
itself, he switched between the first person singular and
plural, and occasionally the third person, referring to
himself as "the Spectator."

In February 1957, Thompson moved briefly towards
a mode of reporting more akin to his later Gonzo efforts.
He recounts the tale of going to the dog-racing track with
his friend, Gene Espeland. The amusing story is obviously
exaggerated and told in such a way as to engage the reader
rather than serve any informative purpose. Every few
sentences, he delivers a punchline of sorts, sometimes
through clearly made-up quotes by other people. Espeland
is portrayed as a hapless buffoon, much like Thompson
would later portray himself, and it is ultimately a story of
comical failure as the two men place doomed bets and lose
their money on foolish theories of gambling.

The following month, Espeland was the subject of
another of Thompson's columns, this time placing him
in a very different light. Here, he is an heroic figure in a
rather more flattering piece of writing. Again, Thompson
shows a clear interest in showing off his literary abilities,
announcing Espeland's departure from Eglin as though it
were a scene in a novel:

A thick blanket of grey fog hung over the

West Gate early Saturday morning, as a green and white Chevrolet rolled past the little gatehouse for the last time. With a characteristic grin, the driver muttered a silent farewell to this Gulf Coast paradise and pointed the nose of the little car down the highway to Pensacola.

It was Gene "The Montana Ace" Espeland, his discharge papers on the seat beside him, heading back to Westby, Montana. Within a week or so, he'll be back at Northern Montana State College, taking up where he left off four years ago.

One of the most colorful athletes ever to wear an Eglin uniform, Gene was what they would call in France "un type." Here, we call them "characters," but they tend to be the same the world over, and without them, life would be intolerably dull.

Espeland later explained to E. Jean Carroll that Thompson's approach to writing even then was fanciful. "He made up the craziest stories! A little something would happen in the gym and he'd make up a great big story." He remembered Thompson as a relatively normal guy but noted: "The only time he got strange was when he started writing."

Shortly after this column was published, Thompson discovered that Bart Starr, a talented quarterback who had been enlisted at Eglin, was being discharged from the military so that he could sign with the Green Bay Packers. His military service had barely begun. Thompson was horrified at the injustice and years later he would claim that he broke into an office, stole the player's discharge papers, and snuck them onto the front page of the paper at the last minute. In truth, however, he wrote a very short article under the heading, "FLASH: Bart Starr To Be Discharged," which arguably contained within its subtext a hint that there was some collusion between Starr, the brass, and the Packers. He switches tenses in order to suggest that Starr's discharge is guaranteed in spite of him not yet having been hospitalized, thereby highlighting the corruption, and ends

29

with a note that neither Starr nor the Athletic Director could be reached for comment, hinting that they were unwilling to answer the journalist's probing questions.

Despite the displeasure that his writing sometimes gave his superiors, Thompson was not often censored during his first six months at Eglin. Aside from a few disciplinary problems unrelated to his writing, he fit in rather well. Thompson and the Air Force were hardly a match made in heaven, but they provided him an opportunity he would never otherwise have gotten, and in return Eglin Air Force Base got its finest ever sportswriter. His writing was lively and sounded more like letters to friends than the stale reportage to which *The Courier*'s readers were used to, giving readers something to look forward to.[6]

Still, although he appreciated the freedom and opportunities presented by his position at *The Command Courier*, Thompson was earning just one hundred and thirty dollars a month. In February 1957, six months after he started as sports editor of *The Courier*, he began moonlighting for the nearby Fort Walton Beach *Playground News*. His salary was double what he earned on base and he was given another weekly column—"The World of Sports." Although Thompson later claimed that he was violating the Air Force's no-moonlighting rule, his former colleagues contend that he had been given permission.

Whether he had permission or not, at the *Playground News* he wrote under various pseudonyms, including Thorne Stockton and Cuubley Cohn. The latter was a reference, of course, to Samuel Taylor Coleridge's poem, "Kubla Khan."[7] The poem refers to the "stately pleasure

---

6   During this period, his letters also changed a great deal. He began writing them in very different styles, clearly using these opportunities as challenges to do something new and different with his words.

7   Thompson was a life-long fan of Coleridge's poetry. His work is littered with references to this and other poems. It is quite possible that it was "Kubla Khan" that prompted his frequent use of the word "savage," as he often picked up words from such sources and incorporated them into his own vocabulary. This word began to appear in his sports reporting around this time, too, with phrases like "savage tackling." "Thorne" may also be reference to Thorne Smith, another hard-drinking humorist.

dome" of "Xanadu," which was the name that Thompson had given to a small beach shack he took over not far from the base. It had been abandoned when he found it, and he turned it into a party shack. He was dating various women at the time, and one even lived with him there for several weeks.

Thompson's life now seemed almost perfect. By Air Force standards he had a tremendous amount of freedom, and between his two jobs he was earning money and honing his skills as a writer. He spent his time flying around the country with sports teams and writing about some of America's greatest sporting heroes. In his articles, which were read by countless enlisted men across the vast Air Force base, he could largely say what he wanted about the world of sports as a means of exercising his ego and espousing his personal philosophies. In several of his later columns, he eloquently spoke out against proposed bans on dangerous sports, echoing his Athenaeum essay, "Security." "Competition is a basic natural instinct," he wrote, "and it will find its own outlets." He was clearly speaking out against censorship and strict rules, both of which were by June 1957 beginning to weigh on him as his time in the Air Force drew to an end.

For all he was improving as a writer, he learned at least one bad habit in Florida that would cause him untold trouble in his future career. By the middle of 1957, he was partying instead of watching the games he was meant to cover. Whether out of boredom or a deeper compulsion for self-sabotage, that year he began reporting based upon secondhand reports rather than what he actually saw. When he was asked to write about a banquet for the Eglin NCO newsletter, he got outrageously drunk and missed the event. This made the perfect fodder for his letters, in which the incorrigible mythmaker excelled at placing himself at the center of the story, not as an heroic figure but rather as an amusing loser. Dr. Rory Patrick Feehan identified this as the beginning of his interest in the non-story and a key development in the use of his own persona in storytelling, saying that his writing about the event

> reveals not only Thompson's flair for hyperbole, but also his tendency to cast

himself in a self-depreciating light in order to endear himself to his audience. He had a penchant for mythologizing his own deeds, but never in such a way as to assume the role of all-conquering hero. Thompson was more comfortable in the role of the serial failure, the miscreant outsider that defiantly thumbs his nose to the establishment, hopelessly blundering from one adventure to the next, yet surviving to tell the tale. As a blueprint for the Hunter Figure, this representation turned his failures and misdeeds into stories that absolved himself of any blame, and that presented his actions in a somewhat honourable light, essentially as an outsider battling against the establishment.

When he did write about sports, he tended to err on the side of the dramatic, as we saw with his "Voodoo at the Orange Bowl" story. He was also using his language to make everything sound incredibly grand. Whilst his writing was usually quite conversational, he could veer off into the sort of phrases that made his ideas sound like epic sagas, a matter of life and death:

> The pages of history are dotted with the stories of "fallen idols" whose exploits lent a little luster and richness to the colorless lives of the millions who cheered them on, paid them homage, and then condemned them to oblivion as a new champion mounted the throne.
>
> The story of Joe Louis is an old one; the story of a star which has outlived its light; the soaring meteor which failed to explode in mid-air at the height of its climb, but plummeted down to the earth with the millions who, moments before, had stared wide-eyed at its beauty.
>
> The world likes to look up at its stars. A meteor which falls out of the skies not

> only is dead when it hits, but digs its own
> grave by the force of its fall. Just as the
> crowd stares curiously at a fallen meteor and
> then wanders off, the crowd is beginning to
> thin around Joe Louis. He stands painfully
> bewildered in a world which he never took
> the trouble to understand. The applause of
> the worshipping thousands has died into
> the whispering of the curious few. The end
> is inevitable.

In passages like this, it is clear Thompson is interested in making his column as grand and literary as possible, tying sports to greater issues. Some biographers have claimed that his writing in the *Courier* tackled politics and other issues, but this is not true. However, in paragraphs like the above, it is obvious that he was eager to go beyond descriptions of boxers bashing each other's skulls and instead explore human nature.

But he was not always interested in such grandiose language. As time went by, his columns became more discursive and conversational, not unlike his letters. Perhaps this was due to his growing confidence. By the time the 1957 Kentucky Derby had come around, he was keen to throw himself into the text a little, albeit as "the Spectator" rather than "Hunter Thompson." He is simultaneously the knowledgeable hometown boy and a comically inept gambler. His reporting is not so much about horses and racing as it is about a man whose "preposterous predictions" have been wrong for eight consecutive years. He is self-effacing but self-obsessed, as he would be in future.

During his time in Florida, Thompson developed a lot as a writer. After just a year and a half, he had gone from having never covered sports to being a sports editor with two columns and thousands of readers. He could write letter-like articles that contained personal adventures, add fake editors' notes to explain his stories, turn insignificant tales into vast sagas, fuse sports and philosophy, and even play with the ridiculous language of the grandiose sports epic, in which every contest seems like an historic battle.

While these were skills and traits that would serve

Thompson well in his later career, they began to irritate his bosses at Eglin and eventually he was reined in by his superiors, making the final months of his service frustrating. When he attacked a TV and radio personality in his column, his bosses told him that he had crossed a line and that he needed to tone down his writing. This put him into a relatively poor mood and he began drinking more and getting himself in trouble.

Thompson realized that his days in the Air Force were rapidly drawing to an end and so, after hearing that a friend had managed to get a discharge, he set about masterminding his own escape. He didn't have to do much to achieve it, though. In late August, Colonel Evans of the Office of Information Services wrote a recommendation that Thompson be discharged from the Air Force and, until that point, forbidden to write for the base paper. Thompson was clearly delighted with this development and used the report frequently in future, perhaps as a way of proving that the *real* Hunter Thompson was as wild and crazed as the fictional version of himself he so often put across in his stories. It didn't hurt that it showed him to be talented and intelligent:

> Airman Thompson possesses outstanding talent in writing. He has imagination, good use of English, and can express his thoughts in a manner that makes interesting reading. […] However, in spite of frequent counseling with explanation of the reasons for the conservative policy on an AF base newspaper, Airman Thompson has consistently written controversial material and leans so strongly to critical editorializing that it was necessary to require that all his writing be thoroughly edited before release. […] In summary, this Airman, although talented, will not be guided by policy or personal advice and guidance. Sometimes his rebel and superior attitude seems to rub off on other airmen staff members. He has little consideration for military bearing or dress and seems to

dislike the service and want out as soon as possible.

In October, he met with an officer to discuss his future. Although he was proud of his service and had at times contemplated continuing in the Air Force in pursuit of even better opportunities, he explained his life philosophy, which largely revolved around a fierce sense of individuality and an outright rejection of military values. It was clear to both parties that Thompson was not going to adopt the Air Force mindset and it was a waste of effort for them to try changing him.

On November 8, Thompson was given his honorable discharge. He had done his service and was free to move on with a host of newly acquired skills. Perhaps he was grateful in his own way for the experiences and opportunities he had gained, but before he left he had one final trick to play. He wrote an absurd story about a riot on base that resulted in planes being burned and women being raped. He left this for the editor of *The Command Courier* and submitted it to the AP and UPI news wires. To friends around the country, he sent a press release that he wrote upon leaving Eglin. In it, Thompson describes himself drunkenly fleeing the base with his discharge papers in hand, hurling a bottle into the gatehouse before speeding off in his beat-up old car. He goes on:

> An immediate search was begun for Hunter S. Thompson, one-time sports editor of the base newspaper and well-known "morale problem." Thompson was known to have a sometimes over-powering affinity for wine and was described by a recent arrival in the base sanatorium as "just the type of bastard who would do a thing like that."
>
> An apparently uncontrollable iconoclast, Thompson was discharged today after one of the most hectic and unusual Air Force careers in recent history. According to Captain Munnington Thurd, who was relieved of his duties as base classification officer yesterday and

admitted to the neuropsychological section of the base hospital, Thompson was "totally unclassifiable" and "one of the most savage and unnatural airmen I've ever come up against."

In fact, Thompson did ride joyously off base with his papers in hand, armed with a year's experience as a sports editor and an ego more commensurate with several decades' work on a major newspaper. As can be seen from his hilarious press release, he was already very adept at spinning a fictionalized version of his own life story and eager to portray himself as a rebel. His use of the letter written by his colonel in various books shows that he was proud of his time in the Air Force and prouder still of the fact that he was too much of a rebel to be tamed by it. He was indeed an "uncontrollable iconoclast," but where does such a person go next in search of success and fulfillment as a writer?

Attempts at Fiction

As things stand now, I am going to be a writer. I'm not sure that I'm going to be a good one or even a self-supporting one, but until the dark thumb of fate presses me to the dust and says, "You are nothing," I will be a writer.
                                                    Hunter S. Thompson

Although it may not have counted for much on a résumé, by 1957 Hunter S. Thompson had some real experience as a writer and editor. In just two years, he had gone from being in jail and having no high school diploma to being a rather talented young sportswriter who now knew that he could make money by putting words on paper. He had found something that he could do well and which he sometimes enjoyed, but most importantly he had recognized that writing would engage him for the rest of his life:

> Events of the past two years have virtually decreed that I shall wrestle with the literary muse for the rest of my days. And so, having tasted the poverty of one end of the scale, I have no choice but to direct my energies toward the acquisition of fame and fortune. Frankly, I have no taste for either poverty or honest labor, so writing is the only recourse left me.

Throughout his whole life, Thompson offered contradictory views on writing, saying often that he hated it and only did it for money, but elsewhere that it was an unrivaled sort of high. He revered great writers and included himself in their ranks, yet also talked of it as a foul vocation for people too degenerate to do anything else. This applied to journalism more than fiction and it applied doubly to sports writing. As we saw in chapter two, Thompson's lucky break came in sports writing and he managed to develop a talent for it quite quickly. But although he would return to this much later in his life and look back fondly on the birth of his career, it was initially fiction that attracted him and, in his mind, a real writer was one who wrote novels.

Before becoming a great novelist, though, Thompson knew he had to cut his teeth as a reporter. It was, after all, far more likely to pay his bills, and it couldn't be that bad of a career move if Hemingway had done it. The older writer had once said that he learned everything he needed to know about writing from *The Kansas City Star* style sheet, a claim that provided Thompson with some hope. But how would he proceed? How does a young and inexperienced writer with a violent personality and a penchant for drunken shenanigans make himself a success? It was time to search for a job tolerable enough to keep him employed for more than a year.

From Eglin, Thompson drove home to Louisville, where he posted an advert in *Editor and Publisher*, declaring himself available for work. He was offered a job in Indiana as a wire editor and accepted, but then a better offer came along so he reneged. He packed his car and headed for a town with a rather misleading name.

On December 9, 1957, Thompson began work as the sports editor of *The Jersey Shore Herald*. He had not realized that Jersey Shore, Pennsylvania, was four hundred miles inland, and he was filled with an immediate sense of regret. Instead of waking up next to the sounds of the Atlantic Ocean, he found himself living in a drab apartment, working for a dull newspaper in "an abandoned coal town" where he could hardly even find a beer to drink.

For work, he wrote articles on professional wrestling matches, in which he more or less fabricated all the details. Instead of writing a basic report of who won and lost, he described the fights as though they were real, just as he had done at Eglin. Gene McGarr recalled Thompson's "Dadaist" style of sports writing:

He wrote everything deadly serious. These things—like pro wrestling matches—were supposed to be laughed at to a certain extent. Everybody knows how it's phony as baloney, but he played it straight. Well, not exactly straight; he was writing things like "People were carried out of the ring with broken backs," "his neck was broken in three places"—stuff like that. Apparently nobody really cared whether it was true or not.

Though this may have seemed the perfect outlet for his deadpan comedic style, Thompson was unhappy from the get-go. "It was a nightmare, really," he said several decades later, when looking back on his time in Jersey Shore. There was only one person in town with whom he could have a pleasant conversation: a man who Thompson said "was an academic, kind of an unemployable poet who might lecture once or twice at the local community college."[1]

As the story goes, when the old poet asked Thompson if he would like to meet his daughter, Hunter jumped at the chance. There were, he noted, no other women "in this barren town [...] between the ages of fifteen and fifty." The poet was less than impressed with Thompson's car—a '49 Chevy called "the Huntermobile"—and offered to lend them his own vehicle for a date. At around two o'clock in the morning, while driving drunkenly through a tremendous rainstorm, Thompson got the car stuck in a bog. He walked to a nearby farm and woke the angry farmer, who pulled them out with his tractor. In the process of doing so, he managed to rip off the car's front bumper and the driver-side door.

Thompson supposedly returned the mangled vehicle and grabbed his own car, but the next day, Christmas Eve, at about seven in the morning, he was looking over the

---

1   Hunter was drawn to these people and usually impressed them with his intelligence and his honest determination to become a great writer. At Eglin, he had also been taken under the wing of a literary old gent, Lieutenant Colonel Frank Campbell, who was willing to talk about great writers and who encouraged Thompson's aspirations.

day's wire stories when he heard an ominous sound. It was the poet bringing his ruined car to work. The whole office witnessed the spectacle of the poor old man limping the water-logged wreck into the car park, with a door hanging by a hinge and the front bumper dragging along the concrete, creating an ungodly noise. Thompson ran out the door, zipped back to his apartment, threw a few things in the Huntermobile, and took off for New York without collecting his paycheck. He had lasted only two weeks.

This is how Thompson told the story and how his biographers have faithfully recounted it. Ten years after his stint in Jersey Shore, however, Thompson's first book was published and a columnist at *The Jersey Shore Express* decided to look into his brief time in Pennsylvania. He noted that Hunter had been unimpressed with the town from the moment of his arrival and, while clearly talented, had been a difficult young man to get along with. Robert J. Evans, the newspaper's editor while Thompson worked there, recalled:

> The boy was ambitious and, I'd say, overly exuberant about his work. He wanted to make a New York Times sports page of our sports page. He was interested in the "national scene" and we were too, to an extent. But I told him the people who bought our paper were just as much interested in the local high school sports – and other high schools in the area – as they were in the University of Oregon's basketball team. […]
>
> Unfortunately, for the two weeks he was there – and that's how long he was with us – he never could seem to understand this concept. Worse than that, it seemed quite odd to me that he would have almost heated arguments with the editor – in this case me – over policy. Our difference of opinion came to a boil over the local vs. national question.

He goes on to explain that Thompson was busy

editing the sports page when the news came in that one of his colleagues had bowled a perfect game. Thompson was not interested in writing about bowling or even including a story that someone else had written, but the editor was adamant that the man's name went in the paper. When the editor changed the sports page to include the perfect game, Thompson was enraged. "I am the sports editor!" he shouted. Evans replied, "Not any more. You're fired."

Through his whole life, Thompson repeated the story about "the poet" and his destroyed car because it was a romantic, dramatic, and ultimately amusing tale that was not easily forgotten. It spoke volumes for his public persona but the real story is just as enlightening. It depicts a young writer and editor with strong opinions about the quality of journalism and the courage to fight for what he thinks is right, rather than a carried-away Casanova who narrowly avoided being bogged down in a Pennsylvania backwater.

Thompson jumped in his car and headed for New York, torn between going to college and getting a job. Ever since being jailed and missing graduation, he had felt embarrassed about his lack of education and clearly attempted to compensate for it with boasts about other accomplishments. He knew that he was intelligent and, even though he did not particularly aspire to a life in academia, he felt that he was smart enough to have gone to a good college. Before his escape to New York, he had asked Air Force officers to send letters to Vanderbilt in Nashville on his behalf, but now that he was on his way to the Big Apple, the logical choice was Columbia. At the same time, he was eager to get ahead in his career as a writer. Despite having only a year's experience prior to his two weeks in Jersey Shore, he first sent an application to *The New York Times*, and then began applying to other newspapers, working his way down the list in terms of prestige. What he lacked in experience, he more than made up for in ambition.

Living with friends in New York, Thompson drank often but continued to make efforts to improve his skill and knowledge as a writer. He would buy newspapers each day and then pick out the best sports stories. He would read them and analyze the way that the writer had put his information on the page, then try to rewrite and improve them by applying his own style. While other young writers attempted to produce standard newspaper copy, Thompson was determined as always to be different.

In mid-January 1958, another golden opportunity presented itself. In the midst of his drunken carousing around New York, Hunter was offered the job of copyboy at *Time* magazine. It may have paid just two hundred dollars a month (much less than his Jersey Shore job) and it lacked the prestige of being a sports editor, but it was an incredible opportunity with, in Thompson's own words, "infinite possibilities." Even though it was entry-level, it was a much sought-after position, and some of the other copyboys were graduates of Ivy League schools. *Time* was also willing to pay half of his tuition if Thompson wanted to take classes at Columbia: the perfect opportunity for this ambitious young writer. He signed up for two classes— "Literary Style & Structure" and "Short Story Writing"— and for two and a half days each week he was a university student. This, he said, "should give me a boost along the road to becoming another D. H. Lawrence."

Being a student allowed him access to the Columbia University library, where he was able to continue his literary education through borrowing classic and contemporary novels. He became obsessed with Sherwood Anderson's *Wineburg, Ohio* and Faulkner's *The Sound and the Fury*. However, undoubtedly the most important book that Thompson read in New York was J.P. Donleavy's *The Ginger Man*. This novel helped permanently shape his writing and, to some extent, his lifestyle.

Published by the infamous Olympia Press in 1955, *The Ginger Man* was immediately banned in Ireland and the United States for obscenity. It tells the story of Sebastian Dangerfield, an American living in Dublin. He cares only for drinking and womanizing and leaves a terrible path of destruction wherever he goes. His actions throughout the book are utterly deplorable as he lies habitually and ruins people's lives. In one scene, he beats his wife and then tries to kill his child. The book is, however, comical. Dangerfield is such an unrepentant, monstrous character that his story can be viewed as a sort of very dark comedy. The sudden, unexpected violence of it is intended to be shocking to the point of humor, much like Thompson's later work.

The novel is also bizarre in how it is written. Donleavy frequently alternates between first- and third-person narrative perspective, sometimes changing twice within a single paragraph. Half of the sentences in the book lack a subject and many lack a verb, leaving fragments of ideas that function instead as a chaotic collage, where nothing is certain. There is a section largely comprised of sentences with just a subject and then the present participle and occasionally an object. It is littered with little rhymes, too, that break up the streams of violent action, amusing dialogue, and bizarre internal monologues that may or may not reflect conversations that have drunkenly taken place. The result is a creative, obscene, but ultimately poetic prose whose sudden jumps in thought or image are disorienting in order to reflect the confused mind of a man gone mad in an absurd modern society. His shocking actions lead the reader to ruminate upon how a rush of social and technological developments have impacted mid-twentieth century morality.

One of Hunter's closest friends in New York, Paul Semonin, thought that he looked to Sebastian Dangerfield as a sort of hero. It wasn't just the dark humor and inventiveness of the book that Thompson admired, but rather Dangerfield was the ultimate rebel—a mixture of Howard Roark and Holden Caulfield, but amped up to another level entirely. His actions throughout the story are utterly abhorrent and indefensible, yet somehow Thompson saw this as a sign of his independence and an admirable, steadfast refusal to bow to social conventions. It really "jelled his personality," Semonin remarked. It is also likely that Thompson saw some of himself in Dangerfield's remark, "Once I heard [his teachers] telling very rich boys to stay away from me because I wasn't a good influence."

It may seem strange to claim that Thompson's personality was "jelled" by a book, particularly because he was already very much a rebellious, aggressive character, but perhaps it is not obvious how much effort he put into being a rebel. Thompson's heroes as a child and teen had been famous outlaws and bad boys—both real and fictional—and he had consciously sought to emulate them. When he was at Eglin, he had even read Colin Wilson's

1956 philosophical inquiry into the rebel mind, *The Outsider*. After reading the book, which discussed writers and artists like Kafka, Nietzsche, Hesse, Sartre, Camus, van Gogh, and Hemingway, he recommended it to his mother. He explained that he had intended to write her a long letter about his own life, but that "after reading that book, you may come closer to understanding just what lies ahead for your Hunter-named son." Rory Patrick Feehan said, "[*The Outsider*] really was the key influence when he was that age, because it allowed him to kind of see how this persona, this type of figure, this type of character, kind of transcended all popular forms of creative expression. It's a part of our mythology and it resonated with Hunter and he saw 'Well, maybe there's a way into literature here where I can actually write about myself or even create myself in that mold.'"

Still, nothing topped Sebastian Dangerfield when it came to rebel role models. Thompson quoted and talked about *The Ginger Man* obsessively throughout his time in New York, emphasizing the parts that highlighted Dangerfield's resistance to being domesticated and forced to go against his natural instincts. It is quite easy to look through his books and see his protagonists as very much inspired by Donleavy's degenerate creation, and there was also some influence upon his use of language.[2] This was permission for Thompson to pursue characters who were unrepentant losers, totally lost in their own intoxication and eager to lead their lives on their terms even if it meant seriously hurting others. Yet, oddly enough, in both Donleavy's and Thompson's books, this would work as a form of brutal humor rather than tragedy.

It was in New York, too, that Thompson first encountered the work of Jack Kerouac and William S. Burroughs. Quite fittingly, it was at a bohemian party that he learned about Beat literature. According to Semonin, a woman called Diti Walker introduced them to Kerouac's books, jazz music, marijuana, and orgone accumulators—an obsession of William S. Burroughs that was going through a fad in hip circles in the late fifties. Thompson read *On the Road*, which had just come out a year earlier, and was impressed. His opinion of Kerouac changed often

---

2   *The Ginger Man* features some typical Hunter Thompson language like "lousy bastard" and "pervert" and "crazy."

throughout his life and he aimed plenty of vicious criticism at the Beat author, but he was initially very inspired by *On the Road*. Even in his later years, he said that Kerouac "remains one of my heroes" and acknowledged that "he was a great influence on me [...] Jack was an artist in every way."

Although at times he talked about Kerouac as writing "sloppy" prose and being overly sentimental (as well as being "a mystic boob with intellectual myopia"), Thompson recognized the genius in *On the Road*. Kerouac had made himself an era-defining icon through his creation of spontaneous prose and his radical confessionalism, depicting his peers in such a way that he inspired generations to come. He wrote about things that you could not write about before, capturing the spirit of his generation by recording his friends' lives and presenting a personal mythology. For these reasons and more, Thompson viewed him as a trailblazer, later explaining:

> Jack Kerouac influenced me quite a bit as a writer ... in the Arab sense that the enemy of my enemy was my friend. Kerouac taught me that you could get away with writing about drugs and get published [...] I wasn't trying to write like him, but I could see that I could get published like him and make the breakthrough, break through the Eastern establishment ice.

It is hard to look at Thompson's writing and see any real influence from Kerouac in terms of language, whereas it is quite easy to note elements of Fitzgerald, Hemingway, Donleavy, and others. Yet Thompson credited Kerouac as being a pioneer of "personal journalism," something he would pursue himself a little later. By this, he meant the innovation of throwing oneself into a story and recording it in a book that lay somewhere between fact and fiction, essentially allowing the author to improvise upon reality.

Thompson was also fascinated by Burroughs' *Naked Lunch*, although he did not read it until a little later as it was released only in 1959. Like *The Ginger Man*, it was published by Olympia Press and subsequently banned in various places, but Thompson's underground savvy meant that he was able to get copies of both. Although he seldom mentioned Burroughs, one can easily see the influence of *Naked Lunch* in his writing from the sixties onwards. Burroughs' disturbing "routines" morphed into Thompson's oddball flights of fancy—sudden rushes of violent but hilarious action and dialogue that went very much over the heads of most readers. He adored the vile, disturbing elements in Burroughs' work and sought to use these in his own writing. From Burroughs, he learned that nothing was too shocking to be included in literature.

In New York, Thompson continued drinking and pranking with his new buddies. Although he had grown up a lot since his arrest in Louisville, he had the same general attitude to life and the same destructive tendencies ran through his synapses. He caused noise and chaos and damage just for the hell of it, and sometimes did things like dump a bag of lime in a packed bar just to see the horrified reactions of people who thought they were being poisoned. In the carnage of his pranks, which often resulted in damage and suffering, it is not hard to see elements of Sebastian Dangerfield. Thompson's attitude was nearly nihilistic at times. He did things just to watch the results, to which he was generally quite detached. After the bag of lime prank, he was beaten badly in the street, but for Thompson this was all just part of the story—a crazy night out that he could boast about in writing or to his friends.

The story, of course, was *his life*. For a long time, Thompson had been writing friends and family about his wild adventures. Sometimes, what he wrote was a relatively faithful account of a real event, but more often than not it was exaggerated or fabricated. Whenever it was real, he was generally stirring up action to amuse himself and, more than likely, to provide material for his writing. From Kerouac, he knew it was possible to write about one's own life and celebrate the debauched, downtrodden elements. From Donleavy and Burroughs, he knew that you could say and do profoundly shocking things as a form of humor. From Hemingway came stoicism and from Fitzgerald came hedonism, and from each came elements of language that will be explored in later chapters.

In preparation for writing his great novel, Thompson continued reading and rereading *The Great Gatsby*. He sat down with the book for hours at a time, underneath a banner inscribed with Fitzgerald's dictum, "Action is Character," making copious notes as he examined each paragraph for clues to its genius.[3] He ended up with a three-page outline of the novel that he intended to use as a model for his own work. He kept this document in his pocket for years.

Although Thompson had been lucky to get his job at *Time*, he did not act as though he was pleased to be there. Before long, he felt he was better than this job. In those innocent days, the company put on a free bar for its employees every Friday evening and Thompson of course took advantage of this, drinking until he became belligerent. He insulted his superiors—and, for a copyboy, that meant almost everyone in the company.

He was annoyed with having to do such low-level work after his experience at *The Command Courier* and pleaded with his bosses to make him a reporter. They pointed out that he would have to work his way up slowly, filling any number of intermediary positions while continually proving his worth to the company. This was not something Hunter Thompson was cut out for. He began dragging his feet, refusing to do tasks he didn't like, and eventually was fired. He had almost made it to the one-year mark.

In his job at *Time*, he lasted longer than he had at Columbia. Although Thompson had been eager to gain an education, he struggled in the classroom. He could not sit still and pay attention with the other students, and he felt that the things he was being taught were not important. After just a few months, he dropped out. It was clear now that, whether in school or university, he was not cut out for conventional education. He learned through the books he read, the people he talked to, and the things he wrote.

For Thompson, it was the last that was the most important. Writing was his way of making sense of the

---

3   This was one of Fitzgerald's final notes while writing *The Last Tycoon*, his unfinished novel. Whitmer records it as "Action Makes Character" but it is not clear whether the mistake was his or Thompson's. [p.177]

world. His volumes of letters are entertaining not just because of his acerbic wit and madcap adventures, but because he wrote long, sprawling descriptions of everything in his life, or about events in the wider world, in order to understand them. Much later, he reflected:

> [...] writing is a kind of therapy. One of the few ways I can almost be certain I'll understand something is by sitting down and writing about it. Because by forcing yourself to write about it and putting it down in words, you can't avoid having to come to grips with it. You might be wrong, but you have to think about it very intensely to write about it. So I use writing as a learning tool.

Throughout 1958, he continued writing letters to friends and lovers and strangers, and in them he was indeed trying to figure himself out and learn about life. He talked about major world issues but also devoted long screeds to working out why he did the awful things he did, dubbing instances of his bad behavior "Thompsonisms." Although he could be boastful and overly macho, he possessed a bitterly self-deprecating wit. Throughout these letters, his voice morphed into his own unique style. The sarcasm, the anger, and the wisdom started to take shape and form the early signs of Gonzo prose.

He also wrote to various publishers and editors around the country (as well as in Canada) looking for employment. He was still at *Time* but deeply dissatisfied with the job and eager to move on to bigger things. In his letters, he was not afraid to explain his faults and viciously assault the wider profession of journalism, even when inquiring about work. To the editors of *The Vancouver Sun*, he admitted that he had poor references, cited his unwillingness to mingle with average people, and then claimed to have "developed a healthy contempt for journalism as a profession." He continued:

> As far as I'm concerned, it's a damned shame that a field as potentially dynamic

and vital as journalism should be overrun with dullards, bums, and hacks, hagridden with myopia, apathy, and complacence, and generally stuck in a bog of stagnant mediocrity. If this is what you're trying to get the *Sun* away from, then I think I'd like to work for you.

Perhaps he was sincere in attempting to win over the editors with his uncompromising honesty, but more likely he was just using this letter as an opportunity to articulate his own views on the profession of which he was now a part. He was also exercising his vocabulary a little, as we can see from that quote.[4] How many negative nouns and adjectives can one cram into a short description? For Hunter Thompson, that was a welcome challenge, particularly when his sights were set on the American press.

He also fired off angry missives about the state of journalism in response to what he perceived as foolish editorials. However, he would still attach a "PS" at the end, offering his services in case anyone had been impressed by his approach. His views on journalism were something that he felt compelled to talk about not only when he had joined the ranks of experienced and celebrated journalists, but when he was an inexperienced nobody. In December 1958, he wrote:

In a nutshell, journalism has lost its primary selling points, the very things which used to make salary a secondary factor. The best American journalists have invariably been respected, envied, and often emulated. Traditionally, they've not only held onto their individuality but capitalized on it, not only maintained their self-respect but commanded the respect of others. [...]
How many newspapers are there in the country today that actually command

---

4   Thompson often become obsessed with certain words ("doomed," "atavistic," etc.) and in 1958 his preferred word was "myopia" or "myopic." He included this in many of his letters from that year.

the respect of anyone who knows a
damned thing about journalism? I'd have a
hard time counting ten. And there's where
we come to the pith and substance of the
whole problem: since journalism has lost its
ability to command respect as a profession,
it has sunk to the level of "just another
job." Where salary used to be secondary it
is now primary.

When it came time to move on from New York, Thompson
was more than prepared. He had been sending off letters
to prospective employers for at least six months, and if he
hadn't insisted upon filling them with bizarre confessions
and angry tirades about the state of the industry, he may
have actually been able to move on earlier.

He did manage to procure an interview with the
copywriting department of an advertising agency. This
was not his ideal profession, but if Fitzgerald had done it,
then so could he. Rather than giving them his own résumé,
Thompson wrote what he thought would be the perfect
one for the job. He gave himself Ivy League qualifications,
publications in *The New York Times* and *The Washington Post*,
and wrote up a reference letter from a senator. When his
amazed interviewer asked, "Have you ever tried your hand
at fiction?" Thompson could contain himself no more and
pointed out that the whole résumé was a work of fiction.
Needless to say, he did not get the job, but the comedic
value made it all worthwhile.

Eventually, Thompson found a job at the *Middletown
Daily Record* in upstate New York. The *Record* was one
of a new breed of newspapers in the United States and
had earned positive reviews from *Time* and others for its
innovations in printing technology. Thompson was excited
to join this new venture and also happy to escape the city
and get into the Catskills.

In what was becoming a well-established pattern, he
quickly found himself in trouble when he started at the
Record. Whilst dining across the street from the newspaper
offices, he sent back a plate of lasagna that he considered
inedible. After sending back the second plate, he was
confronted by the chef, who allegedly attacked him with

a wooden fork. This turned into a fistfight, and the next day he was reprimanded by his editor. As it turned out, the chef was one of the paper's major advertisers, and Hunter was forced to apologize.

He continued to work, doing the usual small-town stories. The editor, Al Romm, observed that Thompson was a talented writer but that he needed a lot more skill to compensate for his weirdness, telling him: "At this point in your career, your idiosyncrasies outweigh your talents." Few of his friends and editors would surely have disagreed with that assessment.

His bosses were willing to put up with idiosyncrasies like his refusal to wear shoes in the office, but when Thompson kicked in a vending machine, it was the final straw. This story, which quickly became part of the Hunter Thompson legend, is another fine example of his self-mythologizing. He would often refer to this incident when talking about his past as a writer, and he even claimed that he was fired from other jobs for the same thing.[5] In reality, after it took his money and did not give him what he paid for, he kicked the office candy machine hard enough for the bottom to fall out. He tried to fix it and assumed no one had noticed, but later his co-workers stole hundreds of candy bars. Thompson had only taken the two that he had paid for, but he was promptly fired and the stolen snacks were deducted from his paycheck.

His letters in search of employment again erred on the aggressive, bizarre, or just overly honest. Considering that he went to lengths to fake his experience and references, he was also shockingly upfront about being "difficult to get along with" and having "no patience with phonies, dolts, or obnoxious incompetents." Unfortunately, none of the editors to whom he wrote were impressed by his Holden Caulfield impression and he was soon so broke that he was forced to move from his apartment into a shack in the woods with no electricity.

Perhaps on some level, Thompson willed this to happen. According to Gene McGarr, one of his friends from New York, "he wanted very much to be a great fiction writer. He felt stuck in journalism" and Bob Bone, a

5 He sometimes claimed that he was fired from *Time* for kicking a Coca-Cola machine.

photographer-reporter friend at the *Herald* suggested that getting fired was "exactly what he wanted." In any case, he certainly recognized it as a pivotal moment in his life. In all of his writing experience so far, he had made bad choices and pushed the people around him to their breaking points. Now it was time to prove himself. No more stories about basketball games or town councils. It was time to finally write a novel.

At this point in his life, despite his self-destructive eccentricities, Thompson was absolutely resolute in his determination to become a successful writer. He grew out his beard in an impersonation of Ernest Hemingway, whose picture he had hanging over his desk, and took countless self-portraits to document the starving artist at work.[6] Living in a cabin in the woods was perfect as it further built his legend. He was not just living the typical life of a young reporter; he was, he felt, a *real writer*. He began writing short stories under the pseudonym Aldous Miller-Mencken, a reference to three other writers that he greatly admired: Aldous Huxley, Henry Miller, and H.L. Mencken. According to Rory Patrick Feehan, Thompson's obsession with image and persona convinced him that being a great writer was about more than just writing:

> It was important to Thompson to look the part, but not just on a surface level; to be a writer, he felt he had to become a writerly persona, so the persona was part of his own creative process more than it was an attempt to project the same image to everyone else.

His walls were covered in rejection slips for his short stories, including "The Cotton Candy Heart" and "The Almost Working Artist." Thompson carefully compared his progress to Hemingway's and Fitzgerald's, telling a girlfriend that Hemingway had sent out stories for eight years before achieving success and Fitzgerald had gotten

---

6   He even had a dog called Pilar, which was also a reference to Hemingway. Pilar was his second wife's nickname, a character in *For Whom the Bell Tolls*, and the name of Hemingway's beloved boat.

one hundred and twenty-two rejection slips before his breakthrough. He calculated that he was six years behind Hemingway but that it would take him just eight weeks to catch up with Fitzgerald. He wrote the occasional angry letter in response to rejections or not hearing anything from a publisher, but overall he remained positive. "I just happen to think I'm going to make it," he said. "I couldn't afford to think otherwise."

He reached out to other authors, even sending a letter to William Faulkner, explaining that "the only choice of the writer in today's 'outer' world is to starve to death as honorably and defiantly as possible." He received no reply but remained undeterred. He was soon spending his every waking hour laboring over the book that he thought would bring him fame and fortune.

The first real attempt Thompson made at writing a novel was *Prince Jellyfish*. In this book, he offers a thinly disguised version of himself as protagonist and places the book in a familiar New York setting. "I'm using the narrator-participant technique—à la *Gatsby*," he told a friend, before admitting the book was "something of a cross between *Gatsby* and *On the Road*." In fact, it sounds more like *The Ginger Man* than either of the other two texts. The protagonist is very similar to Sebastian Dangerfield in as much as he is a drunk and a liar. The book is filled with random outbursts of violence and onomatopoeia (like "Swaacckkk!"), and Thompson has clearly made an effort to use non-standard punctuation and grammar. Just like Donleavy, he occasionally dropped the subject of a sentence and put the verb into its present participle form: "Now moving through traffic, through tunnels of neon sparkling in the rain."

It has elements of the different writers Thompson was reading at the time in it but what is missing is his own voice, and Thompson was well aware of that. While there are definite elements of style cribbed from *The Ginger Man* and *Gatsby*, much of the prose is painfully conventional and there are many weaknesses, including rather corny attempts at profound or romantic ideas, such as this: "her eyes seemed (to Kemp) like dark coals of smoldering sensuality." The story follows a man called Welburn Kemp and introduces people who share names with

Thompson's real-life friends.[7] Kemp is very much modeled upon Thompson, only with his hometown of Louisville swapped for Nashville and his time as a sports editor in the Air Force replaced with the same job but in the Army. He has not made the same mistakes as Thompson, avoiding jail and going to college, and when he is offered a lowly copyboy job, Kemp refuses to demean himself. Thompson enjoyed fictionalizing his own life in order to make himself comically inept, and Kemp definitely falls into this category, but there also seems to be an element of fantasy here, wherein Thompson is attempting to undo the mistakes of his own life.

Some elements of Thompson's later prose attempts feature here, including savage attacks on the state of journalism. Kemp, just like the real Hunter Thompson, is outspoken on the matter of "writing tripe," and the stinging put-down he lays on the industry is an early glimpse of a writing style that would later make him famous:

> The great American press was a babbling joke – an empire built on gossip and clichés – a final resting place for rumor-mongers and pompous boobs.

It is not just the fact that he is attacking the press that makes this very much part of Thompson's development as a writer. The language that he uses is important. The three parts of this sentence—one clause and two fragments, joined by non-standard punctuation—can almost be viewed as three lines in a poetic stanza. The first uses sarcasm coupled with a vivid image to make a coherent statement. It is presented with a specific, strong adjective and a vague noun. It could stand alone, but Thompson liked to double down on his images, layering detail upon detail like Donleavy. The second is a metaphor that links two ideas ("gossip and clichés") and the third invokes the idea of death before connecting another two odd

---

7   Welburn and Kemp were also names belonging to old Louisville friends—Welburn Brown and Kenny Kemp. Both of them had been involved in serious car crashes, with Welburn Brown dying and Kenny Kemp falling into a coma. Thompson admired them both. [*Fear and Loathing*, p.43]

phrases ("rumor-mongers and pompous boobs"). The resulting rhythm—or the musicality of the language—is quintessentially that of Hunter Thompson.

The prose even offers tangents into wild flights of fancy—another key feature of his writing that would gain national attention a decade later:

> Kemp saw himself standing off a whole pack of lunatics with whips, cutting them down like weeds with the back of his hand... nimble and quick, silent and deadly... "Attack *me*, will you!" ... whap! ... slash! ... screams of pain... now standing above a ring of prostrate bodies, wiping the blood off the back of his hand with a handkerchief.

Passages like this show the influence of Donleavy and Joseph Conrad, another of Thompson's favorite writers, more clearly than later attempts, when his own voice somewhat obscured this linguistic template. In particular, the odd combination of exclamation marks and ellipses is something Conrad used extensively in *The Nigger of the Narcissus*:

> The wood split, cracked, gave way. Belfast plunged in head and shoulders and groped viciously. "I've got 'im! Got 'im," he shouted. "Oh! There!... He's gone; I've got 'im!... Pull at my legs!... Pull!" Wamibo hooted unceasingly.

He is capable of handling action and scenes related to action but his prose is mostly awkward. He has captured some interesting moments and copied down some reasonable dialogue, but for the most part the narrative lacks any flair. He is trying hard to bring music to the language, and he succeeds occasionally, but mostly it falls flat. Ultimately, *Prince Jellyfish* is a classic example of a young author's first attempt at a novel—autobiographical, derivative, and sophomoric. It reads more like a series of flashbacks to his past than a coherent novel and is interesting only as a steppingstone on the path Thompson took to literary success.

He worked at *Prince Jellyfish* throughout 1959 but was forced to flee his shack in the woods. He had failed to sell any of his short stories, had lost his unemployment benefits, and could not pay rent or even make insurance payments. Hopelessly impoverished, he had to move in with friends in nearby Otisville. They gave him a room, fed him, and even provided him a little money for cigarettes and beer. Thompson continued hammering away at his typewriter, working mostly at night. When he felt he had become an imposition, he moved back to his mother's house in Louisville to finish his novel. It was an exhausting and depressing process, made worse by a form rejection letter from Viking Press that earned them a trademark vicious reply. Hunter S. Thompson always made time for an angry letter.

Although Faulkner never wrote back, another of his favorite writers, William Styron, did. He was kind enough to share the name of his agent, to whom Thompson then sent *Prince Jellyfish*. This gave him more confidence and spurred him on with his work, but the book was sent around America's finest publishers, earning nothing but rejection letters. Still, he believed that it would sell if he could just rework it in the right way, and so he kept on writing, relying on others to support him through his artistic poverty.

Thompson moved around from friend to friend, occupying their sofas and spare bedrooms as he desperately worked on his novel and short stories. He was becoming more confident and, in both his letters and his articles, he was starting to develop a voice that—while betraying a few major literary influences—was more or less his own. In June, he submitted a piece of satire to *The Village Voice* that previewed his future Gonzo efforts. In a mock press release, he lampoons the Supreme Court's 1959 judgment in the case of Barenblatt vs the United States. Rather than discussing the facts of the case, Thompson creates a character called Benito Kampf, an obvious reference to Benito Mussolini and Adolf Hitler, and then depicts a Nazi takeover of the country, replete with public punishments using the bastinado.[8]

Alas, the life of a starving artist proved debilitating, and so he plotted a return to journalism and at least the occasional paycheck. He began pestering half the editors of the Western Hemisphere with arrogant letters, daring them to reply, and soon he encountered one whose wit was a match for his own.

---

8   Thompson frequently referenced this form of torture throughout his work.

The Great Puerto Rican Novel

His ambition, from the moment that he and I
started dealing with each other, was to be a novelist.
Clifford Ridley

In March 1959, Hunter Thompson wrote to one of his girlfriends to say that he was sick of the cold. He had been living through an icy mountain winter in his tiny shack in the woods and, with just three dollars to his name, he had not been able to afford to keep it heated all of the time. "I have resolved," he wrote, "finally and without reservation, that I shall never again spend a winter further north than Atlanta, Georgia." Inspired by his current reading, Bradley Smith's 1957 *Escape to the West Indies*, he went on to muse over the possibility of traveling abroad, naming a few warm, sunny places, including the Caribbean.

By summer, the temperature had risen but Thompson was no less eager to take off for far-flung locales. His good friend from the *Middletown Daily Record*, Bob Bone, had moved to San Juan in Puerto Rico, where he was working for the newly founded *San Juan Star*. He invited Thompson down, suggesting that it would be a good place to work on a novel. Thompson fired off a rambling letter that was in turns humble and boastful, offering his services as a sports editor. He explained that money was not hugely important when weighed against the quality of a job. "There are some jobs I wouldn't do for two thousand a month," he said, "and others I'd be happy to do for two hundred." He went on to talk about his views on journalism:

> At the moment I am unemployed, and will continue to be until I locate a worthwhile job. Having been a sportswriter, sports

59

editor, editorial trainee, and reporter—in that order—I have given up on American journalism. The decline of the American press has long been obvious, and my time is too valuable to waste in an effort to supply the "man in the street" with his daily quota of clichés, gossip, and erotic tripe. There is another concept of journalism, which you may or may not be familiar with. It's engraved on a bronze plaque on the southeast corner of the Times Tower in New York City.

Most people did not know what to do with the letters they received from Thompson. He concentrated his full literary powers on writing witty, sarcastic, or angry diatribes that were in turns clever and shocking. Even his job applications were full of casual insults and bizarre tirades. It must have been a surprise for him to receive a letter from William Kennedy, managing editor of *The Star* and future Pulitzer Prize winner, that answered him in kind. Although he rejected the job application "somewhat brutally," according to Thompson, his letter was witty and derided the sender's pretentions. Rather than just telling him that he was not hired, Kennedy pulled Thompson's letter apart and mocked it, informing the young writer that he was not as "off beat" as he thought and then ending: "If we ever get a candy machine and need someone to kick it in, we'll get in touch with you."

Thompson, who had received a rejection letter from Viking that same day, was furious and fired back a vicious response, declaring: "your interpretation of my letter was beautifully typical of the cretin-intellect responsible for the dry-rot of the american press." For weeks, Thompson fantasized about flying to Puerto Rico and beating the living hell out of Kennedy, but then another letter arrived from the Caribbean. Unfazed by Thompson's irrational anger, Kennedy continued to jest: "We are still ready to regard you, as you regard yourself, as the bushy-tailed expert on the dry rot of American journalism." He offered Thompson the chance to write a scathing article on the failures of American journalism, an offer he was sure no other publication would extend to an arrogant and inexperienced young writer.

Rather than composing a serious essay on the decline of journalism—a subject Thompson cared deeply about—he chose to write Kennedy a one-act play called "The Dry Rot of American Journalism." Understandably, Kennedy rejected it, explaining:

> You disappointed me. I expected a serious essay on a serious matter. You delivered a batch of warmed-over clichés with barnyard overtones. You raise questions, then trail off into foolishness.
>
> It would not take any guts to publish this piece. Just gall.

Although this was a fair criticism of his work then and often throughout his career, Thompson was enraged at such a savage put-down of his literary efforts. Still, he had gained enough respect for Kennedy in their brief exchanges to begin a friendship that, though awkward at first, blossomed into a fantastic mutual respect, and lasted until Thompson's death, more than four decades later.

In November 1959, Thompson saw the following advert in *Editor and Publisher*, offering recruitment with a new magazine called *El Sportivo*:

> WANT TO WORK FOR THE SPORTS ILLUSTRATED OF THE CARIBBEAN? Now is your chance. Ambitious publisher is looking for journalists who know and love sports and wouldn't mind living in the tropical paradise of Puerto Rico.

Desperate to get to the Caribbean and eager for any sort of paycheck, Thompson jumped at the chance. He lied about his age and embellished his experience a little to impress the editor, then moved to the Caribbean in the first week of 1960.

When he arrived, he was annoyed to find that *El Sportivo* was not exactly "the *Sports Illustrated* of the Caribbean," but instead a crummy bowling journal. After the incident at

The Jersey Shore Herald, Thompson was not exactly keen on bowling, and now he had to attend bowling competitions seven nights a week. His job, it seemed, was to make sure that every bowler in town was mentioned at least once so that they would buy a copy of the magazine. "Ever since then," he wrote thirty years later, "I've hated the word *bowling*." He soon grew to detest his new editor, whom he dubbed "a liar, a cheat, a passer of bad checks, a welshing shyster."

Still, it could have been worse. He wrote his family to say, "I have no hours, no office, one story assignment a week, and I am 98% on my own all the time." This gave him plenty of time for doing other sorts of writing. He managed to find some freelance work writing stories about Puerto Rico for the *New York Herald-Tribune*, the *Milwaukee Journal*, and *The Baltimore Sun*, in addition to writing tourist brochures for the Puerto Rico News Service. Having buried the hatchet with Kennedy, he also produced an article on cockfighting for *The Star*. Mostly, he was just writing puff pieces about tourism on the island and then rewriting that same article to sell to other publications, but with his name in the *Herald-Tribune* he felt a sense of pride and gained some respect among the other reporters on the island. With typical bravado, he took to calling himself "the preeminent writer or journalist on the island."

Before leaving for Puerto Rico, Thompson had written to the editor of the *Louisville Courier-Journal* to pitch a story about "expatriate Louisvillians" living in New York. The story was rejected, but the editor agreed to make Thompson the paper's Caribbean stringer. With his foot in the door, he was able to sell them a piece on his old Atheneum drinking buddy, Paul Semonin, who had followed Hunter to Puerto Rico and was working for *The San Juan Star*. The two men rented a dilapidated shack in a village about an hour outside of the capital, where they were the only white people. The village was surrounded by swamps and buzzed with mosquitos, but the shack was located right on the beach, so it was worth the discomforts that inevitably accompanied it. Thompson's new girlfriend, Sandy Conklin, came down to join them and stayed in the shack with the two men. It quickly became cramped with three people living in the tiny, clothing-optional beach hut—a situation that was doubly awkward because Conklin was Semonin's ex-girlfriend.

Although Semonin claimed to harbor no ill will over Sandy, he was somewhat offended by the article Thompson wrote about him for *The Courier-Journal*. In "A Louisvillian in Voodoo Country," Hunter wrote about Semonin's bohemian life as a painter in Puerto Rico. Semonin had agreed to some sort of article and sat with his friend through several interviews, but when he saw the final draft, he was shocked that Thompson had just made up most of the quotes he used.

He had written the piece in order to present Semonin as a weird but admirable character, footloose and free, but had twisted reality in order to make it an extension of his own vision. In fact, the theme, clearly presented at the end of the article, very much mirrors his old Athenaeum essay, "Security," in which he had argued that a man ought to live his life on his own terms rather than do what is expected of him. In this article, Thompson quotes Semonin as saying, "but just how important is security when you balance it against all the things you can do in the world, and all the places you can see and live? Freedom is a challenge, not something to be shunned and avoided like a dangerous disease." He sounds rather like Thompson in the opening lines of "Security":

> Security ... what does this word mean in relation to life as we know it today? For the most part, it means safety and freedom from worry. It is said to be the end that all men strive for; but is security a utopian goal or is it another word for rut?

In "A Louisvillian in Voodoo Country," Thompson describes Semonin as a Yale graduate from a wealthy family, who has rejected his upper-class identity to live as a beatnik painter in an exotic land, where he earns just fifty-five dollars a week. The personal details were embarrassing, given that his friends and family read *The Courier-Journal*, but it was the fact that his friend had simply fabricated half the story that angered Semonin.

When confronted about the matter, Hunter just

shrugged. It wasn't the first time, and certainly wouldn't be the last, that he would make up quotes or events for the sake of a good story. Years later, Semonin acknowledged that the article was possibly a proto-Gonzo effort in which the lack of truth was implied without being stated, and pointed out that, going forward, Thompson's work tended to become more theatrical and that he would happily invent quotes to take a story where he wanted it to go. He commented that, in his writing, Thompson "creates the drama and escalates the realm of reality. It goes back to that impulse for street theater." Elsewhere, he remarked upon the superficial side of Thompson's writing: "That's what purpose his exaggerations and his buffoonery served— fantastic, eye-grabbing stuff for the reader."

Indeed, it does seem as though writing was for Thompson an extension of the "street theater" of his youth. The elaborate pranks and shocking behavior of his teenage years had evolved into letters, articles, and later books that tore up social conventions and made people confused, repulsed, or delirious with laughter. To say that "A Louisvillian in Voodoo Country" falls into this category is perhaps fanciful, but certainly his fake press releases, many letters, and some of his other articles were extensions of that pranking nature and the urge to shock.

The article, however, is important for another reason. It begins:

> To get to Loiza Aldea, you drive on a sand road between the swamps and the sea, creeping most of the way in second gear. The drive takes almost an hour – through miles of coconut palms, around the swamps, along the dunes, and past an occasional wooden shack full of silent staring natives.

This is not a particularly special piece of writing, but it shows that Thompson was already experimenting with the voice that he would use in his second attempt at a novel. He often tried out new styles or tweaked interesting phrases in his letters, but even in his articles and short stories, he was constantly innovating. When he found something that he liked, he would reuse it in a later, more important piece of work. In the book, the drive to the shack is described:

> He had given me a map to his beach house,
> but I was not prepared for the sand road.
> It looked like something hacked out of a
> Philippine jungle. I went the whole way in
> low gear, the sea on my left, a huge swamp
> on my right – through miles of coconut
> palms, past wood shacks full of silent,
> staring natives.

Prince Jellyfish was still being shopped around in the US, but Hunter had lost faith, calling it "no more than a minor novel." Still, he claimed that he had "learned a hell of a lot writing it" and attempting to have it published. The next book, which he dubbed "the Great Puerto Rican novel," would be based upon his experiences as a journalist in Puerto Rico and would explore the lives of hard-drinking expatriate reporters in San Juan, its seedy capital city. Throughout his time in Puerto Rico, Thompson drank copious amounts of rum and, as such, his novel eventually took the title *The Rum Diary*.

Whilst on the island, he began plotting out the story but the majority of the writing was done later, when he was back in the US. Although the events that occurred in the book did not all happen to Hunter, most of it was based upon what he saw, heard, or experienced during his six months in Puerto Rico. It was again about a man rather like Hunter Thompson, embarking upon a series of misadventures, most of which involved alcohol to some degree. In that sense, it was very similar to *Prince Jellyfish*, although now the characters and events were fictionalized a little more than in his first novel. It would have a plot instead of serving as a series of flashbacks to his own life.

Still, it is hard to read *The Rum Diary* and see it as a work of pure fiction. Aside from a short, Hemingwayesque preamble that sets the scene, the novel is told in a first-person narrative and follows the drunken escapades of a reporter called Paul Kemp, who escapes from his life in New York by working for a newspaper in San Juan. From his personality to his background to his physical descriptions, Paul Kemp, of course, is clearly Thompson, replete with the bizarre, angry outbursts that characterized him in real life as well as most of his literary personas. As he had done in *Prince Jellyfish*, Thompson has changed certain details for his fictionalized self. His hometown is now St. Louis instead of Louisville, he has served in the Army rather than the Air Force, and he has again given himself an Ivy League education. His editor seems to be based upon Thompson's own editor at *El Sportivo*, Philip Kramer, and once again there are various character names that refer to people from Thompson's own past. It is little surprise, then, that in 1998 Thompson remarked, "It's a memoir."

But it is not just the protagonist, Paul Kemp, who is based upon the book's author. Several of the main characters could also be seen as embodying elements of Thompson's own personality. Yeamon, perhaps the second most important character in the novel, seems to be another version of Thompson. He is a tall, fiercely individualistic, hard-drinking Kentuckian, considered a bit of a loose cannon by his colleagues, who contemplates traveling to Europe, writes the sort of articles that Thompson wanted to—and, later, *did*—write, and he makes a bizarre threat that Thompson occasionally threw into his work: to "twist" someone's head. It is Yeamon who lives on the beach in a shack much like Thompson's, with Chenault, a woman that sounds an awful lot like Hunter's girlfriend, Sandy.[1] It is also Yeamon who provokes the fight and arrest that mark the turning point in the story, yet in real life it was Thompson who insisted upon running out on a restaurant bill and getting himself and friends beaten and jailed. Perhaps in this sense, Yeamon was his first "persona"—a proto-Raoul Duke, capable of doing and saying things that Thompson would not willingly attribute to himself, like slapping his girlfriend. However, elements of the character also seem to be based around Semonin, whose portrait

---

1   In 1998, Thompson unconvincingly avoided the question of whether Chenault was based upon Sandy. It is clear from his coy refusal that she was the inspiration, but Thompson simply remarked, "You're in the right direction" and then backpedalled, saying "Nobody is anybody here." [https://www.ewingfilms.com/2-17/]

in "A Louisvillian in Voodoo Country" shows him spear-fishing for lobster off the beach outside their shack, just like Yeamon does in the novel. Another character, Moberg, seems to represent very extreme parts of Thompson's wild side, while Sala also embodies certain other qualities and talks about expecting to die before the age of thirty—a common claim that Thompson made.[2]

Perhaps it was for this reason that Thompson's agent critiqued them as "uninteresting" and one of the writers he greatly admired, Dennis Murphy, criticized the book for lacking any real delineation of minor characters. Certainly, this is a weak point in *The Rum Diary* and almost all of Thompson's fiction. His characters were usually quite one-dimensional, and he tended to insert himself into the text in various ways, making his more fictional efforts rather uninspired. His best works were the ones in which the characters already existed and he just had to describe them rather than create them, or when he attempted completely absurd fantasy that relied more on comic archetypes than realistic characters.

The Rum Diary is an attempt to tell a simple story and for most of the novel Thompson uses fairly conventional language and narrative structures. However, here and there are glimpses of his own innate style that preview the sort of language for which he later became famous. These include random assertions in the middle of otherwise normal paragraphs, such as "a bunch of lunatics ripped the world in half." He uses the same sort of strong verbs and adjectives that he picked up as a sportswriter and would continue to use in his more famous later works, and at one point even explains to the reader that he likes "sharp little words like Punk and Cheap and Phony" rather than more literary ones that apply to bigger concepts.[3]

---

2   Bob Sala is also a composite of two *Star* reporters: Bob Bone and Pete Sala. In his memoir, *Fire Bone!*, Bone recalls asking to read *The Rum Diary* several times but Thompson refusing. He only found out in 1998 that it included a character based on him. [p.122]
3   The capitalization of words such as in this quote is also something that marked his work. He began by capitalizing very important words but by the end of his career he was capitalizing totally at random.

As with almost everything he wrote, Thompson launches searing attacks on the established press. Of course, as a novel set in the offices of a newspaper, the book is one long meditation on problems in journalism, but he also manages to get in some more vicious digs at the contemporary American press. Viewing the profession through Kemp's eyes, the reader is given the impression that the world of expatriate journalism in the fifties was one in which reporters were virtually prostitutes for propagandizing newspapers owned by corrupt groups of wealthy old men. One of the central dilemmas of the novel is whether a young reporter should sell out and become rich or retain his ethics and stay poor. Whatever he chooses to do, he is likely to remain a pawn for powerful men in faraway places.

He also takes his reader along on flights of fancy as straightforward depictions of actions subtly transition into hallucinatory episodes. In one scene, while talking about his past, he casually slips into an imagined interview about why Kemp wanted to leave St. Louis. The dialogue descends into shouting and it is not entirely clear who is even asking him these questions, but both voices seem like Thompson. "Well, fuck you then," Kemp says in a typical explosion of anger.

At its core, *The Rum Diary* is the tale of an intoxicated journalist torn between his motivation to avoid hack work and make a name for himself with real, investigative journalism, and the destructive, hedonistic impulses that compel him from scene to scene, usually clutching a glass or paper cup filled with rum. Major events like riots and carnivals are simply backdrops against which Thompson explores this idea, just as *Hell's Angels*, "The Kentucky Derby is Decadent and Depraved," and *Fear and Loathing in Las Vegas* would become stories of a drunk or drugged-up journalist wandering about against an interesting event or scene.

As we shall see in subsequent chapters, which deal primarily with Thompson's journalism and his ultimate fusion of journalistic and novelistic techniques, he was firmly of the opinion that it was better to look close up at the human aspect of a story rather than deal with the broader themes in wide-ranging approaches. In this sense, as in many others, he was influenced heavily by Ernest Hemingway, who passed away when Thompson was writing the novel. Hemingway famously practiced the "Iceberg Theory" of writing, which he explained in *Death in the Afternoon*:

> If a writer of prose knows enough of what he is writing about he may omit things that he knows and the reader, if the writer is writing truly enough, will have a feeling of those things as strongly as though the writer had stated them. The dignity of movement of an ice-berg is due to only one-eighth of it being above water. A writer who omits things because he does not know them only makes hollow places in his writing.

Hemingway's first novel, *The Sun Also Rises*, was one Thompson greatly admired and actively sought to emulate throughout his life. It was one of the books he had used as a young man when he wanted to know what it felt like to type truly great prose. It also appears to be the primary model for *The Rum Diary*, albeit with a little Fitzgerald, Kerouac, Dos Passos, and Donleavy stirred in for good measure. In fact, during the writing of the book, Thompson even told a friend, "In a twisted way, it will do for San Juan what *The Sun Also Rises* did for Paris."

Hemingway wrote *The Sun Also Rises* in 1926. It was inspired by his trip to Spain the year before, as well as café life in Paris, where Hemingway lived alongside his Lost Generation companions. As Thompson noted countless times in letters and interviews, Hemingway had been a journalist and made the leap to fiction. This was viewed as a valid and common career progression among writers of the era, and even late in his career Thompson talked about following this model himself. For Hemingway, *The Sun Also Rises* was an important breakthrough, in which he realized that he could use his journalism experience to create the plot and characters of a viable novel. He decided to use real people and real events but impose some elements of fiction upon it, once claiming that this was a better method for approaching the truth than an attempt at purely factual, objective writing:

> A writer's job is to tell the truth. His standard of fidelity to the truth should be so high that his invention, out of his experience, should produce a truer account than anything factual can be. For facts can be observed badly, but when a good writer is creating something, he has time and scope to make it an absolute truth.

This was virtually the guiding philosophy of Hunter S. Thompson's writing career.

Of course, the similarities between these two novels go beyond the mere fact that their respective authors held lofty yet peculiar notions about the presentation of truth. *The Sun Also Rises* and *The Rum Diary* were both their author's first published novel, both *roman à clef*, both dealt with journalist protagonists, and both were set among an expatriate society of primarily Americans. Hemingway's protagonist, Jake Barnes, is in love with a promiscuous woman but incapable of having sex with her due to a war wound while Paul Kemp is stunted more by his attitude than any physical issue, and he lusts after a woman called Chenault, who is similarly carefree and uninhibited, and who we find out late in the novel cannot orgasm. Both Chenault and Hemingway's female lead, Brett Ashley, have been written in a way that presents their very existence as having a deleterious effect on the men around them. As women who pursue sex for pleasure, they could each be described as liberated and modern, but for Hemingway and Thompson this places them as accidental troublemakers and sources of pain for the male characters in their books.

In the second half of Hemingway's novel, there is a seven-day fiesta that involves a great deal of drunken revelry, and in Thompson's book this is replaced with the St. Thomas Carnival. Where Hemingway has Brett Ashley dance provocatively with a bullfighter, Thompson remakes the scene with Chenault stripping naked in the middle of a large group of black carnival revelers. As Yeamon and Kemp vainly try to retrieve Chenault from what they assume is a gang rape, the two versions of Thompson are

70

symbolically emasculated, like Jake Barnes, who is incapable of having sex with Ashley regardless of whether or not she has chosen to sleep with a bullfighter.

Throughout the whole carnival scene on St. Thomas, the level of paranoia presented in the text increases. The fun of the event is viewed as inherently criminal through Kemp/Thompson's eyes, with trouble always looming, leading up to the possible gang rape. This is just one of several troubling racial elements within the book. As well as presenting Puerto Rican people in a less-than-favorable light, his original manuscript was littered with the word "nigger." Even in the excerpt printed in the 1990 collection *Songs of the Doomed*, that racial epithet is a frequent occurrence. These are used only in reported speech and so it could be argued that he was highlighting those attitudes among the press and other expatriates in 1960, but it is telling that by the time the book was published in 1998, there were only two instances of the word: one in a piece of speech that is quickly condemned by Thompson's character and the other a reference to a book by Joseph Conrad. In addition, in the version excerpted in 1990, Thompson made frequent reference to skin color in order to make the carnival revelers more menacing, referencing their "black arms" and "black throats," but by 1998 the first had been removed and the second changed to "wild throats."

These last two descriptions come from the infamous scene in which Chenault—the only female character in the novel—strips naked when dancing with a large black man. Whether her acquiescence is due to the old racist trope of the virile, animalistic black person or Thompson's lazy (and equally racist) fallback, voodoo, he depicts Chenault as "in some kind of a trance": she is a helpless, naïve white woman and he is a predatory black "brute" in the middle of a seething, barely human crowd. The whole event is fraught with problems, and Kevin McEneaney quite fairly called Thompson's depiction of the carnival "exploitative consumption."

Semonin was quick to point out that this incident "never happened in Puerto Rico" and was probably a product of Thompson's experiences growing up in the South. As to the question of whether Thompson was in fact racist,

Semonin and others have noted that he had been deeply impressed by seeing Thurgood Marshall speak in New York and had broken a major taboo in both northern and southern states by dating a black woman, suggesting that he was more progressive than his literary efforts suggest. The experience with Marshall quite possibly was Thompson's first major move toward a more progressive attitude to race, and although there are offensive stereotypes and racial slurs used casually in some of his later work, much of his best writing can equally be viewed as firmly anti-racist. Thompson occasionally admitted to saying things that were racially insensitive but contended that this did not make him racist. In 1969, he explained: "My prejudice is pretty general, far too broad and sweeping for any racial limitations." Sandy, meanwhile, stated in the 1990s that his attitudes as of the time of writing *The Rum Diary* were quite regressive, but that he had long since changed his stance.

These issues of race again tie Thompson's novel to *The Sun Also Rises*. A great many criticisms have been lobbied at Ernest Hemingway for presenting Jake Barnes as anti-Semitic, although others defend his portrayal as an attack on anti-Semitism. Like Kemp, Barnes was never intended to be a heroic character with purely admirable qualities. These two men were protagonists, but they were damaged, self-destructive, and often quite unlikeable. Barnes is insecure because of his impotence and this manifests itself in aggression, particularly in anti-Semitic remarks, while Kemp is an early incarnation of Thompson's classic bumbling, incompetent, rude, self-defeating protagonist. After first seeing Chenault, he makes an idiot of himself and then lashes out at an old man on an airplane. Later, he makes frequent violent outbursts and, although he exhibits some admirable traits, can be viewed as an anti-hero—Jake Barnes with a twist of Sebastian Dangerfield and a dash of Holden Caulfield. It was just as Hemingway had said in an early draft of his novel: "Maybe a story is better without any hero."

The nature of masculinity is explored to some extent in each book as the flawed protagonists deal with expatriate life. They both drink heavily, as do the people around them, in order to cope with their situations, and this of course results in fighting and generally debauched behavior. They appear to recognize the problems inherent in their personalities but do little to resolve them. Both are emblems of their tortured generations—Barnes dealing with the physical and mental traumas of war, and Kemp navigating the near-nihilistic early stages of the Cold War, which pitted a disaffected, bohemian youth against an established order that enjoyed unprecedented wealth, all set amidst the continual threat of nuclear holocaust. There is a particular anger in Thompson's book, which was ratcheted up with rewrites that followed the assassination of John F. Kennedy in 1963.

Hemingway's famously sparse style of writing influenced the introduction to *The Rum Diary* more than the main narrative, which differs greatly. While Hemingway had learned to write under the dictum, "Use short sentences. Use short first paragraphs. Use vigorous English," Thompson preferred Fitzgerald's more conventionally literary approach.[4] Coupled with the unconventional prose styles preferred by Dos Passos and Donleavy, this resulted in a wordy narrative that veered away from the "Iceberg Theory" at least in terms of its accompanying exiguous prosody. Hemingway was careful to leave ideas unsaid and avoided the overuse of adjectives, while Thompson took the exact opposite approach.[5] He crammed as many adjectives into each sentence as possible and often said the same thing in different ways to make himself clear. Hemingway avoided sentimentality and, while Thompson is not generally thought of as a sentimental writer, his prose was usually infused with a slight air of nostalgia, with allusions to a paradisiacal, possibly mythical past.

Both Hemingway's novel and Thompson's feature men whose outlook matures during their story, but at the cost of their hope, faith, and honor. They have both sold themselves to some extent and both books have

---

4　These were the first words of *The Kansas City Star* copy sheet that Hemingway claimed had taught him everything he needed to know as a writer. [https://www.kansascity.com/entertainment/books/article10632713.ece/BINARY/The%20Star%20Copy%20Style.pdf]

5　*The Star* style sheet explicitly warned against the sort of language Thompson later favored: "Avoid the use of adjectives, especially such extravagant ones."

ambiguous endings that leave the reader to wonder about their fate. For Thompson, this was a rare instance of real character development. Most of his writing was like William S. Burroughs' in that it presented characters that may undergo sudden changes but do not evolve as a logical result of the events depicted. They are, instead, archetypes frozen in time.

Ultimately, Hemingway's was the more subtle, nuanced novel of the two and his more restrained prose shows an author already matured and gifted, whereas Thompson's was very much a first serious attempt by an author not yet approaching his peak. One of the problems in Thompson's book—and one that could be said to affect many of his works—is an overabundance of themes that are not sufficiently explicated. Like Hemingway, his book deals with large themes like masculinity and love, but he also attempts to tackle land development, issues relating to Puerto Rican politics and relations with the United States, escape from the confines of one's hometown or homeland, and the fulfillment of one's potential. At both the sentence level and the thematic, he often tried to say too much. In his criticism of Thompson's one-act play, William Kennedy had accused the younger writer of asking too many questions and leaving them unanswered, and this was true of the novel that resulted from his Puerto Rican trip as well as many of his later efforts.

One of the overarching themes in this book, and a major area of concern in Thompson's life, was that of land development or human abuse of natural landscapes. In the first chapter of *The Rum Diary*, this is made clear when Thompson compares the raw, natural beauty of the jungle and sea with the crowded, noisy urban landscape. The jungle, at least from a distance, seems to Kemp a peaceful, Edenic place where he can easily grab a slice of pineapple and then fall asleep. In the coffee shop, however, people wore ties—something that Thompson would never do—and talk about the rapid development of land in the region: "… no such thing as cheap beach-front anymore […] we gotta move quick before Castro and that crowd jumps in with…" To them, the land is merely a commodity and the only considerations are money and politics. Hemingway sandwiched a peaceful natural setting between two chaotic urban settings to highlight a similar theme in his novel, but Thompson would make it more explicit. Just as he had done during his stay in Puerto Rico, his protagonist takes freelance assignments writing travel articles and brochures in spite of the fact that he is contributing to the commodification and destruction of the Caribbean. It was an early incarnation of a technique he would often use in his fictional or semi-fictional works: having himself or a character based on himself embody the problem he sought to criticize.

The book also deals with the idea of paranoia, which became a huge component of Thompson's later work. Although the frantic, self-pitying Kemp exudes a slight air of paranoia, and Thompson uses quite a lot of foreshadowing in the first part of the book, the paranoia really begins after Kemp is arrested. "I was beginning to get the fear," he tells Moberg, who responds by telling him to get a gun. Earlier in the book, we can see this phrase, albeit capitalized for emphasis: "I'm a journalist myself, you know – but... well... I get The Fear..." These are perhaps the first examples of Thompson using this phrase, which he often brought up later in his books, and which of course contributed to his many titles beginning "Fear and Loathing..."[6]

Throughout much of the book, Thompson tries to use a fairly romantic sort of language that sounds a little like Fitzgerald, who he was rereading as he wrote *The Rum Diary*, but he is at his best when describing degenerate behavior and weird action. During such scenes, he is hilarious and his vocabulary for such madness is impressive. In describing a cocktail party, the reader is presented with a range of words that became very much a part of the Gonzo lexicon a decade later: "cheap," "greed," "thieves," "hustlers," "quacks," "gimp mentalities." In describing a vicious fight, he is able to call upon his training at *The Command Courier*, where he picked up this sort of language: "savage rush," "swack of bone against bone," "stomped." Elsewhere, his sporting experience aids him in a description of a game of coconut football on the beach, in which the throws and catches are delicately interspersed with philosophical

---

6   He also used this in a letter sent from Big Sur during the writing of *The Rum Diary*. Referring to himself in the third person, he wrote, "I think he has The Fear." [*The Proud Highway*, p.251]

musings.[7] He had, to some extent, attempted this in his sports writing.

Throughout *The Rum Diary*, Thompson has varied success with presenting straight, novelistic descriptions. Sometimes, the prose sounds a little unnatural or overly sentimental, but at other times he manages to produce beautiful descriptions of scenes without resorting to his peculiar, violent vocabulary: "A few big freighters stood at anchor in the bay, waiting for morning and the tugboats that would bring them in." His language occasionally veers into reporter's territory and it sometimes seems as though he is putting together an article rather than a novel: "but Nelson Otto was a man that trade winds never seemed to touch." It sounds rather like the soft leads that he used in much of his early reporting.

While descriptions of debauchery highlight the influence of *The Ginger Man*, it is not hard to find the evidence of *The Great Gatsby* throughout the book, fusing elegiac language with amusing remarks, such as in this line: "And he shuffled off down the street, a small figure in a dirty grey suit, sniffing for his car."[8] Elsewhere, he leaves Yeamon standing on a pier, looking out to sea. He stops short of adding a green light, though. At the end of most chapters, he presents a vivid image that is often romantic or presents some sort of wisdom. The effect is jarring. We can see within the author two distinct paths: pursuing a literary voice or using his own unique voice.

There is an even more obvious reference to Fitzgerald near the end of the book, where Kemp sits down to read Joseph Conrad's *The Nigger of the Narcissus* to get inspiration for an article that he is writing. His hopes of inspiration are quickly dashed: "I was feeling smart, but reading

---

7   Part of this was removed before the book was published in 1998. Thompson ruminated upon the "curse" of professional football, which was "a foolish game with no foundation in reality." [*Songs of the Doomed*, p.79]
8   The rhythm of the language here is quite clearly inspired by Fitzgerald's prose. One similar example from *Gatsby* is this line: "and he had stood on those steps, concealing his incorruptible dream, as he waved them goodbye." For more on Thompson's adoption of Fitzgerald's language, see part one, chapter twelve.

Conrad's preface frightened me so much that I abandoned all hope of ever being anything but a failure..." In 1934, Fitzgerald looked back at his finest novel and concluded, "I had just reread Conrad's preface to *The Nigger*, and I had recently been kidded half haywire by critics who felt that my material was such as to preclude all dealing with mature persons in a mature world. But, my God! it was my material, and it was all I had to deal with."

Of course, Conrad set impossibly high standards. In his introduction to *The Nigger of the Narcissus*, he explained:

> A work that aspires, however humbly, to the condition of art should carry its justification in every line. And art itself may be defined as a single-minded attempt to render the highest kind of justice to the visible universe, by bringing to light the truth, manifold and one, underlying its every aspect.

This introduction ends with Conrad saying, "Art is long and life is short, and success is very far off," a line that Thompson used in his first collection of work, featuring most of his best writing from the 1960s. It captured perfectly the feeling he had during many of these years, when he struggled and struggled but could not quite catch a break. According to William Kennedy, he "considered it dogma for writers" and knew parts of the preface by heart, which Kennedy claimed was "an inheritance from Hemingway."[9]

Thompson labored over *The Rum Diary* for many years but was never able to get it quite right. His aims were surprisingly modest for a man who often boasted about his literary talent. He believed that even great writing did not necessarily have to be flawless; rather, there was more honor in hitting those "high white notes" that Fitzgerald had mentioned in his short story, "Basil and Cleopatra":

There was a flurry of premature snow in

---

9   Hemingway also admired Conrad, saying, "from nothing else than I have ever read have I gotten what every book of Conrad has given me." [*Ernest Hemingway*, p.73]

the air and the stars looked cold. Staring up at them he saw that they were his stars as always— symbols of ambition, struggle and glory. The wind blew through them, trumpeting that high white note for which he always listened and the thin-blown clouds, stripped for battle, passed in review. The scene was of an unparalleled brightness and magnificence, and only the practiced eye of the commander saw that one star was no longer there.

The phrase "high white note" is one that Thompson often used when talking about literature (although often misremembering it as "high white noise" or "high white sound") and he appeared to have various interpretations of it, stemming from one basic idea. When he talked about "high white notes," he primarily meant passages in a piece of writing that were, like Fitzgerald said, of "unparalleled brightness and magnificence." This signified that they possessed a musical quality that transcended merely functional language and induced the same sort of ecstatic response that people received from a rousing piece of music. For Thompson, who studied and typed great passages of literature just to feel the rhythm—much like a pianist might play Chopin—this was a sacred goal and those bits of writing that possessed this quality were treated almost with a worshipper's reverence. When he wrote something, he was happier to know that it had a few sentences of truly great writing than had he written a quite good article from start to finish.

But Thompson's interpretations of an idea were seldom straightforward. Sometimes, he would talk about a "high white note" as just a good idea or something rare and special, but in a non-literary sense. He also meant it in the sense of unique beauty or quality on a larger scale, sometimes referring to a good story as a "high white note" just the same as he would refer to a single line or paragraph within that same story. Late in life, he suggested that a combination of violence and euphoria could cause a "high white FUSION in [his] brain." He seemed to be suggesting, in this case, that the high white note was a matter of blending fact and fiction in just the perfect ratio.

Throughout his entire career, Thompson kept this idea firmly in his mind and variants upon the "high white" phrase abound in his letters and other writings. In November 1961, while writing *The Rum Diary* and also working on various short stories, he considered the merits of these ventures in terms of his "high white note" theory:

> Five good pages in a 15-page story might not win the pennant, but it's a hardnose average and I'll buy it any day. On the other hand, 10 good pages in 200 (with 100 to go) is twice as many good pages as five, but as an average it sucks wind. I guess the moral is pretty obvious—write short-shorts—and that'll do for a while, but every now and then a man needs to launch a real wadbuster and that's about the way I'm feeling. You can hit the target all day with a .22, but when you want to knock a motor-block off its mounts you move in close with a .44 Magnum. Yeah.

He felt that his novel had those moments of greatness but knew fine well that it lacked an overall consistency, which is a reasonable assessment. It is a book with a good story, interesting if incomplete themes, raucous humor, and some fine elegiac passages that belie his age, but it is not a complete, polished work. What we have, then, in Thompson's second novel, is a work that is more mature than *Prince Jellyfish*, but still not yet good enough to be published. Most importantly, *The Rum Diary* is a landmark on Thompson's road to becoming a great writer. If it is him *nearly* finding his own voice and *nearly* writing a great novel, at least he has come a long way since *Prince Jellyfish*.

Thompson's stay in Puerto Rico was not to last long. Within just a few months of his arrival, *El Sportivo* had gone belly-up and he was left broke and scrambling to get any sort of compensation from his former employer. He threw all of his energy into *The Rum Diary*, spending six hours a day writing and rewriting sections of the book that he felt would make him famous. But he was now learning what it meant to be a starving artist. Despite a few other writing gigs, he could hardly afford to eat. "San Juan is rotten," he wrote. "Highest cost of living anywhere in the Western Hemisphere except Caracas."

In *The Rum Diary*, Paul Kemp plots to take off for South America and the real Hunter Thompson was itching to do the same thing. First, though, he had plans to visit Spain, where Gene McGarr was living, but his attempts at maritime hitchhiking only got him as far as Bermuda— an exhausting journey on a boat called Fat City. Hunter and Sandy were stranded there with Semonin for weeks without money. Naturally, Thompson claimed that they lived in a cave and stole cabbages to survive, but in actual fact Sandy's mother's friend owned a motel that they stayed in, while Semonin slept in a park. Thompson managed to spin this adventure into a story that hit the front page of *The Bermuda Gazette Weekly* on July 10, 1960. It had the fairly self-explanatory title: "They Hoped to Reach Spain but are Stranded in Bermuda." He made a little money from his article, but the plan ultimately backfired because, when immigration officials saw the story, they hassled the three illegal immigrants to leave the country quickly.

After borrowing money from McGarr, they flew back to New York, where Sandy took a job to support them and Hunter managed to write a few articles for the *Herald-Tribune* as he continued work on his novel. After just a few months, though, he was eager to hit the road again. This time he set his sights on Big Sur, some three thousand miles away. He and Semonin, channeling Kerouac, agreed to deliver a car to Seattle. They drove there via Louisville, and *en route* they watched the TV debates between Kennedy and Nixon. This fascinated Thompson, who had never before considered that politics had any real relationship with the man in the street. This was the first spark of an interest in politics that would ignite later in the decade and then consume the rest of his life.

In Seattle, they delivered the car, which Thompson had managed for once to avoid wrecking, and then hitchhiked south to San Francisco. Although he had begun to turn away from his Beat infatuation of 1958, he was still keen to hang out at City Lights and watch poets reading their work.

They had a place to stay thanks to his old friend from New York, John Clancy, but were still nearly starving. He spent a month looking for work while shoplifting to feed himself. He was on a mission, though, and determined to see it through to its end, telling Sandy that he was willing to sleep on the beach and beg for food in order to make it as a writer.

Always interested in seeking out unusual people and eager to rub shoulders with great writers, Thompson set off for Big Sur, down the coast from San Francisco. This raw, rugged section of coastline where America met the Pacific Ocean in a violent clash of cliffs and surf had long attracted adventurers and those seeking solace—sometimes even for artistic reasons. Writers and painters had been coming to Big Sur for almost a hundred years, but it was when Henry Miller settled there in 1944 that it began to develop a reputation as a place where a writer or artist *should* go—and wherever artists congregate, so too do hipsters and hedonists. In his 1957 book, *Big Sur and the Oranges of Hieronymus Bosch*, Miller claimed that "almost a hundred painters, writers, dancers, sculptors and musicians have come and gone since I first arrived." Thompson was enamored of the author, whose *Tropic of Cancer* had been published in 1934 in France but was banned in the US until 1961. The blend of fact and fiction inspired him, as well as the beautiful, musical prose and an unwillingness to shy away from so-called obscene material.

Big Sur proved to be an inspiring location for Thompson, even though it turned out that Miller had left the area in April 1960, and the sense of an artistic colony had vanished along with him. The raw natural beauty of the area had, after all, been what brought Miller and others to this isolated part of the country. Although Miller had left, he still owned property there, which Thompson visited in order to "soak up the 'essence'" of a place where a great writer lived and worked. He also met Miller's secretary, Emil White, although the two did not get along.

However, perhaps more than Miller, Thompson wanted to meet Dennis Murphy, whose novel, *The Sergeant*—another tale of hard-drinking expatriates like *The Sun Also Rises*—greatly impressed him. The two writers became friends and Thompson was hired by the Murphy family to work as a caretaker for their property. He could now afford to live at Big Sur and work on *The Rum Diary*. Once again, he grew out his beard and did his best to live like Hemingway. He began his life-long love affair with guns, got himself a dog, and went hunting for wild boar in the hills. In the afternoons, he could sit naked and look out over the Pacific Ocean, and in the evenings he could act out his masculine fantasies by chasing homosexuals away from the hot springs, where they congregated for orgies.[10]

Having set off for the West Coast alone, Thompson now felt secure enough to send for Sandy. The pair lived together, with Sandy doing everything she could to support her writer boyfriend. Throughout most of their relationship, she devoted herself to supporting his literary aspirations, keeping people away from him and making sure that he was fed so that he could spend as much time as possible at his typewriter. When he was sleeping during the morning and afternoon, she would drive all the way to San Francisco for temp work to pay their bills. Hunter would work most of the night and wake late, by which time Sandy was ready with his breakfast. He would read over the work he had produced the previous night and then ask her for feedback, which she never gave except to encourage him. One friend explained:

> He leaned on her for criticism of his work. But as far as I know, she never provided it. She was there to prop him up. And besides, it was too dangerous for her to say that there was something she didn't like in his work.

Hunter was always possessive and aggressive with Sandy and showed a shocking propensity for jealousy. He

---

10   Hunter was never entirely comfortable with the idea of homosexuality, although like his views on race he became increasingly liberal over the course of his life. Still, he often appeared homophobic. After his brother came out to him, Hunter refused to discuss it. When Jim Thompson was dying of AIDS in 1994, it was Sandy—by then a decade and a half divorced from Hunter—who looked after him and begged Hunter to visit.

wrote her petulant, abusive letters demanding her total loyalty to him and would become hysterical if she talked too long with another man. Now that they were living together, he had become physically abusive toward her. She was a loving, supportive peacenik and he was a frustrated brute with little to no control over his temper. Even in that less progressive era, his behavior toward her appalled friends and visitors.

Thompson was frustrated by his progress on *The Rum Diary* and his lack of success publishing fiction. "He worked every night and every day," Sandy recalled. "He was very serious… *very* serious." He was churning out short stories but no one would bite. For the whole of 1960, his income was nine hundred and seventy dollars and he was angry at being paid as little as forty dollars for some of the articles he could get published. Still, he persevered with his craft.

Among all the people he met at Big Sur, perhaps the most important was Lionel Olay. Olay was a gifted writer but never achieved much fame and only really gained a degree of it after Thompson wrote his obituary some years later.[11] He had written one modestly successful pulp novel but mostly survived through freelance work. He valued writing more than money, an attitude that deeply impressed Thompson, and practiced what Hunter called "personal journalism." At Big Sur, the older writer counselled the younger, telling him not to worry so much about editors and sources and all the boring but serious parts of writing—*just work hard to get good at writing.*

To this end, he turned his focus on a book he deeply admired. Dennis Murphy's novel, *The Sergeant*, had blown him away and so he decided to study it as a model for his own fiction. One day, Murphy found Thompson's copy of his book, which he didn't even know that Hunter had read. He had gone through the whole thing, annotating it with ideas that he could use later. Murphy explained:

> He had taken it apart sentence by sentence, underlining, marking in the margins with questions and comments like "notice how this character is introduced – this is a good

---

idea to fit these pieces together."

Of course, this was hardly surprising. He was a very serious young writer and he spent a huge portion of his life attempting to become as good as he possibly could at this skill. From his early experiments in typing pages from Fitzgerald and Hemingway to closely studying Murphy's novel, there can be little doubt that he was entirely dedicated to mastering his craft. Perhaps for this reason, his attitude toward rejection slips had changed from his days in the Catskills. Now he was furious at each one that came in. His anger built as these pieces of paper stacked up.

Thompson continued to beat at the keys of his typewriter, pounding out story after story. In addition to all the fiction, he worked on articles that he was able to sell for some much-needed cash, including another piece that was published in the *Chicago Tribune*, called "California's Big Sur Lures Tourists with its Solitude." It is an intelligent, worldly article that is witty, informative, and restrained, but most importantly it was another piece of writing in another major publication. Thompson would later reuse the idea and sell it to other publications, often repeating key images.

In April, Thompson wrote another article for his hometown paper, *The Courier-Journal*. "Carnival Time on St. Thomas" introduces its reader to the week-long party that takes place in the capital of the Virgin Islands. Thompson compares the event with the Kentucky Derby, and the subheading claims that the carnival "puts Derby hi-jinks to shame"—something that he would disprove in 1970. The scene will be familiar to readers of *The Rum Diary*, as it is this carnival that provides the book with its central moment, as Chenault is led away after dancing nude in a huge crowd. There are four paragraphs in the article, two rendered in italics and two in bold, which are clearly excerpts from a 1961 version of his novel. This is the fourth:

> At 11 o'clock on Saturday morning, after spending a comfortable night on the beach, we came across a scene that was like nothing I've ever witnessed in my life. Several hundred people blocked Main Street. A percussion corps sat on

the curbing, beating on empty crates with beer cans and champagne bottles. Men and women danced wildly in the streets, and from somewhere in the middle of the crowd came the piercing blast of a trumpet, played by a huge Negro wearing red silk pants and no shirt. Farther down the street, in a blue jeep marked "Poleece," a gendarme in a pith helmet watched the scene impassively.

In the book, all of this happens and even some of the language that he used is the same. At one point, he writes, "A percussion corps of drunkards was beating with beer cans on empty scotch crates." Elsewhere, he says, "We hurried off down a side street, passing a blue jeep marked 'Poleece.' In it, a gendarme in a pith helmet sat half asleep, idly scratching himself." Even the "huge Negro wearing red silk pants and no shirt" was resurrected for the description of the man Chenault had danced naked with.

In July 1961, Ernest Hemingway shot himself in Ketchum, Idaho. He was Thompson's literary idol, a man he aimed to emulate both in prose and in life. He was devastated but resolved to push onwards with his efforts in fiction. Finally, he was beginning to make some progress. *The Rum Diary* was half written and he had a number of short stories with his agent, floating around the market and being rejected by well-known publications. He had adapted parts of *Prince Jellyfish* as short stories, too, but he had no luck in placing them. Success with these, he knew, could prove to be an invaluable steppingstone to having a novel published.

Eventually, he managed to sell two pieces of writing to *Rogue*, a men's magazine that operated as a direct competitor to *Playboy* between 1956 and 1965.[12] The first was another article about Big Sur, entitled "Big Sur: The

---

12   Like *Playboy*, it featured pictures of semi-nude women, advice on sex and men's health, comics, essays, and literature. Other successful authors published in *Rogue* included Arthur C. Clarke, J.G. Ballard, Lenny Bruce, and William Saroyan.

Tropic of Henry Miller."[13] From the first words, it is clear that Thompson has now found his voice. He is not trying to sound like Hemingway or Fitzgerald or anyone else. This is a totally new voice and one utterly unique to Hunter S. Thompson. His language is aggressive, his imagery brutal yet absurd, with layers of dark comedy, paranoid foreshadowing, and wild speculation:

> If half the stories about Big Sur were true this place would long since have toppled into the sea, drowning enough madmen and degenerates to make a pontoon bridge of bodies all the way to Honolulu. The vibration of all the orgies would have collapsed the entire Santa Lucia mountain range, making the destruction of Sodom and Gomorrah seem like the work of a piker. The western edge of this nation simply could not support the weight of all the sex fiends and criminals reputed to be living here. The very earth itself would heave and retch in disgust–and down these long, rocky slopes would come a virtual cascade of nudists, queers, junkies, rapists, artists, fugitives, vagrants, thieves, lunatics, sadists, hermits and human chancres of every description.[14]

We can see here a collection of words and images that Thompson was obsessed with during these years, and which he used often in his letters: "queer," "orgy," "chancre," "fiend." Even the phrase "like a piker" is something that he wrote in letters to friends, once using it to describe Kerouac's efforts at hitchhiking, which Thompson believed paled in comparison to his own. This is very much Gonzo lexis, the sort of vocabulary that would set his writing

---

13   When published in *The Proud Highway*, it was retitled as "Big Sur: The Garden of Agony."
14   This is from the full version of the article that Thompson submitted, as printed in his collection, *The Proud Highway*. In *Rogue*, it was substantially edited to make the text a little more conventional and a lot shorter.

apart from others and ensure that anyone who tried to imitate him would fail. These were words that other writers were unable to use with such conviction because outside of Thompson's wild imagination, they seem rather absurd.

His article is in some sense a celebration of Big Sur, yet at the same time a harsh assault on what it had become, and more than anything it is a critique of Big Sur in the popular imagination. After the introductory paragraph, he mentions the hordes of tourists who have come to gawk at the artists living here, and suggests that the combined weight of all these freaks and gawkers would indeed cause the land to collapse into the Pacific and that orcas would come and eat the people as they floundered in the water. It is another good example of him mixing reality and absurdist fiction to make a point:

> None of this is likely to happen, however, because almost everything you hear about Big Sur is rumor, legend or an outright lie. This place is a myth-maker's paradise, so vast and so varied that the imagination is tempted to run wild at the sight of it.

His contention is that Big Sur is a wonderful place but rather spoiled by the myths surrounding it, which he attempts to dispel. He argues that the people who live there are not as odd as you might expect, but that the busloads of tourists that come to see how weird it is are destroying the area. This was fast becoming one of the main themes in his writing.

In the story, Thompson engages in another quirk of his writing that he would use frequently in the future—he made up quotes. As we saw in regard to the article on Paul Semonin, Thompson was not averse to fabricating a quote, but sometimes he did it deliberately with the intention that the reader knew it was not a genuine quote.[15] Sometimes

---

15   Although he did not admit to such things publicly, to friends he would acknowledge inventing quotes. He told William Kennedy, "Actually, I made up that quote in [*Hell's Angels*] that goes: 'for a guy that ain't straight at all, he's pretty goddamn straight. ...' Or something like that." [*Fear and Loathing in America*, p.149]

he said things that were intended as examples of what *could* have been said. This is another instance of his periodic digressions into fantasy, such as in the following excerpt:

> "Where's the art colony, man? I've come all the way from Tennessee to join it."
> "Say, fella, where do I find this nudist colony?"
> "Hello there. My wife and I want to rent a cheap ten-room house for weekends. Could you tell me where to look?"
> "How're ya doin', ace? Where's this marijuana farm I been hearin' about?"

Thompson even adds one quote that he could not possibly have heard, given that he never met Miller: "Or the one that drove Miller half-crazy: 'Ah ha! So you're Henry Miller! Well, my name is Claude Fink and I've come to join the cult of sex and anarchy.'" In fact, this was another entirely made-up quote. Claude Fink was a character Thompson worked on during 1961 and is mentioned in a letter to a prospective literary agent. In a note to Paul Semonin, Thompson suggested that he was working on a "Claude Fink series."[16]

Each of these quotes is clearly an example of something someone *might* have said, albeit with a slight exaggeration for comedic purposes. Already, Thompson has presented the notion of slack-jawed tourists and freaks from all over the country descending upon Big Sur to watch or join the weirdos at play. He has collected their voices into several representative statements. It is a huge leap forward from his March article in the *Chicago Tribune*, which said the same thing in a more conventional way, albeit with a little comedy tossed in:

---

16   He attached a very short and very dark story about Fink, who is described as "a writer – a piss-poor one" who wrote books and articles that he worried no one would read. No one did and he died alone, a failure. [https://natedsanders.com/Hunter_Thompson_Typed_Story_Featuring_His___Claude_Fink___Protagonist____Also_With_an_Autograph_Lett-ITEM52194.aspx]

Some people will tell you it's an art colony, some will tell you it's a state park, others will tell you it's a nudist colony, and still others will say it's a sparsely-populated section of the California coast, a lonely paradise, full of poets and wild boars.

People familiar with his later work might wonder when Thompson is going to appear in the story, but he doesn't. He simply talks about Big Sur and the people living there. There is no first-person narrative pulling us through, yet his voice is familiar and the rambling nature of the prose, too, is a Thompson trait. From start to end, the article is well written but it meanders from topic to topic according to its author's whim. This is because Thompson had written an article not in the style he learned from the journalism textbooks he borrowed at Eglin, but rather like the letters he had written to friends. Instead of cramming key information into the first paragraph or two, he unwinds it slowly and artfully. The tone is informal and even conversational, but occasionally aggressive: he is not afraid to refer to people as "out-and-out bastards."

Throughout the article, Thompson talks often about Miller and quotes his books at length. Toward the end, he makes reference to specific people who live there, such as Lionel Olay, Emil White, and Dennis Murphy, giving details about their lives. He concludes by calling the whole place "a lonely campground for the morally deformed, a pandora's box of human oddities, and a popular sinkhole of idle decadence."

For Thompson, the article was a massive breakthrough. He was paid three hundred and fifty dollars, which was a good sum for him, but he wasn't just glad to make some much-needed money. As he wrote to William Kennedy, it meant much more than that:

> It was not so much the money, but the feeling that I had finally cracked something, the first really valid indication that I might actually make a living at this goddamn writing.

However, it was also going to cause him the loss of his new home—a place that had brought out the best in him as a writer. The article, with all its details about the lives of people who lived there, as well as sleazy gossip and allusions to the gay scene around the hot springs, managed to anger the whole community. "Everyone mentioned in that article is agitating for my immediate departure," he told his mother. Some were offended by his cruel depictions of them but most worried that, despite Thompson's efforts to dispel myths in the article, it would send out a message that would encourage even more creeps to visit the area. Even his landlady, Vinnie Murphy, was upset. Already angry at Thompson for his drinking and violent behavior, she did not appreciate being mentioned and had not wanted it made public that there was a prominent gay scene on the property. Thompson was fired as caretaker and evicted from the property he had overlooking the sea.

In August, *Rogue* printed Thompson's first piece of published fiction, paying him two hundred and fifty dollars for a short story called "Easy Come, Easy Go." He was relieved to have finally made this breakthrough, but annoyed that it had been in a titty mag rather than a serious publication. The story, which was renamed "Burial at Sea" by the *Rogue* editors, fictionalized his journey to Bermuda the previous year and was published in the December 1961 edition of the magazine. As with his check for the Big Sur article, he spent the money from this one on a gun. However, money wasn't everything. His Big Sur article had been heavily edited and he was worried that *Rogue* would cut his short story down. While he respected the edits made on his non-fiction, he was very protective over his fiction.

While Thompson's attempts at novels were very thinly disguised autobiographic efforts, "Burial at Sea" is more heavily fictionalized. It is certainly inspired by his experience traveling to Bermuda with Sandy, but the events that transpire on the boat are obviously figments of his imagination. The story is about a medical student called Bruce Laurenson, who, with his wife Anne, takes a holiday in the Caribbean. They decide to work as crew on a boat for an odd, drunk captain called Chick Maier.[17] Shortly after setting sail, the captain appears to make a move on Anne and Laurenson is filled with jealousy. When they run into a squall, Laurenson is humiliated by his fear and his inability to carry out the orders Maier screams at him. The reader is led to wonder whether Laurenson is paranoid or not, with the truth only revealed in the final paragraphs. Thompson's flair for the dramatic made for good reading. In terms of plot and theme, the story is very similar to Hemingway's "The Short Happy Life of Francis Macomber," in which the titular character experiences a tremendous humiliation on safari in Africa. After he shows himself to be a coward during a hunt, his wife mocks him and then has sex with their guide.

In his Big Sur article, Thompson unleashed his own voice, replete with his usual vituperative and hyperbolic vocabulary, but "Burial at Sea" is far more conventional. Rather than packing his prose with words like "fiend" and "orgy" and offering a rambling, personal narrative, it is a compact story, filled with precise descriptions and littered with sailing jargon. Presented in the third person and following a protagonist that is very different to himself or other characters based upon Thompson, the story's language is terse and simple and it presents a study of masculinity, suggesting that he was not just copying Hemingway with his beard. Although he perhaps uses too many reporting verbs in places, giving the prose at times a repetitive feel, it is still a tighter and more mature effort than *The Rum Diary*. It is a very strong piece of fiction but bears almost no resemblance to any of his other work, and perhaps this is why it was never included in any of his collections.[18]

---

17   Maier is more than likely based upon Donald Street, the captain of the boat that Thompson and Conklin had taken from St. Thomas to Bermuda. During the real journey, Thompson was childish and difficult but in the short story it is Maier who is the antagonist. [*Fear and Loathing*, p.54]

18   Even though Thompson collected and published much of his non-fiction and correspondence from this period of his life, none of his early short stories were included. Perhaps the reason was the gulf in quality between his fiction and other forms of writing. He regularly sent his short stories to a friend, Don Cooke,

The only few lines in the story that sound anything like Thompson's other work come near the end, when describing the captain as "a vicious, ignorant bum," before reflecting on having been "Reduced to jelly by a cheap sea-thug." Finally, Laurenson screams out, "You rotten bastards! You scum!" Aside from this, "Burial at Sea" is very different from almost anything else Thompson published. It was an exercise in discipline that clearly took a tremendous effort, but at this point he was an extraordinarily motivated, hardworking writer. The achievement pushed him to continue improving his craft, but as we shall see in the next chapters, he was eager to move away from this sort of Hemingwayesque prose and determined to create his own inimitable voice.

---

who noted that the accompanying letters were far better. "His letters and newspaper stories were filled with such liveliness," he explained, "but his fiction was totally flat. It didn't go anywhere." He said these were merely "prose snapshots" with no plots. [*Fear and Loathing*, p.83]

Literary Journalism

You say, for instance, that Spain will undoubtedly go Communist and you will get a lot of noisy shit, perhaps even from the editor you send it to. If, on the other hand, you tell exactly how one frustrated Spaniard spends his waking hours, damn few people are going to be in a position to say you're wrong.

Hunter S. Thompson

Both Hunter and Sandy had loved their year at Big Sur but, after being evicted, they were unable to find a new place to stay. That was a challenge for the struggling writer and his girlfriend, particularly because the writer had spent his meagre earnings on guns and Dobermans, with much of their other income having funded several Tijuana abortions.

In late 1961, they left their idyllic Big Sur home and headed back east. Sandy flew to New York to take up yet more temporary work to provide them with an income, while Hunter went home to stay at his mother's house. He took a job delivering a car to Aspen, then traveled most of the rest of the way by train. In Louisville, he wrote that it was "grey and wet and full of so many ghosts and memories that I get the Fear whenever I go outside," but he wasn't back home to go outside. He was busy working on *The Rum Diary*. From his childhood home, he wrote:

> […] lo and behold, I crouch in the bowels of the Highlands, seeking something, mostly waiting, thinking, killing time, procrastinating, drinking instant coffee by the gallon, reading and re-reading my half-born book and wondering now and then if I will ever write anything but the occasional

bright word of the horny traveler.

He wrote a long, rambling letter to a friend, which, at times, sounds like Fitzgerald. He jokes that a previous letter he'd written was so wonderful that he'd tried to get it published but couldn't because "most of it was cribbed from [...] Scott Fitzgerald." Until this point, Thompson's writing owed a huge debt to Fitzgerald, Hemingway, Kerouac, and Donleavy, but with the Big Sur article he had begun to find his own voice and, in the coming few years, he was about to accelerate that process.

Despite his work on *The Rum Diary* and his success in publishing a short story, Thompson was making more headway as a journalist and so it was logical to pursue that career while writing fiction on the side. In October 1961, he managed to sell a short Baja California travel guide to the *Chicago Tribune*. It was a very straight, dull article but ended with two comparatively unconventional paragraphs as Thompson attempted to apply the language of literature—with a slight hipster flair—to his article:

> You drive thru the blue dusk, between empty mountains and a cold sea, past little tin roof shacks where dark skinned men in baggy pants and sandals sit around drinking beer, past rusty wrecks of old American autos, and you keep going until there's nothing to see but cactus and dust and a few lizards beside the road.
> And soon or later you turn around and go back, because soon or later you have to.

With his foot in the door at a major newspaper, he followed up with a story about a bluegrass music festival in Kentucky. This second story—alongside a picture of him smoking a cigarette—made the front page of their "Traveler's Guide" section. It was a huge achievement, further convincing him that he had a viable future in the industry.

Published on February 18, 1962, "Renfro Valley" picked up where his Baja California article had left off.

The first article had ended with two paragraphs written in the second-person perspective, and this new piece was written predominantly in that point of view. It is clearly Hunter attempting to put himself into the heart of the story without explicitly mentioning himself. Instead of detailing his own actions, he uses the reader as a surrogate: "You ask what goes on at Renfro Valley and they shrug and say, 'Not much.'" He mostly uses plain language with none of his typical strong verbs and adjectives, and sometimes appears to imitate local speech patterns, such as in the final paragraph: "Not much to hurry about in the Bluegrass, specially in the winter when the trees are bare and the barns are white with frost and most folks are inside by the stove." Instead of his usual expansive sentences and multiple strands of imagery, he has predominantly short, terse sentences presenting basic information and pertinent images, often missing out parts of conventional grammatical structures or shortening words like "through" to "thru" as he had done in the previous article. It is almost hardboiled prose and it seems Thompson is once again pushing his work in a new direction, experimenting with style. Although he did not pursue this style of writing much further, he had taken another step toward a model for his future reporting: the story of the journalist reporting on a place, trying to find a drink and bumping into a number of colorful local characters along the way.

After writing his bluegrass article for the *Tribune*, he went to New York and wrote about bluegrass musicians there. He noted the irony of people who had fled rural America to live in the big city now watching live "hillbilly music" as though it were exotic. The article, titled "New York Bluegrass," went unpublished until Thompson's 1998 letter collection, *The Proud Highway*, but it is interesting to see him continuing to place himself within a story. Although his impact is negligible and he is purely an observer, he is nonetheless visible throughout, using first-person pronouns and telling the reader his thoughts and actions as a means of framing the story.

In search of work, he put an ad in the "Correspondents" section of *Editor & Publisher*, proudly proclaiming his range of talent and experience, and also stating quite clearly what he was *not* interested in doing:

Politics, travel, features. No hack work.
Young, good experience, contacts. Advise
needs, rates. Box 969.

Thompson's letters to editors tended to be similarly arrogant. Despite later claims about writing purely for money, he was usually unwilling to do work that he considered beneath him, regardless of pay. He considered himself a serious writer and was not willing to do "hack work" even if it helped him pay the rent. It is also notable that he did not mention sports writing, which he now viewed as beneath him, in his ad. If he had to write journalism rather than fiction, then he at least wanted to deal with important issues.

In November, he pitched an article to *The Atlantic Monthly* about the John Birch Society, a far-right organization founded in 1958 and famous for its anti-communist activities. The idea was rejected and the article never written, but it is still worth noting as, in his letter to the editor, Thompson outlined something that would define his best writing and shape his journalism going forward. It was not the political aspect, about which he was still only mildly interested at best, but rather the personal element of these stories that intrigued the ambitious writer: "Politics can be interesting," he explained, "but I prefer people."

Again, this can be viewed as the influence of Ernest Hemingway, whose journalism avoided the bigger picture in favor of immediate details. According to Hemingway's biographer, Jeffrey Meyers, "he objectively reported only the immediate events in order to achieve a concentration and intensity of focus—a spotlight rather than a stage." It was a technique that Thompson would continually work with until he had mastered it, presenting the key themes of his work through the lives of the people he met and the interactions he had with them. In a letter to Paul Semonin, he explained his own interpretation of Hemingway's journalistic approach, advising Semonin to write about:

subjects least likely to be contradicted or
called into question by people who think
they know a lot more about them than you
do. You say, for instance, that Spain will

undoubtedly go Communist and you will get a lot of noisy shit, perhaps even from the editor you send it to. If, on the other hand, you tell exactly how one frustrated Spaniard spends his waking hours, damn few people are going to be in a position to say you're wrong.

Indeed, his early journalism tended to follow a traditional mode of researching facts and then presenting them somewhat objectively, with his own opinions tying the resulting details and quotes together. However, he was beginning to find that when he made grand pronouncements, people could disagree with him by picking apart his evidence. Talking with people, on the other hand, provided him the opportunity to look at the world through someone else's eyes. It was subjective and no one could argue with that person's right to a viewpoint. In the coming years, he would attempt to approach the biggest questions and issues of the era not by explaining them and exploring them through objective facts and his own analysis, but rather through the words and stories of individual people. This was going to be Thompson's approach to journalism, but another problem remained—finding important topics to write about and then finding someone to pay him for it.

While he was pondering his next moves, Thompson's grandmother passed away, leaving him an inheritance. It was a modest sum of money and he had a lot of debts to pay off, but it put him in a position of unexpected freedom. He immediately planned a trip to South America, where he intended to travel widely, writing about what he found and then pitching it to various travel publications.[1] It was, he figured, "the last frontier" and therefore a place ripe for an intrepid young reporter. With fewer English-language journalists working there, it would also be a less competitive job market and the perfect place for a relatively inexperienced reporter to catch a break. He would not

---

1   He also spent several hundred dollars on camera equipment as he found he was able to sell photographs along with his articles. Before heading off to South America, he even pitched an article on photography to the magazine *Pop Photo*.

take Sandy with him, but instead send his articles to her, expecting her to type them up and then forward them to various editors, basically acting as his agent while she also worked full time as a secretary.

In April 1962, Hunter Thompson handed a 366-page manuscript to his agent and set off once again for Puerto Rico—the first stop on a long journey. It was a fitting destination because the manuscript was *The Rum Diary*, a novel filled with "flogging and fighting and fucking" that he had spent eighteen months writing since its inception in those sunny climes. Sitting down for so long had given him a near-permanent case of hemorrhoids and, tired of laboring over the same book for so long, he was glad to be finished and moving on.

Founded in late 1961 and first printed in February 1962, the *National Observer* was still in its infancy when Hunter Thompson wrote to features editor Clifford Ridley. It had started as a Sunday edition of the *Wall Street Journal*, but soon its parent company, Dow Jones, decided to make it a Monday paper. They had a limited budget, so they had only a few reporters sent out to cover stories and thus most of the content was reprinted from elsewhere or written by a few writers in an office. Originally, its publisher, Barney Kilgore, wanted a publication that was written by people who read and regurgitated other reporting, adding intelligent insight to make complex issues understandable for a relatively young readership; however, teething problems led to poor reviews and so the editorial staff were open to new ideas and perspectives, with no set style to limit their writers.

This lack of a unified voice and openness to new ideas made the *National Observer* a perfect fit for Thompson's work. He had worked hard on his journalism, but ultimately his style of writing was unorthodox. He could tell a good story, but—with the exception of his *Tribune* piece—his writing was too loose, peppered with weird language, and his stories typically too wild to sit well with the editors of big newspapers and flashy magazines. Thompson liked to present stories like a novelist, setting the scene and giving some background in a process he called "The Fuse," before having people talk through the issues as he stands by and watches, then gives his own commentary—"the wisdom" as people would later refer to it.[2] It was a slow-building style that worked well when a reader was invested but wasn't exactly appealing to most editors. At the *National Observer*, he found editors willing to respect conversational, rambling prose, happy to let a writer use as many or as few words as he wanted, and—importantly—lacking the resources to fact-check stories.

When Thompson sent a letter to Ridley before leaving the States, the editor was not so much enamored of the clippings as the letter itself. Thompson's style was infectious and his attitude engaging. If he could write like this, Ridley wondered, perhaps his coverage of South American issues would draw readers into his up-close-and-personal style of reporting. He didn't expect much but agreed to read whatever stories Thompson sent him. The first article he wrote was published in June and was not especially interesting. The style of writing is extremely conventional, heavy on facts, and with no intrusion of Hunter's character. It shows him as a competent young journalist able to produce very traditional newspaper material, but he shows no real trace of personality. However, his second piece would capture Ridley's attention.

After spending ten days in Puerto Rico with William Kennedy, Thompson traveled to Aruba, a small island less than twenty miles from Venezuela and the South American mainland. Here, he wrote an article that read almost like a short story and explored the political divisions on the island not through wordy political analysis, but through a conversation between two people in a bar in the island's capital city. He sets the scene and introduces various characters, then reports on the political situation through his sources:

> He turned back to the American: "You ask
> who is who in these elections, well by God

---

2   Thompson explained: "The Fuse: the reader lights it by becoming initially involved in the book – the first few pages – and then he has to be dragged (reluctantly, if possible, so as to traumatize his memory) all the way to the end . . . at which point he may or may not realize that he's been forced, or duped, into reading an essay." [*Fear and Loathing in America*, p.25]

I tell you – it is the decent people against
the cut-throats and the Bolsheviks."

This was a perfect example of the advice he had
given Semonin about describing "a Spaniard" instead of
attempting to deal with Spanish politics. It was believable,
readable, and informative. For once, Thompson had even
covered the five Ws of reporting—who, what, when, where,
and why—although these details were presented more like
elements of a short story than a piece of journalism.

When Ridley read the story, which was accompanied
by photographs Thompson had taken of himself, he
immediately knew that it had to go in the newspaper.[3]
However, before he had a chance to start working on it,
another package arrived—a third article, this time from
Colombia. It was even better than the second.

"A Footloose American" explores the lives of whiskey
smugglers in a Colombian village called Puerto Estrella. In
it, Thompson provides a very straightforward, informative
look at this mysterious corner of the world but also
presents an entertaining account of one man's adventure
into dangerous territory. Particularly in the first paragraphs,
the writing is reserved and reportorial. Again, the influence
of Hemingway is clear. The story is rather similar to one
that Hemingway wrote when he was only twenty-one years
old: "Canuck Whiskey Pouring into U.S.," printed in the
Toronto *Star Weekly*. Thompson is essentially telling the
same story and even imitating Hemingway's language, but
his great breakthrough here was putting himself right into
the middle of the action.

After a few paragraphs of Hemingwayesque
introduction, Thompson appears on the scene. He
describes himself and his interactions with the local people.
Although he is an observer, he is nonetheless important.
He acts as a surrogate for the reader, who would otherwise
struggle to imagine himself in such a place. A photo,
taken by Thompson, who is identified as "the village's
first tourist," provides an intimate view into their lives.
They look into the lens of the camera, almost making eye

---

3   One photo was a self-portrait that would grace the
cover of *The Rum Diary* when it was eventually published in 1998.
In the newspaper, however, Thompson is identified as "a tourist."

contact with the reader. Thompson's depiction of himself continues in this role:

> As I came over the brink of the cliff, a few children laughed, an old hag began screeching, and the men just stared. Here was a white man with 12 Yankee dollars in his pocket and more than $500 worth of camera gear slung over his shoulders, hauling a typewriter, grinning, sweating, no hope of speaking the language, no place to stay – and somehow they were going to have to deal with me.

The image is humorous and yet descriptive. Already, the reader wants to know more about these people and about what happens to the intrepid journalist next. It is an image that would come to define Hunter S. Thompson— the unprepared outsider embarking upon a comic misadventure. He must engage in a drinking contest with the locals, who are vividly described during the ensuing trials.

The article ends with a subtle but witty remark. Thompson had depicted the smugglers drinking Scotch all day and night, so he finishes with an image of him drinking beer at his next destination, where the Scotch has been imported. "And then we would have another beer, because Scotch is so expensive in Barranquilla that only the rich can afford it." It is a conspiratorial wink to the reader, who is left feeling that they have some insider information about smuggling in this part of the world. They are also left curious about the Indians' lives, but most of all they want to know where Thompson went next. He was not just firing off a single article to earn a little money to fund his trip. He had now found an outlet for his work and, more importantly, he had somewhere to work on developing his style.

Thompson's articles were an immediate hit with readers and editors, but despite the enthusiasm for his work, Ridley did have a few doubts. At the time, he wasn't entirely sure that Puerto Estrella was really the wild hub of smuggling that Thompson depicted… or, for that matter, whether it even existed. Years later, he told a biographer that "In light of all Hunter's subsequent journalism, I look back on some of this stuff and wonder how much of it was true." However, in Ridley's own words, it was "quite impossible to check."[4] They were sure that he was presenting things in a somewhat dramatic way but, like millions of readers in the coming decades, they weren't certain how much was real and how much was imagined. Ridley commented later: "hyperbole was Hunter's stock-in-trade, and we understood that."

If articles like "A Footloose American" seemed too good to be true, then one that he wrote a year later raised suspicions even further. In "Why Anti-Gringo Winds Often Blow South of the Border," Thompson starts:

> One of my most vivid memories of South America is that of a man with a golf club—a five-iron, if memory serves— driving golf balls off a penthouse terrace in Cali, Colombia [...] Beside him on a small patio table was a long gin-and-tonic, which he refilled from time to time at the nearby bar.

This image prefaces his description of the political situation in Cali, where an anti-gringo politician has risen to prominence. It seems a little too perfect and his editors wondered whether or not he had just invented the scene in order to present an image of a detestable colonial type, illustrating precisely what it was that many Latin Americans hated about the white man. Throughout the rest of his story, he quotes various people that also seem to say things that were extremely convenient. There are various anonymous sources such as "one young American" who say very hard-to-believe things, such as, "I came down here a real gung-ho liberal..." These sources are more like crudely drawn characters than actual people. One of them is "John," an aid worker whose story Thompson paraphrases. It is a perfect illustration of the frustrations felt by white people in Latin America and it conveniently

---

4   The town was, however, correctly identified on a small map included alongside Thompson's article.

counterbalances the rooftop golfer image. In describing John as "a representative" of an aid organization, one wonders if Thompson was subtly admitting that John was representative of white people in the region.

Later, when Thompson was asked by his editors about the authenticity of the things he mentioned in his articles, he said, "A good journalist hears a lot of things. Maybe I heard some of these stories and didn't see them. But they sure as hell happened." Whether he did in fact watch a British businessman whacking golf balls into a slum, the highly specific details—the five iron and a gin and tonic—lent his story a visual quality that made his readers want badly to believe it was all real. Indeed, he thought highly of the story, saying rather immodestly, it "was one of the best and most original pieces I've ever read on Latin America or any other place" and that it "smacked of authenticity." The latter comment seems a tacit admission that the story had been invented but that the fiction was true due to its author's knowledge, just as Hemingway had once claimed.

At the time, though, his editors didn't even think to question Thompson. For one thing, his stories were so good that one or two small factual inaccuracies could be tolerated; for another, Ridley knew that it would be career suicide for a young journalist to just make things up and try to pass them off as real. He knew Hunter Thompson to be brave, but he certainly was not stupid. In any case, when the "Anti-Gringo Winds" article was printed, it appeared alongside a cartoon of a fat man hitting golf balls off a roof, with a cocktail right beside him. Real or imagined, Thompson had presented the perfect image of privilege run amok. He had either created or invented his own Gatsby—one of many to grace the pages of his fiction-infused reportage.

Thompson's Conradian journey around South America had begun with his boat trip into Puerto Estrella, and from there he traveled through Columbia to Peru, Ecuador, Bolivia, Uruguay, and then finally arrived in Brazil in September 1962, where he wrote for the *Brazil Herald* in addition to the *National Observer*. Throughout his trip, he provided fascinating insights into local culture and politics, constantly developing his narrative style. He mostly provided straight journalism with a restrained voice, but he managed to make his articles dramatic by dropping himself into the fray. In telling his own story, he began to write about the journalistic process. This metajournalistic aspect was becoming a common trope in his work. Between his intense focus on local people and events and his personal involvement in the story, his editors sometimes had to add facts in order to make it more detailed for the reader and remind them that this was journalism.

Still, some of Thompson's best writing was a little more conventional, including a piece from August 1962, called "Democracy Dies in Peru, but Few Seem to Mourn its Passing." The tone throughout is informative yet conversational and the author speaks with tremendous confidence about Peruvian politics and culture. It appears to be extraordinarily well researched and is incredibly detailed, containing more facts and figures than one normally finds in a Hunter S. Thompson article, yet also possesses the same highly readable nature as his other South American articles.

In contrast with his often-toned-down articles, his letters were fantastical and shocking. He wrote hilarious stories to Ridley that inspired the editor to select some of the less offensive parts and print them in the newspaper. Published in the December 31, 1962 issue, these brief excerpts introduced readers to the "the personal experiences of the digging, inquisitive newsman." They were illustrated by a map of South America, showing Thompson's route around the vast continent. Throughout his missives from far-flung places, Thompson bitched about everything from his health to his finances, and sometimes the horrendous insects that plagued him. These were far more colorful than his articles or the toned-down excerpts Ridley chose, as this passage from a letter to Paul Semonin shows:

> The crew is primitive and vicious looking and the captain is an old river toad who can't understand why I'm here and doesn't much care for it. His daughter is here too, but she is scraggy. I was dealing in a whorehouse last night but refused to pay and could not make my concepts understood. I convinced

the lovely, but the chickenheaded madam held firm. Fuck them all. These latins are all whores in their own various ways—even the presidents.

From his letters, one gets the feeling that he starts complaining in order to vent his frustration at, say, "a beetle the size of god's ass," but then he continues to layer fictions upon these observations, getting wilder and wilder with his bizarre descriptions and exaggerations. He is partly venting his frustrations and partly entertaining his friends, but his letters also seem like trial runs at longer pieces of writing. He is learning how to take his pain and suffering and anger, amplify it through his overactive imagination, and turn it into something that can make people laugh out loud.

Shortly after his correspondence appeared in the *National Observer*, he wrote "Brazilshooting," an article that was very different from anything he'd published thus far. In this story, Thompson is the central figure, but he refers to himself in the third person as "an American journalist" or just "the journalist," borrowing another technique from Hemingway.[5] Like his "Renfro Valley" story for the *Chicago Tribune*, this is—in places—written very much like a hardboiled short story:

> Ten minutes later the half-dressed journalist jumped out of a cab a block away from the action. He walked quickly, but very casually, toward the Domino Club, with his camera and flashgun cradled in one arm like a football. In a Latin American country nervous with talk of revolution, no man with good sense runs headlong into a shooting party, because he is likely to get stitched across the chest with Czech machine gun slugs.

It is an incredibly effective piece of writing. His focus

---

5   Although Hemingway famously wrote his fiction in the first person, his early reporting included frequent references to himself as "the editorial writer" or "the reporter."

in this piece is reporting the details of his immediate surroundings—a crime scene—and then linking it to the wider issue of corruption. The immediacy of his participation brings home the brutality and confusion of a shooting in a nightclub, but he is able to tie this to Brazilian politics, offer some insight from media reports on the incident, and insert his own wisdom. Toward the end of the article, he includes several dubious quotes from anonymous sources.

Alas, the story that appears as "Brazilshooting" in his 1979 collection, *The Great Shark Hunt*, was very different when it was published in the *National Observer* on February 11, 1963. Now titled "Daybreak at the Domino: Brazilian Soldiers Stage a Raid in Revenge," it had been stripped down to basics, with all the hard-boiled detective narrative removed, along with most of the unconventional elements, like ending on a George Orwell quote: "In the kingdom of the blind, the one-eyed man is king." The last line was no great loss as it made little sense in the context of the article, but the gritty, noirish prose, with Thompson's journalist racing to the scene and scrabbling to cover it against the wishes of racist officials, was indeed a loss. His editors had turned "the journalist" into Thompson's regular first-person observer, so that "When the journalist arrived…" became "When I arrived…"

Still, Thompson had once again tried a new technique and it would be added to his arsenal. Many of these *National Observer* pieces found him experimenting with his reporting in this sort of way, as did his work at the *Brazil Herald*, where he turned in "an interesting combination of facts, exaggerations, and imagination." The editor, Bill Williamson, believed these efforts to be an early incarnation of Gonzo.

In November, Thompson wrote to William Kennedy with some wisdom he had picked up coving South America:

> Let me warn you to turn in the most bizarre copy imaginable. [...] Never hesitate to editorialize with a vengeance or abuse anyone you disagree with. Mock generals indiscriminately and state flatly that all non-Americans are thieves and queers.

> Drink with as many people as possible, and when they tell you some heinous secret in confidence, quote them directly and if possible get photos of them drunk. And if all else fails, pull a gun and get rough.

This outburst was likely inspired by his views of the English-language press in South America, "where the government ministries hand out statements and communiqués to correspondents who line up to receive them and dutifully relay their contents back home." Though he advocated and practiced ethically dubious methods of reporting, he believed these to be morally superior to the usual press practices.

In total, Thompson wrote sixteen articles for the *National Observer* during his one year in South America, earning him two thousand dollars plus expenses. His work was good enough that it often made the front page, was frequently reprinted in other newspapers around the country, and helped him establish his name as a talented journalist. He also managed to sell an article to *The Courier-Journal* about blagging a free boat ride by doing photography assignments for the owner of a barge. In an amusing piece of reporting, titled "Beer Boat Blues," he describes the journey toward the equator on a boat laden with booze, both Thompson and the crew emptying bottle after bottle in an attempt to slake their thirst. It is quite typical of his reporting at this point. It starts with a sentence that intrigues the reader ("There is a bit of beer shortage here, but nobody really cares except the merchants."), tells the story of his own comical adventures in a strange place, focuses on big issues through the stories of individuals, and ends with a witty remark. He observes that it is cheaper for the barge owner to allow the sailors to steal his beer than to hire guards, who would invariably pilfer his supplies, too.

However, although he certainly exaggerated his discomfort throughout his trip, he did appear to be quite often miserable from poverty and sickness. By mid-1963, he was ready to leave "this rotten continent."

Outsiders and Outlaws

In a prosperous democracy that is also a society of winners and losers, any man without an equalizer or at least the illusion of one is by definition underprivileged.
                                                                Hunter S. Thompson

During his time in Brazil, Thompson had written to a friend about his regret at having spent so much time on Latin American politics: "I am so fucking involved in politics, etc," he wrote, "that I don't have much time for the oddball stuff that is really the most important." Indeed, although his movements around South America had been brave and unpredictable, and although his writing had been unconventional, the subjects about which he wrote were mostly the big topics that interested readers of a Dow Jones newspaper, namely politics and economics. Aside from a few smugglers, the only real outsider in his work was the courageous journalist roughing it across a vast continent.

When he returned to the United States in mid-1963, Thompson was somewhat of a legend among the staff of the *National Observer* and his name was becoming known throughout the wider journalism community. *The Washington Post* and *National Geographic* both wanted to talk with him, and he felt there was "a general opening of doors" upon his return. His travels in South America may not have been particularly comfortable for him, but they had been highly successful in terms of his journalism career.

When he walked into the *Observer* offices in Washington, Thompson was dressed in a tropical shirt and shorts, with aviator sunglasses and a cigarette holder between his teeth. His editors hardly knew what to expect from their oddball correspondent, but they were not disappointed by the man that showed up. Amused and impressed, they put him up at an excellent hotel for a few days, arranged for him to speak at the National Press Club, and then offered him a nice, comfortable office job.

Of course, Hunter S. Thompson was never cut out for office jobs, and he declined their offer. He told them he was going west to see what was happening in San Francisco, which he felt would be the nexus of any coming political or cultural movement. The *Observer* agreed to keep paying him for articles written from his Latin American notes and also for work he did around the United States, and so he ventured westward in search of important and unusual scenes to cover.

Hunter and Sandy traveled from Washington to Louisville, where, on May 19, they piled into a car with Hunter's two brothers. Sandy asked where they were going and Hunter told her, "Jeffersonville, Indiana." She was mystified and asked why. Hunter replied, "To get married."

After a quick ceremony, which was consummated on the backseat of that same car, the newly married couple headed south to Florida to visit Sandy's parents. Here, Thompson raided his Latin American notebooks for ideas and began cranking out articles for the *National Observer*, including one of his best pieces of South American reportage, "The Inca of the Andes: He Haunts the Ruins of His Once-Great Empire." It begins:

> When the cold Andean dusk comes down on Cuzco, the waiters hurry to shut the Venetian blinds in the lounge of the big hotel in the middle of town. They do it because the Indians come up on the stone porch and stare at the people inside. It tends to make tourists uncomfortable, so the blinds are pulled. The tall, oak-paneled room immediately seems more cheerful.
>
> The Indians press their faces between the iron bars that protect the windows. They tap on the glass, hiss, hold up strange gimcracks for sale, plead for "monies," and generally ruin the tourist's appetite for his

inevitable Pisco Sour.

It wasn't always this way. Until 1532 this city of crisp air and cold nights in the Andes Mountains served as the gold-rich capital of the Inca empire [...]

By mid-1963, Thompson had a signature style in his articles: His opening paragraph sets the scene with either a bizarre or poignant image or a grand pronouncement that will be partially explained in the next sentences, before a digression that usually takes the reader back in time. The theme running through much of his work is the loss of values or of innocence, as the past is invariably contrasted with the fast-paced, mechanized modern world. As one of his editors later remarked, "All his writing was about the loss of some mythic world that he may once have inhabited." He then builds slowly to his main point and to something that will either explain or justify the first paragraph. He was not afraid, then, to bury his big ideas, quotes, or facts deep in the article. His slow build captured readers' attention and took them into the heart of the matter like an old storyteller patiently spinning his yarn.

In this story, Thompson is keen to explain the differences between rich and poor, between the old empire and the new. He presents the Incans as a sad, pitiful shadow of their once proud civilization, tormented by the cold, cruel, and excessive white man. At times, he goes a little over the top in his descriptions, but that was his style and it worked for drawing attention to the Indians' plight:

> Today, the Indian is as sad and hopeless a specimen as ever walked in misery. Sick, dirty, barefoot, wrapped in rags, and chewing narcotic coca leaves to dull the pain of reality, he limps through the narrow cobblestone streets of the city that once was the capital of his civilization.
>
> His culture has been reduced to a pile of stones. Archeologists point out it's an interesting pile, but the Indian doesn't have much stomach for poking around in his own ruins.

Although he is talking about things that are certainly tragic, Thompson speaks with a deadpan humor:

> A fine old Indian tradition, now on the wane, was to greet all strangers with a hail of stones, because they invariably meant trouble.

Whilst perhaps a little insensitive by today's standards, it makes for an engaging article that very much places the Incan people as victims and elicits sympathy for their suffering.

Again, Thompson uses stories that appear apocryphal and quotes that are almost certainly made up to represent things he may have heard, but which primarily serve the purpose of propelling his narrative and supporting his views. For example, he reports someone as quoting an Indian farmer rejecting modern methods:

> "Ah, senor," he said, "this is a wonderful plow, but I like my old wooden one and I think I will die with it."

As with the wealthy Brit hammering golf balls out over a favela while drinking a gin and tonic, this quote, accompanied by a photo of an old Incan man, is a little too perfect. It portrays the humble, simple Indian with his rustic values and submissive nature. It was likely an invention based upon a crude stereotype and is clearly intended as an amusing anecdote that would surely get a chuckle from his readers.

After discussing the Spanish occupation of Peru and efforts to bring the indigenous people into the politics and culture of modern South America, Thompson finishes by suggesting that maybe they will do more than just look through the blinds to make diners comfortable. He has brought the ending of this article back around to the beginning, having presented a complex issue in a coherent and entertaining way. The whole plight of the Indians has been summarized in a few images—of them peering at rich folk through windows and of a simple man plowing his fields with ancient farming implements, willing to die with the old ways rather than adapt to the new. The article is Hunter Thompson at his most concise and is one of his best-crafted pieces of non-fiction.

We can compare this to the "Anti-Gringo Winds" article that was published a little later and which was probably written at around the same time. In both articles, Thompson has set up a battle between rich and poor, native and colonist. In each case, he has framed the discussion with a powerful image, both of which are quite possibly imagined but nonetheless effective for drawing the reader's attention to the issues he wishes to raise. After all, a long, boring article on wealth inequality may be informative but it lacks the punch of a rich Brit smacking golf balls into a slum or starving Indians watching white people sip cocktails.

After mining his journals for South American material, Thompson began writing articles for the *Observer* about things he encountered back in the United States, including an hilarious account of his hitchhiking experiences that contained the amusing line, "At age 22 I set what I insist is the all-time record for distance hitchhiking in Bermuda shorts; 3,700 miles in three weeks." The article is funny but also deals with the serious issue of race and offers that tone of lament for the past that had become common in so much of his writing. He also dipped his toes in the pond of literary criticism with an article called "Where Are the Writing Talents of Yesteryear?" As the title suggests, it is an inquiry into the state of contemporary American literature as well as another lament for a world changing for the worst. In this article, he writes:

> [...] it's hard to argue with the rumor that fiction is becoming passé, that the novel is dead as an art form, and that the short story is on its last legs. Running down the list, the only reasonable comment is "Who cares?"

Indeed, fiction was becoming passé and the new world was so big and weird that non-fiction could tackle subjects even a novelist could hardly imagine. A talented journalist, Thompson felt, could take something real and write about it in a way that was as important and as artistic as any novelist working on a story formed purely from his imagination. He bemoaned the state of contemporary reporting again and said that it was imperative that America needed motivated young reporters "to make journalism the great literature it can be." Certainly, that had been his aim throughout most of his reporting from South America and then back in the US. These were attempts to make reporting into an art form rather than simply a way of conveying information. He had made his articles entertaining, original, and occasionally poetic.

After writing an article on the National Folk Festival in Covington, Kentucky, Thompson took off for the West Coast. His first stop, though, was Las Vegas, where the *National Observer* had arranged for him to watch and report on a heavyweight boxing match between Sonny Liston and Floyd Patterson on July 22. It was the second time that the two boxers had fought in a year, and for the second time Liston knocked Patterson out in the first round. Whether it was the predictability or the brevity of the fight, Thompson did not bother to write about it. It was the first time in his career that he had failed to write an assigned article, but it would not be the last.

Paul Semonin was living in Aspen in 1963 and invited the newlyweds to come and visit him. Thompson, who had only previously made a fleeting visit, quickly fell in love with the area, where he was free to hunt and work and drink as he pleased. They stayed with Semonin for two months before renting a house in nearby Woody Creek, a quiet town that had grown out of the Colorado Silver Boom. Soon Sandy was pregnant, and so Hunter began turning down writing assignments that required travel. It seemed it had come time for the footloose journalist to settle down.

He began to ponder writing a book. Having decided that fiction was old-fashioned, he knew that what he had to write was a non-fiction book that possessed the qualities of a great novel—something beautiful, powerful, and original, but grounded in the frenetic world of 1963. Initially, he thought about writing the story of his journey throughout South America, with some of his articles included to pad out the narrative. Then, a publisher suggested writing a book on the ski bum culture in Aspen. However, for Thompson this was just too trivial. His first book had to tackle something important, and the ski bum fad just felt shallow and meaningless.[1] There was nothing he could dig into, so he passed.

While living out west, Thompson penned an article about Louisville, drawing on ideas and notes from his last visit. He had decided that he needed his byline in a bigger publication than the *Observer* and approached *The Reporter* with an investigation into race relations. *The Reporter*, which was published between 1949 and 1968, was one of the biggest and most respected magazines in the US, and Thompson referred to them as "about the best magazine in the country." He was delighted when they published his article, "A Southern City With Northern Problems," in December 1963, but although he continued to pitch articles to them, his friend Dwight Martin, who had been editor for just a brief stint, left in 1964 and his replacement was not as fond of Thompson's style.

For three long paragraphs, Thompson portrays Louisville as a modern, integrated city where black and white people rub shoulders without a hint of animosity. However, he then makes a sudden about-turn: "All this is true – and so it is all the more surprising to visit Louisville and find so much evidence to the contrary." It is a technique he had previously employed to a limited extent, and which would make him famous with his first book, *Hell's Angels*. Thompson is trotting out the official story as though it were true, only to logically and systematically refute it.

In this article, he also manages to combine several voices into one and use it as a quote representative of how people *feel* rather than what any one person actually *said*. This was not the first time that he had done this but now it is clearer that he is combining various voices into

---

1   In 1969, he wrote "The Temptations of Jean-Claude Killy," about the world's most famous skier. He remarked, "Now it is all downhill for the world's richest ski bum." [*The Great Shark Hunt*, p. 95] On the surface, it is a silly and rather obvious piece of wordplay, but it also functions as a put-down of Killy, who had by then retired from professional skiing and was little more than a "ski bum," something of no interest to Thompson.

one singular, representative voice. He again supports his claims with anonymous quotes that sound a little too perfect. These sometimes serve the function of proving his argument and other times they are used to break up the text and make it more readable by having a back and forth between two or more people, like his Aruba article.

Thompson's point is that Louisville may seem to be over its racist history because it is now integrated, but that open or violent racism is not the only kind. Whilst obvious to most Americans in the twenty-first century, this was not a point seriously considered by many in the early sixties. Thompson recounts comparatively subtle instances of racism throughout his article, such as discrimination in real estate. He highlights this by reporting the story of a "Negro executive with adequate funds" who calls up a realtor and asks to view a house. When the executive arrives, the realtor is furious because the black man had sounded white over the phone. It is a witty observation that highlights the absurdity of racist mentalities, much like Mark Twain had done in *Pudd'nhead Wilson*.

On November 22, 1963, President John F. Kennedy was assassinated in Dallas, Texas. Thompson was devastated by the news and wrote William Kennedy that "there is no human being within 500 miles to whom I can communicate anything – much less the fear and loathing that is on me after today's murder." He had been using the phrase "the Fear" occasionally in his writing since at least his time in Big Sur, but this was his first known use of the term "fear and loathing" that would later become synonymous with his style of writing and as a shorthand for his most famous book. There have been various theories about where this term originated, but Douglas Brinkley put it most concisely:

> Hunter used to claim that the phrase "Fear and Loathing" was a derivation of Kierkegaard's *Fear and Trembling*. In actuality he lifted it from Thomas Wolfe's *The Web and the Rock*. He had read the novel when he lived in New York. He used to mark up pages of favorite books, underlining phrases that impressed him. On page sixty-

two of *The Web and the Rock* he found "fear and loathing" and made it his. I asked him why he didn't give Wolfe credit. Essentially he said it was too much of a hassle, that people would think he meant Tom Wolfe, his New Journalism contemporary.

The death of President Kennedy was an enormous blow. Here was a politician Thompson could respect and who might possibly push America in the right direction—and his head had been blown apart in front of the nation. It brought an end to several blissful months and severely dampened any optimism Thompson had for the future of his country. It also convinced him—although he had already considered the possibility—that "Fiction is dead." He told his friend that, from this moment onwards, "every man with balls should be on the firing line. [...] They can count me in." It was the beginning of his politicization and a new resolution to have his impact upon the world with his only saleable skill—writing. But the assassination had changed things. The old rules of journalism no longer applied. Words were weapons that bestowed power that could be wielded against those in positions of authority. "I feel ready for a dirty game," he said.

Just a few days later, the game began as he launched perhaps his first visceral attack on future president, Richard Nixon:

> He is like a hyena that you shoot and gut,
> then see a few hours later, loping along in
> his stinking way, oblivious to the fact that
> he is not only dead, but gutted as well.

This was precisely what he meant by "a dirty game." No more deferring to authority or treading carefully within the confines of traditional, objective journalism. It was the start of a new era, in which calling a politician a "hyena" was perfectly reasonable.

Although they had been happy in Woody Creek, in December Hunter and Sandy were forced to leave after their landlord hiked the rent. They hopped in their car and headed to Glen Ellen, some fifty miles north of San Francisco, which Thompson felt would be a fount of weird stories to report on. Jack London, on whose books he had been raised, had lived there for several years before his death in 1916, building a home he called Wolf House. Thompson did not have the money to buy a vast ranch like London had done, so he and Sandy moved into "a sort of Okie shack" that he called Owl House. He was not exactly enamored of the area, calling Glen Ellen "the Brazil of America."

On March 23, 1964, Sandy gave birth to a boy, Juan Fitzgerald Thompson, named for the president who had been shot a few months previously and for F. Scott Fitzgerald, who remained Thompson's favorite writer. They were, however, soon evicted from their shack because Thompson insisted on shooting gophers at four in the morning. The married couple and their new baby were forced to move in with their friend and neighbor, Dr. Bob Geiger. Thompson and Geiger, who was an aspiring novelist in addition to being a doctor, got along very well, and Sandy became friends with Mrs. Geiger.

In Glen Ellen, Hunter began drinking at a bar called The Rustic Inn. It was a rough place, he noted, but also rather fraudulent. He started work on an article about it for *The Reporter* but it was not published until 1967, in a men's magazine called *Cavalier*. Begun in April and finished in September, the experience soured Thompson on *The Reporter* as they assigned him the job but then backed out and even managed to lose his manuscript. Nonetheless, it is a wonderful story that shows its author's interest in character and setting, as Thompson slowly and with meticulous detail introduces the locals and lets them talk. At this point in his career, he was adept at reporting on what he saw and heard, painstakingly crafting an article that slowly wound out the story, often balancing various themes and characters.

He begins by describing a photo of Hazel Cowan, an old-timer who knew Jack London and used to ride around on a horse. Thompson brings this into the present day and shows Cowan talking with Chester Womack, a soldier of fortune and part-owner of the Rustic. When a tourist couple wander into the bar, Womack grabs a guitar and sings a vulgar song, driving them out. Thompson has thus presented an effective image—we get an idea of the town's history through a photo of Cowan and we know how much things have changed and what the locals feel about it through Womack's attitude toward the tourists. This elicits a smile from the one-eyed bartender—a smile that was "more out of habit than amusement," Thompson notes despite this being something a mere observer could not possibly have known. The story is presented artfully, more like a novel than a piece of journalism. These little glimpses into the characters provide details that, as Hemingway had explained, illuminate the bigger picture better than if the author had carefully articulated the town's history through dates and facts.

As with so many of Thompson's articles, this is about the changing of the times and contains a slight lament for what the world has become.[2] Yet it is not blind nostalgia by any means. Thompson demythologizes the subject of his article, pointing out that the "saloon" in which Jack London supposedly drank was neither Jack London's watering-hole, nor was it even technically a saloon. Still, while he picks apart the false imagery surrounding the Rustic, he observes that it retains the outlaw charm of an old-timey saloon whereas the other carbon copy tourist bars have become rather tame by comparison. In the Rustic, one can reasonably expect to find a good ole barfight, yet without the cars of police officers showing up that one would find in San Francisco.

Although his depictions of some characters are very well rendered, others are clearly just fabrications to insert Thompson's own opinions, which otherwise hide between lines of description. One such imagined person, referred to only as "an ex-patron," goes on at length in a not-very-convincing fashion that is rather reminiscent of other Thompson quotes. It is too succinct to be real, and, of course, ends on a punchline of sorts: "The next time I

---

2   Two months before Thompson began work on the Rustic article, Bob Dylan, whose music Hunter adored, released his album, *The Times They Are a-Changin'*. After listening to it, he said, "I think the blood is moving in my brain again. Dylan is a goddamn phenomenon, pure gold, and mean as a snake." [*The Proud Highway*, p.436]

want to see how it was in the old days, I'll watch Bonanza." There is another character called Wolf Larsen, who is presumably imagined, too, as his name is borrowed from London's novel, *The Sea-Wolf*, and a reference to a stevedore called Clem, which is possibly a nod to Clem Snide—a character in several books by William S. Burroughs.

Thompson's character does not intrude much upon the story and there is no real action involving him. He just sits at a bar and listens as people talk. On the final page of his 1967 *Cavalier* article, which had been renamed from "The Rustic Inn & Jack London & The Valley of the Moon" to the more prosaic "Nights in the Rustic," Thompson finally breaks with the restrained, novelistic style that he had used until this point, and moves more into his usual opinions—"the wisdom." Having taken his reader back and forth between authenticity and phoniness, the final judgment is proffered. In terms of authenticity, the bar is not old enough to have been London's favorite and the old-timers are paid to sit around and talk about him, but still it is a rough place that reminds Thompson of a Bolivian mining camp.

"Nights in the Rustic" is evidence of Thompson's developing style and attempts to fuse journalistic and novelistic modes, as well as his interest in the outsider scene. After being published in 1967, *Cavalier* was sued for five and a half million dollars by the bar's owners, who did not take kindly to his numerous insinuations that the bar was violent and unfriendly toward tourists. No doubt they were offended by lines such as this:

> The 1890s atmosphere is badly addled by 1960-style hoodlums who long for trouble. […] On most weekend nights the place fills up with one of the sleaziest mobs in all Christendom. Along with the regular handful of pot-bellied frumps and the muscular women who work at the nearby hospital for the mentally retarded is a hard core of out-of-control customers who would tax the hospitality of the most venal innkeeper in the mountains of eastern Kentucky.

The *San Francisco Examiner* also suggested that there was an inference in the article of the bar being a resort for swingers, but the quoted dialogue that supposedly proves this is rather ambiguous.

After leaning on the Geigers about as long as they could reasonably do so, the Thompsons moved into the city and took an apartment on Parnassus Street, in the Haight-Ashbury district. Ever since his teens, Thompson had possessed an ability to identify outsider and underground trends, and he had known for a while that something was happening in San Francisco. The Beat Generation was dying away, but the hippies were coming and all sorts of social issues were bubbling to the surface. He was going to be right in the middle of it.

But there was a problem. Whether it was the death of John F. Kennedy or the financial burden of a newborn child, or whether he missed being a rambling, footloose reporter, in 1964 Thompson was starting to feel that he had lost his voice. "I am deep in the grip of a professional collapse," he wrote a friend, "that worries me to the extent that I cannot do any work to cure it." In South America and in the first few months after returning to the States, everything he wrote was golden. He had found a style of writing that worked for him and he could play with it and try new things, always propelling himself forward. Now, however, he had hit a wall.

Certainly, his writing by this point had become a little stale. In 1963, his opening lines would grab a reader by the collar and demand to be read. His stories were witty and informative, filled with sly humor and adventure. Now, they were dry and notably lacking enthusiasm. He had dropped his own voice and replaced it with a more standardized form of reporting. He was writing book reviews and then taking assignments that required him to drive across much of the western half of the country, but nothing really inspired him. Even an article about his teenage hero, Marlon Brando, resulted in a tedious collection of words that could have come from almost any small-town newspaper in the country.

Between *The Reporter* paying him late and the *Observer*'s conservative values severely limiting his freedom to editorialize, he was growing weary of even trying to turn out good writing. To his friend from Big Sur, Lionel Olay, Thompson lamented that:

> I have turned into a fuck-off as far as this journalism is concerned—one of these woodsy types who talks a good article but never writes it. I only write when finances pressure me into it, and not a hell of a lot then.

This was a marked shift in attitude. Prior to this, Thompson had considered journalism to be his saleable talent but he seldom wrote *just* for money. He was high-minded about writing and, even though he viewed the wider American press as a bunch of charlatans, he still believed in the fundamental importance of good, reliable journalism.

For one of his better articles, he drove to Ketchum, Idaho, where he visited Ernest Hemingway's home. One of Thompson's true heroes, Hemingway had shot himself just three years earlier. In the article, he asks locals what brought Hemingway to this strange place and why he stayed. He then looks at the novelist's life and work quite briefly, charting the downward trajectory that brought a brilliant man to a point where he could no longer write. Here, Thompson is weaving together several strands of a story. There is his role (which is relatively minor), the people he talks with, Hemingway's life and work and death, and several greater themes that bind it all together. Sometimes he attempted to include too many threads, but here he is able to handle all of these and weave them seamlessly, crafting a fine article. It was also his first containing "atavistic," a word he would use so often that it became forever associated with his work.[3]

---

3   He told Tom Wolfe: "I picked that up in a Ketchum, Idaho, bar about five years ago and I suspect it's appeared in every article since then." [*Fear and Loathing in America*, p54] However, "atavistic" and "atavism" both appear in Fitzgerald's *Tender is the Night* and several of Fitzgerald's books are discussed in the paragraph preceding Thompson's use of "atavistic," suggesting that perhaps he had found it there. [*Tender*, p. 196; 223]

Thompson is interested not only in what brought Hemingway to Ketchum, but what pushed him to suicide. Regarding Hemingway's view that "conviction" was essential for literary success, Thompson wrote:

> That power of conviction is a hard thing for any writer to sustain, and especially so once he becomes conscious of it. Fitzgerald fell apart when the world no longer danced to his music; Faulkner's conviction faltered when he had to confront Twentieth Century Negroes instead of the black symbols in his books; and when Dos Passos tried to change his convictions he lost all his power. [...]
> Like many another writer, Hemingway did his best work when he felt he was standing on something solid – like an Idaho mountainside, or a sense of conviction.

Thompson suggests that the modern world was moving too fast and was too chaotic for an old writer. He explains, in a line that indicates that he was reflecting on his own recent failures: "The function of art is to bring order out of chaos, a tall order when the chaos is static and a superhuman task when chaos is multiplying." Indeed, Thompson had always written in order to understand the world, and this thought no doubt frightened him. The article is also sadly prophetic. As Thompson charts Hemingway's road from literary brilliance to failure and suicide, he maps out his own path for the future.

The article was written on a tour of the West paid for by the *National Observer*. Thompson was not happy with his writing, except the Hemingway article, which he said "was the only one I still feel like claiming," and the only one that went into the newspaper without heavy editing. It was time for a change.

In San Francisco, he found a vibrant world of freaks and outlaws that was worth writing about, but it was not what the *National Observer* or its readers wanted. He kept pitching them ideas but the newspaper, whose readership was largely Republican, wanted little to do with the counterculture, and certainly nothing that celebrated it or brought its unconventional views uncomfortably close. He was, however, able to sell them an article about the fall of the Beat Generation in "When the Beatniks Were Social Lions," which dealt with a group who now seemed like old news, and therefore safe. His article is on the surface a tame, almost sociological approach that looks from the outside in on the Beats. It begins with a question—"What ever happened to the Beat Generation?"—and then sets out to answer it, focusing on a friend of Thompson's called Willard, "one of the great 'beatniks' of his time." Again, he is using his notion of reporting a single person's story to shed light on a bigger issue.

He begins his story in the conspiratorial tone he had inserted into his South American reporting, telling the readers that what they are about to read is true:

> The story is a classic, and if you travel in the right circles out here you will still hear it told, although not always accurately. The truth, however, goes like this:

Thompson then explains that he had been brewing his own beer when one day it was discovered by Willard and another artist friend. The two men consumed it and, in a fit of drunkenness, decided to repaint Willard's rented house. The police "arrived to find the front of the house looking like a Jackson Pollack canvas" and a fight ensued, with the hulking Willard sentenced to six months in prison.

There is no mention of Willard in any of Thompson's letters or in any of his other writings because Willard did not exist. As Thompson explained to a friend,

> I have discovered the secret of writing fiction, calling it impressionistic journalism, and selling it to people who want "something fresh." I just sold the Observer one on the Beat Generation; it required one hour's work, has a vague base in historical rumor, and they loved it.

Throughout the next decade, Thompson would work on this concept that he sometimes called "impressionistic journalism" or "personal journalism," and which he credited at least once to Jack Kerouac. His definition of this sort of fiction-journalism hybrid would change slightly over the years but it remained close to what he explained in this letter—writing what was essentially a short story based upon something that probably did happen. It involved a loose, conversational style that made him realize "that people would rather read my letters than my work." The degree of fictionalization in this approach varied from year to year, but at least on this first occasion he obviously viewed it as producing a short story that was loosely based upon a real event. "Personal Journalism is the *Wave of the Future*," he wrote in October 1963.

Thompson had been grafting fiction onto reality since childhood, but clearly he had developed this idea further in South America with his fabricated quotes, imagined scenes, and the presentation of himself as a character observing and sometimes participating in events. He would take a story that had some truth to it and then write a fictionalized version, perhaps making the narrative more engaging for the reader while still conveying the important truths of the issue. This, he felt, was not too far from regular journalism, later explaining, "All journalists improvise on the skeletal truths they drag up – the trick is to do it right and truthfully." He once explained to William Kennedy that "Objectivity is impossible in journalism" because of certain legal quandaries, which could make reporting with total accuracy impossible. "Fiction is the only way to get around this roadblock," he claimed, suggesting that a degree of fictionalization could bridge the gap and allow for a purer truth to emerge.

More than once, he said that this idea was cribbed from Faulkner, whom he quoted as saying, "the best fiction is far more *true* than any kind of journalism – and the best journalists have always known this." Still, he was aware that there were major problems inherent in the idea of blending fantasy and reality, not least the issue of being a relatively unknown journalist, writing for serious publications:

> You cannot write like that—and get paid for it—until your name rings bells; then you can foam to your heart's content. I have the same continuing problem, and am constantly hung on it. Whether you are a journalist or not, the only way to attempt journalism is to assume you know nothing at the start, and then only write what you find evidence to support—along with the evidence, so neither the editor nor the reader is forced to take your word for it.

In a sense, the journalist still had to deal in truths that could be proven even if he fictionalized parts of the story. It was a challenging concept and one that he would refine often throughout his career and explain at great lengths to befuddled editors, publishers, readers, and interviewers.

We will return to the interplay of fact and fiction later, but in Thompson's article on the Beat Generation, we can see the journalist also developing something akin to the sidekick and persona devices that he would employ with great success in his most famous books. Aware that one man's adventures could get a little tedious, he has either invented or borrowed the character of Willard to liven up the prose. Automatically, having another person there makes the text more interesting and also allows Thompson to bring some weird and wild behavior to the story without actually seeing and reporting it or doing it himself. In some of his later stories, he would present a sidekick or temporary companion as a perspective on his own insane actions, and in others he would play the relatively straight observer role while his character—often a version of Thompson himself—would raise hell. It seems that Willard is an early instance of the latter.

As for Thompson's own role in the story, he plays the detached observer, looking back to a point in recent history and reflecting upon those heady days. He tells his reader that the wild story that transpires was all about Willard, but in fact it is Thompson who leaves this giant artist character alone with a five-gallon jug of beer. In a sense, he is the instigator—a literary prankster. Just as Young Hunter flicked lit matches into piles of leaves around suburban

Louisville, Literary Hunter is subtly starting fires and then watching them rage. Now, of course, he had more than just his neighbors watching the carnage.

Despite his recent successes in journalism, Thompson was good at burning bridges and managed to insult some of his publishing contacts. As a result, he was forced to line up for temporary work with homeless people, hoping that he could earn a few dollars by handing out flyers. He also had to drive a cab on occasion and sometimes sold his blood to feed his family. Still, he was asked by the *National Observer* to attend the Republican Convention in San Francisco in August 1963. Here, he embarrassed himself by displaying an unforgivably poor knowledge of national politics in front of other reporters, but, worse than that, word about his obnoxious, drunken behavior made its way back to his *Observer* bosses and earned him a letter of warning about his behavior. He explained to a friend: "They wrote and told me to straighten up or fuck off—and I still haven't decided which way to swing."

He had been upset with them for not allowing him to write the interesting stories that he wanted and then had failed to turn in an article on the Liston vs Patterson fight. He had also been turning in large invoices for expenses—something that would sour his relationships with even the most tolerant editors in the future. When he was eager to head east for a wedding, he convinced them to fund a long train ride across the country, promising a story in return. The *Observer* initially sent him off with an expensive train ticket and several hundred dollars, but on the first day he sent a telegram asking for two hundred more. He did the same several days later, and again and again, until eventually he had received two thousand dollars from the newspaper. Feeling that Thompson had taken advantage of them, the editors deducted this money against his future articles, causing a major rift between the newspaper and its rogue reporter.

The resulting story, which was only published in Thompson's 1997 letter collection, *The Proud Highway*, was called "Dr. Slow; Or, How I Learned to Save Money,

Lose Weight, and Love the Airplane…"[4] It is the story of a journalist attempting to travel across the United States by train and being thoroughly bored and annoyed by the whole journey. He gives a reasonably interesting description of the train and its inhabitants, as well as some of the landscapes and landmarks that they pass along the way. At one point, Thompson bemoans the fact that everything has changed since the days of *The Great Gatsby*, and that traveling by rail has become something that most people avoid if at all possible. He explains:

> No doubt there are several good reasons for crossing the country by rail, instead of by plane, but once you've done it a few times, that's it, you've done it, and the next step is to admit that airplanes have as many basic advantages over trains as television has over radio. For good or ill, the space age is very much with us, and if Wolfe and Fitzgerald were alive today they'd surely be traveling by jet.

Thompson's biographer, William McKeen called it:

> a prototype for what would become known as a Hunter Thompson story [that was part] literary reflection, part mad-dog screed at the foibles of modern life [and] in the end a diary of an insane cross-country trip with club cars full of people whose sole purpose was making Hunter's life miserable.

However, there is nothing "insane" about this cross-country trip and, as he just sits in a chair and offers obvious comments on the time it takes to cross the country, it hardly could be viewed as a prototype of a classic Gonzo tale. The journey is pretty much devoid of action or events, save for a baby crying or Thompson trying to put his seat

4   The title is an obvious reference to Stanley Kubrick's 1964 masterpiece, *Dr. Strangelove or: How I Learned to Stop Worrying and Love the Bomb*. He made various references to this movie in his letters, too.

back and then deciding against it. He remembers a few arguments that other people had but mostly he weighs the merits of train travel in the jet era in what reads very much like a dull high school essay.

In any case, it did not sit well with the *Observer* editors, many of whom were now calling for time on Thompson's tenure. Although this one was surely dull enough to believe, they claimed that many of his articles now had a "fairy-story aura" and that he was "unreliable" as a reporter. When Clifford Ridley found that Thompson had quoted the Bible but gotten the wrong verse, Thompson replied, "Well hell, one verse or another." In his own mind, such details were not of any significance to the story he was trying to tell.

In an article about Butte, Montana, more serious accusations emerged. In "Whither the Old Copper Town of the West? To Boom or Bust?" Thompson savaged the town but defended all of his observations with quotes from people on the street. It was the "frustrated Spaniard" idea that he had told Semonin about. Soon, though, people began to call in and complain that they had been misquoted. Some words had merely been taken out of context, but others had been changed entirely. When it was discovered that he had also made up information about the town's population and the number of employees at the factories he wrote about, the editors confronted him. All he had to say was, "Who cares about these kinds of facts?" It did not exactly give them confidence in their journalist. Nonetheless, many years later, he defended his approach to journalism as factual, but in a different way from conventional reporting: "My concern with accuracy is on a higher level than nickels and dimes, in a word, line by line."

When he turned in "Dr. Slow," the story was pulled due to concerns over whether Thompson had plagiarized it. Editor Bill Giles, who had been one of Hunter's biggest supporters at the paper, told one biographer that "There was some discussion that [the train story] came from a writer who did the same sort of thing, going cross-country on trains, in the twenties." He explained that they could never definitively confirm that Thompson had plagiarized his story, but that they could not afford the risk.[5]

Of course, Thompson told the story of his departure another way. He claimed that one of the book reviews he had written for the newspaper was spiked due to an editor's personal grudge. He had positively reviewed Tom Wolfe's *Kandy-Kolored Tangerine-Flake Streamline Baby*, but the editor supposedly loathed Wolfe and refused to run it. Thompson, incensed by this, sent the review to Wolfe and thus ended his relationship with the *Observer*.[6] His last article appeared in December 1964. He had bigger things to write about.

One of Thompson's major gripes with the *National Observer* had been their refusal to consider an article on the burgeoning Free Speech Movement around Berkley. They may have considered it if Thompson had promised to expose the movement as a hissy fit among empty-headed students that would soon die away—but Hunter was certain that this was the start of something bigger.

In December 1964, he received a letter from Cary McWilliams, editor of *The Nation*, who said he greatly admired Hunter's work for the *National Observer*. Today, *The Nation* touts itself as "the oldest continuously published weekly magazine in the United States" and at the time it was a very progressive outlet that had been banned in certain libraries during the fifties for its allegedly pro-communist leanings. Thompson respected McWilliams for

---

5   It is not clear to what work they were referring, but Sinclair Lewis' 1919 novel, *Free Air*, is thematically similar, though stylistically very different. In *Free Air*, the car is championed over the railway as a democratizing force. This book also echoes a life-long theme in Thompson's work: it attacks the wealthy, privileged classes. This also links it with *The Great Gatsby*, to which Thompson's story bears more similarity. Indeed, he acknowledges that in the text and it appears that this voice is a deliberate affectation.

6   Thompson claimed in an interview with *Playboy* that he was "fired" and *Playboy* added that it was after a "bitter dispute," which earned a letter of reply from Roscoe C. Born, an editor at the *Observer*. "As a fascinating figure flitting about on the periphery of journalism," he explained, "Hunter has a certain value as long as he is not taken too seriously." [*Fear and Loathing in America*, p.596]

his 1939 book, *Factories in the Field: The Story of Migratory Farm Labor in California,* and felt honored to join the ranks of *The Nation's* contributors, such as Albert Einstein and Jean-Paul Sartre.

Thompson was in deep poverty at this point and *The Nation* didn't pay much, but he was excited enough by the prospect of writing for them that he put aside the matter of money. He was free from the *Observer* and could write about the sort of things that really interested him. Five years earlier, he had claimed that "There are some jobs I wouldn't do for two thousand a month and others I'd be happy to do for two hundred." *The Nation* paid even less than that, but he stayed true to his word.

He pitched McWilliams his Free Speech article, agreeing that they would publish this in the magazine in late 1965, but first the editor had another idea. He sent Thompson a note about the Hell's Angels and told him to pick up a copy of the California Attorney General's report on motorcycle gangs. The idea was perhaps not terribly original, as the media was already obsessed with biker gangs in 1965, but when Thompson read the report, he had an idea that was very much unique. He wanted to embed himself in the Angels, just like a war correspondent. It was something no other journalist had attempted due to the gang's notorious propensity for violence. Most importantly, though, he wanted to tell the real story rather than the absurd fictions presented in the report.

This is where one of the great contradictions of Hunter Thompson's life really enters the story. Thus far, we have seen him bend the truth for the purposes of comedy or drama, and then claim that fiction can be a gateway to truth or a way to fight back against injustice by highlighting greater truths than could be told in straight reporting. We have also seen that he made up quotes and facts possibly out of laziness or just a lack of interest. Here is a man who would readily lie in some stories but who was paradoxically obsessed with uncovering *the truth*. It was a journalist's job, he knew, to expose the truth and then explain it for the world. In Hunter's mind, fictional elements only came into play when presenting that truth in order to explain it better than traditional modes. Likewise, novelistic elements may work when exploding falsehoods or dealing with insidious propaganda.

Despite what we have seen of his reporting methods so far, it is clear that in most cases Thompson was eager to drive at the truth, and he did pursue it with a reckless passion. When he learned about the Hell's Angels, the obvious question for him was whether these outlaws were as bad as they seemed. Everywhere you looked, they were in the headlines and none of the reporters churning out these articles for a minute considered that they could be anything less than the devil incarnate. But could this really be true? Thompson knew all about presenting a rebellious image in the media—he had been doing it since his days as a sportswriter at Eglin. Perhaps the bikers were putting on an act and the newspapers were just playing along with it.

At his local bar, Thompson asked a *San Francisco Chronicle* reporter called Denny Beckler about the Angels. Beckler introduced him to Birney Jarvis, another *Chronicle* reporter, who used to be a member of the biker gang. Thompson had an in, and he was about to write the book that would launch his career.

Hell's Angels

I think you miss the point by focusing on the word "courage." I never thought of it that way, at the time—it was simply an assignment: to write a true book, and to write the truth I had to get close to it.

Hunter S. Thompson

In early 1965, Hunter Thompson wrote Cary McWilliams to say that he was "long past the point of simple poverty, and well into a state of hysterical destitution." He pitched various article ideas, including one about the decline of San Francisco and one on racism that built upon a single image he had included in his article for *The Reporter* the previous year. They did not, however, manage to agree on any of these.

On March 18, McWilliams had sent the starving journalist a note that changed his life. Writing about the world's most notorious motorcycle gang was the perfect assignment for the erstwhile street punk. Thompson agreed, saying "this one is right up my alley," and he went immediately to the Attorney General's office to talk with the staff there. A report on an investigation into motorcycle gangs, compiled by Thomas Lynch, had just been published that month. After consulting with the staff there and reading the Lynch Report, he was appalled to find that no one had actually spoken to the Angels before publishing it—the only sources were police. "I can't imagine doing a story without their point of view," he said to his editor.

After a week of mostly conventional research, on March 25, Thompson walked into the DePau Hotel bar and confronted the world's most notorious biker gang. He had been pointed in this direction by Birney Jarvis,

133

a former vice president and life-time Hell's Angel, but Jarvis did not come along for this crucial meeting. It was a daunting task. He had to convince a group of murderous thugs to cooperate with a journalist they had never met before, and he had little reason to believe they would do anything but beat him to a pulp there and then.

The Angels were not immediately convinced, but they admired the courage it took for a man to walk in alone and address them. It probably helped that he looked different from other reporters and was quite drunk, too. In "a beautifully wasted speech," he savagely attacked the establishment press that had thus far offered only inaccurate, sensationalistic reporting on the Angels without ever communicating with them. Referring to himself as part of the "outlaw press," he told them he intended to be the first journalist to get the truth and present a fair and balanced story. He managed to win them over.

They won him over, too. Thompson was surprised to find that "they're human and, in fact, peculiarly decent when they're off guard and relaxed." Or maybe they just saw in each other something familiar: "Crazies always recognize each other," he explained. Later that night, in a story often told by Thompson and included in pretty much every book about him, he invited some of the Hell's Angels over to his house, where his wife and infant child were sleeping. Before letting them in, he warned them that he had a shotgun and was not afraid to use it. That seemed to earn their respect, and certainly added to Hunter's legend as a wild man.

He immediately recognized that he was onto something with these people and became obsessed with learning about their lives. Paul Semonin worried that he was being sucked into their world, saying, "If you look at his writings about the Hells Angels, there's not a more unsavory kind of bunch of characters, and yet he somehow idolizes them. He does it in a very subtle way, but he makes their struggles something that reflects both a failure and a rebellion against certain things in American culture and society." In his audio recordings, which were as much a personal journal as they were professional notes, Thompson admits to having a "romantic idea" of the Hell's Angels that he acknowledges is at odds with their penchant for brutal crimes like rape. Bob Geiger also worried about his younger friend:

> I would say, "Hunter, why are you writing about these losers? These guys are crazies, and you're glorifying them. They're nothing. You wouldn't stop to piss on them if they were on fire, so why the hell are you writing a book about them? In essence, you're kind of glorifying them in this book. Even though you're not saying positive things, you're giving them all kinds of publicity." […] But he said, "No, these guys are really showing us where society is going." And I totally missed it, because he was absolutely right.

This was Thompson's angle with the article and with the book. He wanted to write about "fringe types" but it had to connect to a bigger theme. It had to mean something. He later said:

> The Hell's Angels are an ugly phenomenon; they are also an ominous symptom of something wrong at the roots of the society that breeds them. This is what I tried to write about; the Angels themselves were only a vehicle.

Over the two weeks it took Thompson to write his article, he met often with the biker gang. He would purchase beer or wine and then get the Angels drunk as he scribbled copious notes, recording every detail of their lives that they were willing to share. One day, Thompson's primary contact among the Angels, a man called Frenchy, took the reporter to a bar called El Adobe to meet Sonny Barger, the group's leader. He was more intelligent than the other Angels and wary of Hunter's motives. Still, the pair warmed up to one another and Thompson soon had Barger's blessing for the article. "We weren't friends,"

Thompson made clear, "but there was a mutual respect."[1]

On April 9, Thompson submitted his article to *The Nation*. It was, he said, "a sociology-type piece" that examined the attraction of the motorcycle gang to disaffected men and explored why they were so fascinating to middle America. He also took the approach of running through the charges brought against them by the Lynch Report and then either confirming or denying them. These were both techniques that he had practiced in his *National Observer* articles, where he would present a claim that was generally believed to be true and then set out to prove or disprove it.

Years later, he explained that this was the article that altered his opinions on journalism as an artform. He wrote:

> Of course, I had already written two novels… I'd always regarded journalism as a lower form of work, a left-handed thing to make money. But of course I'd never seen any journalism that struck me as being special. It was all the same, newspaper writing.
>
> But this subject was so strange that for the first time in any kind of journalism, I could have the same kind of fun with writing that I had had in the past with fiction. I could bring the same kind of intensity and have the same involvement with what I was writing about, because there were characters so weird that I couldn't even make them up. […] In a way it was like having a novel handed to you with the characters already developed.

In a letter to McWilliams that accompanied the article on April 9, he admitted making "seemingly authoritative but frequently unsupported remarks"—a hallmark of his journalism ever since Eglin. However, he explained that all

---

1   In his private notes, Thompson fawns over Barger, remarking that he is a natural leader and highly intelligent. However, he observes that the Hell's Angel is quite inarticulate. [*Gonzo Tapes*, CD1 track 2]

claims about the history of the club were vetted by Birney Jarvis, who as a life-time member and also a reporter for a major publication was uniquely qualified. He had also put in serious legwork in terms of research and so his authoritative voice was, for once, firmly backed by reliable sources. When quoting the Angels, he was careful to observe that they were as likely to tell vile stories about their own actions as the press were—but that didn't necessarily make those stories true. "A lot of this is a pose," he said of their enthusiasm for putting on a tough image.

Hunter S. Thompson seldom ignored an opportunity to lash out at the American press and with this new piece he was going for the jugular: "The difference between the Hell's Angels in the paper and the Hell's Angels for real is enough to make a man wonder what newsprint is for." He trots out the claims by *Newsweek* and *Time* and then thoroughly picks them apart, claiming that they "make a clanging good article for a national news magazine" but lack any substance and are far from reflecting the truth of the situation. He mocks the unoriginality of the headline writers by acknowledging that *Newsweek* had used "The Wild Ones" and the *Times* had gone with "The Wilder Ones." As for the claims made in either of these articles, Thompson allows an Angel to speak for him: "It's all bullshit."

The Hell's Angels piece includes many of the best features of his previous reporting. He begins with an arresting opening (briefly mentioning "a heinous gang rape in the moonlit sand dunes"), attempts to weigh accusations against reality, and interjects himself into the story. He even manages to reference *The Great Gatsby*. Thompson is not a major participant in this article but he is continuously present. The reader is aware that he has infiltrated the group and is on speaking terms with its terrifying members, but he does not boast of this, nor does he celebrate his own outlaw actions as he would do in later articles. He is an observer and little else.

The article also ends with a one-on-one conversation over a pool table with an unnamed Angel, finishing with the line, "Hell, these days we have more action than we can handle." He avoids saying that the news media is making the Hell's Angels into something they otherwise would not be by having one of his interviewees say it in an ominous, cryptic way. It is a classic Hunter Thompson device and a fitting end to one of his best pieces of writing. For years, he had known he could advance his own views and push a story where he wanted it to go by putting words into his subjects' mouths, later explaining that he "paraphrased a lot of dialogue without giving it a second thought" when writing about the Angels.

In this article, Thompson also advances a method of reporting speech that he had only begun to explore in previous works. After having spent so much time around the Hell's Angels, gathering information and collecting quotes, he decided that it was better to roll all of their voices into one singular representation than to present them separately. As such, he writes:

> This, in effect, was what the Hell's Angels had been saying all along. Here is their version of what happened, as told by several who were there:
>
> One girl was white and pregnant, the other was colored, and they were with five colored studs. They hung around our bar– Nick's Place on Del Monte Avenue–for about three hours Saturday night, drinking and talking with our riders, then they came out to the beach with us–them and their five boyfriends.

The origins of this reporting technique are most likely in a book that Thompson mentioned in *The Rum Diary*, and whose author was one of Hunter's great literary heroes. Joseph Conrad, in *The Nigger of the Narcissus*, used the same technique to describe the sailors aboard a ship traveling from Bombay to London:

> [...] the growling voices hummed steady amongst bursts of laughter and hoarse calls. "Here, sonny, take that bunk!... Don't you do it!... What's your last ship?... I know her... Three years ago, in Puget Sound... This here berth leaks, I tell you!... Come

on; give us a chance to swing that chest... Did you bring a bottle, any of you shore toffs? Give us a bit of 'baccy... I know her; her skipper drank himself to death... He was a dandy boy!... Liked his lotion inside, he did!... No!... Hold your row, you chaps!... I tell you, you came on board a hooked, where they get their money's worth out of poor Jack, by—!..."

At the end of their collective speech, the Angels say "—and that's all it was." Thompson brings the narrative back to his own weighing of the law vs the Hell's Angels by beginning a new paragraph, "But not quite all." This informal quirk is a sentence fragment and, as you would learn in any basic guide to English grammar, it is a major grammatical error.

In his letters, he often trialed ideas before attempting to fit them into his articles. As he had the habit of going off on tangents in his letters, he would attempt to bring his narrative from one point to another or back to a previous point by saying "Anyway" at the start of a new paragraph. It was conversational and could work in some forms of writing, but it was a little too lazy for inclusion in serious journalism. However, a year earlier, in an article called "Living in the Time of Alger, Greeley, Debs," he had done something very similar, refocusing his narrative with another sentence fragment: "Which may be a valid question."[2] While working on his Hell's Angels article, he wrote to a friend and, toward the end of the letter, suddenly changed the direction of the narrative by starting a new paragraph: "And that's that."

From "Anyway" to "And that's that" and "But not quite all," we can see a very subtle development. Thompson had now learned the rules of writing well enough to know that good writers break them, and when he did so it was

---

2   This is at least how Thompson had intended it and how it appears in his 1979 collection, *The Great Shark Hunt*. However, the editors removed the first four paragraphs of his article, including this interesting transition.

in a conscious effort to find his own literary voice.[3] After his death, his widow, Anita Thompson, explained: "Here is the secret: *Hell's Angels* owes its genre-busting success to the previous fifteen years Hunter had spent studying the art and craft of writing." Indeed, he continued to develop these odd, stylistic quirks that ultimately forged his own inimitable style, making his writing easily identifiable. But it was not just a matter of style. These unconventional transitions helped him to structure his stories, weaving the strands of the plot neatly, and guiding his reader seamlessly from scene to scene, idea to idea. By beginning paragraphs with certain sentence fragments, he was able to include more wisdom through digressions and tangents before bringing the reader suddenly back to the main track. It would become a major feature of his writing over the coming years.

His article, "The Motorcycle Gangs: Losers and Outsiders" was published in *The Nation* on May 17, 1965. "It is probably too long," he had told his editor, of the four-thousand-word article, "but my main feeling is that too much has been left out. A one-hundred-page piece would have been much easier." Fortunately, Thompson was going to have the chance to write a longer version because, within a week, there was a giant pile of letters under the letter box in his front door. The self-proclaimed outlaw journalist had suddenly become hot property.

In the days that followed the article's publication, offers came pouring in from big-name magazines and newspapers, hoping there was more to come from the world's leading expert on the Hell's Angels. The editors of publications like *Playboy*, *Esquire*, *The Saturday Evening Post*, and *Cavalier* all wanted to speak with the daring journalist that had gotten the scoop of the year and see if he would write for them. Each of them promised far more than the hundred dollars he had been paid for the original article, so they made for tempting offers.

These were soon followed by notes from publishers wondering if he was interested in turning the story into

3   Late in life, he offered some invaluable advice: "I think you have to learn the craft and learn to respect it before you set out to break all the rules." [*Ancient Gonzo Wisdom*, p.484]

a book. The offers varied greatly in terms of what was expected from Thompson. Although some publishers wanted him to expand the article into a full-length book, most hoped that he would be able to turn his attentions to other "fringe types." He had wanted to write a book for a long time and so he had plenty of ideas bottled up, drawing upon old articles he had written about outsiders and rebels who lived in the dark shadows of society—"a non-publishable hellbroth of vagrant interests," in his own words.

Money, of course, had long been the roadblock between Hunter and his book. He had not been able to afford to put aside paid writing and work on something that took months or years of his life, but now he had a range of offers to consider. Poverty, however, robbed him of the chance to fully explore his options and so he quickly signed a contract with Ballantine Books, who offered him an immediate one thousand five hundred dollars for agreeing to write a book on the Hell's Angels. In total, the contract was worth six thousand dollars, which was ten times Thompson's income for the first half of 1965. Bernard Shir-Cliff, his editor at Ballantine, evidently spoke Hunter's language.

With this newfound wealth, the terminally impoverished writer paid for several months' rent, retrieved his gun and camera from the pawnshop, and purchased health insurance for his family, knowing fine well that there was a good chance he would be hospitalized before the book was written. He also bought a motorcycle on the premise that if he wanted to write a book about the Angels, he needed to *ride* with the Angels. He didn't want to follow them around in a beat-up old car. Still, he was determined to avoid becoming too close, so he bought a BSA 650 Lightning—a bike guaranteed to upset at least a few Angels, who exclusively rode Harley-Davidsons. They offered him several stolen Harleys, but even among outsiders Thompson needed to be different.

He was not only keen to differentiate himself from the Angels, however. As he embarked upon the task of writing his first book, he no longer felt he had to walk in the footsteps of those great writers who had inspired him. He still respected them and would—consciously or otherwise—attempt to emulate them to some extent, but already he had begun to walk his own path. In July, he explained:

> It has finally come home to me that I am not going to be either the Fitzgerald or the Hemingway of this generation … I am going to be the Thompson of this generation, and that makes me more nervous than anything else I can think of.

Despite being referred to as "losers" in both the headline and text of the article, the Hell's Angels were pretty happy with what Thompson had written. He had been fair and honest, and that was all they had wanted. They hadn't asked him to write a puff piece to improve their image; they had only asked that he tell the truth, which he had done. "The club agreed to let him write the book," Sonny Barger said. "I think the majority of people really, really got along with him." The Hell's Angels took a vote, held among members of all the club's chapters, and formally gave him permission to write his book.

Before he could start, however, Thompson sped off for Berkeley, where he spent a week researching and writing the article he had wanted to do for a whole year—the Free Speech Movement. Now that he had an editor who was willing to run articles on progressive causes and open to his editorializing and quirkiness, Thompson knew he had to write the piece. And, despite his advance on the book, a hundred dollars was still not something he could afford to pass up.

In "The Nonstudent Left," Thompson wrote about the college campus tensions at Berkeley. As the political heat rose in the mid-sixties, authorities had passed a law banning nonstudents from participating in protests that originated on campus. This angered the writer, who used his article as a way of criticizing what he perceived as a gross injustice. Once again, he laid out an accusation—that the protestors were merely troublemakers—and then set out to refute it.

"The Nonstudent Left" is a fantastic article and proof

that "The Motorcycle Gangs" was no one-off triumph. Thompson had further refined his literary-journalistic voice, incorporating much of what he had experimented with in old pieces and pushing these techniques as far as he could. With McWilliams allowing more freedom than editors before him, he was able to include more of his darkly satirical statements. When dealing with people he dislikes or distrusts, he is savage and often hilarious. In describing the establishment view of the protests, he refers to one Don Mulford and says, "He thinks he knows that the outburst last fall was caused by New York Communists, beatnik perverts and other godless elements beyond his ken." In criticizing the origins of anti-protest ideas, he claims, "*The Examiner* is particularly influential among those who fear King George III might still be alive in Argentina." When Thompson wants to satirize the media coverage of the student protests, he paraphrases them in his own unique way:

> These people, it was said, were whipping the campus into a frenzy, goading the students to revolt, harassing the administration, and all the while working for their own fiendish ends. You could almost see them loping along the midnight streets with bags of seditious leaflets, strike orders, red banners of protest and cablegrams from Moscow, Peking or Havana.

Notice the peculiar choice of verbs: "whipping," "goading," "harassing," and "loping"; as well as the outrageous adjectives: "fiendish," "seditious." The image is absurd enough but the language—entirely over the top—brings home the foolishness of the mocked viewpoint. In this form of journalism, there is no need to feign objectivity, and so he speaks his mind freely throughout the article, even calling the law "a defective rattrap."

In a letter to McWilliams that accompanied the article, he explained: "I think it is a good piece and maybe closer to the truth than something 'objective' might be." To Paul Semonin, he said that it was "the most biased, violent and wholly political piece I've ever written." Still, despite him putting his cards on the table, most of the article is quite balanced and offers straightforward information about the lives of nonstudents, exploring their politics and backgrounds thoroughly and fairly.

He asks who these "nonstudents" are and brings in his own experience at Columbia to explain. By doing this, he justifies a subsequent passage that claims to speak for the nonstudent. When he says, "It never occurred to [the nonstudent] to jump into campus politics," he is talking on behalf of nonstudents precisely because he was one. He does not need to lean on statistics and quotations for this section because personal experience makes him the expert.

Although Thompson briefly references his own experience, he is notably absent throughout the rest of the article, still an observer rather than a participant. When talking with nonstudents and explaining their lives, there is no mention of the process of getting the story. It is a well-crafted and informative article that shows a mature writer gaining confidence in his work while writing about something that deeply interests him. "It is a far cry from my *Observer* stuff," he said of it, and he was right. *The Nation* provided him the freedom necessary to push his style of writing further.

While on campus and talking with the people at *Spider*, a magazine considered to be the voice of the Free Speech Movement, Thompson gave them a poem he had written. This was not his first poem, nor his last, but he did not often write poetry.[4] Still, he was proud of this effort, entitled "Collect Telegram from a Mad Dog," in which we can see a more familiar Hunter Thompson voice emerge than that in his comparatively restrained articles:

> I wanted rhetoric
> but could only howl the rotten truth
> Norman Luboff[5]
> should have his nuts ripped off with a plastic fork.

---

4   Thompson had written a poem called "The Night-Watch" for *The Spectator* in 1955. It is collected in *Proud Highway*.
5   Norman Luboff is a musician who worked with Bing Crosby. It is not clear why Thompson hated him, but in the book he mentions that the Angels would listen to Luboff before leaving a bar in search of trouble. [p.89]

In a sense, this poem could be viewed as an early form of Gonzo, with "Mad Dog" his alter ego.[6] In his true Gonzo work, beginning in 1970, Hunter inserted himself into the text as a participator or instigator, but in 1965 this was not really something he could afford to do in anything he intended to publish. Yet here we have a short poem in which a violent man howls his rage and seems to be on a quest for someone to rape. It is the sort of deplorable character that Donleavy had employed in *The Ginger Man* and very much what Thompson himself did with *Fear and Loathing in Las Vegas*. In Vegas, he could blame much of the bad behavior on "my attorney," but in his poem it is "The legal man" who sanctions the madness.

In "Collect Telegram from a Mag Dog," he also coins the word "slumfeeders." This is the beginning of a habit he would develop for taking two words and jamming them together into an ugly, offensive new term like "greedhead," "suckfish," or "swinesucker." Such terms became staples of his work.

Soon enough, though, Thompson would have little time for poetry. He was so tired of being broke that he took advantage of his Hell's Angels article success and agreed to write numerous versions of it for different publications. In August, he explained the pressure he had brought upon himself:

> As things stand now, I have a (to be revised) piece due at *The Nation* by September 1, also a book review for them on the same date. Also a 5000-word piece to *Playboy* by then, and a short but pithy thing for *Stanford Literary Review*. The first half of the book is due September 15, and so far I haven't written a word.

He had not yet started work on the book and already he was struggling.

***

6 He later decided that he wanted "Collect Telegram from a Mad Dog" included in *Hell's Angels* alongside "a short note on why the use of fictious names is not coincidental" (HA Letters, p.22).

While writing *Hell's Angels,* Thompson was still living in San Francisco. He was a regular fixture at the Matrix, where he hung out with his favorite band, Jefferson Airplane. Exploring the innumerable countercultural happenings in the area, he met other literary and cultural figures, including Ken Kesey and Allen Ginsberg. When Kesey wanted to meet the Angels, Thompson introduced them, and the bikers were invited to a party at his La Honda home on August 7. Hunter, who knew the Angels as well as anyone, was understandably concerned by the prospect of this meeting of subcultures. There was, he felt, a very real chance that the drug-crazed thugs would end up murdering some of the drug-addled hippies. Nonetheless, he could not overlook it as potential material for his book. Incredibly, rather than violence, the party resulted in a bizarre—albeit temporary—friendship between Kesey's Merry Pranksters and Barger's biker gang.

Thompson continued to drink with and spend time with the Angels as he worked on the book between the summer of 1965 and February 1966. Typically, he spent about three or four days per week with them, and the rest of the time he was reading police reports or planning out how to structure the book. Sometimes the Angels would come over to his house, gobble pills, and read aloud early drafts of the text. The fragments he sent off to his editors typically earned praise, even though it was "a little disorganized." Still, what he wrote was impressive enough that they began to wonder if it might be an altogether more important book, and in September it was sold to Random House for a hardcover edition along with the rights to *The Rum Diary.*[7] The pressure was on.

The first half of the book was researched and written over many months as Thompson continued his investigation into the outlaw bikers and their violent world. However, as the deadline loomed, and with Random House editor, Jim Silberman, breathing down his neck for the final manuscript, he panicked. He feared that failure to deliver might mean he would have to pay back his advance (which, of course, was long gone) and so he set off for a period

---

7   It has been claimed in various publications that Ballantine was a part of Random House, but this did not happen until 1973.

of enforced isolation. At a motel in Monterey, he unloaded his typewriter and set about finishing the book. For four days, he lived on a diet of McDonald's hamburgers, Wild Turkey, and Dexedrine. When he got into the swing of writing, he wrote at a tremendous pace and sent the book away in chunks of thirty or sixty pages. He listened to rock music and wrote for a hundred consecutive hours until it was complete. Finally, he was able to send off the final pages. He just had to hope that the world was ready for what he had to say and how he said it.

When talking over the Hell's Angels book idea with various publishers, Thompson had given a lot of time to Angus Cameron at Alfred E. Knopf. He wanted to keep open the possibility of another book after *Hell's Angels* was finished. While they debated a book on the topic of losers and outsiders, Thompson set forth his ideas on fact and fiction in clearer terms than anywhere else. He explained that straight non-fiction was too limited to handle a topic like this and that he would go insane trying to do it through normal journalism. He went on:

> Fiction is a bridge to the truth that journalism can't reach. Facts are lies when they're added up, and the only kind of journalism I can pay much attention to is something like *Down and Out in Paris and London*. The title story in Tom Wolfe's new book is a hell of a fine thing, I think, and so is the one on Junior Johnson. But in order to write that kind of punch-out stuff you have to add up the facts in your own fuzzy way, and to hell with the hired swine who use adding machines.

This quotation is often used by people in discussing the degree to which Hunter Thompson was a journalist or a novelist because, although he explained it often over the rest of his life, this was perhaps his clearest and most concise explanation. Throughout his book, he puts forth the facts regarding crimes committed by the Hell's Angels, yet they all add up to nothing more than a falsehood—

the true story of the Hell's Angels was shocking but very different to the version depicted in the Lynch Report and the popular press. In Thompson's mind, his own interpretation was far more truthful for the elements of fiction included.

Naturally, some of the claims that Thompson made in the book were disputed. Sonny Barger, in his 2001 autobiography, makes reference to Thompson's liberties with the truth. He had enjoyed the article, which he felt was a fair representation of the club, but the book did not get his approval:

> I read the book, *Hell's Angels: A Strange and Terrible Saga*, when it came out in 1967. It was junk. The worst part is that it became a law enforcement guide on the club. There was a lot of writer's exaggeration along with a writer's dream-and-drug-induced commentary, like when he talked about members pissing on their patches or members having to wear pants dipped in oil and piss. Blood in, blood out. The cops claimed that for years after. That kind of stupid mythology came right out of Hunter's book.

Others have observed that Thompson's approach to mixing fact and fiction appears to be a description of New Journalism, a style of writing that arose around this period, but Thompson rejected the comparison.[8] Although he admired the writing of other New Journalists, including Wolfe, he said that his work was fundamentally different. New Journalists took a story and then pieced it together later, figuring out what happened and telling it with novelistic features, but his style was to actually be there in the moment, writing more or less as it happened, and observing so closely that he sometimes impacted events. "Wolfe's problem is that he is too crusty to participate in his stories," Thompson explained. "The people he feels comfortable with are dull as stale dogshit, and the people

---

8   Although New Journalism was being practiced at this point, it did not earn its moniker until 1973.

who seem to fascinate him as a writer are so weird they make him nervous."

Still, it is hard to view Gonzo as entirely separate from New Journalism and perhaps it could be viewed as a sub-genre rather than a distinct entity. John Hellman, in *Fables of Fact: The New Journalism's New Fiction*, argues that New Journalism can easily be split into two categories: those who participate and those who observe. However, there is one uniting quality: "Above all, the New Journalist wishes to use his imaginative powers and fictional craft to seek out and construct meaning."

When Thompson says, "The title story in Tom Wolfe's new book is a hell of a fine thing," he is referring to "There Goes (VAROOM! VAROOM!) That Kandy-Kolored (THPHHHHHH!) Tangerine-Flake Streamline Baby (RAHGHHH!) Around the Bend (BRUMMMMMMMMMMMMMMM)..." from Wolfe's 1964 book, *The Kandy-Kolored Tangerine-Flake Streamline Baby*. In this article, like the others in the book, Wolfe has attempted to utilize highly experimental prose techniques. In *The Art of Fact*, Ben Yagoda says that Wolfe was eager "to give any trope try" and went on to explain why:

> For Wolfe, traditional cadences and structure simply could not do justice to the sheer manic energy of the early- and mid-sixties zeitgeist, and so here he gives us present-tense scenes, over-the-top cinematic lap dissolves, a narrative voice bordering on the hysterical, and high-octane punctuation (dashes, ellipses, exclamation points, and italics) that collectively evoke the era.

Thompson was impressed by Wolfe's prose and it is clear from his letters that he took inspiration from his friend when preparing to write *Hell's Angels*. Wolfe's example proved to Hunter that he did not have to adhere to the formal strictures of journalism in order to succeed. It was now possible to write a "nonfiction novel," to blend the true and the imagined, and to really push one's literary abilities to the limit even in the previously staid confines of journalism.

It was very much the route he would take in writing *Hell's Angels*. He sought to work out the truth, put it into a coherent order, and then tell it using the language of the novelist rather than the journalist. Although he did not realize it at first, by adding himself into the narrative, he also provided an additional thread of plot and gave the reader a surrogate through which they could view the violent characters he encountered.

It had been Ernest Hemingway who provided the model for *The Rum Diary*, but now Thompson would look to George Orwell's first book as inspiration for what he called "another down-and-out assignment."[9] For years, he had been influenced by *Down and Out in Paris and London*, and when he was tasked with writing a book about people living on the very fringes of society, often in some degree of poverty, he naturally turned to Orwell's masterpiece for clues to how it could be done.

George Orwell, who was then Eric Blair, had spent time living amongst the very poorest people in London and then Paris. He had written an essay on his experiences in the former city but soon decided that he could incorporate Paris, too. When he did, he reversed the order of events and imposed some elements of fiction upon the reality of his experiences—something Thompson would later do in *Fear and Loathing in Las Vegas*. The role of fact and fiction is often discussed in reference to *Down and Out in Paris and London*, and in the introduction to its 1935 French edition, Orwell addressed the issue:

> I think I can say that I have exaggerated nothing except in so far as all writers exaggerate by selecting. I did not feel that I had to describe events in the exact order in which they happened, but everything I have described did take place at one time or another.

In his annotations to one copy of the book, Orwell

---

9 Thompson frequently made literary references in his letters, and "down and out" is one that appears at least since 1960.

admitted that many of the events that happened to him in the story really happened to others, but that they were still true because he had heard about them. It was an explanation that Thompson had used when defending his reporting for the *National Observer*: "Maybe I heard some of these stories and didn't see them. But they sure as hell happened."

To Thompson, *Down and Out in Paris and London* was the finest sort of journalism. It was personal, mostly honest, and it focused on people rather than overtly discussing its major themes. Orwell had written numerous wonderful sketches of characters in the dark recesses of these major cities, using anecdotes about their lives to examine the issue of poverty and the gulf that existed between the privileged and the desperate. It was the perfect template for *Hell's Angels*, in which Thompson uses the colorful characters he finds to illuminate larger issues, with the resulting book as much a comment on the direction of society as a sociological study of a single motorcycle gang.

Another inspiration was Mark Twain's *The Innocents Abroad*, a humorous travelogue recounting the author's trip around Europe and the Middle East. Twain offers a view of the world that he feels is more realistic than those of contemporary travel writers, who grossly embellished their own experiences and the foreign sights they encountered. His book also highlights the falsehoods found in history and he mocks them in much the same way that Thompson would mock the press and police in his book. He even makes a reference to Twain in noting that one location in the book was the setting for "The Celebrated Jumping Frog of Calaveras County," an amusing short story that was Twain's first big success. When his book was finally published, he placed it next to *The Complete Essays of Mark Twain* on his bookshelf.

Hell's Angels begins with one of the great passages of Hunter Thompson's career:

> California, Labor Day weekend. . . early, with ocean fog still in the streets, outlaw motorcyclists wearing chains, shades and greasy Levi's roll out from damp garages,

all-night diners and cast-off one-night pads in Frisco, Hollywood, Berdoo and East Oakland, heading for the Monterey peninsula, north of Big Sur... The Menace is loose again, the Hell's Angels, the hundredcarat headline, running fast and loud on the early morning freeway, low in the saddle, nobody smiles, jamming crazy through traffic and ninety miles an hour down the center stripe, missing by inches . . . like Genghis Khan on an iron horse, a monster steed with a fiery anus, flat out through the eye of a beer can and up your daughter's leg with no quarter asked and none given; show the squares some class, give em a whiff of those kicks they'll never know. . .

This is perhaps the perfect illustration of what he explained to Cameron. He has written an introduction that defies all journalistic convention. It sounds more like a novel, a poem, or even the voiceover to a movie than the start to a piece of non-fiction. It is totally ungrammatical—just a collection of images building upon each other as though seen through a movie camera drifting across a landscape and zooming in on the most frightening characters ever to grace the screen. The punctuation tells us that this was meant to be read aloud as it guides the breath rather than being used in any true grammatical sense, with the ellipses demarcating a shift in image as well as a pause in breath—much like Louis-Ferdinand Céline in *Death on the Installment Plan*. Thompson often said that he listened for musicality in his prose, asking friends, family, and visitors to read his work aloud for this purpose, and in these opening paragraphs he has succeeded mightily in producing his own rock 'n' roll prose. William Stephenson, in *Gonzo Republic*, connected his unconventional approach to punctuation and grammar with his libertarianism, suggesting that it

allowed Thompson's quest for freedom to find expression not just in what he wrote, but in how he wrote it. He flouted the conventions of journalism and fiction and violated the rules of syntax in order not only to represent drugged consciousness, but also to subvert the premises of the state.

In passages like this, it is also easy to see the influence of Tom Wolfe in the creative use of language. In 1964, Wolfe wrote an article called "The Girl of the Year" for the *New York Herald Tribune*. It begins with the sort of playful language that Thompson used for his own first paragraphs:

> Bangs manes bouffants beehives Beatle caps butter faces brush-on lashes decal eyes puffy sweaters French thrust bras flailing leather blue jeans stretch pants stretch jeans honeydew bottoms eclair shanks elf boots ballerinas Knight slippers, hundreds of them, these flaming little buds, bobbing and screaming, rocketing around inside the Academic of Music Theater underneath that vast old mouldering cherub dome up there – aren't they super-marvelous!

Like Wolfe, Thompson sought the presentation of images through a layering of ideas in a non-grammatical way, more interested in playing with sound than adhering to any prior expectations.

There is nothing in this passage that indicates journalistic objectivity, either. From referring to the bikers as "The Menace" to comparing them to "Genghis Khan on an iron horse, a monster steed with a fiery anus," the text is shocking and hilarious and prepares the reader for the horrific events described later. Rather than presenting a straight image, he has gone for hyperbole and specific, bizarre, grotesque imagery. It is literature rather than reporting, presenting a fictional or fictionalized scene that conveys an image more accurately and completely than "objective journalism" ever could.

Although this section is stylistically different from the rest of the book, the notion of completely subjective writing presented in novelistic terms continued to varying degrees throughout the text. In relatively straight, sensible sections, he uses literary language to draw the reader into his descriptions of the Angels ("They rode with a fine, unwashed arrogance, secure in their reputation as the rottenest motorcycle gang in the whole history of Christendom") but elsewhere he throws in comical or vile language in order to shock, amuse, or otherwise engage the reader, juxtaposing straight facts with utterly subjective assessments like "tender young blondes with lobotomy eyes" and "crotch-busting fools." They are hardly phrases learned in a journalism textbook.

All through the book, Thompson shows off his skill as a writer and, in some instances, journalism seems to play second fiddle to his determination to include a phrase that is intelligent or musical. This is another example of Fitzgerald's "high white note."[10] In one passage, he describes "the wary expression of half-bright souls turned mean and nervous from too much bitter wisdom in too few years." There is an unusually high volume of adjectives in this cluster of words—something that marked Thompson's prose throughout his career. He liked to make sure that as many of his nouns had a strong adjective before them as possible and preferably more than one. One quirk of his writing was to link two adjectives with "and" in the middle, like "mean and nervous" above. Even the subtitle of his book included this newfound technique: *Hell's Angels: A Strange and Terrible Saga*. This was another allusion to Fitzgerald, who included the phrase "strange and terrible" twice in his 1922 novel, *The Beautiful and Damned*, and it became a feature of Thompson's writing that was often imitated and parodied.

To see how Thompson approached this element of his writing, we can briefly skip forward to 1998 and look

---

10   Thompson directly refers to this near the end of the book, using the phrase to describe a speech made by Terry the Tramp: "He got hold of a microphone tied up to some powerful speakers and used the opportunity to unburden his mind. . . addressing the police in a very direct way, speaking of morals and music and madness, and finishing on a high, white note which the San Mateo sheriffs department will not soon forget." [*Hell's Angels*, p.243]

at a blurb he wrote for fellow Kentuckian, the poet Ron
Whitehead. In blue ink, he wrote:

> I have long admired Ron Whitehead. He
> is crazy as nine loons, but his poetry is
> wonderful mathematics.

This was later edited in red marker, with "wonderful
mathematics" scored out and replaced by more specific
imagery:

> I have long admired Ron Whitehead. He
> is crazy as nine loons, and his poetry is
> a dazzling mix of folk wisdom + pure
> mathematics.

The difference between these two notes is that the
second has essentially been *Hunterized*. In the former, the
phrase "crazy as nine loons" is very much in Thompson's
style, but the addition of superfluous imagery, comprised
of that ADJECTIVE + NOUN structure, gives it an extra
punch. Moreover, he has replaced one adjective-noun
phrase with three. This is the sort of stylistic change that
he often made to improve his writing, and which made his
prose highly recognizable.

While researching his book on the Hell's Angels,
Thompson recorded his notes and thoughts on audio
tape—a practice that he continued well into the future. These
show a man trying to find the right words and ideas, but
not quite managing. His descriptions of his surroundings
are rather uninspiring and he falls back too easily on his
favored phrases, like "loon." It is obvious that his literary
style came through the process of careful revision that we
can see in his note for Whitehead. Although he later came
to rely heavily upon spontaneous compositions, it was the
process of consciously improving his work that made it
wonderfully unique.

Thompson also managed to include the phrase
"fear and loathing" in the book, as well as "atavistic,"
which he had been using since Ketchum. Consciously or
unconsciously, he was developing habits that included the
adoption of certain uncommon lexical items such as these.

He would repeat them in his work and this is partly what made him such an identifiable figure in literature.

Like John Dos Passos, whom he admired and studied as a young man, Thompson litters the first half of the book with quotations and excerpts from documents.[11] There are literary quotes like François Villon and Henry Miller, as well as quotes from police officers and jailers, newspaper excerpts and government documents, a poem by Allen Ginsberg, and of course the Angels themselves. Many of these are used simply for something to refute while some are included to illustrate Thompson's ideas and opinions. In at least one instance, he quotes himself, but uses a made-up name: Sr. Cazador. This imagined person repeats a line that Thompson had initially written into an early draft of his Hell's Angels article: "In a prosperous democracy that is also a society of winners and losers, any man without an equalizer or at least the illusion of one is by definition underprivileged."

From his extensive use of quotations attributed to police and news reports, juxtaposed against actual facts dug up by the roving reporter, the reader is led on a long and complex search for the truth. Thompson keeps them wondering throughout most of the book whether the Hell's Angels are really as nightmarish as they are presented because there is, in fact, no simple answer. The Angels are a mix of angry, disaffected men with different pasts and motivations. They are extraordinarily violent but probably nowhere near as violent as people think; they commit atrocities, but not the atrocities of which they are accused.

He nurtures this sense of uncertainty, keeping the reader interested through a continual sense of unease, interspersed with sudden shocks when he talks about women being raped or having their teeth ripped out with pliers by a man who simply thinks it is funny. The menace and uncertainty are compounded because these sadistic brutes are often presented as polite, decent human beings—just normal people gone a little too far down the wrong path. The reader feels he gets to know some of these

---

11   When his book was published, Thompson placed it next to Dos Passos' *USA* and the aforementioned Twain collection. In an audio recording, he notes that Dos Passos was "weird." [*Gonzo Tapes*, CD 1, track 21]

characters as Thompson describes them convincingly and often records their dialogue, bringing them to life. For this, of course, he was using his tape recorder and transcribing what they said, giving the book a sense of immediacy at times. Even the characters who are just passed over briefly seem real because Thompson is able to convey serious depth in just a few lines.

Throughout the book, he weaves various threads and themes masterfully, like a novelist handling different character arcs. The reader is presented with the history of the Hell's Angels, then sees them preparing for a "run" as the characters are introduced. Important ones are given backstories that illustrate Thompson's views on who the Angels are and why they exist. He tells us about their jobs, their families, their hobbies, their sex lives, and their violent proclivities. The reader gets to know certain characters like Terry the Tramp, while others are only identified due to their amusing or shocking nicknames (like Charger Charlie the Child Molester), and yet more are simply brushed off with descriptions in order not to weigh down the narrative.

His attacks on the press are extensive and vicious. For the first half of the book, one sometimes wonders whether the focus is really the Angels or whether it is the meditation on the American press that he had promised William Kennedy in 1959, with the Angels simply used to illustrate shoddy reportage.[12] In chapter two, Thompson explains how his old employers, *Time*, are guilty of "flagrant libel" by skipping over truths and fixating on falsehoods. He contrasts different accounts of events and uses verifiable figures to disprove false media reports. Using crime statistics, he points out that the Hell's Angels are responsible for statistically insignificant numbers of crimes and that their reputation is instead just a creation of publications like *Time* and *The New York Times*. Diving further into this critique, he explains one method of pulling the wool over readers' eyes. He says that reporters and editors often use "alleged" and other similar qualifiers to get away with saying things that they *feel* are true but which they cannot prove. He cites a *New York Times* article that

---

12   In some of Thompson's own correspondence, he describes the book more as though it were about the press than a biker gang.

uses nine such qualifiers in fourteen short paragraphs, and even uses this technique to mock irresponsible reporting, at one point saying, "For some reason it was impossible for the press to divine how many alleged rioters had been arrested."

When it came to action and madness, Thompson was already a formidable writer. Even at the lowest points in his career, he could produce enthralling descriptions of vehicles of all kinds and he was especially gifted when those vehicles were racing or crashing. In one stand-out passage of this book, he recounts his own experience of "going over the high side," which was biker talk for taking a bad fall. He vividly describes a crash that left his friend with a destroyed leg:

> The bike was going sideways toward a bank of railroad tracks and there was nothing I could do except hang on. For an instant it was very peaceful. . . and then it was like being shot off the road by a bazooka, but with no noise. Neither a deer on a hillside nor a man on a battlefield ever hears the shot that kills him, and a man going over the high side on a motorcycle hears the same kind of high-speed silence. There are sparks, as the chromed steel grinds down on the road, an awful jerk when your body starts cartwheeling on the first impact. . . and after that, if you're lucky, there is nothing at all until you wake up in some hospital emergency ward with your scalp hanging down in your eyes and a blood-soaked shirt sticking to your chest while official looking people stare down at you and assure each other that "these crazy bastards won't learn."

The incident itself must have occurred in less than a second, but Thompson's description goes on for several paragraphs as he recounts it in vivid detail. His descriptions of injuries due to motorcycles are shockingly casual, just like when he describes injuries sustained due to fighting or other Angel activities.

In his article, Thompson was an observer but he was not highly visible and did not really participate in the story. The book, however, was a different matter. The first half, which took him many months to research and write, is fundamentally an extension of the article. It is only in the latter half of the book—the part written in a four-day flurry of amphetamine-fueled writing—that Thompson really enters the fray in a recognizable way.

In the first half, he appears a few times to illustrate certain points. Firstly, when he wants to show that motorcyclists are discriminated against, he cites his own experiences as a responsible journalist who happens to own a motorcycle. A little later, he criticizes journalists attempting to pay for stories by talking about himself and the fact that he would never pay a source.[13] He introduces himself when trying to buy a bike so that he can educate his reader about motorcycles from a purely lay perspective. Talking about bikes, he presents himself as ignorant and cowardly, while the knowledge and bravery of the Angels appears as a stark contrast.

Although he often portrayed himself as a bumbling fool, ignorant and woefully unprepared, he also tended to write about himself in ways that built his legend. He had always sent letters to friends boasting about his weird habits or shocking behavior, and some of this had—in a quite restrained way—slipped into his articles. He had frequently written about his unconventional appearance, actions, and attitude. Now that he had a book that he felt might be read by tens of thousands of people, he was keen to prove his machismo on paper. The back cover describes him as "America's most brazen and ballsy journalist" and in the book he tells the story of first meeting the Angels and trying to impress them by shooting out the windows of his own San Francisco home.[14] Such moments of bravado tend to enter the story very briefly and seem to serve little

---

13   The Hell's Angels maintained that they were paid by Thompson. He promised them one keg of beer in return for their cooperation.
14   Sonny Barger was less than impressed by Thompson's bravado: "He would fire a gun out the window of his apartment in San Francisco trying to impress people—to me, that is the

purpose beyond this self-mythologizing.

The second half of the book, which largely concerns a Hell's Angels "run" to Bass Lake, continues to present and critique media or police reports and also discusses certain elements of the Angels' lives, but its style is quite different. This section features the writer in a much more prominent position. Thompson is now the journalist that is following the Angels on a potentially dangerous journey and his sense of unease is key to making the reader understand what happens. The turning point occurs when Thompson announces: "and then, Sweet Jesus, it dawned on me that I was right in the middle of it." From this point on, he is embedded with the Angels like a war correspondent in a beleaguered army. This first-person perspective brings a greater sense of immediacy to the narrative as the story becomes increasingly dangerous and Thompson builds tension over whether or not violence will erupt by the lake. The chapter of the title, "The Hoodlum Circus and The Statutory Rape of Bass Lake," makes clear his intention.

This perspective was a breakthrough for Thompson's journalism. He realized that he could put himself into a story and then witness it up close to give his reader a more intimate view. It also allowed him to take unconventional approaches, such as focusing on the crowd of spectators that gathered to watch the Angels. Just as he would do in his first real Gonzo story at the Kentucky Derby, he has found the value of turning his back on the subject to see something totally new.

Aside from the run to Bass Lake, in the second half of the book Thompson engages in a number of long digressions to explain subjects as they arise. In one such instance, he mocks the Lynch Report for calling the Angels' women "sheep." Thompson did not just correct this error, but quipped, "It sounds like the creation of some police inspector with intensely rural memories." This sparks a long section in which he carefully explains the different kinds of women associated with the biker gang, noting the distinction between an "Old Lady" and a "Mama."

---

stupidest thing anybody can do—and he would talk himself up that he was a tough guy, when he wasn't. When anything happened, he would run and hide, like what he did at Bass Lake." [*Gonzo*, p.81]

As in all of his very best writing, Thompson's digressions begin seamlessly and return to the main thread of the story without any loss of coherence. Although the book was well researched and usually very truthful, Thompson also took the chance to deploy his fiendish imagination. His best writing was always characterized by oddly specific images often in the middle of larger flights of fancy, and *Hell's Angels* was no different. Occasionally, he would employ multiple metaphors to describe something, such as:

> Together they looked like figures in some ominous painting, a doomsday portrait of the human animal confronting itself. . . as if a double-yolked egg had hatched both a chicken and a wildebeest.

When he is asked to go along on a beer run with some Angels, he unleashes his imagination, inventing an hysterical woman screaming that the Angels were invading their store and begging for her husband to shoot them. It is just a brief image and the rest is a presumably faithful account of a real beer run. Elsewhere, he is more subtle when entering into the part that is purely imagined, but the fantasy is so utterly absurd that the reader knows it to be untrue. In one such instance, he is satirizing news coverage of the Angels once again, laughing at the notion of them traveling from San Francisco to New York just to raise hell and spook the locals. He goes on:

> If the *News* had put two and two together they would have known who caused the great power blackout that autumn. It was a Hell's Angels plot to take over the subway system and triple the fares. After weeks of intricate sabotage and recircuiting the power rails, the outlaws were attempting a final tie-off under the Yale Club when one of their number, afflicted with bad hives, was overcome by abulia and wired the main subway voltage to the root of the Empire State Building's lightning rod. The

resulting explosion killed them all, but their
bones were carried off by water rats and
there was no other evidence. As usual, the
Angels beat the rap. And the *News* missed
a hell of a story.

It is obviously imagined and, in that last line, just
dripping with sarcasm. Hopefully, all but the most ignorant
or gullible reader would understand his intention. Later in
his career, Thompson would do the same thing but instead
of making it clear that it was a hypothetical situation and
instead of letting his imagination run for several sentences,
he would write page after page of bizarre fantasy presented
as reality. The balance of fact and fiction in his work was
always in flux.

Of course, this book was never entirely fact *or* fiction.
It was journalism; Thompson knew that much. But then,
in the book he also listed the 1953 movie, *The Wild One*,
as "an inspired piece of film journalism." What we have
is journalism as Thompson envisioned it—a mixture of
serious reporting with lots of opinion, the observations
of a person who is actually present and knows what is
going on, even if he is an outsider, and presented with the
trappings of a novel or short story. It was like Hemingway
and Orwell had done, but with Thompson's own rhythm,
lexis, and persona foisted upon it. Besides, he explained that
some things were just "not in the realm of the five W's."
This included taking acid with the Angels—something that
surely no other journalist would have dared try and which
traditional journalism might have struggled to describe
with accuracy.

Although he occasionally threw himself into the
story, when it came to drugs Thompson was relatively
circumspect at this point. He admitted to using Benzedrine
and LSD, both of which were legal when he began writing
the book, but he was not yet willing to admit to the use of
illegal substances.[15] One of the key scenes is a party at Ken
Kesey's home in La Honda, where Thompson mixes with

15   LSD was prohibited in California early in 1966 and a
nationwide ban followed in July. In his letters, he talks about
taking Dexedrine but in the book he admits to Benzedrine. It is
likely he had used both amphetamines.

the Merry Pranksters and the Hell's Angels as everyone drops acid, including the author, who claimed to take it himself for the first time that night.[16] He recorded the events of the evening on his tape recorder and used the recordings later when he had to write about it. He also lent the tapes to Tom Wolfe, who then wrote about the party for his book, *The Electric Kool-Aid Acid Test.*

In the penultimate chapter, Thompson tries to tie together all the threads he has so masterfully woven through the book—the Hell's Angels, LSD, the media, and wider issues of the sixties. He offers a concluding thought on what the Angels really were:

> For nearly a year I had lived in a world that seemed, at first, like something original. It was obvious from the beginning that the menace bore little resemblance to its publicized image, but there was a certain pleasure in sharing the Angels' amusement at the stir they'd created. Later, as they attracted more and more attention, the mystique was stretched so thin that it finally became transparent. [...] I realized that the roots of this act were not in any time-honored American myth but right beneath my feet in a new kind of society that is only beginning to take shape. To see the Hell's Angels as caretakers of the old "individualist" tradition "that made this country great" is only a painless way to get around seeing them for what they really are – not some romantic leftover, but the first wave of a future that nothing in our history has prepared us to cope with.

---

16   Hunter often made this claim, but Sandy said that he had taken it for the first time shortly before then. He became violent and she was terrified he would kill their child, so she scratched his face. Thompson ran away and was deeply embarrassed by the incident, which is presumably why he claimed that the La Honda party was his first time using acid. [*Gonzo*, p.74]

He states that most people would—if given the choice—love the power that comes with the bullying nature of the Angels, so it is hardly a surprise that some people reach a point in their life when they have nothing left to lose and make that leap. Those who resolutely condemn the Angels, meanwhile, are engaged in the "psychic masturbation" of their own fascination. It is the wisdom of the book that he has been working toward, slowly leading the reader through the workings of the motorcycle club, the failings of the press, and the corruption of the police, to this horrifying conclusion. It was a fitting denouement to a truly shocking book, but there was still more left to say.

The book ends with a stunning passage that sees the author get on his BSA 650 Lightning and hit the road. It was written immediately after he got back home, with tears still drying on his face from the exhilarating ride, and is one of his best pieces of writing. Thompson later referred to it as "Midnight on the Coast Highway." In this extraordinary passage, he zooms along the dark highway and comes to realize that it is a quest for "the Edge":

> You can barely see at a hundred; the tears blow back so fast that they vaporize before they get to your ears. The only sounds are wind and a dull roar floating back from the mufflers. You watch the white line and try to lean with it. . . howling through a turn to the right, then to the left and down the long hill to Pacifica. . . letting off now, watching for cops, but only until the next dark stretch and another few seconds on the edge. . . The Edge. . . There is no honest way to explain it because the only people who really know where it is are the ones who have gone over. The others – the living – are those who pushed their control as far as they felt they could handle it, and then pulled back, or slowed down, or did whatever they had to when it came time to choose between Now and Later.

Thompson always claimed that it was an inspired piece of writing—the immediate product of a profound experience that remained unaltered: "I sat and wrote the whole thing, right through, and never changed a word of it," he recalled in 1990. It was a perfect example of the "high white note" that he often talked about—a moment of pure brilliance in a piece of writing, when the words sound so perfect when put together that they are practically musical notes. He explained:

> [...] until the Angels I had always been writing in the same mold as other newspaper hacks and I thought that was the way to do it. With the Angels, however, there was a freedom to use words. I'm a word freak. I like words. I've always compared writing to music. That's the way I feel about good paragraphs. When it really works, it's like music.

Hell's Angels was bookended by such passages, for we can view this as the counterpart to the opening paragraphs that show the Angels tearing across the landscape as Thompson compares them to Genghis Khan.

All through the book, we can see Hunter Thompson moving from an invisible narrator to an occasionally mentioned observer to a participant and, finally, out on the road in the middle of the night, he is the whole story.[17] In retrospect, he would realize just how important his involvement was. There was no going back. From here on out, Hunter Thompson's writing would almost always revolve to some extent around Hunter Thompson.

The book finally comes to a postscript, in which the author recounts being brutally "stomped" by the Hell's Angels. From the beginning, the reader has been brought behind the scenes of journalistic procedure—into the violent but thrilling world of an embedded journalist—

---

17   He shows an awareness of this early in the book, saying, "By the middle of summer I had become so involved in the outlaw scene that I was no longer sure whether I was doing research on the Hell's Angels or being slowly absorbed by them." [*Hell's Angels*, p.46]

and this is the logical conclusion. He has become the things that he was studying all along—a biker, a victim of the Hell's Angels, and a journalist who slipped up. By becoming all of these things, he adds legitimacy and perspective to his own reporting. The final insider-insight into the journalistic process is in the last sentences of the book, when he says, "I tried to compose a fitting epitaph" but he cannot think of anything more appropriate than Conrad's last line in *Heart of Darkness*: "The horror! The horror!... Exterminate the brutes!" Not only has the focus of the book shifted toward its narrator, but any claim he may have had to balance and objectivity is now out the window; he is a part of the story, submerged within it, and given over to the emotions and biases that follow being savagely beaten.

He gives little away about why the beating occurred except to say two ambiguous things. Firstly, the Angels felt that he was taking advantage of them, and secondly, "a minor disagreement suddenly became very serious." As with so many stories in the life of Hunter Thompson, it is hard to get to the truth of what really happened. Certainly, no one who was there or who knew about the beating ever agreed much with Thompson's assessment, and his version of it changed often. He sometimes claimed that the Angels were annoyed about the price sticker on his book, feeling that they had been cheated out of what they perceived as their share. Other times, he said that he stepped in when a man was beating his wife and dog. On another occasion, he explained that he had been arguing over the virtues of a BSA compared with a Harley. Sonny Barger confirmed that Thompson had intervened after one Angel beat his wife and dog, but there are various inconsistencies with his story, too. He sometimes said that Thompson never went to the police after his beating and sometimes that he did. Sometimes he claimed that there had been just one punch thrown, and elsewhere that everyone joined in. Nonetheless, it was his contention that Thompson had provoked one of the Angels, confident in the knowledge that he would be beaten but not severely. "The problem I have is that it just really isn't a true story, but it is a very, very good story," he said of Thompson's version of events.

In the end, it probably does not matter much what

caused him to be beaten. However, as a man whose journalistic career was a strange search for truth that was largely filtered through layers of fiction, or at least accompanied by bizarre flights of fancy, it is perhaps worth looking into just where and how and why he distorted the truth. In most cases, it seems that he lied or exaggerated in order to advance his legend. Thompson had been self-mythologizing since his childhood and, in *Hell's Angels* as well as many of his articles, he was clearly interested in presenting an image of himself as a fearless iconoclast. He was a serious journalist and yet he took acid with the world's most notorious biker gang, fired guns out of his windows, and got himself in trouble with the police while partying with Beat poet and countercultural icon, Allen Ginsberg.

It is impossible to know to what extent Thompson really did aim to get at the truth in his stories, but we can assume that he presented fantasies for the purpose of satire or to otherwise draw his reader's attention toward a greater truth. But undoubtedly he lied to make himself look like an outlaw. That is not to say that he wasn't one, or that he didn't act that way. There are countless eyewitnesses to his crazed antics and substance abuse issues, but his writing celebrates and—presumably—exaggerates these aspects of his personality. It was much like his letter-writing bravado, his self-portraits, and his reckless actions. As he admitted on many occasions, he was an "egomaniac." Of course, that is not to say there was no literary or even journalistic merit in his depictions of himself, but writing was an ego trip for Hunter S. Thompson, which adds a layer of complexity over the search for meaning in his work.

It is little surprise, then, that tucked away in the final pages of the book is a reference to himself as an heroic outlaw:

> In a nation of frightened dullards there is a sorry shortage of outlaws, and those few who make the grade are always welcome: Frank Sinatra, Alexander King, Elizabeth Taylor, Raoul Duke.

This odd reference would no doubt have baffled his readers as it was the first time that the name "Raoul Duke," Thompson's future literary persona, had appeared in print.[18] Duke would be his passage to total freedom of speech, but also the prison that would trap him and cause the stagnation that led to his spectacular downfall as a writer.

Being beaten by the Hell's Angels may have been a terrifying and painful experience, but at least it only lasted a few seconds and yielded a fitting end to a great book (not to mention a great story for the Hunter legend). The process of writing, editing, and promoting the book, however, was a far worse torture. This was vastly more complex than anything he had previously attempted. On November 1, 1965, he explained his situation to Norman Mailer, an author whose work Thompson respected, and asked for a few words he might use to promote his book. He told Mailer that he had just one month to turn in eighty thousand words but all he had so far was thirty-four pages. These were, he said, "a grab-bag of word-photos, libel, straight narrative, and occasional wisdom." In his audio notes, he speculated that it would be near impossible to meet his deadline "unless I get on one wild blasting red hot perfect streak that really needs no rewriting at all"—the sort of "blast out narrative" that he called a "zing zong wing ding rush." In the end, the deadline was pushed back

---

18   Douglas Brinkley, in his commentary for *Fear and Loathing in America*, claims that Thompson invented Duke after the 1968 Democratic Convention, but we can see that he already existed in some form as early as 1965. William McKeen claims that Thompson had used Duke in his *Command Courier* articles, but this is also untrue. Thompson once claimed in an interview once that he had possibly invented the name in order to check into a hotel. [*Ancient Gonzo Wisdom*, p.272] Sandy said, "Raoul Duke has always been one of his fantasy personalities." [*Hunter*, p.154] However, during Thompson's work on *Hell's Angels,* there were various newspaper stories about a Calgary businessman named Raoul "Duke" Duquette, and one must wonder whether Thompson, who had read newspapers from all across North America in his search for insights into the press' infatuation with the Angels, had borrowed this name from an unassuming shop manager.

from December 1 to March 1, but even with that extra time, he struggled to get the book written.

Another author that Thompson very much admired was Nelson Algren. *Hell's Angels* was filled with quotations from all sorts of different places (and a whole poem by Allen Ginsberg) but he wanted to include around five hundred words from Algren's novel, *A Walk on the Wild Side*. When Algren politely refused, Thompson was shocked. Extremely disappointed, he pleaded with the author for permission. None was granted, and Thompson was forced to paraphrase the story. In a footnote, he took a swipe at Algren, saying that his story lacked "the dimension of humanity" found in William Faulkner's work.

On March 1, Thompson submitted his manuscript just in time to make the deadline—quite possibly the last time that ever happened. He was thus infuriated when he felt that his publishers were pushing the publication date back further and further in order to give his book sufficient attention. However, according to Margaret Harrell, who later copyedited *Hell's Angels*, "he did not really understand the production process in a book" given that his only prior experience had been with magazines and newspapers. In any case, he hadn't realized that there was still much work to do. "Books are too slow," he said. "Only old men should write them."

Over the coming months, his manuscript was passed from the developmental editing team of Bernard Shir-Cliff and Jim Silberman to Margaret Harrell, who worked under Silberman at Random House to gently prompt Thompson to perfect his book. Thompson, of course, was never a fan of being edited, particularly due to his experiences with heavy-handed magazine editors, and the more he had invested in a story, the more he resented any little change to it. However, he would take suggestions and accept cuts if they were fair and reasonable, and if he thought the editor knew best, which was the case at Random House. Though he initially tested Harrell with an angry letter that aggressively rejected proposed changes, saying "I won't have that kind of writing in my book. I'd rather be obscure," he was in fact very appreciative of her suggestions and agreed to most of them. Harrell explains:

He had never gone through a copy-editing stage in a publishing house. He did not really trust that in our system, nothing would ever be forced on him. No deletions forced on him, as in magazine writing. But in fact, the copy editing was to stimulate him and help him see problem spots. He could always take my penciled suggestions or think of his own. He soon realized that we were a team.

Though in his letters, Thompson complained that the process had "turned into a nightmare of long haggling and desperate work," he was treated quite well by his publishers, who were eager to keep their young author happy. Certainly, his choices were respected more than they had been at the various magazines and newspapers he had worked for.[19] Silberman even took the highly unusual step of allowing unlimited expenses for phone calls between Hunter and Margaret, some of which cost more than five hundred dollars when adjusted for inflation. This was because Thompson had not been brought out to New York, which was standard practice at Random House in order to keep their authors happy and assure them that their books were in the right hands.

Random House was, however, worried about lawsuits. They asked Thompson to find evidence to justify just about every statement made in his book, a process that he knew would take a long time—and, in some cases, would be totally impossible. He was angry that his wisdom and his sources had been questioned, and infuriated that the company's "ignorant, old-womanish lawyers" wanted him to provide criminal records to support his claims about the Angels' pasts. This was not legally possible, but they insisted and so Thompson was forced to hire someone to

---

19   Particularly toward the end of his tenure with the *National Observer*, his work was cut substantially before being printed. One article in particular, printed as "Living in the Time of Alger, Greeley, Debs" in *The Great Shark Hunt*, was cut to just six short paragraphs, around 350 words, when it appeared in the newspaper. In his anthology, it is a lengthy piece of about four pages.

acquire the documents extralegally.

This aspect of publishing a book brought out a righteous anger in Thompson (and some measure of childishness, too). In his mind, everything he had written in the book was true and he deeply resented his judgments being called into question. Besides, any uncertainties had been made clear in the text, which he believed was fair and reasonable. As for his research, he said, "My sources are not always reputable, but they are not given to conscious lying." The implication of the lawyers' requirements was fundamentally the same as the editors of the *National Observer* pointing out his falsifying quotes or facts, which Thompson considered trivial matters at best. Besides, this time he had invested an enormous amount of effort into the book and had "researched it about as well as any human could." *Why should I be forced to go through all this work again?* he wondered. Worse still, it seemed to Hunter as though Silberman and the lawyers had waited for him to leave San Francisco and move twelve hundred miles away to the mountains before asking him to do a lot of footwork that they could have insisted upon when he was in the thick of the story. He was livid.

All his life, Thompson faced these legal issues but he took great care to keep people out of trouble. He frequently boasted about his ability to write journalism that did not lead to convictions, presenting truths without giving evidence. In explaining this to a high school student who had asked him about his book, Thompson invoked Hemingway's Iceberg Theory again, telling her that a reader must go into the subtext of a book, as legal problems often hinder what can be said explicitly. It is a different interpretation of Hemingway's concept and it shows the depth of thought he invested in understanding great writers.

He got into another dispute with the lawyers over the phrase "Pepsi Generation" and won, but they could not, however, be persuaded about other things. Neal Cassady had been at the La Honda party but they insisted his name be removed. In response, Thompson (possibly joking, but probably not) sent a half-nude photograph of himself for the back of the book. His editor laughed it off and returned the photo.

The process dragged on and on as he worked to

comply with legal demands. According to Thompson's letters, Random House kept pushing back the date of release, which angered him immensely, as he was again utterly broke.[20] He was eagerly awaiting his first royalty check, but he started to realize that it could be a long time before he ever saw another penny from the book he felt he had long ago finished. He detested working so hard for an advance that had been long since spent. After the Random House hardback and Ballentine paperback, the book was published by Penguin, with countless typos added and its dedication page removed, making Thompson wonder whether there had been any point to the whole process or if it was all an effort in busy-work.

Then followed a torturous publicity tour that resulted in various disasters. For one thing, the publishers had grossly underestimated demand and only printed twenty thousand copies, so Thompson had to go on tour with no books for people to buy or him to sign. He had to sit and answer stupid questions day after day without even knowing whether he had made new sales.[21] That is not to suggest that he invested much effort in the publicity part of the book. Paul Krassner remarked that Thompson was "either a blathering drunk or an insane mumbler" when he showed up for an event—and he didn't always show up.

There were also excerpts to piece together and articles to write—both for money and to help promote the book. *Pageant, Esquire*, the *LA Times*, and *The Courier-Journal* all wanted something from him. In the *Courier* story, which is an excellent reflection on the whole process of researching and writing the book, Thompson claims, "I know more than any other writer, and more than most other people – including the outlaws, for that matter" about the Angels.

---

20 Margaret Harrell points out that this, like many other of Thompson's claims about the publication process, was possibly inaccurate as this is not consistent with how Random House (or other publishers) operated at that time. [E-mail to author] It is likely that he was again confused or simply exaggerating in his letters

21 One person asked him, "Are [the Hell's Angels] homosexuals?" Thompson replied, "How latent is latent?" and then added, "To me the whole question is irrelevant." [*The Hell's Angels Letters*, p. 101]

He says that when people ask him questions, he is annoyed: "Read the book, dammit; that's why I wrote it – to answer the questions."

Despite all of these troubles, the book had sold out and another printing saw good sales, too. He was invited onto TV and radio shows, and it was during these appearances that he really began to cultivate his image—turning himself into a character and a brand. Tellingly, in a letter to Margaret Harrell, he referred to his TV appearances as "performance," though he implied that it was a cover for his nerves. His old friend, William Kennedy said:

> I noted the transformation of Hunter into a public personality for the first time when he was doing publicity for *Hell's Angels* in 1968. He was in New York and he turned up with a cowboy hat and very bizarre sunglasses, bright red or green, glow in the dark. It was a costume for Halloween, and that persona was what he was after, that look. I asked him, "What are you made up for? What are you trying to prove?" He had always shown up at my house wearing sweaters, slacks—clothes, not costumes. But now the image was foremost. I believe Hunter was captured by that persona, and that his writing was transformed. More and more it was about that persona, not about what it used to be about. And it seemed he was reveling in it.

Although this process certainly accelerated during the *Hell's Angels* press campaign, it had been ongoing for some time. He had always enjoyed playing the rebel and there are any number of examples of him attempting to appear like a renegade during his writing career and even before it. When he came back from South America, he certainly made an impact through his dress sense, and he made an effort to describe his clothes in both published writing and his letters. At this point, Thompson also began taking his pranking into the professional world by making bizarre appearances at the Random House offices, sometimes with a maritime foghorn that he used to startle people, and in one case a large snake that subsequently escaped and was killed. There are numerous accounts of people who experienced these theatrical displays, and one can reasonably assume that it was partly for fun and partly for presenting that zany Hunter image that he made his personal brand. Wayne Ewing confirmed this after Thompson's death, saying that "From the beginning, he had an instinctual sense that branding himself properly was a key to success and fame."

Despite his savaging of the press, early reviews of *Hell's Angels* were very positive and the book soon became a best-seller. By the end of 1967, the combined hardcover and paperback sales were more than half a million copies. Studs Terkel of the *Chicago Tribune* called it "a terribly important piece of journalism" and Eliot Fremont-Smith of *The New York Times* said Thompson was "a spirited, witty, observant, and original writer." Leo Litwak of *The New York Times Review of Books* said: "Thompson has presented us with a close view of a world most of us would never encounter. His language is brilliant, his eye remarkable." It was incredible praise for an author's first book and it made his name as a writer—but not just any sort of writer. He was already one of the outlaws, a literary tough guy in the mold of Hemingway and Mailer. His star was quickly rising but the question remained—what would he do next?

Origins of Gonzo

Journalism, to me, is just another drug—a free ride to scenes I'd probably miss if I stayed straight.
                                                        Hunter S. Thompson

As the exciting young author of a best-selling book, Hunter S. Thompson now had the world at his feet and so he began to plot his next move. With his publishers, he discussed the idea of yet more work on "fringe type" people. They wanted a book on right-wing militants but Thompson refused and suggested living in Mexico for six months and writing a book about expatriate life south of the border. Perhaps seeing that this may have been a ruse to have the company fund an extended holiday, Random House rejected his suggestion.[1] To *The Saturday Evening Post*, he suggested trying to get aboard a Russian naval fleet so that he could write about Cold War tensions. "I have a talent for getting into strange places," he explained. He also informed the editors that he had moved on from the style he used when writing for the *Observer*, emphasizing that any future work would be more similar to the articles he had written for *The Nation*.

In spite of all his options, he was still stone broke, so he hastily signed a new contract with Random House to write a book on a yet-to-be-decided subject. They offered him what seemed like a fair contract that also gave them the rights to his still-unpublished novel, *The Rum Diary*, but they made clear they would only publish it on the condition

---

1   In letters to family, he did indeed announce that he would take a vacation in Mexico and, knowing his relationship with expense accounts, their guess was probably correct.

that it was largely rewritten.[2] Although he was delighted to have it finally placed with a major publisher, he was less than enthusiastic about the contract:

> At a glance it looks like a $10,000 advance for two books, but what it really amounts to is ill-paid bondage for an indefinite period of time. I am very discouraged with the book business. The money is illusory and the cheap realities are all the more shocking because they are hidden, like rocks in the surf, by decades of paternalistic myth.

Still, he was keen to make this next book count. *Hell's Angels* had provided him with a modest degree of fame but he was not yet a household name. He wrote a friend that "since I already have a contract for another non-fiction book I think it should be on the most pertinent subject I can find." For months, he scrabbled around for ideas but found nothing, and began to seriously regret his choices. The book was due by the summer of the following year, but he didn't even know what it was about. In all of the articles he considered writing, he looked for topics that might potentially be expanded into a book, hoping to repeat the success of *Hell's Angels*. He was aware of his reputation as "a sort of hoodlum-writer" with the ability to investigate underground or dangerous groups, but he was reluctant to be pigeon-holed and hoped to branch out and cover something totally different.

Pretty soon, he was working on an article for *The Nation* and had agreed to do another for *Playboy*. A year later, however, he had still not submitted his work to *The Nation*. He had first promised them an article on extreme right-wing groups, but then when he could not write that he promised them a profile of a rock band. He figured that this would be easier because he had an unused interview

---

2   Thompson was happy with the idea of his novel being rewritten but seemed reluctant to actually do it given the pressures of other work. As time went by, he became less enamored of it, later saying it was a "hopelessly naïve and half-conceived book" whose "first 100 pages are worthless." [*Fear and Loathing in America*, p. 134, 133]

with the manager of Country Joe and the Fish, which he had conducted during the research for an older piece. Still, he struggled badly, restarting four times before eventually writing to his editor in shame, saying that he only had one sentence.

The *Playboy* story was a straightforward article on the Hell's Angels, which he was able to write easily from his notes. However, they ended up rejecting it because he had already sold another version to *The Saturday Evening Post*. Now that he was becoming well known, it was harder to hide the fact that he often attempted to spin the same article to two different outlets. He was also failing to meet deadlines for articles he had been paid to write by *The New York Times Magazine*, *Ramparts*, *Pageant*, and *The Realist*. His problem, he claimed, was that every project he took on spiraled into a lengthy screed. "Anything less than 100 pages seems like a meatless outline," he wrote. He was looking for the right lens through which to explore each issue he tackled, but these just led him to expansive and unsatisfactory discussions on a violent, chaotic, and confusing world.

Already, Thompson's observations about Hemingway's decline were proving prophetic. He had written, "Like many another writer, Hemingway did his best work when he felt he was standing on something solid – like an Idaho mountainside, or a sense of conviction," and now Thompson himself was struggling to keep up with a rapidly changing world. He was distracted by events in the news and overwhelmed by the tasks in front of him, constantly changing what he was working on. In explaining his inability to be concise or stay focused, he explained, "It keeps changing... but then so do I." Yet he was also experiencing the first hints of a problem that would plague him throughout the seventies and beyond. He just could not focus on anything long enough to complete it. *The Rum Diary*, he felt, just need a surface rewrite, and various other stories should have been easy for him to knock out and send off. Somehow, though, he kept jumping from project to project. By October, he had even agreed to write a monthly column for *Ramparts*—twelve hundred words for the reasonable sum of one hundred and fifty dollars. But time and time again he simply failed to finish what he had started. He wrote a friend to say his "writing block [was] getting worse with every new article."

There were also factors closer to home that limited his literary output. Thompson was angry with the Scott Meredith Literary Agency for a number of reasons, but mainly he felt that they had ruined or nearly ruined several opportunities for him and then finally allowed him to sign what he considered a terrible deal with Random House. He hired lawyers to resolve the issue but ultimately decided to let his contract with Meredith expire on December 15, 1967. Meanwhile, Sandy was going through a painful, protracted miscarriage.

When he was evicted from his San Francisco home, Thompson felt that it was time to retreat to the mountains. He had milked the Bay Area for a lot of material but its heyday, he felt, was in the past. It was time for him to move on, and there was nowhere he would rather do it than Woody Creek, Colorado. He had spent a happy few months there before arriving in California, and now was the time to move back and find a home. He moved into a modest ranch house with lots of land and called it Owl Farm. He quickly began to refer to it as his "fortress," and in another attempt to build his own legend, he would put that (or "fortified compound") onto the back cover or inside flap of all his books.[3] Owl Farm would be his home for the rest of his life.

In turns desperate for work and overstretched by work, Thompson was eager to find the next big story—something made just for him and ripe for his burgeoning style. After looking through the various possibilities for more "fringe" work, he crafted a long pitch for an exposé on professional football. It is a manic piece of writing, written as though by a man on amphetamines (which he most likely was), and in it he introduces himself as "HST"—the abbreviated form he would use often in future, including when signing books. Written in December 1966, more than three years before the term "Gonzo" was coined, Thompson was very much pitching a Gonzo story. It even began in proto-Gonzo fashion with a flurry of subheaders, joined with

---

3   However, "for publicity reasons" he initially kept his move to the mountains quiet and advertised himself as "a 'San Francisco writer.'" [*The Hell's Angels Letters*, p.26]

odd punctuation marks:

A THESIS—TO BE WRITTEN BY A RABID FAN—IN WHICH IT IS ARGUED, RESEARCHED, PROVEN AND OPENLY DISPLAYED THAT PROFESSIONAL FOOTBALL IS A VICIOUS UN-SPORTING HOAX—A VIOLENT SICK JOKE, BEING PERPETRATED ON A SICK SOCIETY—WITH THE FEELING FOR ULTIMATE GALL—IN THE PERSON OF PETE ROZELLE—THAT CAN ONLY BE MAINTAINED ON A LEVEL BEYOND THE WILDEST DREAMS OF HISTORY'S GREATEST HYPE-SELLERS.... AND A SECONDARY THEORY THAT SUCKERS IN THIS COUNTRY ARE MADE, NOT BORN.... A MERCILESS EXPOSÉ ON THE ROLE OF SPORTSWRITERS IN THE GREAT INDUSTRY OF SPORTS-PROMOTING....

He proudly touted his "weird background" as a writer and suggested that he essentially infiltrate the summer training camp of the San Francisco 49ers and then talk with the players. He promised to get the "real" stories from the players and made it clear that he would not be writing "a PR puff."

For many months, he also worked on a story for Paul Krassner of *The Realist*, based upon his farcical experiences on the *Hell's Angels* book tour. Although it had been excruciating, he had seen in the phony, repetitive, sycophantic routine the seeds of a wonderful satire. Thompson took two hundred dollars for the story, which was worked out over dinner one night, but after much struggling, it was never written. Margaret Harrell, who had been present when the idea was hatched, said "It would be a forecast of 'The Temptations of Jean-Claude Killy,'" referring to a breakthrough story from 1969 that also scrutinized the growing PR industry.

In early 1967, he wrote an obituary for his good friend, Lionel Olay, who had recently died at an age Hunter guessed at little over forty. He wrote of Olay as part of the already dying myth of the sixties:

> Lionel was one of the original anarchist-head-beatnik-free-lancers of the 1950s … a bruised forerunner of [Timothy] Leary's would-be "drop-out generation" of the 1960s. The Head Generation … a loud, cannibalistic gig where the best are fucked for the worst reasons, and the worst make a pile by feeding off the best. Promoters, narcs, con men—all selling the New Scene to *Time* magazine and the Elks Club.

It is a touching but angry piece of writing, in which Thompson recalls his old friend as an outlaw of literature—clearly a model for his own later approaches to writing. He describes an opportunity Olay had to make money and become successful by writing a flattering feature on a Hollywood producer, but instead Olay ran up a big expense bill and then wrote a scathing attack, in which he called the man a "pompous toad." Thompson compares him to H.L. Mencken for his integrity, describes him as "a man who makes his own rules," and pitches him as the antithesis of what Hunter considered the negative elements of the sixties counterculture: phony gurus, half-baked ideas, and an unwillingness to fight the power. In short, Olay was a hero battling quietly against a sadistic world.

Thompson's literary output in 1967 was not prodigious. Even though the success of *Hell's Angels* had opened doors for him, he could not bring himself to cross the threshold. There was a litany of agreements made, including an article about Aspen for *Harper's*, but most of them were later broken as he lost focus and moved on to other projects. The spat with his agent had also caused him to avoid anything that might put money in Scott Meredith's pocket. Still, he wrote long letters, often filled with vitriol, that showed him continuing to play with language and develop his style. In one letter, he wrote, "It's a mockery of every decent idea and instinct that might exist in journalism."

This was a sentence structure that he frequently used in later work. The line "*x* is a mockery of *y*" became very common in his language, as did "*x* is a monument to *y*." He had actually used the latter as far back as *Prince Jellyfish*, when he described the Empire State Building as:

> that great phallic symbol, a monument to the proud dream of potency that is the spirit of New York.

He had also used this phrase in 1958:

> [his procrastination was] a symbolic experience, I think, when you realize that most people's lives are virtual monuments to cowardly indecision.

In 1967, he again used it in a letter to Paul Krassner:

> The Scott Meredith Literary Agency is a stinking, shit-spined monument to everything that sinks to the bottom in the sediment pool of human responsibility.

The phrase "a monument to" became such a part of Thompson's vocabulary around this time that when his first collection of work was brought out, *The Great Shark Hunt* (1979), it contained thirteen instances of those words. In most cases, these referred to Richard Nixon, including one that was taken from an article written just four months after his Krassner letter:

> For years I've regarded his very existence as a monument to all the rancid genes and broken chromosomes that corrupt the possibilities of the American Dream.

In 1967, Thompson only sold six articles and made a total of fifteen hundred dollars.[4] The best of these pieces

---

4   He claimed that he sold three, but in fact he published six articles during 1967. The reason why he said that he only

was "The 'Hashbury' Is the Capital of the Hippies," which appeared in *The New York Times Magazine* in May 1967. In it, Thompson, in his own words "a known confidant of all undergrounds," gives a simple, anthropological guide to the counterculture, explaining beatniks and hippies to the average person just as he had done with motorcycle gangs. Here again, he seems knowledgeable and lets the reader in on dirty secrets like drug world jargon.

As with the Angels article and book, he uses collective quotation to capture the voice of a group:

> They reject any kinship with the Beat Generation on the ground that "those cats were negative, but our thing is positive."

He has also returned to the technique of simply making up quotes to fit his narrative, as we can see when he cites a young radio engineer called "Brent Dangerfield." Thompson trained in the Air Force as a radio engineer and the name is an obvious reference to Sebastian Dangerfield. When Dangerfield quips, "I'm 22, but I used to be much older," it is most likely a reference to Bob Dylan's 1964 song, "My Back Pages," and the line, "Ah, but I was so much older then/I'm younger than that now."

In August, *Pageant* published Thompson's article, "Why Boys Will Be Girls."[5] It was very similar to the "Hashbury" article, functioning as a sociological overview of countercultural elements. As the title suggests, it focuses on why young people appeared to be engaging in transvestitism. Thompson delineates the Beats and hippies, talks a little about drugs, and argues that there is essentially nothing wrong with the weird dress sense and habits of the youth. His style is conversational, with some dry humor, and he is not afraid to insert his own opinion or even odd

---

wrote three was that some of the material was excerpted or rehashed parts of *Hell's Angels*.

5   Thompson had first worked with *Pageant* in 1965, writing articles called "It Ain't Hardly That Way No More" and "The 450-Square-Mile Parking Lot" for the September and December issues. Both were quite tame, conventional efforts. The latter contained a lot more statistics than normally appeared in his articles.

facts about his own life, such as claiming that he enjoys wearing women's hats. He finishes with the evidence of Dr. Robert Geiger, who Thompson fails to mention was a close friend.[6] Thompson, who liked to end his articles on a witty or poignant line has Geiger remark: "If there is any sexual confusion involved, I would say it is in the minds of people who get hysterical when they see a man with long hair."

These articles were followed up by a long piece for the *1968 Collier's Encyclopedia Yearbook Covering the Year 1967* called "The Hippies." Not exactly typical encyclopedia fare, Thompson recounts a very subjective history of the hippie movement, tying it to the Beats and beatniks of the fifties, before then recounting his own adventures with the Hell's Angels. Some sentences were reused from his May 1967 *New York Times* article on the same topic. In the "Hashbury" article, he wrote:

> The Digger ethic of mass sharing goes along with the American Indian motif that is basic to the Hashbury scene. The cult of "tribalism" is regarded by many of the older hippies as the key to survival. Poet Gary Snyder, a hippy guru, sees a "back to the land" movement as the answer to the food and lodging problem. He urges hippies to move out of the cities, form tribes, purchase land and live communally in remote areas.

This is reworked for his *Collier's* piece:

> The concept of mass sharing goes along with the American Indian tribal motif that is basic to the whole hippie movement. The cult of tribalism is regarded by many as the key to survival. Poet Gary Snyder, one of the hippie gurus, or spiritual guides, sees a "back to the land" movement as the

---

6   Geiger had also been the focus of Thompson's final *National Observer* article, "A Surgeon's Fingers Fashion a Literary Career," in 1964.

answer to the food and lodging problem. He urges hippies to move out of the cities, form tribes, purchase land, and live communally in remote areas.

Although the two pieces are very similar and indeed contain some sections that he had rewritten, the *Collier's* article is more playful and personal. Thompson seems eager to drop himself into the story, again exaggerating his own life experiences. He claims to have lived in San Francisco in 1959 when in fact he merely passed through in 1960, says that he lived at Big Sur for three years when he actually spent just one year, and then tells the reader that he lived in South America for two years rather than the six months he spent there. One can hardly fail to note the irony here: He presented these falsified facts to position himself as a more reliable guide to the counterculture, but in doing so he was effectively showing his willingness to say whatever he felt would best support his version of a story.

At the beginning of 1968, Thompson was free of his agent and so he flew to New York to renegotiate the contract for his next book with Random House. They had agreed the year before to an unnamed project on some element of outsider culture, but now the publisher and writer decided upon "the Death of the American Dream" as the subject. Thompson would always attribute this to Jim Silberman, referring to it as "Silberman's lame idea" and sometimes "Silberman's book." However, according to Silberman, the idea emerged from a phone call, in which Hunter explained his various ideas for subjects and Silberman remarked, "You're really writing one book." Thompson somehow took this to mean that he was contractually obliged to write a book on the Death of the American Dream.

He almost immediately regretted taking the American Dream as his subject as it made him "nervous because it's so vast & weighty." Originally envisaged as a profile of the Joint Chiefs of Staff, the book quickly spiraled out of his control. He knew that the first chapter would be a simple series of profiles, but beyond that he had no idea. The topic was too difficult to pin down. Even a year and a half into his work on the book, he complained:

> I still have no idea what I'm supposed to be
> writing about—in terms of titles, chapters,
> jacket blurbs and that sort of thing. I see
> a lot of connections in my head that I
> can't make on paper, and consequently
> I have no real image of what I'm doing.
> That "American Dream" notion becomes
> increasingly meaningless—mainly because
> it fits everything I write, and most of what
> I read.

The single book deal had also morphed into an agreement for three books, including a total rewrite of *The Rum Diary* by July 1. The other one was a look at President Lyndon B. Johnson's re-election campaign, either told through Thompson's "impressionistic journalism" style or in the form of a satirical novel. In any case, the Johnson book would have to be finished by June 1 but the "American Dream" book wasn't due until July of the following year.

Thompson's plans for both new books took shape over the coming months but neither of them was ever written and, after various delays and difficulties, *The Rum Diary* was largely forgotten about until 1998. The Johnson book seemed much more straightforward but it also transformed a great deal in the planning stages. However, one thing that Thompson often mused over for both books was the mix of fact and fiction and the fusion of novelistic and journalistic techniques. At one stage, he considered writing a report on attempts to derail the 1968 Democratic Convention through protest and pranks. He aimed to find out in advance what was going to happen and then publish it—but mix both real plans and fake ones. He explained to his publisher:

> I'd have to mix up fact and fantasy so totally
> that nobody could be sure which was which.
> We could bill it as a fantastic piece of root-
> hog journalism—The Thompson Report,
> as it were. This courageous journalist
> crept into the sewers of the American

underground and emerged with a stinking heap of enemy battle plans—and just in time, by god, to warn the good guys what to watch out for.

His concept involved imagining interviews with politicians, including Johnson, and then reporting them as though they really happened. This was a step beyond the fact-fiction dynamic in *Hell's Angels*, but still Thompson defended his concept by saying, "most of the fantasy content would be based on fact." He even pointed out to his editor that he had removed similar material from his first book, lamenting that "some of the best parts of the H.A. book never made it past the first-draft."

He also realized that the book needed a narrative structure that most likely involved him as a participant. He told Jim Silberman that "my involvement will have to serve as the beginning of a narrative" in order to better guide his reader through the story. It harkened back to an old dilemma: Is he a writer of thought or of action? With himself as the protagonist, it could well be both. He discussed the book's need for "a beginning and an end," much like a novel, in order to keep the reader interested. He had no intention of merely writing a collection of essays, which would not be as engaging, he felt, as *Hell's Angels*. Instead, *writing the story* was going to be part of the story. He aimed to attempt contact with the Joint Chiefs and fully expected to be ignored. As with much of his writing, he felt that the failure would be part of the narrative, and in this case the beginning of the story. It would lead into the greater questions of:

> Who are these people who won't talk to me? Where did they come from and why are they in charge? How far does their power extend? Where does their power originate? Why them, and not me?

It would be a book packed with "Details, madness, action" and it would lead to him ruminating on the Death of the American Dream as he savaged the "swine" who had led the country down a dark path and who kept people like Thompson perennially out of power.

When planning out these next books, Thompson was fortunate to have talented and tolerant editors that would consider his view on fictionalizing real events. However, most magazine editors were not so open to his peculiar brand of journalism and he struggled to explain to them why he wanted to incorporate seemingly random and libelous flights of fancy within his work.

For many months, he had been working on an article about the Nevada prison system for *The New York Times*. Although the topic certainly seemed to call for traditional reporting, Thompson believed that the chaos created at a conference he had attended was outside the realm of straight journalism. He said that the editors were "asking for an account of something that didn't happen" because a straightforward account was no way to represent something that was not at all straightforward:

> I'll be fucked if I'm going to try to pass it off as a 1, 2, 3, 4 ... sort of a thing. If anything, it was 3, 2, 4, 1 ... and that's the way I tried to write it, because that's the way I saw it.
>
> [...] I can't get over the feeling that you're asking me for an article that you never should have assigned me to in the first place ... some sort of legally logical exercise in straight-grey journalism, which is what I'm trying to do right now, if for no other reason than a deadweight sense of obligation all around.

In the end, Thompson did not rewrite the article for the *Times* and it was never published. Another long article, this one on "the Oil Shale menace," was written for the *Los Angeles Times*, but they declined to published it after it was submitted. In a rare burst of optimism, Thompson wrote it off as "another chapter in my education." He knew fine well that sometimes good writing was rejected, having once lamented that "most of the best things I wrote were never published."

Amidst these unpublished articles, there was at least

one success. He agreed to "a fluff assignment to do a piece on Nixon for *Pageant*" that would allow him the freedom to write in his new style as well as gain material for both the Johnson and American Dream books. Already, he was sure that Nixon was tied into its death.

To write his profile on Richard Nixon, then running for president, Thompson flew to New Hampshire on February 11, 1968 and stayed at the Manchester Holiday Inn, which also served as Nixon's campaign headquarters. Nixon was the Republican frontrunner and in the middle of an incredible political comeback, despite having seemingly ended his political career in 1962 with a failed campaign for governor of California. Thompson traveled on Nixon's press bus, where he befriended *Boston Globe* journalist, Bill Cardoso, and then managed to get a private interview with Nixon in a limousine that was taking the candidate to an airport. Thompson's hostility toward Nixon was known but he was chosen because of his experience in sports writing. Nixon wanted to talk football and Thompson was the only reporter there who knew enough to hold a decent conversation. They talked for about a half hour, with the writer deeply impressed by the candidate's knowledge of professional football.

The resulting article was published by *Pageant* in July 1968, as "Presenting: The Richard Nixon Doll (Overhauled 1968 Model)." Thompson had submitted a forty-five-page manuscript, from which the editors cut fifteen of the first twenty pages. He was livid. He demanded that his name be removed, but the magazine would not agree. At this point, Thompson exerted great effort over his writing and cared deeply for every word he wrote—including "pig-fucker," which the editors refused to allow.

The Nixon article starts in a quite disjointed fashion (no doubt because of the extensive editing) and the commentary is reasonably tame. However, soon enough the author's usual voice emerges. It begins with him attempting to get the story but encountering some problems—namely, that he is not trusted by Nixon's handlers. Then, suddenly, he launches into attack mode:

> Richard Nixon has never been one of my
> favorite people, anyway. For years I've

regarded his very existence as a monument to all the rancid genes and broken chromosomes that corrupt the possibilities of the American Dream; he was a foul caricature of himself, a man with no soul, no inner convictions, with the integrity of a hyena and the style of a poison toad. The Nixon I remembered was absolutely humorless; I couldn't imagine him laughing at anything except maybe a paraplegic who wanted to vote Democratic but couldn't quite reach the lever on the voting machine.

Here, he starts with comic understatement and then writes a long, vicious sentence that includes unique and horrible imagery. It is the sort of description that Thompson excelled at—completely disregarding journalistic convention and using language that is utterly merciless. He then adds another long sentence that suggests Nixon would laugh at a handicapped person. Image is heaped upon image, creating a repugnant description.

Is it a fair and reasonable journalistic technique to make such suggestions? After all, in *Hell's Angels*, Thompson had attacked the press for using words like "allegedly" to make suggestions that were not necessarily true. In this case, he would probably have defended himself in two ways: First of all, he did say "imagine" and so it is clear that the image is a figment of his own imagination. Secondly, he would point out that, with people like Richard Nixon, their image is so carefully controlled that nothing they say is credible. This sort of reporting is, then, a method of fighting back. Writing was one way of leveling the playing field.

For the rest of the article, he slips back into a more restrained mode, content with gently and humorously mocking Nixon and his campaign people. Throughout a coherent article, he weaves Nixon's past with the present and with his own movements as a journalist on the campaign trail. The reader is not just presented with an attack on Nixon, but the story of trying to report on him. Thompson repeatedly encounters unreasonable obstacles in his attempts to report and can never seem to get a grasp on what the New Nixon is all about. In a sense, it was something he had been doing since his days on *The Command Courier*, but now it was ratcheted up and he had thrown off most of the shackles of convention, happy to accuse Nixon of having "the integrity of a hyena."

We hear very little of what Nixon actually says because Thompson's aim is to go beyond the carefully managed façade that has remained intact because other journalists had simply regurgitated his lies. Instead, he wants to present a different perspective, offering a non-traditional view of a presidential candidate, and from comparing him to a "poison toad" to showing the difficulty a reporter faces in getting the truth, he certainly managed that.[7]

This article features yet more self-mythologizing from Thompson, who was keen to tell his readers that he had almost blown up Richard Nixon by smoking a cigarette too close to the engine of his airplane.[8] He also drops in a name that might have been familiar to readers of *Hell's Angels*: Raoul Duke. Thompson again mentions Duke just briefly, this time to deliver a quote about only trusting a drunk used-car salesman. Years later, Thompson said that he used Duke because he wanted an Angel to say something but none of them would say exactly what he needed. He either confused this with the Nixon profile for *Pageant* (in which Duke is referenced as a source) or used a different name for a made-up quote in *Hell's Angels* (most likely Sr. Cazador, mentioned in the previous chapter).

Regardless of his anger with the editors at *Pageant*, Thompson was relatively happy with what he had written about the New Hampshire trip. In continued discussions over his next book, he told his Random House editor that the article demonstrated his new style and the approach he planned to take for his American Dream book—it would have a narrative based upon "a participant's point of view."

***

7   The "poison toad" line may be a reference to Lionel Olay, whose use of "pompous toad" impressed and amused Hunter.
8   In the *Pageant* article, he says that he was told later that he had been smoking by the plane, but in later versions he played up the drama of the incident. In *Fear and Loathing on the Campaign Trail '72*, he claimed that the cigarette had been snatched from his mouth in a flurry of action.

When Lyndon Johnson suddenly dropped out of the presidential race on March 31, 1968, Thompson's book on him died, too. Whether he would have managed to write it or not is doubtful, but his concern at the time was having lost a ten-thousand-dollar advance. That was, however, just one event in a tumultuous and often tragic year. In January, there was the Tet Offensive in Vietnam, the My Lai massacre took place in March, Martin Luther King and Robert Kennedy were assassinated in April and June, and then in August there was the Democratic Convention.

In pursuit of material for his American Dream book, Thompson headed to Chicago. He expected trouble and brought a motorcycle helmet as protection, but what he found was far worse than even his violent imagination foresaw. In the streets, Mayor Richard Daley's police viciously beat not only protestors but members of the press. Anyone that went outside was liable to have their teeth knocked out and their skulls cracked. You did not have to be a protester to incur the wrath of the Chicago Police Department—a gang of thugs every bit as violent and cruel as the Hell's Angels. To a friend, he said it was "the Fourth Reich out in the open for the first time." Thompson was rammed in the stomach with a billy club and then pushed through a plate glass window, and all this in spite—or perhaps because—of his press credentials. His experiences there compounded the hopelessness he'd felt at Robert Kennedy's death, confirming for him the fact that the American Dream was dead and his beloved country was being run by brutal fascists. Thompson claimed to have been forever changed by the events of that day. "It permanently altered my brain chemistry," he wrote. "I went to the Democratic Convention as a journalist and returned a raving beast."

Although his experiences in Chicago were among the most important of his life, he published relatively little about them. They were discussed in letters to friends, mentioned in interviews, and alluded to in some articles, but there was nothing devoted solely to the events that so profoundly marked him. This seems strange, of course, but Thompson tended to struggle when it came to writing that was highly personal, and by all accounts the violence he witnessed and experienced hurt him deeply. Still, there were some efforts to put this most significant of times into print. He told Margaret Harrell, "I'm writing bags of pages every day on Chicago," but it seems these pages were intended "as part of a book tentatively titled 'Eight Years on the Road to Chicago: Notes on the Death of the American Dream – or, once again, Which Side Are You On?'"

His only extended piece of published writing about the Democratic Convention was released thirty-two years later in his letter collection, *Fear and Loathing in America*. In the untitled piece, he describes being beaten by cops and then getting high with a photographer. It is a jumpy, unpolished story that seems half a faithful account of the beatings and half a short story that introduces his friend, Raoul Duke.[9] The second half is strange and it is not clear what Thompson wants to say. Duke is nothing like his later incarnations and not much happens. However, it is interesting to see his early descriptions of the effects of drugs. He encounters a "500 pound cop with blue fangs" as he trips on synthetic weed and tries to escape the madness of the street, which is compounded by distortion through a hallucinatory lens. Rory Feehan believes this was an important moment in the creation of Gonzo:

> Thompson had certainly written about drugs before, both in *Hell's Angels*, and his article "The 'Hashbury' Is the Capital of the Hippies," yet in both instances, the writing is more journalistic and informative in nature, with Thompson serving as a cultural interpreter of sorts. [...] Thompson's Chicago essay [...] marks his explicit embrace of the drug culture as a mark of defiance against the political establishment. The use of drugs is presented as a political identifier in terms

---

9   From Chicago, he even wrote a letter to Paul Semonin that he signed, "Fear + loathing [...] Raoul." Already, Duke existed not just as an imagined character but as an alter ego. [https://www.theguardian.com/books/2018/sep/25/hell-and-slander-hunter-s-thompsons-letters-to-childhood-friend-to-be-sold#img-2]

of answering the question "Which Side Are You On?"

It is quite likely that this story was part of the "bags of pages" that he wrote after returning from Chicago, suggesting that Raoul Duke was meant to be involved in *Eight Years on the Road to Chicago*. This makes a lot of sense because, as time went by, Thompson continued to play with the idea of Duke as some sort of character in his writing. In a letter sent just one month after the *Eight Years on the Road to Chicago* suggestion, he refers to his Death of the American Dream book as a "Fictional Documentary Novel" called *Hey Rube! The Memoirs of Raoul Duke … or a report on the rape and looting of the American Dream by a gang of Vicious Swine.*

When Thompson went back to Woody Creek, he felt that he finally had a new focus for his book. He had witnessed the American Dream dying in Chicago and, tragic as it was, it made for a good story. He was still determined to focus the book on something tangible that represented the Death of the American Dream and told his editor that it was "a far extension of Faulkner's idea of 'seeing the world in a grain of sand.'" Though he repeated this quote several times, he always confused Faulkner with William Blake, whose "Auguries of Innocence" begins: "To see a World in a Grain of Sand/And a Heaven in a Wild Flower/Hold Infinity in the palm of your hand/And Eternity in an hour." In any case, it was essentially another example of what he had told Paul Semonin—it is better to write about a "frustrated Spaniard" in the street than say Spain will "go Communist." He pursued the "grain of sand" idea for a long time, but eventually realized "I don't even have a beach to write about."

When *Esquire* asked him to write a story on the NRA, Thompson somewhat exceeded their three-thousand-word limit. The "article" that he submitted was around eighty thousand words and had taken him four months of writing. It was, in fact, a fully developed book, which Thompson later called *The Gun Lobby*. According to Douglas Brinkley, it is "the bridge book" that links *Hell's Angels* and *Fear and Loathing in Las Vegas*. He explained that "[it] has a lot of things that are similar to the *Vegas* book, but it's a little more straight journalism than *Vegas*." The book is serious and factual, yet it has a first-person narrative that takes the reader through cocktail parties. It is also deeply personal, as Thompson attempts to reconcile the part of him devastated by the violent deaths of the Kennedys and the part perversely attracted to guns.

Writing *Hell's Angels* had been an eye-opener for Thompson, as had all his planning for the next book. "The space and freedom of book-writing has completely spoiled me for articles," he explained. "Everything I start turns into a 100-page screed of some kind." He had been aware for some time of his tendency to insert too much of himself, his ego, or his wisdom into a piece of writing, even when he knew that the focus should have been someplace else. It was probably, he speculated, due to "a maddening compulsion to do all my thinking in print." In the case of *The Gun Lobby,* he was deeply conflicted between his liberal values and his love of firearms. Frustrated, he explained to Silberman:

> I'm as aware of this problem as you are, but it continues to plague me, and cripple my articles, which would certainly be a hell of a lot more saleable if I could keep the focus on people, words and action—rather than the internal dialogues of HST.

Although he was hammering out lengthy pieces of writing, Thompson was aware that not everything he wrote was golden. He regularly read *The Great Gatsby* and admired the concise descriptions Fitzgerald could give, and the fact that it was such a short book but said so much about the era, the country, and the human condition. He compared himself to Normal Mailer, saying, "I am writing great sentences and paragraphs, but when I get beyond a page I go all to pieces." It did not bother him too much as his interpretation of Fitzgerald's "high white note" was that it is better to have a few stand-out phrases or sentences in an article than to have a whole article that is just quite good.

Brinkley observed that the final year of the sixties was perhaps Thompson's most productive period, when he was able to write for hours, producing a huge volume of work. "He could type twenty flawless pages without missing a comma or a dash," he said. Even when he wasn't writing for money, he was working on projects just for fun, like "a piece of nightmare fiction set in SF, LA and Tijuana" that was never published. He was also eager to have Random House fund these projects, which gave him access to worlds he would not otherwise have been able to enter. Luckily for him, they continued to pay his ludicrous expenses for several years, enabling him to get close to almost everything that interested him that could be tied in even the loosest sense to the American Dream. "Journalism, to me," he told a friend, "is just another drug—a free ride to scenes I'd probably miss if I stayed straight."

Alas, *Esquire* declined to publish an eighty-thousand-word article and, more than fifty years later, *The Gun Lobby* remains unpublished. Perhaps Thompson vetoed its publication during his lifetime for fears over his reputation, as he quickly became synonymous with firearms, but as with many of his projects between 1967 and 1968, it just never made it into print. It was only in 1969—two years after *Hell's Angels* was published and four years after he had started writing it—that he began having major work published again.

In New Hampshire, Thompson had met Bill Cardoso of *The Boston Globe*, and the editor hired him to cover Nixon's inauguration in January. It was another opportunity for him to hurl invective at the politician he was coming to view as his mortal enemy, and his attacks would have to be even more vicious now that Nixon had regrettably been elected president. The resulting article, "Memoirs of a Wretched Weekend in Washington," was what Thompson described as "almost pure impressionistic journalism, larded here and there with a few old cudgels and HST bias points."[10] In it, he openly states that "Neutrality is obsolete," abandoning even the feintest pretext of objectivity.

Again, Thompson is in the center of the action, reporting on what he can see around him: "As I backed away from the brawl, two dogs began fighting behind me

---

10   It is worth noting that there is a caption on the first page of the article claiming that Thompson "has spent the last 12 months with Nixon," which was of course totally untrue.

and a march leader shouting 'Peace!' into his bullhorn was attacked by a freak wearing a Prussian helmet." The chaos of the event is conveyed effectively and the result is dizzying. He talks about the process of getting the story, referencing his past troubles with press credentials, and he twice includes his own notes, something he would use more extensively in future work. Both of these techniques were central to Gonzo writing, just a year away from being discovered.

Given more freedom to experiment, Thompson plays with punctuation, making frequent use of ellipses, and throws in some words that would become hallmarks of his writing: *king-hell, hellbroth, geek*. There are also two references to the "bastinado," a form of torture that he would often allude to in future works, and a mention of a "banshee screaming," an image he would sometimes conjure in his writing. He is playful with his words, too, making up compound nouns like "swineherds." There is even another brief reference to Raoul Duke, this time referred to as "a visiting dignitary," before he is allowed to deliver a witty quote.

In describing the events and people around him, Thompson is not afraid to use his imagination and create truly bizarre descriptions. In once such instance, he compares an angry police officer, who had been stripped almost naked by the crowd, to "a guinea hen just worked over by a pack of wild dogs." It is oddly specific, something that marked the imagery in most of his best work, and it harkens back to his early pranks, like having a boy beat a rubber frog in front of his school. He has concocted something so bizarre that no one would ever think of it, and for that reason it grabs the reader's attention and sticks in his mind.

Of course, he also descends into flights of fancy:

> My first idea was to load up on LSD and cover the Inauguration that way, but the possibilities were ominous: a scene that bad could only be compounded to the realm of mega-horrors by something as powerful as acid. No... it had to be done straight, or at least with a few joints in calm moments...

like fast-stepping across the Mall, bearing down on the Smithsonian Institution with a frenzied crowd chanting obscenities about Spiro Agnew... mounted police shouting 'Back! Back!'... and the man next to me, an accredited New York journalist, hands me a weird cigarette, saying, "Why not? It's all over anyway..."

To bring the focus back from his imaginative digression, he uses another recent innovation: a sudden, ungrammatical sentence beginning a new paragraph. He simply restarts, "Indeed. He was right. From my point of view [...]" By blending past, present, and imagined scenes, he needs these devices for refocusing the narrative.

With the inauguration of Richard Nixon in January 1969, Thompson felt that the spirit of the decade had come to an end. He was nearing the peak of his literary abilities and was making a real name for himself in the journalistic community, but already he had begun to hate the sight of his typewriter. For a year, he had been bogged down with the task of writing about the Death of the American Dream—a topic that evolved too fast for him to grasp. He complained:

> In truth, I find myself constantly grappling with senseless, ill-conceived notions for book-chapters and other garbage. ... Bottomless pits that keep me writing desperately and accomplishing nothing.

By mid-1969, Thompson had convinced himself that he had been scammed by Random House and Jim Silberman, and referred to his ongoing book as "Silberman's lame idea." In August, he called it "several hundred scrambled pages" of "doomed bullshit." He claimed that "I have never had the vaguest idea what the book was supposed to be 'about,'" and said that even the title had changed fifteen times. "At times it looks like a series of articles," he worried, "but sometimes it looks like a novel with a few article fragments thrown in for fillers."

Still, he acknowledged that this painful affair had at least spawned "a few high points."

Indeed, although the Death of the American Dream book seemed hopeless at times, Thompson had cunningly used it as a means of finding other stories to write about—various potential grains of sand. This allowed him access to an endless array of important events and scenes, but also provided him the necessary opportunities to further develop his style of writing. He was churning out countless pages of writing and constantly refining his voice, but there were still a few pieces that remained to be set in place before he reached what millions of fans would come to know as Gonzo.

Despite his rage at the editing work that they had done on his Nixon profile, Thompson returned to *Pageant* to do another article. He had written three other articles for the magazine—two in 1965 and one in 1967. This time, he took off for Edwards Air Force Base in California on the tenth anniversary of his Air Force discharge. He spent a few days on base, researching his story, and then retired to the Continental Hyatt House in Los Angeles. There, he spent time with old friend Gene McGarr and relatively new acquaintance, Oscar Zeta Acosta. When Thompson sat down to write at two or three in the morning, he found himself struggling. It was the first time he had really come to feel the hopelessness of writer's block. He admitted that being drunk and high on pills and weed was not helping him much and said that "trying to mix writing and fucking around with old friends don't work no more." He had to wait until he was back in Woody Creek before he managed to write the article.

Published in September 1969, "Those Daring Young Men in Their Flying Machines" was another triumph and showed Hunter Thompson (the middle initial oddly dropped) honing his own voice further. It begins with a piece of wisdom that became one of his most famous quotes, adorning T-shirts, posters, tattoos, and later memes around the world:

> Myths and legends die hard in America.
> We love them for the extra dimension
> they provide, the illusion of near-infinite

possibility to erase the narrow confines of most men's reality. Weird heroes and mold-breaking champions exist as living proof to those who need it that the tyranny of "the rat race" is not yet final.

The first paragraph features Thompson's wisdom, the second brings the topic into focus, and in the third, he adds himself into the mix as an observer-participant. He deliberately presents himself as an incompetent, clumsy outsider, acknowledging that he had asked the wrong questions to the wrong people and then telling these incredibly cautious pilots that he breaks the bones in his hands on average once per year. Thompson portrays himself as a careless, foolhardy, daredevil idiot in order to highlight the caution within the new generation of pilots.

Whilst venerating the pilots of the past, who undertook impossibly dangerous tasks, Thompson presents the new Air Force as sterile and subdued. He is pitting past against present, as he did in more than a few of his articles from the sixties and, as in those other articles, the present does not look quite as appealing as the past did. This article could well have shared the title of his first *Pageant* piece, written four years earlier: "It Ain't Hardly That Way No More."

In a letter to the Air Force's press department, Thompson explained his article, calling it "a necessarily incomplete distillation of the impressions" he gained at Edwards, showing that he was still working on his impressionistic journalism concept. He acknowledged the efforts he had made to avoid trouble with the Air Force "truth squad" and expressed a rare willingness to address "any factual mistakes" in his work. He clarified, though, that his opinions were "not subject to censorship," demonstrating his perception that factual and subjective writing were not mutually exclusive.

The article is interesting and Thompson's own voice rings out despite the fact that *Pageant* was looking something very bland compared to his usual style. He is restrained but subtly funny, and he has managed to squeeze in a few wild phrases and lots of wisdom about courage and motorcycles.

His article was accompanied by a short biography titled "A Writing Ace," which presents the author in a rather flattering light. It further builds his legend and sets him apart from his fellow writers, identifying him once again with his subjects:

> Hunter Thompson, already a legend at an unpretentious but absolutely with-it 32 years of age, has in him some of the daredevil style that characterized the old-time test pilots he reminisces about in this article. He calls himself an "unemployable writer" (he hasn't held a job since 1958); the fact is, he is a skilled and professional freelance who had the guts to ride with the wild motorcycle gangs for a year, as research for a best-selling book, *Hell's Angels.*

It goes on to say that his "next book, *The Rum Diary*, will be published by Random House – probably next year."

Ever since he had lived at Big Sur and tried his hand at writing short stories, Hunter Thompson had been keen to work with *Playboy*, which in addition to half-naked women was known for its good writing. Unfortunately, anything he had tried to do with them before had fallen through. In early 1969, though, they asked him to write a profile of Jean-Claude Killy, a French skier who had come to dominate the sport in 1967 – 68. In 1968, the Winter Olympics were broadcast in color throughout the United States, making the handsome Frenchman into a celebrity. He retired as a hero at age twenty-five and began a new career endorsing products for major brands.

Thompson followed the skier around but struggled to write about his subject. After more than three months of research, he said "The Killy thing was a bomb from the start, a stupid, wasteful thing to work on." Deadlines kept coming and going. At one point, he found himself several days past deadline and had not even begun his article, but *Playboy* granted him extension after extension, having already paid him four hundred dollars. This only encouraged Thompson's tendency to procrastinate, and

200

another month later he had become hopelessly mired in self-doubt, calling the article "a long, embittered harangue – not fit for print in any commercial medium." Eventually, he wrote what he thought was an excellent article, but it was rejected by the editors. Thompson was furious as he had struggled over the story and believed it was good enough for the two-thousand-dollar payment he was promised— even though he had submitted it two months late.

In his piece, Thompson had attacked Chevrolet, which *Playboy* wanted as an advertiser. One of their editors, clearly unhappy with Thompson's developing style, said that his "stupid arrogance is an insult to everything we stand for," and swore they would never work with him again. Fortunately, Thompson was able to sell the article to another editor—one who appreciated and nurtured the writer's evolving, original style. In 1967, he had befriended Warren Hinckle, then working at *Ramparts*. He had long planned on writing something for that magazine, but now Hinckle had founded a new publication, *Scanlan's Monthly,* and he wanted Thompson's Killy article.

"The Temptations of Jean-Claude Killy" appeared in the first issue of *Scanlan's* in March 1970. It is Thompson's best and most original piece of writing until this point and is just a short step away from his Gonzo breakthrough, "The Kentucky Derby is Decadent and Depraved." In it, most of the devices that he had developed over the past decade are present, and a few more emerge that would later come to dominate his writing.

The article begins with a terse description of the weather before Thompson introduces a new device— the sidekick. In this case, it is his *Boston Globe* friend, Bill Cardoso. His purpose is to allow Thompson to introduce himself, and through Cardoso we get a physical description of the reporter, who is also going to be our protagonist. More than a mere observer or even casual participant, Thompson is now Nick Carraway to Killy's Jay Gatsby and absolutely at the center of the story. As for the plot, it is again the process of getting a story. This had of course been a feature of his earlier work, but in "The Temptations of Jean-Claude Killy," it has become the whole story.

From the very start, it is clear that Thompson is struggling with his mission of finding out who Jean-

Claude Killy really is. Like Nixon in his *Pageant* profile, it seems that the man is just a projection created by his press team. As he had done with Nixon, Thompson attempts to compare the old Killy with the new, but he also uses himself as a comparison as he had done in his article about test pilots. Killy's personality (if he has one) seems the very antithesis to Thompson's. This is demonstrated when Thompson wants to order a vast breakfast spread, but Killy opts for a simple prune juice. Though likely true, the image is something one might expect from a novel rather than an article. It is another example of his use of Hemingway's methodology—showing an image that highlights an idea more effectively than an extensive explanation—and of Fitzgerald's notion that "Action is Character.".

As the struggling journalist, Thompson aims to get close to the skier and find out what he is really like, but even when he gets past the press team it is a challenge. There seems to be nothing behind the image, and what little Thompson can see suggests an incredibly boring man. When he finally becomes exasperated and tells Killy his problem, the skier laughs and says, "Well, maybe you could write about how hard it is to write about me." It was an unlikely source for the advice that would change Thompson's approach to journalism.

Just as he had done with the Hell's Angels, Thompson recounts for the reader his subject's public image and then attempts a thorough demythologizing of it, in this case attempting to establish whether Killy was really as impassive as he seemed. The result was a systematic but unconventional peeling back of the layers of bullshit obscuring the truth about Killy while at the same time exposing the cozy relationship between corporate greed, sports, and public relations.

Throughout the article, Thompson presents himself as an oddball character and freely admits his ignorance about certain things. When one of Killy's press team suggests that there is a dark secret that all the press know about but won't discuss, Thompson plays along, feigning knowledge of the alleged accusation. He tells the reader that he offered "a fine eyebrow shrug to cover my puzzlement."

Enjoying the freedom he had in this story, Thompson plays the role of the prankster. When three young boys approach him and ask if he is Jean-Claude Killy, he tells them that he is and then reports the following:

> Well, you goddamn silly little waterhead, what the hell does it look like I'm doing? But I didn't say that. I gave the question some thought. "Well," I said finally, "I'm just sitting here smoking marijuana." I held up my pipe. "This is what makes me ski so fast." Their eyes swelled up like young grapefruits. They stared at me – waiting for a laugh, I think – then backed away.

What purpose does this serve in a profile of Killy? On the surface, it appears to be comedy for the sake of comedy but in fact it is a comment on the nature of celebrity and in particular Killy's empty-figurehead status. No one seems to know anything about the skier and evidently some people don't even know what he looks like. It seems like a strange story to insert into an article until one digs into it and unpacks its purpose. Indeed, this is true of much of Thompson's writing, which often seemed juvenile and filled with pointless bragging.

The scene is funny not just because of its absurdity or social commentary, but because he was so adept at presenting an implausible yet somehow vivid and believable scene within a more prosaic reality. Thompson's descriptions are peculiarly accurate thanks to their specificity, and his incredibly original imagination constantly takes the reader by surprise as he makes odd suggestions, observations, and statements. Here, the description of the children's eyes as "young grapefruit" is peculiar and memorable. Coupled with the comedic line, "This is what makes me ski so fast," it creates a scene that leaves the reader uncertain whether this really happened and yet very much amused.

We can see this sort of approach elsewhere in the article. When Thompson is warned by one of Killy's press agents not to embarrass the skier and instead be "discreet" by not digging into his past, the writer states that it "was hard to imagine him as a sex freak" whose kink involves "a cattle prod and two female iguanas." The result is hilarious because of its specificity and subtlety. A later Thompson would likely have accused the skier of being a "pig-fucker" or "Pervert" (capital P) but the young writer was keenly aware that this hyper-specific description—very definitely *not* an accusation—was much funnier. It puts a distinct idea into the reader's mind—an idea that the reader had almost certainly never thought of before. When helping Craig Vetter edit his *Playboy* interview five years later, Thompson told the younger writer not to mention that the price of his beer was twenty-five cents, but to change it to twenty-four cents. It was the sort of fine detail that made an image more real.

Elsewhere in his article, he compares a room hosting a bored Killy to "a bingo parlor in Tulsa." The effect is far greater than describing what the room actually looked like, which would be comparatively mundane. When talking about traveling with United Airlines, rather than saying it was an uncomfortable or unpleasant experience, he simply says that it "is like crossing the Andes in a prison bus." Again, he has imparted in the mind of his readers a distinct and unforgettable visual image, bringing them into the story as he had done with his conspiratorial asides in previous articles.

But perhaps the most brilliant description in the article is of the evasive Jean-Claude Killy himself, who Thompson describes as possessing a smile like James Dean mixed with "a teen-age bank clerk with a foolproof embezzlement scheme." Every writer knows that it is hard to describe a man's appearance in a way that will resonate with readers, but in this short sentence Thompson has succeeded mightily not just in conveying his appearance but in hinting at his personality. He has placed an image in the head of his reader that will stick there permanently. It was something F. Scott Fitzgerald achieved, albeit in more words, when he had Nick Carraway describe Jay Gatsby's smile:

> He smiled understandingly—much more than understandingly. It was one of those rare smiles with a quality of eternal reassurance in it, that you may come across four or five times in life. It faced—or seemed to face—the whole eternal world

for an instant, and then concentrated on you with an irresistible prejudice in your favor. It understood you just as far as you wanted to be understood, believed in you as you would like to believe in yourself, and assured you that it had precisely the impression of you that, at your best, you hoped to convey.

In Thompson's mind, he had bypassed conventional journalism to get the real story. Rather than accept memorized answers or repeat what was written in press releases, he had persevered and written a truly unique story that came as close as any to reaching the real Killy. His unconventional approach had paid off and it was clear to him that he could push the idea further.

There are other quirks of Thompson's writing that occur in "The Temptations of Jean-Claude Killy," including the capitalization of significant words (Weird Person, Money Game), a reference to snow leopards, the use of favored words like "waterhead," the phrase "monument to," and even certain patterns that would repeat themselves later, like: "My decision to quit the Killy story came suddenly," which is very similar to "The decision to flee came suddenly," a line from *Fear and Loathing in Las Vegas*. There is even a small amount of swearing, which most of his previous employers would not permit.

Indeed, the writing style that defined Hunter Thompson was more or less in place when he wrote the Killy story, and thankfully Hinckle did not chop his article up trying to suppress Hunter's voice.[11] Thompson's friends said that he had finally learned to write like he spoke, and Hunter seems to have realized this too. Certainly, his writing was now far more like the exciting, aggressive, and humorous tales he typically included in letters to friends.

---

11   He did, however, cut part of the ending, which made Thompson a little upset because he felt it was "high-white prose" that really completed the article. He felt that his actions in that article were unexplainable without the ending, and he begged his editor to let him decide what parts to cut. "Hell, I may be crazy as a fucking loon, but it seems only fair to let me testify." [*Fear and Loathing in America*, p.270]

The result earned a positive reception from the magazine's readers and showed him that he need not try so hard to emulate other writers; instead, his own style had an appeal as great as any of them. This article, in a sense, was a short version of the American Dream book he had planned for two years. It featured him at the center of the plot, writing in his own strange way, while exploring a bigger issue through the problems he faced and the people he met.

After years of struggling with what he considered bad editors, Thompson was now working with one whom he thought was the very best. Although *Scanlan's* only lasted for nine months, it would be a fertile period for Thompson's writing. He was already flush with ideas when, one night, he suddenly hit upon the big one.

Gonzo is Born

Gonzo was an approach to the immediate vagaries of life, not a disciplined program to create a single vision or unified work of art.

Kevin T. McEneaney

It had been Warren Hinckle who approached Thompson and asked for permission to publish "The Temptations of Jean-Claude Killy," but for their next collaboration, the idea was Hunter's. At three-thirty one morning, he called the *Scanlan's* editor and told him he wanted to go home to Louisville and cover the Kentucky Derby. Hinckle agreed and the rest was history.

Hunter Thompson had grown up in Louisville and was proud of his Southern manners, but toward his hometown he felt some degree of antipathy. It was the place where he had been the token poor friend of the rich kids, who had finally turned their backs on him when he had been sent to jail. It was a place of painful memories and personal failure. When he had escaped to the Air Force, it had been an accomplishment and whenever he returned home it had usually been out of desperation or necessity.

Now he wanted to go back and revenge was firmly on his mind. There was nothing new to say about the Derby; it had been exhaustively covered by the mainstream press since its inception. But Thompson had no intention of writing the same thing as thousands of journalists had done over the previous ninety-five years. Following his savage takedown of Richard Nixon, he now viewed his writing as a weapon, an equalizer that bent the powerful to his level. He was going back "to whip the shit out of everything [he] was raised and brought up to hold dear." He would take Kentucky's proudest moment and savage

207

it, evening the score against those that had let him rot in jail during his high school graduation. He could not have cared less about a bunch of horses. "The story, as I see it," he explained to Hinckle, "is mainly in the vicious-drunk Southern bourbon horse-shit mentality that surrounds the Derby than in the Derby itself."

To capture the true horror of his surroundings, he needed an illustrator. Photographers, he felt, were too strait-laced and conservative, and their work tended to capture moments too literally, which did not match well with Thompson's creative and subjective approach to reporting. Illustrators tended to be freaks like him and could see things in a subject that a camera could never bring out. Thompson wanted Pulitzer Prize-winning illustrator, Pat Oliphant, but instead found himself hunting for a Welshman called Ralph Steadman.

Thompson's work had appeared alongside cartoons before. Even at the *Playground News*, in Florida, his writing had been featured alongside an illustrator called Hartley. Later, lacking a photo of a British man whacking golf balls into a favela, his *National Observer* editors had placed a cartoon into the article, while in 1969 his *Pageant* article on test pilots had also been illustrated. But never before had an artist complemented his words and captured his weird vision as well as Ralph Steadman would.

Steadman had been working for *Private Eye* in England during the sixties and in April 1970 flew to the United States in search of work. An editor at *Scanlan's* had read his book, *Still Life with Raspberry*, and asked him if he was interested in covering the Kentucky Derby as a last-minute assignment. He agreed and they rushed him to the airport for a flight to Louisville. *En route*, he realized he had left his pencils and paint brushes behind, so they stopped at an editor's apartment and he borrowed some lipstick and eyebrow pencils. He would have to make do.

When he could not find Thompson at their Louisville hotel, Steadman made his way to the Churchill Downs. He had been told to find a tall, bald Hell's Angel in a hunting jacket, so he wandered around, asking people for "Hunter Johnson." Eventually, Steadman talked his way into the press room and stopped for a drink. Here, the two freaks finally found each other—Thompson with his head newly shaved, clasping a drink and a cigarette holder, and Steadman with mountains of hair and a pointy beard. "I met the strangest man in America," Ralph later said, no doubt echoing Hunter's thoughts.

For several days, the two men drank together and observed the debauchery, all the time recording the scene in their notebooks. Steadman drew fantastic, warped drawings of the people he encountered. None of them were remotely flattering, with hideous faces and skeletal bodies. As the editors of *Scanlan's* had known from his previous work, Steadman had a habit of drawing things in a way that made them seem even more repugnant than they appeared to others. It was one of the qualities that made Thompson's writing so recognizable—he, too, found crises where there were none and portrayed things he disliked with absolute contempt. Yet Steadman's work was even darker than Thompson's and Hunter had to tell him to stop drawing people on several occasions. He explained that he liked the sketches but that they were ugly and would offend people. Indeed, during their week in Louisville, Ralph supposedly made several people cry.

Thompson also remarked that Ralph's drawings were so dark that they made him "see things that I had forgotten about." In fact, throughout the whole Derby week, it was Steadman's perspective that opened the scene up to the writer. "I could tell from his notes that he was looking at things through my eyes," Steadman explained later. He said that, as a foreigner, his naïve questions helped Thompson understand the world he had grown up in. In numerous interviews, he called himself an "innocent abroad," referring to the Twain book that had proven influential on Thompson. Steadman wandered around, sketching what he saw and explaining it aloud while Thompson made notes on a big yellow notepad. He scrawled quickly and filled countless pages with notes that Ralph thought were very similar to how Hunter talked.

When the Derby was over, *Scanlan's* flew both men to New York to finish the job. In two days, Steadman turned his sketches into full works of art for the magazine, but Thompson struggled badly. "I arrived in NY in a state of crazed angst," he explained to his editor, "far gone in pill stupor and barely able to think, much less write." It could have been the drink and drugs he had consumed during that frenetic week or maybe it was the news from Kent State University, where the National Guard had shot dead four students on May 4, but something distracted him and made it impossible for him to write.[1]

For six days, he was locked in a hotel room with whiskey and room service, attempting to compose a story on his typewriter, taking amphetamines to keep himself awake and as focused as possible. But he couldn't write. According to his wife, Sandy, it was the first time that this had happened to him. The man who had stayed up late writing about anything and everything had suddenly been struck by the complete inability to commit words to paper. Copyboys and even editors showed up and all left without the pages needed to fill the big blank space in the next issue. He moved from his desk to the bathtub and sat there drinking whiskey straight from the bottle, certain that he had finally ruined his career.

Eventually, no matter how much he told the editors that the story was gibberish, they demanded that he send it. In a panic, he tore pages out of his notebook and sent them away in lieu of real writing. This, he thought, might buy him a little time to get the story onto paper. But still it didn't come. When the copyboy returned, much to Thompson's surprise, he asked for more pages. The notes had somehow been enough. He tore more pages from his notebook, added handwritten inserts, and sent them away, too.[2]

Hinckle called from San Francisco. Instead of screaming at Thompson, he said he loved what was being sent in. *Keep it coming.*

***

---

1   The Kent State shootings were alluded to at the beginning of his article and explicitly mentioned at the end. As Thompson and Steadman drive to the airport, the news is broken over the radio. However, this line was cut from the magazine version of the article along with much political commentary.
2   As Steadman had observed, his notes tended to be quite developed, presented in his unusual patterns of speech rather than more basic, conventional note forms.

"The Kentucky Derby is Decadent and Depraved" can be viewed as the culmination of Thompson's literary innovations until this point. Everything that he had learned as a journalist had been the product of his training and experiences but fed through the bizarre computer of his mind, which spat out a form of writing so weird that there would be a new word coined just to describe it. It was a style of writing based upon his past efforts but, through the desperate act he was pushed to in that New York hotel room, it had been coalesced by the chance addition of his notes into something even more original: *Gonzo*.

It is obvious from the very first word that this article would be a story about Hunter Thompson rather than the Derby. As so many of his later stories would do, it begins with him and travel: "I got off the plane around midnight…" From there, he stops at an airport lounge and meets a man called Jimbo. It is soon clear that Jimbo is not a real person but a device that allows Thompson to introduce himself (clutching a cigarette holder, of course) and to set the scene. Jimbo is obviously a caricature of the loud, brash whiskey gentry he sought to lampoon. Even though he is a Texan, rather than a Kentuckian, he is nonetheless a regular Derby attendee and in Thompson—a local boy—he sees someone he can trust.

Big mistake. Repeating the ruse that he had played upon the gullible boys in his Killy story, the reporter tells Jimbo a lie—that he is attending the Derby to cover a violent riot that is sure to break out. Jimbo, of course, falls for it hook, line, and sinker. Thompson proceeds to comically wind the man up, informing him that this will be the result of boiling racial tensions in America. Jimbo is heartbroken that his beloved Derby would be sullied in this way. "Don't they respect *anything*?" he asks. It is a classic Thompson introduction—funny and gripping. The reader, wondering where the hell a story like this could possibly go, is compelled to continue.

Thompson then announces that he has to go to the race and "get [his] act together for the awful spectacle." By pranking the locals and admitting that this event will be "awful," he has again thrown off the shackles of objectivity. Indeed, that was very much the aim of his story. As Steadman observed years later: "He was back to settle a score [with] the people that he really despised in Louisville—the establishment that had rejected him many years ago." William Kennedy, meanwhile, explained:

> I think that that was a moment where he used all his fictional talent to describe and anatomize those characters and just make it all up. I'm sure some of it was real.

It was the perfect assignment for fusing fact and fiction. Thompson already knew this place and these people, so whatever fiction he heaped upon the scenario would be grounded in his interpretation of reality. Hemingway had once explained that "If a man is making a story up it will be true in proportion to the amount of knowledge of life that he has and how conscientious he is; so that if he makes something up it is as it truly would be," which is very similar to something Thompson said, years later: "If I'm going to go into the fantastic, I have to have a firm grounding in the truth." When he tells Steadman that you can recognize a genuine Kentucky Colonel by the whiskey and vomit stains on his shoes, it is an exaggeration of the truth—a piece of comedy that contains within it some real wisdom.

The story, from there, is again largely about *getting the story*, and in a Gonzo tale this is seldom a straightforward procedure. Thompson's literary journalism was a response to the chaos of the world that Hemingway could not cope with, and which had only been tackled by the abstract expressionist action painting of Jackson Pollack or the passionate, desperate anaphora of Allen Ginsberg. Like Jack Kerouac's spontaneous prose—a lyrical jazz composition sketched in the moment—Thompson's Gonzo writing would involve improvisation upon chaos. Grounded in the first-person perspective, guided by a stream-of-consciousness narrative transcribed straight from the participant-narrator's head, the reader is set down right amidst the carnage of Derby day.

It was his innovation with the Killy article that told him this could work. The reader is taken through the hassles of everything a journalist must battle in order to report a story, starting with renting a car during Derby week. Again, Thompson's narrator tells a lie and this time dupes a boy at the Hertz rental office into thinking he works for *Playboy*. He explains that flashing a *Playboy* press tag can be an incredible tool for a reporter. The reader is drawn further into what is essentially a non-story thanks to Thompson's conspiratorial tone.

The article continues with comic misadventure as Thompson struggles to find Steadman. When they meet, they begin looking for an angle to cover the race. Hunter tells Ralph that they are looking for something specific:

> He had done a few good sketches, but so far we hadn't seen that special kind of face that I felt we would need for the lead drawing. It was a face I'd seen a thousand times at every Derby I'd ever been to. I saw it, in my head, as the mask of the whiskey gentry – a pretentious mix of booze, failed dreams and a terminal identity crisis; the inevitable result of too much inbreeding in a closed and ignorant culture.

The quest for "that special kind of face" guides the story. They explore the Churchill Downs and witness drunken idiocy, whilst partaking to no small measure. Thompson frequently uses foreshadowing, building a sense of paranoia by alluding to violence coming later. There are flurries of madness as he imagines macing people and offers random, explosive outbursts like "Fuck England" and "Creeping Jesus." He also makes sure to mention those words that now marked most of his writing: "atavistic," "swinish," "doomed," and the phrase "fear and loathing," which had become increasingly common in his letters by this point.

Of course, there also the mandatory flights of fancy that creep into each of his articles now. In this single article, there are five instances of Thompson simply wandering off into imagined scenes, including this one:

> Thousands of raving, stumbling drunks, getting angrier and angrier as they lose more and more money. By midafternoon

they'll be guzzling mint juleps with both hands and vomiting on each other between races. The whole place will be jammed with bodies, shoulder to shoulder. It's hard to move around. The aisles will be slick with vomit; people falling down and grabbing at your legs to keep from being stomped. Drunks pissing on themselves in the betting lines. Dropping handfuls of money and fighting to stoop over and pick it up.

Although he is not reporting something that has happened, he—as an insider—is speculating on what *could* or probably *will* happen. It starts subtly and the reader is drawn into the fantasy and left slightly disoriented, eventually realizing that it is satire rather than a faithful account of real events. He carefully uses verb tenses to switch between present and imagined future, employing the present participle, sometimes without a subject, like Donleavy had done in *The Ginger Man*, to merge the real and the imagined. We can assume the first sentence is intended as a bridge between what is happening and what could happen, with the use of the future continuous and then future simple tenses following as the author includes more fantasy. This switches to subject and present participle and then by the final line the subject is gone. This is intended to convey a sense of disorientation, mimicking the inebriation of the crowd. When Thompson does this, he is artfully challenging the reader. It functions as comedy but also highlights in an effective way the propensity for sloppy drunkenness within these people.

The first half of the story, while soaked in mace and madness, was told in a relatively straightforward fashion. It had Thompson's now-inimitable footprint all over it, and some of the abovementioned playful use of language, but it was still told with more or less complete sentences and paragraphs. This all changes at the point where he had gotten such severe writer's block that he sent in pages from his notebook. In the article, he explains:

> But now, looking at the big red notebook
> I carried all through the scene, I see more

or less what happened. The book itself is somewhat mangled and bent; some of the pages are torn, others are shriveled and stained by what appears to be whiskey, but taken as a whole, with sporadic memory flashes, the notes seem to tell the story.

From that point on, Thompson's notes *are* the story. This was a completely new and accidental addition to his repertoire. Like William Burroughs and Brion Gysin discovering the Cut-up Method, Thompson stumbled into Gonzo purely by accident, but took to it with enthusiasm. They begin:

> Rain all nite until dawn. No sleep. Christ, here we go, a nightmare of mud and madness. . . but no. By noon the sun burns through – perfect day, not even humid.
> Steadman is now worried about fire. Somebody told him about the clubhouse catching on fire two years ago. Could it happen again? Horrible. Trapped in the press box. Holocaust. A hundred thousand people fighting to get out.

His notes were detailed, coherent, and oddly descriptive. They carry important ideas that he would have later developed in most circumstances. However, even without the grammar that would have been placed upon these fragmentary word sketches, they convey everything Thompson wanted the reader to know—and without the philosophical rambling he felt marred his other work. It was like Hemingway had said: "After you learn to write your whole object is to convey everything, every sensation, sight, feeling, place, and emotion to the reader." That is what these notes were—immediate observations and interpretations of his surroundings. Statements like "pink faces with a stylish Southern sag, old Ivy styles, seersucker coat and buttondown collars" tell the reader what he sees and present an image of Southern aristocracy. Far from being simple reporter's notes, these included literary techniques such as alliteration. Elsewhere, of course, it is more hideous: "banshees on the lawn at night, screaming out there beside that little iron nigger in jockey clothes." Sometimes it carries important ideas necessary to move the narrative, such as this: "The rest of that day blurs into madness. The rest of that night too. And all the next day and night."

Through all of the second half of the article, his notes create a startling sense of immediacy. They make it far more real, conveying the frantic nature of their search for a particular face and replicating the confusion felt by the protagonist and his sidekick. It is a wonder that this method of composing a story was so strange to Thompson. As a teenager, he had realized he could record his thoughts on a tape recorder and had been impressed by his own creations. In his research for *Hell's Angels* and other projects, he had also worked from a tape recorder and made copious notes, which had been used to provide the material for his work. When he had lent his tapes to Tom Wolfe, he discussed the value of such material and told his friend, "I think the instant/verbal notes were better and more real than either one of our interpretations." What's more, a year earlier, he had pondered "the writer's eye as a camera lens"—which sounds very much like John Dos Passos' "Camera Eye" sections in his *USA* trilogy, or even Jack Kerouac's "spontaneous prose." Evidently, the idea of written or recorded notes containing such descriptive or creative value had been in his head for at least a few years.

Although it was ostensibly an article on a horse race, the details of the race are conspicuously absent. He explains: "Total chaos, no way to see the race, not even the track. . . nobody cares." But of course, as Thompson knew even before going to Louisville, the race was never going to be the focus of the article. His grains of sand were faces in the crowd, through which he could see the whole of the race, not to mention the society that had created a spectacle such as the Kentucky Derby.

Near the end of the article, Thompson switches back to a comparatively normal style of writing and then finishes off with a dramatic turn. They finally find the one face that they have been looking for throughout the whole event— the perfect image to capture the decadence and depravity of the Derby:

> There he was, by God – a puffy, drink-ravaged, disease-ridden caricature... like an awful cartoon version of an old snapshot in some once-proud mother's fancy photo album. It was the face we'd been looking for – and it was, of course, my own.

In his article, Thompson has utilized every weapon in his literary arsenal and even added a few extras. He had found in his Richard Nixon profile piece that a sidekick figure offered various possibilities for presenting information or just having a little fun. He could introduce himself to the reader, thereby setting himself as the protagonist, but it also allowed him to present witty or informative dialogue, which made an article much more readable than just presenting the writer's internal monologue, broken up with a few facts. In Steadman, he had found the perfect sidekick—someone who was opposite to him in many ways and who could be presented as a naïve foreigner witnessing this peculiarly American institution.

Of course, sometimes he had just made up dialogue in order to further his own views of a story or to introduce an idea that had not organically arisen. He had also combined numerous voices (whether real or imagined) in some of his previous work, and he used these techniques here as well. Jimbo, for example, serves the purpose of allowing Thompson to be shocking and weird, but mostly to reflect on a group of people—in this case, rich Derby folk. He and the faceless people around him say and do what Thompson wants the reader to believe of everyone at the Derby. In the opening paragraph, he writes:

> Inside, people hugged each other and shook hands ... big grins and a whoop here and there: "By God! You old bastard! Good to see you, boy! Damn good ... and I mean it!"

There is no one person to whom this quote is attributed because it is once again the voice of the collective. It is what someone at the Derby is *likely* to say.

Indeed, most of the characters in his Kentucky

Derby article are a blend of faces rather than individuals. Thompson often picks out voices from the crowd and presents them as representative of Louisville's whiskey gentry: "Goddam, did you hear about Smitty's daughter? She went crazy in Boston last week and married a nigger!" Despite his own troubling use of racial epithets and perhaps a few racist characters in his stories, Thompson was a supporter of civil rights and opposed to what he perceived as real racism. When Thompson tells Jimbo that there will be a race war at the beginning of the piece, the implication is that Jimbo—the representative Derby attendee—is at least partly racist and likely to be deeply offended by the idea of black militants storming the Derby—an icon of white, southern pride. It is clear from the get-go that this attack on the Louisville Establishment is an attack on racism.[3]

Had readers wondered about the extent to which fiction pervaded the ostensibly true story of two men covering the Kentucky Derby, they would hopefully have realized by the end that it had been infused with more than a little fantasy. Although the Jimbo story should have been a major clue, the final lines tell us that Thompson was more interested in a wild story and cultivating his insane persona than actually recording reality:

> The journalist rams the big car through traffic and into a spot in front of the terminal, then he reaches over to open the door on the passenger's side and shoves the Englishman out, snarling: "Bug off, you worthless faggot! You twisted pigfucker! [Crazed laughter.] If I weren't sick I'd kick your ass all the way to Bowling Green – you scumsucking foreign geek. Mace is too good for you. . . We can do without your kind in Kentucky."

It is too manic, too ridiculous to be real, and of course it wasn't. In addition to the flurry of hard-to-believe action

---

3   In an earlier article about race in Louisville, he had strongly suggested that racism was a trait held more by the wealthy than the poor.

and over-the-top screaming, there are also some factual inaccuracies here. Thompson states early in his article that Steadman had just flown in from London and here at the end it appears he is heading back to England, but in fact he had been staying in New York.[4] Still, it was important for Thompson to present him as an outsider in order to get just the right perspective on the Derby—and for Thompson to use himself as a mode of conveying insider information. There is also his reference to "the journalist." This is something Hemingway used but the switch in perspective from first to third is something Donleavy did constantly throughout *The Ginger Man*. Perhaps this was a subtle reference to two of his great influences.

Throughout the article, Thompson goes to lengths to present himself as not just an anonymous journalist covering a sporting event, but a freak and a prankster who should be viewed as a character in a story as much as the writer. From pranking Jimbo to pushing Steadman out of a moving car and screaming "twisted pigfucker" at him, Thompson is at his lunatic best in this article. His actions, like Sebastian Dangerfield's, are often abhorrent, but he constantly seems proud of them. He frequently refers to mace and after a particularly blurry period of drunkenness, Ralph tells him that he maced a waiter.[5]

What significance, if any, did this have in "The Kentucky Derby is Decadent and Depraved" or any of his other work? In a sense, Thompson plays the role of jester, offering his audience clever satire from the safety of his idiot's disguise. He has become what he hated in order to criticize it better. He visited the Derby and was swept up in the depravity, and that has allowed him to present an altogether more accurate and insulting depiction. Beyond that, his rampant bad behavior added to the depravity of his surroundings, ultimately creating a story that was as chaotic as the actual event.

---

4 Ralph Steadman is Welsh but Thompson referred to him here and in most other places as English.

5 Steadman confirmed that Thompson really did mace an entire restaurant full of people. [*Gonzo*, p.120] Thompson also claimed in an interview to have sprayed mace into the governor's box, but it is not known whether that is true. [*Ancient Gonzo Wisdom*, p.90]

After the last of his notes were sent away with the copyboy and Thompson flew home to Woody Creek, he felt ashamed of his perceived failure. He had cut some corners in the past and definitely played loose with the rules of journalism, but he had never before resorted to submitting his barely edited notes. He wasn't sure why *Scanlan's* had accepted them, but he felt it was a catastrophic disaster and that he was finished as a writer. He told Bill Cardoso, "It's a shitty article, a classic of irresponsible journalism." He hadn't even made copies of his notes, so he couldn't look back to see what had gone into the story he had given them.

He wrote to Hinckle to explain his disappointment in himself and the perceived failure of this article. "I wish there'd been time to do it better," he wrote. "With another week I might have honed it down to a finer, meatier edge." With another editor, Donald Goddard, Thompson worked to remove an extraneous four thousand words from the first half of the article, but ultimately the effort of cutting it to a "finer, meatier edge" fell to Hinckle, who sat in a booth at Tosca's in San Francisco and rearranged the article until it ran together smoothly. He explained: "Editing Hunter was like picking up the pieces of a jigsaw puzzle that had been dropped on the floor and trying to put them back together to make sense without having the benefit of the picture on the cover of the puzzle box." It was a familiar refrain. Most editors who spoke publicly about working with Hunter Thompson complained that the biggest challenge (aside from just getting him to write) was piecing together the disjointed fragments that he submitted.

Editing Hunter Thompson had always posed challenges, but as his work became more experimental, the work left to editors became more difficult. He was also beginning to lose his focus and, while he was getting better at certain elements of his writing, he was also beginning to struggle with others. His wife, Sandy, explained:

> When he wrote the Kentucky Derby article for *Scanlan's,* the drugs and the booze and all that stuff was getting involved in his life. This was no longer the Hunter who would sit down and rewrite a piece three

times. He could get out a page, maybe, or a paragraph, a really neat, wild paragraph—and then some gibberish. He couldn't come out with a full piece.

Nonetheless, when it appeared in the fourth issue of *Scanlan's* in June, "The Kentucky Derby is Decadent and Depraved" was considered a triumph. Readers loved it and the completely new style of writing, which worked in combination with Steadman's grotesquely insulting images of Derby spectators, earned *Scanlan's* and its star writer a great deal of attention.

It was also the first of Thompson's works to be called "Gonzo." There is some confusion over the origins of the term, like so many stories about Hunter Thompson. Various books and essays claim that it means "courage" or "the last man standing" in various languages and dialects, but in fact the truth may be rather mundane. Douglas Brinkley explained what he believed to be the true origins of the word in *Gonzo: The Life of Hunter S. Thompson*:

> The legendary New Orleans R&B piano player James Booker recorded an instrumental song called "Gonzo" in 1960. The term "gonzo" was Cajun slang that had floated around the French Quarter jazz scene for decades and meant, roughly, "to play unhinged." [...] From 1960 to 1969 [...] "Gonzo" was Hunter's favorite song.
>
> When Nixon ran for president in 1968, Hunter had an assignment to cover him for Pageant and found himself holed up in a New Hampshire motel with a columnist [...] named Bill Cardoso. Hunter had brought a cassette of Booker's music and played "Gonzo" over, and over, and over—it drove Cardoso crazy, and that night, Cardoso jokingly derided Hunter as "the 'Gonzo' man." Later, when Hunter sent Cardoso his Kentucky Derby piece, he got a note back saying something like, "Hunter, that was pure Gonzo journalism!"

It is unclear whether or not this claim is accurate. Certainly, it is surprising that Thompson never once mentioned this song in writing, despite it allegedly being his favorite during his most prolific period. He did not even include Booker's name in a list of his favorite albums of the 1960s, which makes Brinkley's claim dubious. Cardoso, who passed away in 2006, gave no definitive answers, offering only joke explanations or avoiding the question entirely when asked. The term was popular in his home state of Massachusetts during his teenage years and signified something cool, so perhaps it is as simple as him resurrecting it two decades later.

Whatever the reason for Cardoso's choice of word, that totally new style of writing Thompson had unleashed on the world—the fusion of fact and fiction, totally subjective, dripping with vitriol, peppered with violence and wisdom and obscene or obscure words, with its manic narrator at the center of a quest for any sort of story— had a name. This was not just journalism; it was not even typical satire. There was no one doing anything like it, and thus a one-man literary genre was born.

Thompson's feelings toward the article shifted until the consensus came in. He was embarrassed at first but then later realized that there may be some quality to it. At one time, he thought it could be a good article and maybe even the sort of thing someone could turn into a movie. For a while, he worried that "the writing is lame bullshit" but then the article was released and he changed his mind. It was a breakthrough. He was now a Gonzo journalist.

Though he was not yet a household name, Thompson was now becoming famous in the world of journalism. He recognized quickly that Gonzo was going to be his signature style and he moved to mark out his territory. At the *Middletown Daily Record*, he had been told that, if he wanted to be an iconoclast, he would need more talent. Ten years later, he was on the cusp of being the country's most iconoclastic journalist. He knew how to market himself, even going as far as to describe his clothes in many of his articles, often when there had been no real reason to do so. He had been fiercely individualistic since childhood and now he had his own literary turf. Besides, he had been trying for years to crack the traditional journalism markets and it had always meant sacrificing his personal style or views to please their editors. After the Kentucky Derby, he asked: "Holy shit, if I can write like this and get away with it, why should I keep trying to write like *The New York Times*?"

He decided that Gonzo needed to be pushed further. Despite his massive ego, he recognized in this case that Steadman's drawings were a huge part of his success and he began to plan future Gonzo adventures. Since they had launched a vicious attack on the Kentucky Derby, Thompson wanted to continue to "rape" "sacred American institutions" in a collaborative book project called *Amerikan Dreams* or a regular feature in *Scanlan's* called "The Thompson-Steadman Report." Hinckle gave the go-ahead for this promising venture. He had recognized the potential of Gonzo even before Hunter.

Thompson wrote to Steadman to convince him that they should continue to work together and gave an example of the sort of prose that would come out of a trip to Mardis Gras:

> As we buckled down for the approach to New Orleans I snorted the last of our cocaine. Steadman, far gone on acid, had locked himself in the men's room somewhere over St. Louis & the head stewardess was frantic. I knew I would need psychic strength & energy when we landed—to meet the press limousine & get on with our heinous work. ...

They finally settled upon the America's Cup yacht race, where they embarked upon predictably chaotic Gonzo adventures, but unfortunately *Scanlan's* folded before either of them had time to finish their version of events. They caused mayhem as they sought to get among the challengers to find an angle for the story. This resulted in them attempting to write "FUCK THE POPE" on the side of an expensive boat and turning vast expanses of water bright orange before they fled the scene. The two men ate psilocybin and for Ralph this was the first and last experiment with hallucinogens. It made him sick for days. In search of comic misadventure, Thompson shot flares into the sky, then explained to Steadman that their failure was "a better story" than if they had succeeded in covering the race. Indeed, the shocking behavior, resulting in a flight from justice, created the sort of paranoid scene that Thompson specialized in describing. Steadman later speculated that the failed America's Cup story was "the genesis of 'Fear and Loathing in Las Vegas.'"

Unfortunately, although their adventures would have been a good follow-up to the Derby piece, in the end nothing was written and Ralph's illustrations only appeared years later in one of his collections. Thompson was left in debt by the magazine's collapse as he had run up more than five thousand dollars' worth of expenses, partly because they chartered a flight to avoid arrest. His attempts to recover this money were unsuccessful as he had not written anything, making his claim legally invalid. Part of the problem was that he had included all of his daily expenses (and those of his associates) for three separate articles over a period of three months, only one of which was ever published—not even in *Scanlan's*; that ended up in *Rolling Stone*. The people at *Scanlan's* thought Thompson's claims were too excessive to justify anything more than a good-will payment of five hundred dollars, and so he was left with vast, unpayable debts on his credit cards, which he believed would make it nearly impossible to function as a freelance journalist.

Before *Scanlan's* folded, Thompson wrote one more article for them. In the September 1970 issue, he contributed a review of a magazine for police chiefs. This was not credited to Hunter S. Thompson, however. It was allegedly written by Raoul Duke, who in this instance is described as a veteran law enforcement officer now serving as a weapons consultant.

"Police Chief – The Indispensable Magazine of Law Enforcement" is an hilarious review that features plenty of strange and violent digressions, as well as Thompson's usual aggressive language, like "scumsucker" and "dope addict." It begins with Duke saying that he does not want to write a review, but that he will because he is a patriot. He cites obviously fake sources, one of whom testifies to the power of a weapon:

> Last week I had to chase a nigger downtown, and when he got so far away that he couldn't even hear my warning yell, I just pulled down on the bastard with this .44 Magnum and blew the head clean off his body with one shot. All we found were some teeth and one eyeball. The rest was all mush and bone splinters.

Duke complains that the weapons advertised in this magazine are not nearly powerful enough and recounts a number of violent stories about better weapons like the "Nutcracker Flail," which could grab a man by the testicles and squeeze until he surrendered. In the article, we can see Thompson's imagination let loose to an even greater extent, which was one of the purposes for which he used this persona.[6]

The name Raoul Duke had first appeared in the writings of Hunter S. Thompson in a list near the end of *Hell's Angels*, written in 1966 and published in 1967. Later, it was used as a source in an article, as a name on a letter, and as a character in a story about the 1968 Democratic Convention. He had considered inserting Duke into *The Gun Lobby* to meet the president of the NRA and, in August 1969, as part of his Death of the American Dream book, he had written about his 1960 cross-country journey with Paul Semonin, but in that version it was Thompson and Duke riding across America. In his story, the two men drive from the Bronx to Seattle and then hitchhike down to San Francisco, becoming politicized along the way.

By 1970, then, Raoul Duke had been in Thompson's mind for at least four years, slowing developing. He frequently changed his mind over how Duke should be used, but now it was clear that Duke was at least partly his alter ego. In February of that year, he wrote to his editor at Random House to say that Duke was his "foil"

---

6   The other was a legitimate fear that the violence in the article (and in subsequent ones that he planned but never had time to write) would earn his name a place on the FBI's watchlist.

and that he was "slipping more and more into the role of" this character. When his editor expressed encouragement, Thompson went on to explain more about his reasons for creating Duke:

> You have focused on my root problem in the new book—combining controlled (and formal) journalism with the jangled reality of my day to day thing. That was my original reason for bringing in Raoul Duke—to let me sit back and play reasonable, while he freaks out. Or maybe those roles should be reversed …?

He goes on to express some uncertainty about how his alter ego would actually work as journalism or literature. Clearly, it offered him a new avenue in his hybridization of fact and fiction, allowing him to take real events and issues and explore them in new ways with Duke. He wrote that using this persona gave him "far more leeway to improvise on reality, without distorting it, than I'd have without Duke."

Thompson clarifies this by giving an example. When he was on Nixon's press bus, he witnessed a journalist smoking a joint but he could not use this in his article because the journalist would lose his job. However, using Raoul Duke, he could have assigned the blame to a fictional person. The reader would know that pot-smoking occurred on the bus, but no one would have their career ended.

He even wondered if Duke was a device that could be used in rewriting his old novels. He still wanted to be a novelist, which he considered to be the great vocation. In the late sixties, he was eager to dig up and fix *The Rum Diary* so that he could make his mark in terms of fiction, but as the years went by it became harder and harder to sit down and attempt the necessary rewrites required to make it publishable. In September 1968, he explained:

> I've about decided that it would be dishonest to re-write the book in any serious way; it seems like it would be the same as giving it to a ghost-writer – an

older and balder HST. So I'm thinking very seriously of doing a surface, mechanical re-write job, mainly cutting and clarifying, rather than re-thinking.

He could barely relate to the experiences of the young man in that book, living just ten years earlier. It was a different era. A different world. The late sixties were an altogether darker time, and Paul Kemp was not the man to explore this fast-paced age. It was becoming clear that Raoul Duke was needed.

In 1968, he had considered taking his experiences throughout the sixties and fictionalizing them, then using the year's heinous events to show the death of an era. He called these "quasi-biographical notes, courtesy of Raoul Duke." By 1970, the idea had evolved a little but Thompson was struggling to make Duke believable. He explained to Silberman:

> I haven't been able, so far, to make Duke
> a human being; he hasn't come to life—
> not even for me. So the narrative still looks
> like a phoney gimmick to string a bunch of
> articles together.

That was another problem with Gonzo journalism. Once you inserted fictional elements into the prose, how would they interact with the real world? Thompson's depictions of himself and others often seemed exaggerated, so how would he pass off a completely fictional character placed into a real scene? Still, he was positive about its potential and explained one possibility for the American Dream book:

> There's the Raoul Duke approach, which is
> essentially a very contemporary novel with
> straight, factual journalism as a background.
> I don't know any precedents to cite for this
> one … which is probably why I like it best.

Ever since his creation of Duke, Thompson had pondered using him to bridge the gap between fiction and non-fiction—those supposedly artificial terms. By the beginning of the seventies, Duke was ready to make his mark on the world and Thompson was ready to unleash him. But how? In letters to his editors, he considered the merits of taking a fictional character and placing him into a very real scene, replacing Thompson himself as the real journalist.

At the Kentucky Derby, Thompson realized the value of having "a straight man" in Ralph Steadman. He said that Steadman was "someone to bounce reactions off of" but soon he realized that this limited him. You could only act so wild as the journalist in a story and dodge the consequences. Thompson realized that Duke's function could be the opposite of Steadman's: "Sometimes I'd bring Duke in because I wanted to use myself for the other character."

Although he had been playing with the character of Raoul Duke for some time, his role was still not entirely clear to anyone, Thompson included. However, the confusion was about to become even greater, as Thompson and Duke began to blend into one.

Freak Power and Brown Power

Unfortunately, I proved what I set out to prove… that the American Dream really is fucked.
Hunter S. Thompson

Aspen in the late 1960s was still a quiet, peaceful place where a man and his family could retreat from the fast-moving world, but change was very much in the air. The outside world seemed determined to catch up and bring this mountain town into the stressful, frenetic modern era. Many in the community were determined to stop this from happening, but others were more than willing to take the huge sums of money on offer from developers and sell their little piece of paradise. As such, it became a place where public debate was valued and where tensions were often high between competing ideologies.

It was an odd town with a mix of very progressive and very conservative inhabitants, and in the letters pages of two Aspen newspapers, the liberal *Times* and the conservative *Illustrated News*, one could easily find colorful, passionate screeds on local issues. In March 1968, a letter that began "Herr Editor" and was signed by "Hunter S. Thompson (for Martin Bormann)" was sent to both newspapers. It heaped praise upon the Aspen Sheriff's Department for possessing the same sort of values as the Third Reich. The letter was, of course, amusing satire by a man who had been using "Martin Bormann" as a pseudonym for many years.[1]

This was neither Thompson's first nor last letter to the editor, but it is wonderfully representative of his style

---

1   Bormann was Hitler's personal secretary and some believed that he had escaped to Argentina after the Nazis were defeated.

of writing and his intentions at the time. He cared deeply about the valley he called home and he was unhappy with the local government and land developers. In the late sixties, he sent various letters to these newspapers in order to draw attention to issues that he found important, often using comedy to highlight the absurdity of arguments put forth by his opponents. Sometimes he would write under his own name and sometimes he would pretend to be Martin Bormann, but regardless, his letters were always fiercely intelligent and often quite brutal. He took the same approach to these letters as he had done to some of his best writing, applying techniques like hyperbole, satire, and sarcasm.

These were not just quick notes fired off in the dead of night, either. His friend and neighbor, Jay Cowan, greatly admired those letters and so Thompson gifted him the original version of one. Cowan was amazed by how much editing Thompson had done in order to find just the right words. He also felt that Thompson's letters were a sort of self-introduction to the community. As a moderately well-known writer, he wanted to become a figure of local importance and so he made sure that his wit and eccentricities were on display in the one place to which the whole town paid attention.

But this was not simply an ego trip. In Woody Creek, Thompson had found a place to call home and he felt as though it was under threat. Writing, which was not just a way of earning a living, but a weapon, could perhaps be used to tackle injustice and effect real change. His experiences writing about national politics had been enlightening, but there was not a great deal he could do to change the course of presidential elections. Instead, it was time to turn toward local action, and here politics and literature would begin to fuse.

In 1967, the year Thompson had moved to Woody Creek, a prominent restauranteur and police magistrate, Guido Meyer, was embarking upon a campaign to rid his town of the hippie scourge. A local lawyer, Joe Edwards, took up the hippies' cause and brought the case to court, where Meyer, always an outspoken figure, confessed his prejudices with an hysterical outburst, bellowing "Those dirty hippies! They're all over the place, and they're filthy, and they haven't washed, and they smoke dope!" The judge came down on the side of the hippies but Meyer kept up his campaign of intolerance.

Two years later, well into the wee hours of the morning, Edwards was awoken by a phone call from the still-nocturnal journalist, who proceeded to give a mumbling speech that explained why he should run for mayor of Aspen with Thompson as his campaign manager. The pair had never met, but Edwards agreed. Three weeks later, he ended up losing to the Republican candidate, Eve Homeyer, by just six votes. This was a tremendous lesson for Thompson, who realized that he had made a serious impact upon the local political landscape. If the absentee ballot papers had been sent out on time, they would have won.

The campaign energized Thompson and also gave him hope that his long-awaited Death of the American Dream book had finally found its "grain of sand." In September 1969, he wrote an article for the *Aspen Illustrated News* that he forwarded to Jim Silberman with the explanation: "For the first time in nearly two years, I see a gimmick for tying all my wasted bullshit together in a book—titled 'Joe Edwards for Mayor.'" By this time, the book was envisaged as a collection of failed and successful articles from the past four or five years, including his NRA story, the Jean-Claude Killy piece, and the oil shale article that he had worked on for the *LA Times*, and he believed that Joe Edwards was the lens through which he could look at a bigger picture. It was "that tight-focused chunk of absolute reality that even the craziest, weirdest kind of journalism needs to hold it together."

Thompson, Edwards, and a local artist called Tom Benton had attempted to galvanize the youth of Aspen with a campaign called "Freak Power." Born of the hippie movement that had swept the nation just a few years earlier, this extended "Flower Power" into an altogether more coherent and aggressive political movement.[2]

2 Thompson is on record as disliking hippies, but he certainly felt an affinity with some of their values as well as their taste in music and drugs. The *LA Times* referred to him as a "hippie cultist" after he conceded the election in November. It was an opinion shared by much of the press.

Thompson aimed to use it at the local level first and then possibly take it national. While Benton produced art for the campaign posters, Thompson outlined his ideas in the aforementioned *Illustrated News* article. In it, he is eloquent but argumentative. His tone is serious and the prose packed with facts and evidence, yet he manages to throw in some typical Gonzo phrases: "a hellbroth of graceless thieves"; "rapacious greedheads."

One of Thompson's promises during the Edwards campaign had been that, if they lost, he would run for sheriff the following year. In 1970, he made good on his promise and entered the race for sheriff of Pitkin County, soon after adopting a two-thumbed fist clutching a peyote button as his campaign symbol. After the campaign, the symbol, designed by Benton, became the official Gonzo logo and would adorn most of his books.

Together, Tom Benton and Hunter Thompson founded the Meat Possum Press and ordered doctorates of divinity from the Church of the New Truth, which advertised on the back page of the *Los Angeles Free Press*. For ten dollars, they each became doctors. Thompson later claimed to have a doctorate of chemotherapy from Berkeley and a doctorate of journalism from Columbia, but of course this was a joke that he played on interviewers. The divinity doctorate, however, despite being purchased, grew to become more than just a joke. For the rest of his life, Thompson was known as "the Doctor," "the good Doctor," or just "Doc" by his friends and fans and he often referred to himself as Dr. Hunter S. Thompson. In fact, Thompson had referred to himself as "your friendly doctor" when writing for his column at Eglin and even before that, in high school, he had been known as Dr. Hunto, so this was not much of a change for him. Still, he loved it, telling Benton, "This is great, because you get cut rates on hotels. And you know, it always sounds good in an airport when you hear 'Paging Dr. Thompson.'"

One day, as the two men plotted the rise of Freak Power, Thompson suggested publishing something through the Meat Possum Press that they had founded. "We should do an Aspen wallposter," he said.

"What the hell is that?" Benton asked.

Thompson explained: "It's gonna be a single-sheet

thing, and it'll have your graphics on one side and my writing on the other."

The concept has been described as revolutionary, but in fact Thompson had gotten the idea from Warren Hinckle, who printed wallposters to hand out at the 1968 Democratic Convention while editor of *Ramparts*. As Hunter had explained, there would be a poster on one side with Benton's graphics capturing people's attention and on the other side Thompson would write about whatever took his interest. This would vary from wallposter to wallposter. In the first edition, he attacked corrupt attorney, Robert Delany, who subsequently resigned. For the second, he wrote more broadly about the Death of the American Dream, as well as an obituary for Terry the Tramp—one of the Hell's Angels whom Thompson had considered a friend. The third wallposter was about what Thompson called "land rape" and featured a story about the dynamiting of a windmill, while the fourth included a photograph of a naked woman and a discussion of obscenity, juxtaposing the innocence of nudity with the horrors of the My Lai massacre. Over time, they grew in size and complexity, eventually featuring adverts.

They were, however, a hit from the moment they first went on sale. *Aspen Wallposter #1*, published in March 1970, was an immediate success. Thompson and Benton, who had both stayed up all night working on their collaborative endeavor, produced a thousand copies and they quickly sold out. As with his regular journalism, Thompson believed that he should put his biases out in the open. True objectivity may be impossible, he thought, but it was still possible to be fair and reasonable. He told his readers that they would consider "any relevant, coherent and even outrageous counterpoint to our own clearly biased opinions" even if they came from a "Nazi greedhead with the money to hire a good ghostwriter."

This new form of writing brought out the best of Thompson. He was now his own editor and publisher and he could say pretty much anything he wanted, freeing him to push his experimental style further. He excitedly told a friend that it "may or may not be the leading edge for a whole new kind of journalism." He viewed it as half journalism and half political education, and it made

Hunter, in his own words, "the voice of Aspen's counter-culture."

The first edition was rather like his reporting at this point, blending historical and factual details with clearly made-up quotes. It also featured many of those words that were now part of the Gonzo lexicon ("weird," "rape," "atavistic," "half-bright") while the second took a different approach and partly told the story of making the first one, detailing their arguments with the printer. It also featured the tale of Thompson and Benton running amok after taking acid—a precursor to the adventures of Duke and Gonzo the following year. By *Wallposter #4*, Hunter was finding his Gonzo feet with more satirical efforts. He even wrote a profile of Raoul Duke, who is depicted as thoroughly insane—not to mention deceased.

Thompson's writing is coherent, logical, discursive, and well researched, but of course there are the usual flights of fancy. When gleefully telling his readers that *Wallposter #1* has sold out, he claims to have gotten wildly rich and spent all the money on drugs. He is eager to present his own legend to the readers and he is not afraid to play up his drug use and craziness, which in this case he attributes to Jack Kerouac.[3] Thompson also refers to Kerouac as "a young Columbia refugee who ran amok and still made it big, on his own terms," citing this as the inspiration for his own adventures in the world of literary journalism.

Thompson's campaign for sheriff drew major media attention, and it appears that in speaking with the likes of the BBC, *The New York Times*, *Time*, and others he used wishful thinking when answering their questions about his own life. The *Aspen Times* reporter was under the impression that Thompson was a graduate of Columbia University and *The Washington Post* refers to him as the author of two novels—but fails to mention that neither of them had been published.[4] In interviews, Thompson had the tendency to say what he wanted to be true rather than what was in fact true, and even in 1988 a *Boston Globe* journalist noted that he was "vague" about his education background, "mumbling

---

3   He claims that, after seeing Kerouac on TV, "I decided to quit my job and go into full-time craziness." [*Freak Power*, p.46]
4   Another newspaper reported that he had attended the University of Kentucky. [FBI file]

something about attending Columbia University and other institutions of higher learning."

Some of the media picked up on this. In an *LA Times* article on his campaign, the reporter points out that it "is difficult to distinguish put-on from dead-earnest"—a statement that applies equally to Thompson's writing and politics. He then asks, "Or is the whole bit merely to publicize Thompson, the writer of provocative prose?" It is a good question and one that others have often asked. Despite the success of *Hell's Angels* in 1967, Thompson's career had not quite taken off, but the attention that came with the Freak Power campaign brought infamy—just what an outlaw writer needed.

The *Aspen Wallposter* series, which ended after seven editions rather than the planned twelve, was a sandbox for Thompson to practice his new writing style. Over time, these revolutionary publications evolved, allowing him not just a single article without editorial controls, but the freedom to write various articles and include fake letters and references to the apparently deceased Raoul Duke. His writing is often satirical and for the fourth edition he wrote an article called "Aspen, Summer of Hate, 1970... Will the Sheriff be Killed?" It played upon the incumbent sheriff's paranoia. Sheriff Whitmire had claimed that his life was under threat, so Thompson exaggerated the threat tenfold, emphasizing the stupidity of the original claim by suggesting that the threat was "a full-scale invasion of the town [by] several thousand drug crazed motorcycle thugs."

In the seventh issue, Thompson claimed that the FBI had interfered to stop the publication of his wallposter. Indeed, the Bureau was investigating him at the time but their interest had begun some years earlier when he signed up for a communist newspaper, presumably as part of his voluminous research into fringe political or cultural movements. They had quickly decided that he was not worth investigating, but his campaign for sheriff reignited their interest. In particular, they noted that *Wallposter #4* featured the words "Impeach Nixon" and included a hidden swastika in the "x" that could only be seen when the poster was held up to strong light. The FBI continued to compile information on Thompson until February 1971, by which

235

time they had decided he was not a serious threat.[5]

At the beginning of his campaign, Thompson had not seriously considered that he would become sheriff. He was making a political point rather than trying to get elected for office, and was almost certainly attempting to distract the media and his opponents from other, more legitimate candidates, such as Ned Vare, who was running for county commissioner. He knew that, by playing up his role as a freak, he would make more conventionally progressive candidates appear moderate and acceptable to the voters. However, as the weeks went by, it became more and more likely that he would win and so he prepared for the eventuality of being elected sheriff. To this end, he planned to act as a "sociologist-type ombudsman" and then hire an experienced person to take up the traditional duties of sheriff.

Thompson's statements were incendiary and Benton's graphics shocked the community, but perhaps the biggest issue was his political platform, which suggested tearing up the streets and replacing them with grass, punishing unscrupulous drug dealers by placing them in public stocks, and renaming Aspen "Fat City" in order to deter land developers.[6] This was all laid out in his first piece of writing for *Rolling Stone,* a relatively new rock 'n' roll magazine headquartered in San Francisco.

Thompson had not been a particular fan of *Rolling Stone* magazine, believing it to be "a magazine for pansies," but he had been subscribed to it on the Random House expense account for his research into the Death of the American Dream, and when he read their coverage of the tragic events at Altamont in December 1969, he wrote to the publisher and editor, Jann Wenner, to congratulate him. Thankfully, he was not aware that Wenner had reviewed *Hell's Angels* for Berkeley's school newspaper, *The Daily Cal.*

---

5   His FBI file was released several years ago but a number of pages were destroyed in the 1990s. There is little information available, but several copies of the *Wallposter* were included.
6   Fat City was the name of the boat on which Thompson traveled to Bermuda. He had been reminded of this journey when first traveling to Aspen and clearly kept it in mind until 1970.

Wenner had dismissed it as the work of "another hippie journalist," but in his first letter to Thompson, he claimed to have "really dug it in its pre-cut form."

In their first letters, Wenner and Thompson discussed an article about Terry the Tramp, but before they could agree upon it, Hunter was invited to San Francisco to meet with the head honchos—Wenner and John Lombardi. Lombardi had spoken to Thompson before as the editor of the *Los Angeles Free Press*. He had seen Thompson's obituary for Lionel Olay and called to ask if he could reprint it. "Sure, print the fucker," Thompson had said. Now he was at *Rolling Stone*, Lombardi wanted to bring talented, subversive writers and Thompson seemed like the perfect candidate.

When Thompson arrived (late, of course) at the San Francisco meeting, he was dressed very much on-brand in his aviators, a Hawaiian shirt, and a woman's wig, whilst holding a cigarette holder and two six-packs of beer. He proceeded to put on a show that he would often repeat when meeting important people for the first time—pulling out an assortment of weird items from his bag, including an air horn. His life, like his writing, was always an opportunity for theater.

There was no conversation. Thompson just launched into a monologue about his campaign for sheriff. He talked at length about his bizarre platform, their unconventional tactics, and the need to mobilize the youth vote. As he talked, Lombardi noticed that he was "inventing vocabulary" like "greedheads" and "fun-hogs." Neither man knew what to make of the certified lunatic in front of them, guzzling beer and most likely high on any number of other substances. Lombardi recalled that Thompson spoke like he wrote—a sort of "oral rock 'n' roll."

On April 16, Wenner wrote and suggested that the campaign for sheriff be the focus of Thompson's first article for the magazine. Thompson wrote back to say that he agreed, but that his campaign would just be a part of it. He viewed Freak Power as a much bigger entity. Explaining that he did not want to win his campaign for sheriff, he went on to say that it could inspire similar efforts across the nation that likely would be successful. He saw *Rolling Stone* as the perfect launchpad for a national movement of connected grass-roots efforts to wrest control away from an entrenched establishment.

Jann Wenner had founded *Rolling Stone* in 1967 as a counter-cultural magazine focused on rock 'n' roll music, but he had never been entirely comfortable with the politics of the underground. The magazine had taken some flak during the late sixties for its perceived neutrality, particularly in comparison with more radical publications like the *Berkeley Barb* or *Ramparts*. If this bothered Thompson in any way, he was very much appeased by the financial situation. *The Nation* may have fostered the advent of Gonzo with its progressive views and open-minded editors, but they only paid a hundred dollars per article. With its comparatively neutral political stance, *Rolling Stone* could attract far bigger advertisers, and in turn offer writers much better renumeration.

This, of course, appealed to Thompson, but it was also an opportunity for the shrewd businessman at the helm of a rising empire. Wenner had deliberately plotted this course and avoided courting controversy, but by hiring a maverick writer he could evade some of the stones thrown by his critics. Besides, Freak Power was the sort of off-beat nonsense that even the mainstream media were reporting on. It didn't pose a real threat to the establishment, did it?

Initially, Thompson had been inclined to write about his campaign for *Scanlan's*, which at this point had not yet gone bust, but he didn't feel that *Scanlan's* was the right venue for it. It was extremely progressive, but he wanted a larger, younger audience. When he began talking with Wenner, he realized that *Rolling Stone* was the right place. It had a young, hip readership who, if motivated, could become a sizeable voting bloc.

In "The Battle of Aspen," published on October 1, 1970, Thompson described his Freak Power campaign and presented his platform. He also showed his unusual style of writing (and personality) to the readers of *Rolling Stone* for the first time. This made him feel a little uneasy as he was not sure how he would be perceived. In a phone call to John Clancy, he expressed serious doubts: "Well, unfortunately, I'm locked into this terrible honesty in this article... I've lost all track of it... it may be craziness… Does it come through as a speed trip to some people?"

The article begins with a series of subheaders connected by ellipses that act as a sort of summary of the section that follows. Thompson had introduced this technique to a limited extent, but now he had produced a much longer version that conformed to the style he would later use, breaking apart the grammar of proper sentences into shorter fragments that tease the reader about what will follow. Appearing almost like notes copied from his notebook, the individual parts of the title can be viewed as single images or summaries of sections of the article. This time, they began:

> A Memoir and Rambling Discussion (with Rude Slogans) of Freak Power in the Rockies. . . on the Weird Mechanics of Running a Takeover Bid on a Small Town . . . and a Vulgar Argument for Seizing Political Power and Using It like a Gun Ripped Away from a Cop. . .

He starts his article by looking back at the campaign to elect Joe Edwards for mayor, one year earlier. He paints the scene as the results are about to be announced, explaining their techniques for watching the polls in order to avoid voter intimidation. It is the story of a plucky underdog campaign standing up to an entrenched and immoral establishment comprised of wealthy old men. He then switches over to the present day to talk about their fight for registering voters, and then back to the campaign, where he informs his readers that his candidate has lost by just six votes. Finally, he turns to his present campaign for sheriff and outlines his tactics and "Tentative Platform," both of which are a mix of serious and comical ideas. He explains that he intends to disarm the police but that they should be allowed to use high explosives and trained wolverines.

It is a long article despite Wenner having initially asked for just twenty-five hundred words, but it is engaging, informative, amusing, and even inspiring.[7] It is also very much a Hunter S. Thompson piece of writing as he is now in Gonzo mode and embracing every rebellious aspect of

---

7   The article was long enough, in fact, that Thompson attempted to expand it slightly into a book.

it. Naturally, the author's usual vocabulary was on display, as he refers to "fun-hogs" and "land-rapers," and again trots out the idea of using "a bastinado platform." He also uses his wild flights of fancy, and in this instance begins it with "I have a nightmare vision of our whole act coming to a massive orgiastic climax…" before describing a riot and his own arrest.[8]

He once again uses a collective quote, although this time he provides a voice that is clearly his own: "Your whole act is doomed… We're going to beat your ass like a gong."[9] There are other quotes that are more than likely Thompson's own creations, as well as accusations of Nazism and other outrageous charges. It is also another effort in myth-building, as Thompson presents himself as an outlaw throughout the article. He makes it clear that he is a gun-freak who likes to roam naked and indulge in illegal substances. Of course, that is exactly what one would expect from a candidate under the banner of Freak Power.

All of the attention gained through his *Rolling Stone* article, the *Aspen Wallposters*, and the regular media, which was very interested in the election, helped catapult Thompson from a relatively unknown author to a major name in journalism. However, they also ensured that his political campaign was unsuccessful. The attention caused his opponents to work together and Thompson was defeated by a rare bipartisan effort of Republicans, Independents, and Democrats called RID. An illegal mailing campaign was carried out to defeat the Freaks at the final hurdle. "Unfortunately," he said in his concession speech, "I proved what I set out to prove… that the American Dream really is fucked." Nonetheless, he was always quick to observe that he had started in motion a movement toward serious political reform in Aspen. Just

---

8   The phrase "orgiastic climax" appears to be yet another reference to Fitzgerald: "Gatsby believed in the green light, the orgastic future that year by year recedes before us." [*The Great Gatsby*, p.180] This uncommon word, spelled "orgastic" in the first edition but "orgiastic" in others, appears occasionally in Thompson's writing.
9   The expression "beat (something) like a gong" is used frequently throughout Thompson's letters and articles.

two years later, Joe Edwards won his next campaign for mayor, and eventually the progressive Bob Braudis, a good friend of Thompson's, became sheriff. Freak Power proved successful in the end.

During his Freak Power campaign, Thompson had relied upon the help of a friend called Oscar Zeta Acosta. The two men had met at the Daisy Duck bar in Aspen in 1967 and been friends ever since. Acosta was a lawyer and, like Thompson, a prodigious user of drugs. He was a large human being with a forceful personality and had become a prominent figure in the Los Angeles Hispanic community after defending Chicano activists in various trials in the late sixties. As a lawyer and former preacher, he could deliver terrifying proclamations and would captivate and horrify anyone who dared listen—particularly when he then projectile-vomited blood due to a persistent stomach ulcer. Thompson was enthralled by his violent, Biblical prophecy and penchant for hallucinogens.

In 1970, Acosta ran for sheriff of Los Angeles and received just a tenth of the number of votes the winning candidate had, having been jailed for several days in the middle of the campaign. When he retreated to the mountains in defeat, Hunter recruited him to help with his own campaign. They put their warped minds together to invent unusual methods for grabbing the public's attention. In one instance, Thompson wrote twisted scripts that Acosta would read out on local radio. These were, however, soon taken off the air after listeners failed to see them as fictional stories intended to satirize anti-Freak sentiment in the area.

Thompson and Acosta were drawn toward each other by their radical politics, towering personalities, and superhuman tolerance for alcohol and drugs. Acosta, however, was even more extreme than Thompson in terms of politics and almost everything else. While Hunter was engaged in his bizarre bid for political power, Acosta was playing a game that was altogether more deadly. He was a leader in the Chicano Rights movement—less famous than Cesar Chavez, but still well known and enough of a target to require the protection of a bodyguard.

After helping out his friend's Freak Power campaign,

Acosta hoped for something in return. Racial tensions were high in Los Angeles and a Chicano-led anti-war protest had turned ugly with the sudden, suspicious death of Ruben Salazar, a reporter for the *Los Angeles Times*. Salazar had been a vocal critic of the city government and Acosta felt his death was clearly a deliberate hit job, carried out by the LAPD. He wanted Thompson to write about it and bring the story to a wider audience.

The opportunity to uncover a potential conspiracy and expose police criminality appealed to Thompson. He sold the idea to Warren Hinckle at *Scanlan's* but then the magazine collapsed, leaving him "infamous & stone broke." Thankfully, "The Battle of Aspen" had proven a hit with the readers of *Rolling Stone* and so he was able to sell the piece to Wenner. Most of the writing had been done in 1970 but, early in the following year, Wenner agreed to pay Thompson's expenses to return and expand the story.[10]

Thompson traveled to East Los Angeles in February and checked into the Hotel Ashmun, where Acosta and several intimidating friends would show up in the afternoon. They would sit around, drinking rum and taking pills while they planned radical political action. They were mostly street thugs and not happy with the presence of a white journalist in their neighborhood. One of them shouted, "What the hell is this goddamn gabacho pig writer doing here?"

It was not an easy article to research but, just as he had done with the Hell's Angels, Thompson managed to infiltrate a hostile group that viewed him as an outsider. He finished the article, which became "Strange Rumblings in Aztlan," and was published in *Rolling Stone* on April 29, 1971.[11] At twenty thousand words, it was the longest piece of writing the magazine had yet published.

Thompson's article looks at the events that occurred before and after Salazar's death, profiles Acosta and the

10   Already, Wenner considered Thompson his golden goose. Timothy Crouse remarked: "I think it would be fair to say [that Wenner was] in love. [...] Jann really worshipped Hunter." [*Sticky Fingers*, p.204]
11   "Aztlan" means the home of the Aztec people, but the term was adopted by Chicano activists to refer to lands taken from Mexico by the United States.

various elements of the Chicano rights movement, and presents an exploration of the LAPD's reactions. In an article that differs massively from his usual work, he examines the case in great detail, making it increasingly obvious that something was wrong with the official story. As in *Hell's Angels*, he methodically deconstructs various stories in order to show them as utterly absurd. He does not, however, condemn the killing as a deliberate murder, even though it is clear from his investigation that Salazar had been murdered. Eschewing the bold statements and total subjectivity of his recent writing, he is more cautious and balanced in "Strange Rumblings." This article could perhaps be viewed as New Journalism more than Gonzo Journalism and is surely his best relatively straight piece of writing after *Hell's Angels*.

The story begins, as all of Thompson's work from this period, with a series of subheaders strung together. This time, however, they are more fragmented than in the past, which is odd because the article itself is more coherent than others. These begin with two individual words separated by ellipses:

> The. . . Murder. . . and Resurrection of Ruben Salazar by the Los Angeles County Sheriff's Department. . . Savage Polarization & the Making of a Martyr . . . Bad News for the Mexican-American . . . Worse News for the Pig. . .

Despite this familiar style of heading, it is clear from the offset that Thompson is digging back into his more conventional journalistic capacity. His first line sounds more like his *National Observer* work than anything recent, as he presents a teasing image that will later be explained: "Morning comes hard to the Hotel Ashmun; this is not a place where the guests spring eagerly out of bed to greet the fresh new day." He goes on to describe the scene as angry Hispanic men attempt to kick in the door of a communal bathroom while screaming racial abuse at the manager, who is attempting to bring some calm to the scene. It is the sort of opening at which Thompson had always excelled. The scene is dramatic and it makes the reader curious: Who are these people? Why are they so aggressive? As the story progresses, Thompson inserts himself as a man safely ensconced in another room at the Hotel Ashmun, trusting that these violent people will not think to kick in *his* door.

The story moves at a quick pace and soon we are introduced to Acosta and his associates. Thompson is there but has moved back to an observer's role and does not engage in any wild activities or bizarre outbursts. Any craziness in the article comes from other characters, with Thompson as the relative straight man, almost reversing the roles found in his Kentucky Derby article. He is restrained and simply narrates necessary events and dialogue. The narrative is unusually lucid and straightforward, heavy with wisdom, background, and conversation. Aside from a racist joke about lazy Mexicans, it is a quite responsible piece of journalism.

The story is also extremely objective when compared to most of Thompson's other writing, beginning in the mid-sixties. Essentially, this article was his effort to shed light on an issue raised by his friend, but early on in the story he expresses doubts about Acosta's version of events. Throughout the article, he explains the facts of the case very carefully and without his usual bias because he is eager to expose the truth. Whenever he brings in his own views, they are positioned as the entirely biased views of an observer, lacking the absolute certainty he brought to, for example, his assessment of political figures. Toward the end, he concludes that the official version of the story is impossible to believe, but this is the measured conclusion of a man who has demonstrably weighed the evidence.

In a sense, then, it is a more conventional story than one might expect; however, it is still marked by features peculiar to Thompson. For a start, the text is littered with aggressive verbs and adjectives: "pounding," "wild," "terrible," "ripped," "hysterical." Thompson has also used the features of a novel instead of a typical journalist's structure. Rather than giving context and then details, he starts with gripping action, then sets the scene in terms of location, and then finally—taking his time, as always—he explains the reason for the article. There is, of course, an obligatory reference to Fitzgerald, when Thompson talks about the "high white summer of 1967," and he again litters his text with quotes from signs, news articles, and press releases. He even manages to attack the press, this time turning his attentions to the *Herald-Examiner*, which he says is "a monument to everything cheap, corrupt and vicious in the realm of journalistic possibility."

In the late sixties, Thompson had become better at weaving different threads of a story, bringing background, current events, digressions, explanations, dialogue, and fantasies together into coherent narratives. "Strange Rumblings" involves an even more complicated array of threads, showing a far greater vision. Thompson himself realized this, calling it "a natural framework & a good narrative," and this was no exaggeration, for it is his most mature and complex piece of writing. Once again, he uses sentence fragments (often beginning with "Which…" or simply the word "Indeed") to refocus the narrative or jump into new ideas when necessary, but the cuts are not as jarring as they often were in his writing. Digressions and fantasy sequences are rare, with the narrative following the relevant details only. It is important to him that the reader fully understands the facts of the investigation and so everything is presented clearly and the timelines are deftly entwined, without his usual indulgent pontification.

It must be noted here that this was not all Thompson's work. He was mostly producing short bursts of writing from different parts of the story and sending them for his editors to piece together. In this case, it was the highly skilled but achingly methodical David "Stonecutter" Felton that did the arranging. Thompson, who had written part of the article at the *Rolling Stone* offices, sat and grudgingly gave permission for Felton to move sections of the story for greater clarity. [12] He was still not entirely enamored of being edited.

In a passage that acts as a conclusion, Thompson

---

12   He was brought into the *Rolling Stone* offices and given space to finish the article in order to ensure he did not break deadline. Charles Perry recalled finding him buzzing with energy and proudly announcing that he was on a roll. But soon he hit a wall: "I lost my momentum. I've been up for two days on speed. I haven't changed my clothes. I think my feet are rotting." [*Outlaw Journalist*, p.160]

states that the police version of events is idiotic and that it is hard to believe any of what they said. On the other hand, while Salazar's death was definitely a murder, it was not a conspiracy. He argues that the incompetence of the police confirms that it was not possible for them to conduct a targeted assassination. He writes:

> The malignant reality of Ruben Salazar's death is that he was murdered by angry cops for no reason at all – and that the L.A. sheriff's department was and still is prepared to defend that murder on grounds that it was entirely justified.

He goes on to demonstrate that, even if it had not been a targeted murder, it was still very much the product of racial violence perpetrated by a bigoted police force. Here, he chooses to use the collective quote method again, only this time he is clearly paraphrasing his interpretation of their words and actions rather than using actual quotations:

> What the cops are saying is that Salazar got what he deserved – for a lot of reasons, but mainly because he happened to be in their way when they had to do their duty. His death was unfortunate, but if they had to do it all over again they wouldn't change a note.
> This is the point they want to make. It is a local variation on the standard Mitchell-Agnew theme: Don't fuck around, boy – and if you want to hang around with people who do, don't be surprised when the bill comes due – whistling in through the curtains of some darkened barroom on a sunny afternoon when the cops decide to make an example of somebody.

He provides another story after his conclusion. In it, he recounts the death of a young, gay, Chicano man killed in a jail cell. Everyone *knows* that he was murdered but no one can prove it. It is impossible to say for sure that his death was a murder, but at the same time no sane person could claim otherwise. This story seems to justify the idea that Salazar was surely murdered even if there is no hard evidence to prove it. It also seems to justify Thompson's own approaches to journalism, from this relatively conventional piece to his more Gonzo efforts. Sometimes the truth cannot be pinned down through traditional methods, particularly when it is being purposefully obscured by those who abuse their power, but a writer is able to present his version of reality through a careful presentation of the facts. The reader now *knows* the truth, even if it is nearly impossible to bring law enforcement to justice.

There is a tone of hopelessness close to the surface of the article that is usually a deeper theme within his work. Normally, Thompson's wacky antics and the crazed subjects he examines hide the serious issues raised, such as the brutality of institutional power over the individual or, sometimes, over minority groups. Here, that feeling is ever-present, from Thompson's own fear as a *gabacho* journalist in the barrio to the intimidating presence of the unrepentant, malevolent LAPD.

The article ends with a short passage in which the journalist hears about a bombing at City Hall. He calls the police to ask if they know anything, and when he presses them they say that the Chicano Liberation Front is responsible.[13] They have no hard evidence to prove it, but they *know*. The inference is that for the police *knowing* something is enough, but for everyone else there needs to be hard evidence. The system is rigged.

---

13   There is some speculation that Acosta was involved in this or another bombing. In Ian Lopez's *Racism on Trial*, he goes into some discussion and concludes that Acosta most likely did plant bombs, one of which resulted in the death of a Hispanic man. [p.122] Later, Thompson alluded to this in *Fear and Loathing in Las Vegas* when Acosta's character shouts "One of these days I'll toss a fucking bomb into this place!" [p.13] and elsewhere Thompson remembers him showing up for work smelling of gasoline and with "charred soap-flakes" on his boots. [*Great Shark Hunt*, p.497] Acosta appears to admit to this in a cryptic letter from 1972 in which he claims Thompson "called a halt to the bombings." [*Uncollected Works*, p.106] He does not, though, say anything more specific.

Fact and Fiction in Las Vegas

Let's keep in mind that this was never a commissioned work of journalism; it was a strange neo-fictional outburst [...] It's been an instinct trip from the start, and I suspect it's going to stay that way—for good or ill.

Hunter S. Thompson

In 1971, while investigating the death of Ruben Salazar in Los Angeles, Hunter S. Thompson had been viewed with the utmost suspicion by Oscar Zeta Acosta's militant friends. Even though Acosta had invited him in order to present their side of the story, the idea of trusting a white journalist was too much for many of them. Neither man felt free to talk, which put the article in jeopardy, and Thompson felt that he was in greater danger of being beaten or murdered than when he had rolled with the Angels up the coast. The militants around them wanted the "gabacho pig writer" gone and there was also some fear that the police might be attempting to listen in on their conversations.

Thompson and Acosta retreated to the Polo Lounge of the Beverley Hills Hotel to talk in private, and while they were there Thompson had an idea. One of his old friends, Tom Vanderschmidt, was now working at *Sports Illustrated* and had offered him a plum job—a quick trip to the city of sin to write a 250-word caption for a photo essay about the Mint 400 motorcycle race, which took place March 21 – 23, 1971. It was the perfect excuse to get out of town for the weekend and have it all covered by an expense account.

From the Polo Lounge, Thompson called Vanderschmidt but got no reply. He left a message and soon thereafter a dwarf emerged with a pink telephone. It was agreed; they would set off immediately. With little time to prepare, they rented a car to carry them across the desert. As Acosta was particularly paranoid about being spied on, they hired a convertible, which they reasoned would be harder to bug.

The race was a blow-out. It was just a bunch of motorcycles and dune buggies scrambling about in the desert, totally obscured from view by the sand that they kicked up. This was not hugely important to Thompson, who had learned at Eglin that you didn't need to *see* a sports event in order to write about it. You could just piece it together later from what you had heard. Or, alternatively, there was the Kentucky Derby approach—load up on mind-altering substances, run amok, and not even bother with the sports side of the story at all.

What happened in Las Vegas is unclear and I will discuss the finer points of what is and isn't known later in this chapter, but the most widely reported version of events is this: The two men discussed the Salazar case and Thompson got what he needed to finish his article. There may have been some drug use and no doubt they drank heavily before Acosta returned to Los Angeles, leaving Thompson to deal with the consequences of their sybaritism.

When he was on assignment, Thompson normally filled notebooks with his observations. His ultimate aim was to record his surroundings at the moment he saw them, with "the eye & mind [...] functioning as a camera." He continued: "The writing would be selective & necessarily interpretative – but once the image was written the words would be final; in same way that a Cartier-Bresson photograph is always (he says) the full-frame negative. No alterations in the dark room, no cutting or cropping, no spotting... no editing." We have seen this with his notes from the Kentucky Derby, which were supposedly used verbatim in his final article. However, while with Acosta, he wrote nothing. It was only when his friend left that Hunter holed-up in his room at the Mint Hotel and spent nearly two days trying to remember everything that had happened.

Normally, when Thompson wrote he smoked cigarettes and drank beer or whiskey. If he became tired, he would take some form of amphetamine to keep him going, allowing him to work for days at a time. While he obviously enjoyed recreational drug use, he did not view these substances as a tool for writing and believed that even marijuana was detrimental to his writing process. In 1969, he had written an account of taking mescaline for the first time, but it was just a private experiment that was only included in his 1990 collection, *Songs of the Doomed*. When he wanted to write about the effects of drugs, he would normally do so when he was *not* high.

In his hotel room, Thompson made notes about his trip to Las Vegas that suggest there were some hallucinogens consumed: "Pterodactyls lumbering around the corridors in pools of fresh blood [...] a half-naked fourteen-year-old girl being chased through the air by snarling wolverines." He scrawled these weird images on notepaper and cocktail napkins, trying to capture the sensations of a real acid trip. During the drive back across the desert, he stopped often in order to write down more ideas that came to him, including an imagined scene featuring Raoul Duke being pulled over by the California Highway Patrol.[1]

Thompson claimed that he wrote the whole of the first draft of part one of *Fear and Loathing in Las Vegas* on Mint Hotel stationery "during an all-night drunk/drug frenzy" and that, when he returned to Los Angeles to continue working on it, he "changed hardly anything." As we will see later, that was not true. Certainly, from other accounts, it appears that he wrote mostly notes in Las Vegas and then typed them up in Pasadena, and he claimed in an interview that the first paragraphs of the story were written somewhere between Las Vegas and Los Angeles, in a "honkytonk joint." The book was, instead, the product of careful drafting and Thompson was probably trying to build a legend around it, just like Kerouac's *On the Road* scroll.[2]

---

1   Thompson had been recording his own thoughts on audio tape when the cop began following him. It does not appear that he was ever pulled over, but his mind ran wild during those tense moments. It inspired him to write a fictional account for his book.

2   Kerouac claimed to have written several important works, including *On the Road*, in more or less single bursts of writing. However, the final published versions were in fact the product of more methodical drafting.

When he returned from Las Vegas, Thompson supposedly typed up a two-thousand-word report of his trip, which he claimed was "aggressively rejected" by *Sports Illustrated*.[3] For once, though, he was not angry, and even thanked Vanderschmidt for rejecting the piece, telling his friend that he was working on something much greater, which this assignment had "set in motion." What he had submitted to Vanderschmidt, however, was not the story readers would later come to know. It was a drug-free version of a single weekend at the Mint 400, padded out with a bit of local history. This evolved as Thompson continued to experiment. He pushed boundaries and—for the first time—let his fiendish imagination run completely wild. Whenever he had a spare moment from writing about the Salazar case, he added more to his outlandish tale. It was fun, it was educational, it was different, and—most importantly—it was *good*.

Thompson often referred to writing as a painful, exhausting process that he did mostly for money, but now the words were flowing from him—and they were hilarious. He wasn't writing to a deadline or for any editors; he was just writing for himself. It wasn't an article, it wasn't a short story, but none of that mattered. He was feeling playful. This *thing*—this astoundingly weird story—took many of the features of his Gonzo writing style but it was told much more like a novel.

Before long, he knew that he was on to something significant and he showed it to people whose opinion he respected in order to confirm that it really was as special as he imagined. There are various accounts of how Thompson introduced the *Rolling Stone* staff to his new story but it was soon passed around the office and nearly everyone knew that he was working on something groundbreaking. David Felton, Jann Wenner, and Paul Scanlon all recalled reading those pages for the first time and laughing out loud, then

---

3   There are various versions of this rejection, and Thompson's own estimates differ wildly. In one letter, he claims he submitted fifteen thousand words, a major biography claims it was twenty-five thousand, and elsewhere he says that it was five hundred words. In some letters, he says he never even submitted it. Two thousand words, however, seems to be the most believable claim.

encouraging Thompson to continue. They all knew that he was onto something, even if they didn't quite know what it was. Wenner liked it so much that he claims to have immediately offered to buy the serialization rights, and when Jim Silberman at Random House read parts of it, he quickly offered one hundred thousand dollars for the rights to publish it as a book.

Thompson had soon written up a full version of the Vegas trip, but a month later he was told about the National District Attorneys' Conference on Narcotics and Dangerous Drugs, on April 25 – 29, which was also set to take place in Las Vegas. Felton suggested that he go back and write about it, but he was not suggesting it for inclusion in the book. "We weren't trying to get him to write a novel," he explained. "It just came together naturally." Thompson thought it would be hilarious to get outrageously stoned and then go listen to cops talk about drugs. It was precisely the sort of risky, subversive act that he found entertaining.

Thompson and Acosta returned to Las Vegas for the DA convention and proceeded to load up on drink and drugs. This time, Thompson was prepared and he brought a tape recorder to capture events that he might otherwise forget. As they rambled around Sin City, they took turns talking into the recorder, collecting their thoughts and conducting interviews with various people. Both men felt that they were somehow on a quest to find the American Dream, which ultimately became the theme of Thompson's book.

When the second Vegas trip was over, Thompson returned to Woody Creek to be with his wife and son. For months, he had been living in hotels and motels in Las Vegas and Los Angeles. He was delighted to be back at his "fortress," but this also brought problems. Felton thought that the brilliance of Thompson's reporting came from its immediacy. He called it "a personalized form of journalism, happening at the moment of the action, not later." Like Kerouac had done, Thompson's stream-of-consciousness prose dragged the reader into the story, but Thompson's included frequent comments on the writing process and conspiratorial asides, working to bridge the gap and bring the reader closer to the action. He acknowledged, though, that much of what he wrote about was "provoked" and that there would probably have been no story without his efforts to stir it up. In that sense, he was creating a novel out of real life and then writing it down as it happened. This was the strength of Gonzo:

> What I was trying to get at in this was [the] mind-warp/photo technique of instant journalism: One draft, written on the spot at top speed and basically un-revised, edited, chopped, larded, etc. for publication. Ideally, I'd like to walk away from a scene and mail my notebook to the editor, who will then carry it, un-touched, to the printer.

Clearly, then, he viewed the Vegas story as carrying on from his Kentucky Derby piece.

When removed from the scene itself, Thompson felt that the rush of the events and the feel of the surroundings were nearly impossible to recapture and put into words. He always found it harder to write accurately about what had happened once moved to another physical location, and this was compounded by the fact that he was writing about experiences on drugs in a very unusual environment. Back home, in the relative peace and quiet of Woody Creek, he was not so easily able to draw upon the energy he had found in Las Vegas.

Still, when he sat down and began pounding the keys of his typewriter, the words somehow came to him. In the past, writing had been hard, but now it was fun. In the basement of Owl Farm, he placed a door on top of two sawhorses and established the War Room, where he would write for eight to twelve hours per day on a mixture of Dexedrine and bourbon. The writing continued all through the summer, taking about six months in total.

Thompson's story follows Raoul Duke (a "doctor of journalism") and his Samoan attorney, Doctor Gonzo, as they search for the American Dream whilst under the influence of various mind-bending substances.[4] It is told

---

4   Thompson mostly renders Gonzo's name as "Doctor Gonzo" but once slips and calls him "Dr. Gonzo," while other

in two parts but there is no coherent plot, and the book is largely a series of episodes sewn together in a loosely chronological fashion.

In part one, Duke and Gonzo are first seen crossing the desert from Los Angeles to Las Vegas. They pick up a hitchhiker, whom they soon scare off with their maniacal ranting. Duke, who is narrating, takes us back to the Beverly Hills Hotel and the dwarf with the pink phone, before describing their sloppy arrival in Las Vegas. Their first task is to check into their hotel, but Duke is starting to hallucinate badly and envisions lizards fornicating in the foyer. Later, he calms down but Gonzo spirals out of control. He asks Duke to kill him by throwing a radio into the bathtub during a Jefferson Airplane song; however, Duke tosses a grapefruit into the tub instead. Gonzo then flees Las Vegas, leaving Duke to fend for himself with a suitcase full of drugs and a gun that is most likely unregistered.

In part two, Duke also attempts to flee Las Vegas, but then turns and goes back after being stopped by a cop in California. When he arrives at his new hotel, he finds Gonzo shacked up with a girl called Savage Lucy, before they attend the DA convention and listen to absurd propaganda about drugs.[5] The second half of the book is far more disjointed than the first, and consists largely of flashbacks, fantasies, and digressions, rather than the comparatively straightforward Part One.[6] Much of what happens in this section of the book takes place in Duke's head rather than in the streets or casinos of Las Vegas.

The story begins with what is now one of the most famous lines in twentieth century American literature: "We were somewhere around Barstow on the edge of the desert when the drugs began to take hold." The opening

doctors (including Duke and a speaker at the DA convention called Bloomquist) are referred to by the abbreviated "Dr."
5   The girl is called "Savage Lucy" in the chapter headings but is simply referred to as "Lucy" in the text. There are, however, various references to "a scag baron named Savage Henry."
6   For some time, these were considered as two separate stories. Part one would have been a stand-alone book and part two could have become part of the American Dream book project.

scene is ridiculous, hilarious, and now iconic. Thompson presents two utterly unbelievable characters tearing across the desert on their way to Las Vegas, raving like madmen whilst indulging in rare pharmaceuticals. The narrator can see bats flying around the car, but even he knows he is probably hallucinating. Meanwhile, his attorney has "taken his shirt off and was pouring beer on his chest, to facilitate the tanning process."[7]

When Thompson describes the contents of the trunk of their car, he reels off a list of illegal substances and their quantities. As in his other writing, its specificity and outrageousness made it hilarious:

> The sporting editors had also given me $300 in cash, most of which was already spent on extremely dangerous drugs. The trunk of the car looked like a mobile police narcotics lab. We had two bags of grass, seventy-five pellets of mescaline, five sheets of high-powered blotter acid, a salt shaker half full of cocaine, and a whole galaxy of multi-colored uppers, downers, screamers, laughers … and also a quart of tequila, a quart of rum, a case of Budweiser, a pint of raw ether and two dozen amyls.

Iconic though this image may now be, their fantastic pharmacopoeia never existed and any actual drug use in Las Vegas was comparatively tame, but the point is that the list was funny and shocking. Gerald Tyrell, Thompson's childhood friend, recalls him treating high school parties in much the same way. Quoting Thompson, he said,

> "We have seventy-one beers!" The important thing wasn't that we had beer, but that we had *seventy-one* beers, and we had two and a half quarts of bourbon and

---

7   There are numerous parallels between "The Kentucky Derby is Decadent and Depraved" and *Fear and Loathing in Las Vegas*, including this scene. At the end of the Derby piece, Steadman pours beer on his chest as they race to the airport. In that case, he was trying to get the mace off his skin.

we had a pint and a half of gin [...] when I read that part in the book, I said, "Same old guy."

It also speaks to Thompson's methods of describing almost anything in his writing when he really considered it interesting in one way or another. He would begin with a simple description and then often double-down with another that either built upon the first or restated it. In this case, he says they have "extremely dangerous drugs" and then adds a more specific image. After that, the first two become redundant as he explains in great detail what they have. Most of those drugs are not simply listed but, as Tyrell noted, described in terms of quantity. He had always been fond of adding as many descriptive words to his sentences as possible to create the most immediate and vivid images. Indeed, there is no other description in literature quite like this one.

Thompson had possessed a gift for comedy since early childhood. He would constantly say things that were shocking, absurd, or just plain silly, but he possessed a talent for more nuanced satire and could plant subtly amusing images through understated language. In his writing, he transformed real life into a cartoonish world where anything could happen, sometimes by presenting a ridiculous image out of place in the middle of an otherwise normal scene. This is true of his main characters. In *Fear and Loathing in Las Vegas*, from the very beginning, it is clear that Duke and Gonzo are so completely over the top as to be comedic.[8] Their thoughts, actions, and speech are all twisted versions of reality.

The dialogue in particular is often hilarious, especially when Doctor Gonzo is involved, such as the phone call to Lucy in part two, in which he acts as though he is being attacked before hanging up. In such cases, the humor comes from his characters saying things that are so shocking as

---

8   Other characters that appear are largely two-dimensional, like in most of Thompson's writing. Neal Stephenson, in *Gonzo Republic*, argues that the minor characters in *Vegas* are simply repetitions of one another: the hitchhiker and the cop; Lucy, the waitress, and the maid. [p.31]

to be unbelievable.[9] Of course, in many cases it is quite possible that Thompson was describing or exaggerating a real event. From Las Vegas, Thompson and Acosta really did make weird prank phone calls to people, including the *Rolling Stone* office. The sort of humor that they employed was very much like the humor in this call to Lucy.

Thompson relied upon a number of different comic devices to keep his reader constantly laughing. He often built up ideas, making use of foreshadowing and using punctuation to create a rhythm until he finally reached a punchline. In this respect, he wrote much like a standup comic speaks, timing his punchlines and using callbacks to elicit laughter. Certain ideas, characters, or objects reappear unexpectedly through the book, such as the hitchhiker from the first chapter or the song that first plays in their car: "One Toke Over the Line." At one point, the two main characters discuss eating pineal glands to get high, but this is too much for Doctor Gonzo: "Man, I'll try just about anything; but I'd never in hell touch a pineal gland." Later on, when they are tormenting a hick cop with stories of witchcraft and decapitation, they casually mention that junkies are murdering people to eat their pineal glands. It adds another layer of comedy to an already funny scene.

Elsewhere, the humor is much more subtle. In an amusing scene where Duke frightens a garage owner by pumping his tires to a dangerous level of pressure, he casually drops in the line, "Sandoz laboratories designed these tires. They're special." Sandoz was a pharmaceutical company that produced LSD until 1965. Most of Thompson's readers would be aware of this fact, but evidently the garage attendant was not. It was a hip joke that squares could not have understood.

The story is told from the perspective of Raoul Duke, who is clearly based upon Hunter Thompson, as we can see from his appearance, his speech, and some elements of his background. Doctor Gonzo, of course, is meant

---

9   During the editing of this book, Thompson reflected on passages from *Hell's Angels* that had been excerpted and was shocked to see how different he sounded when the comedy was excised from his writing: "All it takes is a few cuts on the Humor to make the rest seem like the ravings of a dangerous lunatic." [*Fear and Loathing in America*, p.410]

to be Oscar Acosta and is constantly referred to as "my attorney" by Duke. As we have seen in previous chapters, Thompson had been developing the character of Duke for some time and had been unsure of how to use him, but in this case he is clearly just a fictionalized version of Thompson himself. Doctor Gonzo, however, is entirely new and had appeared nowhere prior to *Vegas*. His name obviously originates in the style of writing Thompson had developed in 1970 at the Kentucky Derby, but there is little doubt that the character is based upon Acosta. In *The Gonzo Tapes*, we can even hear Acosta giving his name as "Doctor Gonzo" when calling to ask about the existence of a business called "the American Dream."[10]

Despite the fact that Gonzo was obviously based upon Acosta, there are some elements obscuring the true identity of Gonzo's character—namely, Thompson's insistence upon referring to Gonzo as Samoan, when Acosta himself was American and supposedly a full-blooded descendent of the Aztecs. There are two reasons for Thompson changing Acosta into "a 300-pound Samoan" for his novel. First and foremost, he was interested in protecting his close friend. He had seen what happened to Neal Cassady after Kerouac used him in *On the Road*, and he knew that just changing a name wasn't enough to stop Acosta being disbarred.[11] He knew that the elements of fiction that he used within this book would be necessary due to the legal consequences of admitting to countless criminal acts, and in this case he was keen to ensure that there was more than one layer of fiction obscuring the truth.

Another reason, though, is the fact that Doctor Gonzo was the latest incarnation of Thompson's sidekick-companion device, and so he could not be viewed as an American. He had to be an outsider. In a sense, Acosta was the next Ralph Steadman—another foreigner to whom Thompson could explain America and its culture of greed. His foreignness is emphasized from the start of the book,

10   By the second trip, Thompson had already written the first part of *Vegas* and it appears Acosta was comfortable with his appellation.
11   Neal Cassady was arrested and imprisoned for possession of marijuana after Kerouac's novel had drawn police attention to him.

and at one point Duke uses him to explain a larger theme to the reader:

> "You Samoans are all the same," I told him. "You have no faith in the essential decency of the white man's culture. Jesus, just one hour ago we were sitting over there in that stinking baiginio, stone broke and paralyzed for the weekend, when a call comes through from some total stranger in New York, telling me to go to Las Vegas and expenses be damned—and then he sends me over to some office in Beverly Hills where another total stranger gives me $300 raw cash for no reason at all … I tell you, my man, this is the American Dream in action! We'd be fools not to ride this strange torpedo all the way out to the end."

Another temporary companion character arrives in the form of a hitchhiker, to whom Duke explains the premise of the book and the relationship between the two main characters. Duke accuses the hitchhiker of being prejudiced against foreigners, but when the hitchhiker denies it, Duke says, "in spite of his race, this man is extremely valuable to me." A little later, he says something similar: "My attorney understood this concept, despite his racial handicap." These are ironic remarks, comedic for being false and intended to satirize American racism.

The role of the hitchhiker is partly as an outsider to whom Duke can explain the premise of the book ("I want you to know that we're on our way to Las Vegas to find the American Dream."), but at the same time he is the straight man against whom the depravity of these two drug freaks is highlighted. From his first words ("Hot damn! I never rode in a convertible before!") it is clear that he is an inexperienced, naïve character, in stark contrast with the raving lunatics in the vehicle—an emblem of corny Americana against which this new chapter of the American Dream is contrasted.

The accidentally bizarre behavior of the car's occupants immediately sets the boy on edge. Gonzo introduces himself by saying, "We're your friends... We're not like the others," which even Duke recognizes is a creepy thing to say. However, Duke replies by threatening to "put the leeches on" Gonzo, compounding their disturbing appearance. From there, they become more and more twisted until the hitchhiker finally jumps out of the vehicle and makes his escape. His purpose has been served: Thompson's main characters have been firmly established and his reader has been hooked by this hilarious and totally unprecedented story.

There is some small measure of similarity between the hitchhiker and Jimbo from "The Kentucky Derby is Decadent and Depraved." He is another device for explaining the premise of the story, and a naïve person against whom the twisted comedy of Thompson/Duke can be employed. In this case, however, Duke and Gonzo are merely under the influence of various substances; they are not deliberately attempting to mess with this poor young man. In part two, on the other hand, they meet a DA from Georgia and tell him that Californian junkies and Satanists routinely cut people's heads off and that the problem will soon spread to the rest of the country. As he had done with Jimbo, Thompson alludes to the idea of a coming race war, again inferring institutional southern racism and tying it to a gullible moron. In the end, they explain that the police in California have begun decapitating these people as the last line of defense. The poor DA falls for the whole thing.

Once again, this is a comedy routine. The ideas they express are so ridiculous that even the most incredulous country bumpkin is unlikely to believe them, highlighting how dim-witted and out of touch law enforcement are. The cop is meant to know about drugs and crime, but his ignorance is shown up amusingly by these two drug fiends. This scene follows on from another in which Thompson lampoons the DA conference for hiring speakers that think the ends of joints are called roaches because they look like insects. His attacks on the police establishment here may not be as methodical as in "Strange Rumblings," but the comic aspect works equally well in making them look incompetent.

As with Jimbo at the Derby, the conversations with

the Georgia DA and the hitchhiker were almost certainly not real.[12] The dialogue is too perfect and can therefore be viewed as a device rather than a genuine account of events. In the Vegas book, it blends in well with a long string of fantasy scenes.

In *Fear and Loathing in Las Vegas*, Thompson was free to use his prodigious imagination to an extent he had never done before in writing, leaving the real and the imagined interwoven throughout the text. Some fantasy scenes are presented in italics to make it clearer to the reader that these are not meant to be viewed as events that genuinely occurred. Although most of them are, one way or another, introduced as figments of Duke's imagination, the book is essentially a series of drug-fueled incidents and so they involve hallucinations and imagined conversations. Their purpose is to explore the effects of the drugs taken, thereby highlighting the madness of Las Vegas. As Duke says, "Psychedelics are almost irrelevant in a town where you can wander into a casino any time of the day or night and witness the crucifixion of a gorilla."

Several times throughout the book, the horrors of drug visions are compared to normal scenes in Las Vegas either implicitly or through Duke's commentary. At one point, he very clearly articulates the similarities between taking acid and looking out your hotel window at the Vegas skyline:

> Hallucinations are bad enough. But after a while you learn to cope with things like seeing your dead grandmother crawling up your leg with a knife in her teeth. Most acid fanciers can handle this sort of thing.
>
> But nobody can handle that other trip—the possibility that any freak with $1.98 can walk into the Circus-Circus and suddenly appear in the sky over downtown

---

12   Thompson certainly claimed that they picked up a hitchhiker who claimed to have never been in a convertible before. [*Ancient Gonzo Wisdom*, p.209] However, their interactions with him were almost certainly fabricated for the book.

Las Vegas twelve times the size of God, howling anything that comes into his head. No, this is not a good town for psychedelic drugs. Reality itself is too twisted.

In those six sentences, we can see several of the hallmarks of Thompson's writing. He breaks grammatical rules in order to emphasize a point, which we can see from the two sentences beginning "But." The second begins a new paragraph in a way that jarringly changes the focus from drugs to Las Vegas. After a fantasy scene or a digression, Thompson often relies upon unconventional grammar or vocabulary to draw attention back to the main narrative. In one instance, he simply dismisses the fantasy by starting a new paragraph with "Madness, madness…" and then continuing the story. Sentence length is also used very effectively to help the ideas expressed pack a greater punch.

We also see his comic understatement ("Most acid fanciers can handle this sort of thing.") and his understanding that very specific details make a scene more vivid, believable, and hilarious. In the Jean-Claude Killy story, he used this to devastating effect, and it is constantly used throughout *Vegas*. The reference here to being "twelve times the size of God" is a good example of how much more effective the image is with this precise measurement.

Despite this essentially being a novel, Thompson makes it clear throughout that a major part of the story is to "*cover the story*" and so he often talks about being a journalist. Early on, Duke explains to the reader that he is going to Las Vegas to write about the Mint 400, but he tells the hitchhiker, "we're on our way to Las Vegas to cover the main story of our generation," which they explain is the search for the American Dream. In a sense, both were entirely true. Thompson went to Vegas to cover the Mint 400 and this later expanded into what he perceived as an exploration of the Death of the American Dream.

He repeatedly talks about trying to cover the story and explains his difficulties in doing this, which largely included his drug use. One chapter is called "Covering the

Story,"[13] but although Duke tries to follow the race, he later acknowledges that he had no idea what had happened:

> I didn't even know who'd won the race. Maybe nobody. For all I knew, the whole spectacle had been aborted by a terrible riot—an orgy of senseless violence, kicked off by drunken hoodlums who refused to abide by the rules.

From the references to covering the Mint 400, it is obvious that Thompson is Duke. To what extent this character is a fictionalization of the real Hunter Thompson is unclear, but at various times he makes little effort to hide the fact that this is a story about him. When talking about his assignment, he asks himself:

> But what *was* the story? Nobody had bothered to say. So we would have to drum it up on our own. Free Enterprise. The American Dream. Horatio Alger gone mad on drugs in Las Vegas. Do it *now*: pure Gonzo journalism.

He is admitting early on that this will not be a book about the Mint 400—it would be a book about two lunatics set loose in Las Vegas as part of a bizarre investigation into the American Dream. In a sense, it was a satire of the Horatio Alger myth. Alger is mentioned several times in the book, including the final line, where Duke says, "I felt like a monster reincarnation of Horatio Alger." In many of his books and stories, Thompson refers to Alger, author of rags-to-riches tales about hardworking young boys who pluck themselves from poverty without sacrificing their all-American values. For Thompson, this was a laughable incarnation of the American Dream that was either ancient history or pure myth.

Although he often claimed to be annoyed that

---

13   The chapters here were written in a familiar form, with different ideas (often lyrics from songs) joined by ellipses. The full chapter title here was "Covering the Story … A Glimpse of the Press in Action … Ugliness & Failure."

people wondered how much of *Fear and Loathing in Las Vegas* was true, Thompson no doubt sowed the seeds of confusion himself. In the previous quote, he mentions Gonzo journalism and he later refers to himself twice as a Gonzo journalist. He describes himself as wearing the usual Hunter Thompson attire (aviators, cigarette holder, sneakers) and also mentions his "crippled, loping walk"—a trait that made him instantly recognizable, even when out of costume. At the end of part one, he receives a telegram addressed to "Hunter S. Thompson c/o Raoul Duke," which provokes a comically confusing conversation with a hotel clerk, and in part two Duke refers to the photo of Thompson and Acosta on the back of the book and explains "That's a guy named Thompson. He works for *Rolling Stone*... a really vicious, crazy kind of person."[14] Perhaps it is understandable, then, that a reviewer for the *Los Angeles Times* repeatedly referred to the protagonists of the book as "Hunter S. Thompson and Dr. Gonzo."

In confusing author and protagonist, Thompson is again drawing attention to the interplay of fact and fiction by deliberately challenging his readers with the questions, *Is this a novel or is it journalism?*[15] and *If it is real, how much was fictionalized, and if it is fictional, how much of it really happened?* Although he grew tired of fielding these questions from interviewers over the next decades, it was obviously something he consciously inserted into his book. Some of what was described in the book genuinely happened and there is evidence for it, but of course many parts were almost certainly fictional, as we have seen.

Although the only eyewitnesses to what happened in Vegas were Thompson and Acosta, there are countless people who have confirmed Thompson's propensity for

---

14   Thompson identifies himself here but hides Acosta's identify by referring to him as "a hit-man for the Mafia in Hollywood." He asks, "What kind of a maniac would roam around Vegas wearing *one black glove?*" in reference to the single black glove Acosta is wearing in the photo. [p.195]

15   Thompson once explained that "the only real difference between 'journalism' and 'fiction' is in my own mind *legalistic*," and elsewhere claimed that "some of the country's best young writers no longer recognized 'the line' between fiction and journalism." [*Fear and Loathing in America*, p.72; p.420]

drug use, so it is tempting to view this element of the book as an exaggeration rather than pure fabrication. However, some of it was undoubtedly made up. In the book, he wrote about a drug called adrenochrome, which is in fact a real substance that he probably read about in an obscure publication, but he completely invented its effects and the fact that it needed to be extracted from a fresh human corpse.

Perhaps his deliberate confusion of fact and fiction was intended as a vessel for comedy, which is surely how Thompson thought of the adrenochrome section. His description of Duke succumbing to the effects of the drug was total fabrication but utterly hysterical, and his claim that adrenochrome needs to come from a dead body was the sort of shocking statement that he found funny. It was an extension of his pranking, where he did weird or terrible or surprising things just to watch people's horrified reactions. He found it amusing to make claims that were almost believable, but not quite, and it was a tremendous surprise to him whenever someone took his words at face value and failed to see the joke.

Fear and Loathing in Las Vegas is and always has been known as a drug book, and probably the first to take a different approach from the spiritual notion of psychedelics espoused by the likes of Timothy Leary and Allen Ginsberg. Thompson used them as a device to highlight the absurdity of Las Vegas and explore the end of the 1960s counterculture, but they were also central to the story. At its heart, this is the tale of two men doing truly vast quantities of different mind-bending substances. There is not a scene in the book where both men are sober and clear-headed.

Describing the effects of drugs was something Thompson could do well, but due to the strait-laced nature of the publications he had mostly worked for, he hadn't really had the chance. He claimed to have written the book with just Dexedrine and whiskey, but he had years of drug use to look back upon and mine for details. In particular, he was a huge fan of LSD and dabbled in mescaline, so he was familiar enough with these to draw upon the visions and sensations they cause users to experience, and these provide some of the highlights of *Fear and Loathing in Las*

Vegas. More than anything else, it was the terrifying and yet hilarious images of giant lizards that captivated readers around the world:

> Terrible things were happening all around us. Right next to me a huge reptile was gnawing on a woman's neck, the carpet was a blood-soaked sponge—impossible to walk on it, no footing at all. "Order some golf shoes," I whispered. "Otherwise, we'll never get out of this place alive. You notice these lizards don't have any trouble moving around in this muck—that's because they have claws on their feet."
>
> "Lizards?" he said. "If you think we're in trouble now, wait till you see what's happening in the elevators."

It is not all visions, of course. There is paranoia as well—the *Fear* part of the title. Although comical, Gonzo's inference that something monstrous was taking place in the elevators only heightens Duke's hallucinatory terror. Indeed, the whole book is propelled forward at a furious pace by the ever-looming specter of an unknown catastrophe. Thompson manages to convey this fear whilst at the same time presenting its absurdity in purely comedic terms to his reader. The fear and loathing of the book generally remain between the lines, with comedy on the surface.

While Thompson has long been known for his vivid descriptions of drug experiences, it is usually the shocking imagery that is credited. However, his use of language in simulating the effects and reflecting the mind of the narrator is masterful. Whenever Duke is in a relatively sober frame of mind (as in the hallucinogens are either coming on or wearing off), the prose is comparatively straight. The punctuation tends toward the conventional and his grammar is standard with only slight quirks. When Duke is confused, though, this all changes:

> The decision to flee came suddenly. Or maybe not. Maybe I'd planned it all

along—subconsciously waiting for the right moment. The bill was a factor, I think. Because I had no money to pay it. And no more of these devilish credit-card/reimbursement deals. Not after dealing with Sidney Zion.

Here, he is simulating the rapid changing of ideas in a person's head when they suddenly awaken after a long bender and are still suffering from the lingering effects of the substances they have imbibed. The short sentences in rapid succession replicate the heartbeat of someone with "the Fear." The effect is deliberately disorienting, compelling the reader to feel what Duke feels. Near the beginning of the book, the reader is introduced to this sort of confusion as narrative and reported speech blur. While going off on a standard flight of fancy, he brings the reader back by saying "Jesus! Did I *say* that? Or just think it?"

The purpose is not just to convey paranoia and confusion more effectively. What we have is an unreliable narrator, just like Thompson's old idol, Sebastian Dangerfield, and another of Thompson's favorites, Edgar Allen Poe. The reader is taken back and forth between the competing ideas within Duke's mind just as Donleavy and Poe toyed with their readers. Poe often used narrators driven by their unconscious and therefore presented the reader with information that was at odds with the reality of the world in which the story took place. An example of this is "The Tell-Tale Heart," in which the narrator is a murderer who boasts about his ability to "calmly [...] tell you the whole story," while offering an erratic and contradictory perspective told with unintuitive punctuation. Donleavy achieved the same sort of effect in *The Ginger Man.*[16] As the reader continues, he becomes increasingly aware that he cannot trust what Dangerfield tells him, so he has to guess and usually the truth comes out later when Dangerfield is caught in his lies or contradicts himself. In *Fear and Loathing in Las Vegas*, the unreliability of Duke

16   In Part Two, there is a reference to this book. Gonzo tells a maid, "Don't try to tell us you never heard of the Grange Gorman." [p. 182] Grangegorman is a suburb in Dublin that is mentioned several times in Donleavy's book.

is made clear throughout the text. In chapter one, Duke mentions his photographer, Lacerda, but by chapter three he has already forgotten: "Lacerda? The name rang a bell, but I couldn't concentrate."

The use of an unreliable narrator allows Thompson to insert more uncertainty into the text, bringing the reader further into his drug trip while providing further opportunity for comedy and paranoia. Many of his Gonzo techniques were intended to make the reader question perceived truths, and here the reader is asked to go beyond the surface details. One cannot simply believe what Raoul Duke says, as the DA from Georgia does. He lies for fun and when he tries to report the facts, he is too inebriated to do so with accuracy. Perhaps this was Thompson's point— the reader should always question the reporter or narrator.

Another benefit of having Duke as a fictional character and unreliable narrator was that it allowed Thompson to commit even more terrible acts and say worse things than in his previous work. He is able to boast about his drug use, show his reckless disregard for other people's property, and even suggest (jokingly, one assumes) that they have Lucy gang-raped by a bunch of hick cops. It is all utterly appalling behavior and yet Duke is unrepentant. Like Sebastian Dangerfield, he is a man that has total freedom because he answers to nobody but himself. The only time he comes close to an explanation is when he calls his depraved behavior part of an "act" that is essential to his "life-style."

Was this a part of his method of satirizing the regular tourists that visit Las Vegas? Or was this Hunter just continuing to do what he had done throughout his whole life, only now he could brag about it to millions of readers? If the latter point is true, it would hardly be surprising. Many people who knew Thompson during this period have commented on his cruel pranks and his unquenchable thirst for attention. He liked to push a fake hypodermic needle into his stomach and pretend to inject rum, just to make people queasy, and when invited to a fancy restaurant for dinner with an exceedingly wealthy man, he proudly dumped a bag of maggot-ridden liver on the table. His pranks could be vicious, disgusting, or careless, and as a result many people around the *Rolling Stone* offices were afraid of him.

However, it is more likely that Thompson deliberately had his characters do and say shocking things for the first of those two reasons. The despicable actions of Duke and Gonzo are not merely an indulgence on the part of the author, nor are they just a nod to *The Ginger Man*, but rather they are intended as another device. This time, the author is holding a mirror up to America. Just as in *Hell's Angels* and "The Kentucky Derby is Decadent and Depraved," Thompson's version of himself is precisely the thing he criticizes. Duke and Gonzo experience plenty of fear throughout the book, but they are never punished for their actions in any legal sense. "The mentality of Las Vegas," Duke explains, "is so grossly atavistic that a really massive crime often slips by unrecognized." Thompson's point is that Las Vegas is a place that welcomes people who are blind drunk because they are easier to fleece. No matter how terrible their behavior, they are largely accepted. Casinos tolerate them because they know drunks will lose money, and their hotels tolerate them because they are running up vast bills.

Near the end of the book, however, Thompson tells the story of an idealistic man seeking the hippie values that had seemingly been lost in the final years of that turbulent decade. This character appears to be the polar opposite of Raoul Duke and perhaps represents a version of Thompson that could have been—innocent, naïve, too far gone in the hippie mentality. Of course, when this version of Duke arrives in Vegas, he is not welcomed; he is immediately arrested, stripped naked, and when he is wired money for bail, the police steal it. In a sense, his tale is presented as the counterpoint to the story of Duke and Gonzo. This is a vicious town that welcomes those who are rich and depraved but destroys those who are poor and decent.

It is moments like this when Thompson's critique of the dominant culture bubbles to the surface and his lament for the loss of older values becomes more obvious. Although he was not a hippie, Thompson recognized in these people traditional ethics that had begun to fade from society. While some viewed them as anti-American, Thompson believed that within the hippie ethos lay a resurgence of Jeffersonian values. They made mistakes, and those are examined in the book through Thompson's assaults on Timothy Leary and his followers, but he knows that they were optimistic people with good hearts. On the other hand, he says that "The Circus-Circus is what the whole hep world would be doing on Saturday night if the Nazis had won the war." He adds "This is the Sixth Reich" to suggest that the Nixon administration is twice as evil as Adolf Hitler's Third Reich.[17] Elsewhere, he makes repeated references to the Manson family, another symbol of the end of the sixties and a reminder of how the hippie ethos had been coopted and subverted.

In *Fear and Loathing in Las Vegas*, Thompson has written a book that seeks to explain or demonstrate the loss of the American Dream in much the same way as Fitzgerald did in *The Great Gatsby*, but for Thompson it was the optimism of the sixties that represented the Dream. In Vegas, he finds the antithesis of the values and culture of this era. It is a conservative town, where "People like Sinatra and Dean Martin are still considered 'far out'…" It is a town for people who voted Nixon into office, who supported the war in Vietnam, and who laughed when protesters were shot at Kent State and beaten half to death in Chicago. These are the same people he saw at the Derby and against whom his Freak Power movement was aimed. These are the folks who gawped at the Hell's Angels, wishing that they had the guts to live the outlaw life.

Toward the end of part one, Thompson dedicates a whole chapter of the book to reflections on the sixties, which he referred to during the writing of the book as the "definitive epitaph" for the decade. Until this point, it had been a fairly linear narrative, aside from a few flashbacks. Here, however, he suddenly cuts from the story and muses on acid, looking back to his days living in San Francisco. He remembers spilling LSD on his sleeve and then imagines someone's life ruined after he walks in on another man licking the acid from Duke's sweater. This transitions into one of the most beautiful and important images in the literature of that era—a section of the book usually

---

17   In 1968, he had referred to Mayor Daley's police as "the Fourth Reich," suggesting they were worse than Nazis, but now has stepped up his assault. [*Fear and Loathing in America*, p.108]

referred to as "the wave passage," which begins:

> Strange memories on this nervous night in Las Vegas. Five years later? Six? It seems like a lifetime, or at least a Main Era— the kind of peak that never comes again. San Francisco in the middle sixties was a very special time and place to be a part of. Maybe it meant something. Maybe not, in the long run ... but no explanation, no mix of words or music or memories can touch that sense of knowing that you were there and alive in that corner of time and the world. Whatever it meant....

The first sentence has no verb, the second and third are also fragments but not even close to full sentences, and the fourth is missing a clause and ends in a preposition. Thompson switches from asyndeton to polysyndeton in the middle of the paragraph and uses the words "maybe" and "whatever" along with ellipses in order to highlight a lack of certainty, the fading sound of a word denoting its speculative nature. Though there is some alliteration— specifically of the "m" sound—to give the text a softer, almost poetic feel, it sounds more like his spoken voice than any regular literary style, and that is no accident. All of this marks a sudden shift in rhythm that signifies the beginning of an important passage, and its total disregard for grammar shows that Thompson was looking for something beyond just the nuts and bolts of language to convey feeling and meaning. This passage will be about ideas presented through sound rather than actual concrete realities.

It also tells us that Thompson was still actively mining his own letters for ideas and phrases and styles of writing that he could incorporate into his major works, as he has clearly cribbed this from a 1970 letter to Jann Wenner: "San Francisco in the mid-Sixties was a very special time ..." Beyond just those words, this paragraph is quite different from other paragraphs in that letter or others at the time, which typically did not rely so heavily upon ellipses. In that letter, he was writing about a deceased friend and recalling their time together in San Francisco's heyday—the same theme as the "wave passage." He evidently realized that using this punctuation gave him a greater degree of control over the reader's pace, allowing him to elicit a feeling of loss. The ellipses are less abrupt, less transitional than periods, semi-colons, and dashes, and they naturally invoke a drawing out of the breath, causing the words preceding it to taper off and then the pause to become longer, pregnant with meaning.

Even the idea of the sixties counterculture as a wave of optimism had been experimented with in his letters since at least 1969, when he wrote "[The 1967 'Summer of Love'] was a wild and incredible freak show here, but when winter came the crest of that wave broke and drifted on the shoals of local problems such as jobs, housing and deep snow on the roads to shacks that had, a few months earlier, been easily accessible." He used the same metaphor in 1970 when describing the potential of his Freak Power campaign: "Looking back, it's easy to say we obviously had a wave building for us—but, shit, the wave wasn't even visible to me until less than a week before the election." By the middle of 1971, while writing the book, he was still playing with wave imagery in his letters, now suggesting that he may take his own experiences exploring the 1960s acid scene and attribute it all to Raoul Duke, who is described as "riding the crest of an energy wave."

In *Fear and Loathing in Las Vegas*, he would finally bring these words and ideas together into a beautiful, extended piece of writing that possessed a musicality that surpassed almost any of his other work. For Thompson, music and literature were bound together, and the rhythm of the prose was as important as the words chosen to convey meaning, if not more so. He was always chasing the "high white note" that he sometimes called a "high white sound" or "high white noise." To him, it was the keys of a typewriter playing the most sublime music imaginable. For this reason, he considered "the wave passage" to be his best. It was the achievement of that "high white note." Just as the wave reaches its peak, he even refers to it by a telling metaphor: a "long fine flash."

His son, Juan, explained:

> He wasn't just accidentally a great writer,
> this wasn't just "I sat down and wrote Fear
> and Loathing in Las Vegas," [...] he spent a
> long time trying to get the right words and
> the right rhythm, to get it so it flowed, so
> it sounded just right. And not just how it
> read, he really thought about the rhythm,
> how it sounded.

Thompson's prose leant well to dramatic reading precisely because of its musicality. He liked to hear his work read aloud, particularly by famous actors, such as Johnny Depp, who played him in the movie version of this novel. But one doesn't have to be a talented actor to make this passage sound beautiful. His mastery of cadence in this passage to create evocative sentences is stunning and, even reading it silently, it brings chills to the spine. It is not just an incredibly beautiful, and yet terribly sad, image; Thompson's use of sentence structure, which has been entirely overlooked, is essential to making this passage so effective. His ability to compose sentences in such a poetic, musical fashion was something he had long sought to achieve, and ultimately it came handed down through the pages of other great novels.

The fact that Thompson typed out *The Great Gatsby* to "get the feel" for writing a masterpiece is important. While perhaps the influence of Hemingway (or even Dos Passos or Mailer) is more obvious, it is precisely Thompson's interest in matching Fitzgerald that gave him the sense of rhythm that marked his writing as special and elevated him above other talented and ground-breaking authors. In Fitzgerald, Thompson found a musicality that leant itself to literature and gave him the ability to create prose possessing a natural rhythm and pacing that would captivate readers. One clue to this is a quote from an early letter, in which he observes that Fitzgerald "could make a typewriter sound like a piano." Elsewhere, he mentioned picking up a Portuguese translation in Brazil, and claimed that if "Fitzgerald had been a Brazilian he'd have had that country dancing to words instead of music."[18] There can

---

18   Thompson had refused to learn Portuguese whilst living in Brazil. He explained that "a writer should not learn too

be little doubt that Thompson had found in Fitzgerald's work some musicality he wished to emulate. In attempting to understand just why this passage works so well, I decided to look at the number of syllables Thompson used per sentence. I did this because throughout his entire body of work I have felt that he had a special gift for varying sentence length. Of course, all writers do this to some extent, but I felt that Thompson's use was particularly effective, and that in certain parts of certain stories he would utilize a certain rhythm to lead his reader, stringing together clauses to build impatience like a showman building up excitement for his grand finale. What I noticed was hardly surprising. In this case, the length of the sentences actually mimics his imagery pretty accurately:

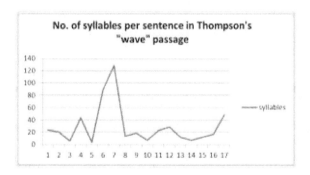

In other words, it looks very much like a wave, and a wave that peaks during his description of the cultural heyday to which his metaphor refers. But it is not just sentence length. Thompson's punctuation could be quite unconventional, but it always reflected how he believed his work should be read aloud. If we break the passage into breaths according to some basic rules of his punctuation, we can see it looks very similar to the above syllabic breakdown:

---

much of a foreign language." [*Fire Bone!* p. 151]

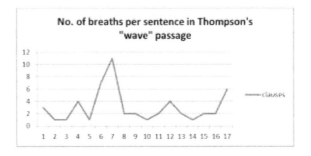

What is the significance of this, if any? To my mind, it shows a level of craftsmanship Thompson possessed that is not normally acknowledged. Here is an author whose prose is as carefully polished (at times) as any poet. As we saw previously with his shifting use of punctuation to reflect the mental state of his narrator, he was able to write in a way that reflects the underlying meaning of his story. These were not words on paper; this was music. Indeed, Thompson once told his friend, P.J. O'Rourke: "I see my work as essentially music... If it fits musically, it will go to almost any ear."

Thompson's wave can be compared to another of the twentieth century's most enduring literary images: Fitzgerald's green light. The final page of Gatsby brings us face to face with that green light, and ends with a somewhat cryptic, but rather pessimistic line: "So we beat on, boats against the current, borne back ceaselessly into the past." Thompson had always considered those "some of the highest and purest and cleanest words ever written about the real beauty of" the American Dream—Fitzgerald's own high white note. He wanted to emulate this and in *Fear and Loathing in Las Vegas* he did. Not only did he deliberately seek to write a book that was the same length as Fitzgerald's, but he also seems to have absorbed the rhythm of its famous final lines:[19]

---

19   Thompson claimed that in both *Gatsby* and *Vegas*, there was "not a wasted word" and talked about competing with Fitzgerald to write a full but short novel. [*Ancient Gonzo Wisdom*, p.205] Both books are roughly fifty-five thousand words.

On the last night, with my trunk packed and my car sold to the grocer, I went over and looked at that huge incoherent failure of a house once more. On the white steps an obscene word, scrawled by some boy with a piece of brick, stood out clearly in the moonlight and I erased it, drawing my shoe raspingly along the stone. Then I wandered down to the beach and sprawled out on the sand.

Most of the big shore places were closed now and there were hardly any lights except the shadowy, moving glow of a ferryboat across the Sound. And as the moon rose higher the inessential houses began to melt away until gradually I became aware of the old island here that flowered once for Dutch sailors' eyes — a fresh, green breast of the new world. Its vanished trees, the trees that had made way for Gatsby's house, had once pandered in whispers to the last and greatest of all human dreams; for a transitory enchanted moment man must have held his breath in the presence of this continent, compelled into an aesthetic contemplation he neither understood nor desired, face to face for the last time in history with something commensurate to his capacity for wonder.

And as I sat there, brooding on the old unknown world, I thought of Gatsby's wonder when he first picked out the green light at the end of Daisy's dock. He had come a long way to this blue lawn and his dream must have seemed so close that he could hardly fail to grasp it. He did not know that it was already behind him, somewhere back in that vast obscurity beyond the city, where the dark fields of the republic rolled on under the night.

Gatsby believed in the green light, the orgastic future that year by year recedes before us. It eluded us then, but that's no matter — tomorrow we will run faster, stretch out our arms farther…. And one fine morning —

So we beat on, boats against the current, borne back ceaselessly into the past.

Both passages describe, in quite similar terms, the near achievement of a dream that brings unprecedented hope and excitement, but which ultimately ends in failure. For Thompson, that dream was represented by a wave which "finally broke and rolled back" across America, but for Fitzgerald it disappeared into the dark fields of America and "rolled on under the night." In both cases, the authors are talking about the American Dream and the end of a period of hope for a character that represents a group of people (dreamers, optimists) in the real world. Thompson and Fitzgerald also use geography and the notion of movement across—or toward—a continent in order to symbolize the life and death of hope.

The rhythm of both passages is unmistakably similar. They begin with several sentences of varying length, setting the scene. Then they develop into far longer compound-complex sentences, layering details and ideas in multiple clauses, before finally breaking into shorter fragments, divided by odd punctuation. Both Thompson and Fitzgerald use em dashes and aposiopesis in their penultimate paragraphs, and their antepenultimate paragraphs are marked by a jumbled variety of different sentences types. It is an ellipsis for both passages that marks the breaking of a misguided sense of hope—in Thompson's it is the wave breaking, and in Fitzgerald's it is a switch from focusing on Gatsby's hopeful quest to a bleak wider reality. Both passages conclude with final paragraphs beginning with the word "So" and featuring a hypothetical person looking west, into the past. Thompson's gazes at a "high water mark" where a wave "broke and rolled back" while Fitzgerald's is "borne back" despite struggling "against the current," the flow of water in each case a metaphor for cultural progression.

If we return to the notion of syllabic construction, we can see just how similar they were:

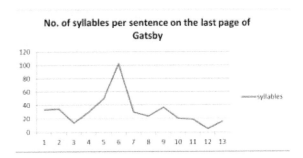

No. of syllables per sentence on the last page of Gatsby

The main difference is that Thompson's final sentence is far longer, whereas Fitzgerald's stops rather abruptly—a fittingly jarring end to the story. The extended final sentence is common in Thompson's work when a particular thread of the story reaches its denouement, and is something that had marked many of his *National Observer* articles.

To take one final close look at the composition of these passages, and to appreciate just how alike they are, we shall look at the penultimate paragraphs more closely:

> And that, I think, was the handle — that sense of inevitable victory over the forces of Old and Evil. Not in any mean or military sense; we didn't need that. Our energy would simply prevail. There was no point in fighting — on our side or theirs. We had all the momentum; we were riding the crest of a high and beautiful wave...

> Gatsby believed in the green light, the orgastic future that year by year recedes before us. It eluded us then, but that's no matter — tomorrow we will run faster, stretch out our arms farther.... And one fine morning —

The structure of these lines is remarkably similar. Both first sentences begin with a statement (of eight syllables), followed by clause that gives a definition. In that second clause, although there are a different number of syllables, the word stress pattern is essentially the same, with six content words: sense/inevitable/victory/forces/

old/evil; orgastic/future/year/year/recedes/before. What follows is a negative statement ("not in…"/ "it eluded…") followed by statements that may as well have been directly paraphrased: "we didn't need that"/ "that's no matter." These are less similar in a structural sense, but nonetheless thematically related. These short clauses build a sense of hope that is about to be dashed going into the final paragraph.

In a "letter-article" that Thompson wrote for the *National Observer* back in his early journalist days, but which was not published until his 1998 letter collection, *The Proud Highway*, he talks a lot about Fitzgerald, saying that he had recently reread *The Great Gatsby*. He starts off joking about whether the story that follows is a product of his mind or Fitzgerald's, and later he quotes a passage from *Gatsby* that blends into the article almost imperceptibly. Thompson's voice is—consciously or otherwise—very similar to Fitzgerald's. The rhythm simply doesn't change from one paragraph to the next, and this should not be a surprise given his history of typing out pages from *Gatsby* and studying it at the sentence level.

The "wave passage" may well be Thompson at his finest, but a quick look through his best works shows that this particular rhythm was not isolated. This pattern may well look, when mapped out as I have done here, like a wave, and it is likely that the rhythm followed such a pattern in order to convey the metaphor in terms of sound, but it is also a storytelling device for building interest and emotion. When he wanted, Thompson could write in this captivating manner and, as I have demonstrated, he likely took it from Fitzgerald. It is most commonly used at the end of a text, or at the end of a section within a larger piece of writing, to deliver an emotional gut-punch. It is usually used in a wistful, nostalgic sense, with twists and turns that lead us to his insightful final thought.

While much has been made of the more obvious references to *The Great Gatsby*, such as the desert and Valley of Ashes, the neon signs and TJ Eckleberg's eyes, and the Circus-Circus and Gatsby's mansion, the more subtle allusions are the more fascinating. It is this sort of craftsmanship that makes the characterization of Gonzo as mindless drug writing so unfair.

It is not just the rhythm of Thompson's prose that makes it unique or impressive. Throughout this book, we have seen the development of his style in various ways, including his frequent use of favored words. In *Fear and Loathing in Las Vegas*, of course, he uses these again. The word "swine" appears five times; "atavistic" is in there twice; "freak" is said twenty-five times; "doom" or "doomed" appears eight times, and there are eleven occurrences of "savage." He also continues to make new words, oddly coining both "doom-struck" and "doomstruck," as well as "scumsucker," "chicken-sucker," "skullsucker," and "saltsucker." The phrase "fear and loathing" appears twice within the text as does "the Fear."

In his writing, Thompson often used interjections and these reflected his real-life, spoken outbursts. In *Vegas*, he twice uses "ZANG" and "BOOM," once says "HELP!" and often includes "No!" when narrating in order to show shock at something that has occurred. Again, the function is reducing the distance between the reader and writer, putting Hunter's voice right into the reader's skull. He tended to go through phases of these words, and "ZANG" was his preferred term for the sixties and early seventies, but this was replaced later by "CAZART!" He would say the latter aloud when surprised or annoyed.

There are also references to Martin Bormann and Yail Bloor, two of Thompson's favorite names for pranking people. Bormann was the Nazi whose name Thompson often invoked when writing letters and Bloor was sometimes a character like Duke, but other times just a reference or pseudonym. The latter is used in a fake article about a riot on a ship in the Pacific, in which several members of the US Navy were "diced up like pineapple." This is, of course, another example of Thompson's violent humor and a continuation of his infatuation for weird language that had begun at Eglin.

Of course, as in almost all of his writing, he manages to find space to attack the press:

> The press is a gang of cruel faggots.
> Journalism is not a performance or a trade.

It is a cheap catch-all for fuckoffs and misfits—a false doorway to the backside of life, a filthy piss-ridden little hole nailed off by the building inspector, but just deep enough for a wino to curl up from the sidewalk and masturbate like a chimp in a zoo-cage.

Like so many of his more descriptive passages, and particularly the ones used as weapons, Thompson begins with a short sentence that makes a pretty clear point, but then builds upon this by adding a longer sentence and then a really long one that is comprised of various clauses, each adding another layer to the image. In the above quoted paragraph, Thompson has provided six different descriptions of journalism, with the last two each an image that is then modified by a subsequent detail: it is not just a "filthy piss-ridden little hole" but one that has been nailed off; it is not just "deep enough for a wino to curl up" but the wino is jerking off like a chimpanzee in a zoo. It is oddly specific and grotesque, like so much of Thompson's writing.

In his books and articles, he often used quotes—short and long—from newspapers, books, poems, songs, and so on. There are various purposes to this, including his continual assault on the traditional press and his attempt to locate the events of his story within a particular time. In "The Kentucky Derby," for example, Thompson saw newspaper headlines about "student unrest" and the "ugly war" and *Hell's Angels* featured a great many quoted materials that broke up the text. In *Vegas*, he presents numerous sources, some of which are real but most of which are fake. He includes newspaper stories that he reads, referring to drug use and torture in Vietnam, as well as sports news about Bart Starr, the quarterback whose discharge papers Thompson allegedly snuck onto the front page of *The Command Courier* at Eglin, and another football player who "destroyed a Greyhound bus with his bare hands." In part two of *Vegas*, Thompson critiques a book called *Marijuana*, written by the conference speaker, Dr. Bloomquist. Duke ridicules the book:

Dr. Bloomquist's book is a compendium of state bullshit. On page 49 he explains, the "four states of being" in the cannabis society: "Cool, Groovy, Hip & Square"— in that descending order. "The square is seldom if ever cool," says Bloomquist. "He is 'not with it,' that is, he doesn't know 'what's happening.' But if he manages to figure it out, he moves up a notch to 'hip.' And if he can bring himself to approve of what's happening, he becomes 'groovy.' And after that, with much luck and perseverance, he can rise to the rank of 'cool.'"

It is the inclusion of real material like this that makes the reader question the authenticity of made-up ones such as the following:

Indeed: KNOW YOUR DOPE FIEND. YOUR LIFE MAY DEPEND ON IT! You will not be able to see his eyes because of Tea-Shades, but his knuckles will be white from inner tension and his pants will be crusted with semen from constantly jacking off when he can't find a rape victim. He will stagger and babble when questioned. He will not respect your badge. The Dope Fiend fears nothing. He will attack, for no reason, with every weapon at his command—including yours. BEWARE. Any officer apprehending a suspected marijuana addict should use all necessary force immediately. One stitch in time (on him) will usually save nine on you. Good luck.

This passage was written by Thompson as a satire of typical warnings from police chiefs to their officers. It might seem hard to believe, but when mixed in with genuine anti-drug hysteria, it becomes difficult to know what is and isn't real. This is precisely the point. By fusing the real and the imagined, Thompson is asking his reader to use his brain—unlike the police at the convention—to decide whether a text functions as propaganda or is a faithful account of reality.

When writing "The Kentucky Derby is Decadent and Depraved," Thompson had accidentally stumbled upon the idea of using his notes to complete a story. When he saw the effect that it had, he realized that this was an effective way of presenting a scene. It kept the story moving at a quick pace and focused on details rather than the wisdom he liked to cram into his paragraphs. In the Derby story, he included whole pages from his notebook, but in *Vegas* he mostly just refers to his notes in the middle of more coherent passages. At one point, he scribbles "KILL THE BODY AND THE HEAD WILL DIE" and then remarks, "This line appears in my notebook, for some reason."

Chapter nine of part two, however, pushes this technique further. Here, Thompson begins with that classic device—the fake editor's note. It explains:

> *At this point in the chronology, Dr. Duke appears to have broken down completely; the original manuscript is so splintered that we were forced to seek out the original tape recording and transcribe it verbatim.*

It explains that this is done for *"journalistic purity"* and what follows is indeed a transcription of a recorded conversation between Duke, Gonzo, and the staff of a taco restaurant. The woman who transcribed the tapes for *Rolling Stone* years later admitted that she could barely understand what was being said in the recordings, particularly Hunter's notorious mumbles. She had to guess at some words and was very surprised when she read the story and found that the transcription was printed exactly as she had written it. However, the original tape was released in 2008 and certainly is not replicated verbatim in the book. Many small changes have been made, though mostly for the sake of clarity and brevity. As for the claim in the fake editor's note about the tape being broken, this was untrue. The quality of the recording is quite good and although they were running low on tape, they recorded what they needed and then bought more.

In the transcribed interview, Duke and Gonzo discuss with two waitresses the current state of the American Dream, with a simple misunderstanding leading to the waitresses suggesting a location. They are under the impression that "the American Dream" is the name of a nightclub that burned down. The editor's note explains that the tape had been destroyed before they found the club, but that it is possible to determine certain parts. It explains that "The owner of a gas station across the road said the place had 'burned down about three years ago,'" which would have been 1968—the year Thompson believed the American Dream had died. It was the year King and Kennedy were assassinated, the Democratic Convention turned to violence in Chicago, and Richard Nixon was elected as president. The sixties had felt like an era when anything was possible, but what few had noticed was that, despite all the talk of peace and consciousness-expansion, the American Dream had been withering away all along. *Fear and Loathing in Las Vegas* was its autopsy report.

It is possible to view *Fear and Loathing in Las Vegas* as a continuation of the work Thompson had done in the late sixties. Certainly, as I have detailed in this chapter, it includes many of his favored devices and themes from previous works, but it is also possible to view this book as a much longer version of the Kentucky Derby story. Once again, we have two men run amok in a place that represents the values of conservative America. Two completely overblown characters abuse their minds and bodies with strong substances, toy with the locals, and exhibit the most terrible behavior. Both stories feature made-up characters, events, and conversations, as well as digressions and fantasy, even though they are allegedly based upon real events. They both include a car screeching across the tarmac at an airport, with Thompson delivering his companion to the door of an airplane. There is, of course, also the subject of mace, and the Derby story even seems to end in a way that is picked up at the beginning of Vegas, with Thompson's companion pouring beer on his chest.

While it is possible to see *Fear and Loathing in Las*

Vegas as a book-length rewrite of "The Kentucky Derby is Decadent and Depraved," transposed on a similar but different environment with a different companion, Thompson believed that the Vegas story was in fact a "failed experiment in Gonzo Journalism." He explained in the jacket copy for the book that his intention "was to buy a fat notebook and record the whole thing, as it happened, then send in the notebook for publication – without editing." He goes on:

> But this is a hard thing to do, and in the end I found myself imposing an essentially fictional framework on what began as a piece of straight/crazy journalism. True Gonzo reporting needs the talents of a master journalist, the eye of an artist/photographer and the heavy balls of an actor. Because the writer must be a participant in the scene, while he's writing it.

As a piece of pure Gonzo journalism, then, the book was a failure, but as a work of literature it was a tremendous achievement and recognized as the finest early commentary on the end of the era that Thompson described with his "wave passage." His book was revolutionary for many reasons, including the fact that no one knew whether to stock it in the fiction or non-fiction section of a bookstore or library. He had created something totally original and, while most people that read it enjoyed it, few really understood what he was doing or why. Keven T. McEneaney perhaps explained it best when he wrote:

> Thompson's great achievement in *Fear and Loathing in Las Vegas* was to run simultaneous myriad intellectual threads in a synthetic manner made accessible to a large audience through its humor.

It is certainly true that this book possesses far more than most people take away from it. Yes, it concerns drugs and it is funny but, while the surface story is admittedly somewhat adolescent, the subtext is vast and complex. He may have included some notes and a whole chapter of transcribed tape recordings, but the finished version of the story was very much a polished product—the result of many revisions.

Thompson often talked about *Fear and Loathing in Las Vegas* as though it were the result of a Kerouacian marathon writing jag and delivered in one piece, with no help from anyone else, but this is not exactly true. Early on, he shared his ideas and writing with people at *Rolling Stone*, including Jann Wenner, and they gave him encouragement and feedback. Although Thompson never publicly acknowledged it, recordings of phone calls between he and Wenner that were released after his death show that his editor had a significant input on the writing process and indeed guided the story and its themes, and that Thompson was unusually receptive to changes and suggestions, even admitting that "a lot of stuff [he had previously written] is going to have to go." Of course, later he preferred to call it a "spontaneous outburst that almost wrote itself," marginalizing Wenner's input. Perhaps most interestingly, Wenner pushed Thompson to make the story about the American Dream. Thompson had already given it the subtitle, "A Savage Journey to the Heart of the American Dream," but said that this was "a joke." He had ostensibly been working on his Death of the American Dream book for several years but the Vegas story, he felt, was absolutely *not* a part of that project. It was something entirely different and the story's subtitle was intended to mock the absurdity of any attempt at covering such an amorphous subject. Wenner, however, felt that it was only logical to have the characters pursue this angle, physically searching for the American Dream in Las Vegas. Thompson agreed but stalled for a long time, with Wenner repeatedly pushing him to include this in the second part of the story. They both knew it was the right thing to do, but Thompson was reluctant.

Perhaps his hesitance stemmed from the fact that the American Dream angle had never really been his own. Tape recordings made by Thompson and Acosta in Las Vegas show that Hunter had simply wanted to goof around and see what happened, but that Oscar proactively sought out and guided their inquiry into the American Dream, taking charge of the bizarre search. It is quite possible that Thompson felt a degree of resentment at Acosta's input, much as he later resented Ralph Steadman's contributions to stories whenever he felt his primacy was challenged. He was very possessive and defensive when it came to his finest book, and eagerly downplayed any input but his own. Prodigious talents are often encumbered by unwieldy egos.

Still, despite the guidance of Wenner and the numerous contributions by Acosta, *Fear and Loathing in Las Vegas* was ultimately the product of Thompson's own warped mind and the result of many months of intensive efforts. With *Hell's Angels*, he had felt control slipping away under pressure from publishers and lawyers, but this one was his own. Some editorial input aside, this was the first and last time that Thompson had written and edited a book almost entirely by himself. No one had to rearrange the events that took place; no one had to force him to write or rewrite anything. Maybe it was four drafts, maybe it was five. The story differs. But the important thing is that it was purely the product of Hunter S. Thompson and it was like nothing the world had ever seen before.

Although tape recordings of their phone calls show that Thompson was happy with Wenner's edits on part one of *Vegas*, he was at times very defensive when it came to his writing, later telling his editor, "I seem to resent any attempts to tell me how I should write my gonzo journalism." He continued:

> Let's keep in mind that this was never a commissioned work of journalism; it was a strange neo-fictional outburst that was deemed so rotten and wasteful, journalistically, that neither RS nor Spts. Illustrated would even reimburse me for my expenses. So I'm not in much of a mood, right now, to act grateful for any editorial direction. [...] the way this thing developed has made me feel sort of personal about it; irrationally possessive, as it were [and] I'm not real hungry for advice about how the thing should be handled. It's been an

instinct trip from the start, and I suspect it's going to stay that way—for good or ill.

"Fear and Loathing in Las Vegas: A Savage Journey to the Heart of the American Dream" appeared in the November 11 and November 25 issues of *Rolling Stone* magazine and, eight months later, it was published in book form by Random House. Both versions were illustrated by Ralph Steadman, whose work was even more brilliant than for "The Kentucky Derby is Decadent and Depraved."[20] Despite having not been in Vegas with Thompson, he was able to perfectly capture the vile images described in the book, like a stark-naked Doctor Gonzo vomiting into a shoe as a horrified maid walks into the room.[21] Even if it was imperfect Gonzo journalism, the Thompson-Steadman connection was still there.

According to Thompson's widow, Anita, only seven sentences were removed from the story that appeared in *Rolling Stone*, but in fact there were a few other minor changes that occurred between the magazine and book versions. Most obviously, the *Rolling Stone* story was credited to Raoul Duke, who is in fact the narrator of the story, while Thompson chose to use his real name for the book version. Two names were also omitted from the book version at the insistence of the publisher's lawyers.

The long gap between the publication of the article and the book was for legal reasons. Acosta was unhappy with how he had been treated by Thompson and threatened to derail the whole book by suing the publishers. At the core of his dissatisfaction was the feeling that he had been used by his friend. The words and actions of Doctor Gonzo were, he felt, his own, but Thompson had not only taken them, he had changed Acosta into some

20　　Some accounts suggest Thompson invited Steadman to Las Vegas but that he declined; however, in a phone call to Steadman, Thompson said "I was going to ask you, but after [the America's Cup] I reckoned you would have had enough." [https://gonzotoday.com/2015/05/03/gonzoyesterdaze-w-ralph-steadman-drawing-vegas/]
21　　The maid is called Alice—another reference to Jefferson Airplane's "White Rabbit." She tells the men to "ask for Alice." [p.183]

clownish character. To one of the editors at *Rolling Stone*, he complained, "Hunter has stolen my soul. He has taken my best lines and has used me." Thompson had never shown Acosta the story, asked him for his opinion, or even sought his friend's permission to use his words and likeness. In Oscar's mind, Hunter thought of him as "some fucking native, a noble savage [he] discovered in the woods."

Most biographers and critics acknowledge Acosta's attempts to hinder the publication process but they come to the issue from the perspective of Thompson's letters, which excoriate his former friend as greedy and irrational. However, the tapes of their adventures in Las Vegas show that Acosta was not just a sidekick but in fact the instigator of much of what was depicted in the book. While Thompson was happy to screw around in casinos, talking endlessly about grapefruit, Acosta insisted that they pursue the American Dream story. He was not just being recorded by Thompson but much of the time directly making notes using the tape recorder, taking control of the titular "Journey to the Heart of the American Dream." It was Acosta who suggested interviewing people and it was he who conducted most of the interviews that led to the discovery of the burnt-out nightclub, but once he had left Las Vegas, Thompson dismissed him as "useless." While driving around by himself, he muttered into his tape recorder that Acosta "became the kind of monster I created in the first half [of the book]." He was referring to Acosta's increasingly erratic behavior, which saw him attend the DA's convention wearing a yellow fishnet vest, with a large hunting knife on his belt. It was once remarked that Ernest Hemingway never let a good deed go unpunished, and Thompson had a similar mentality to his hero, often throwing his friends under the bus for a shot at literary success.

Acosta was upset, too, that his identity had been obscured and that he had been turned into a Samoan. "I can sink the whole publishing house for *defaming me*, trying to pass me off as one of those waterhead South Sea mongrels," he said.[22] Even though Thompson claimed that he was protecting his friend, Acosta felt that he should

---

22   Despite this claim, Acosta sometimes pretended to be Samoan to hide his own identity.

be credited for the words and actions of Doctor Gonzo, which he believed to be his intellectual property. In the end, the book was only published after Acosta insisted that he be credited on the cover, alongside a photo of the two men. It may seem like a strange move for a man with his own legal troubles to worry about, but Acosta was not just a lawyer and sometime political figure; he was an author in his own right and determined to receive fair attribution for his contribution to literary history.

Notably, the book was dedicated not to Acosta, but to two men called Bob—his friend from Glen Ellen, Bob Geiger, and Bob Dylan, whose music had been an inspiration through the writing of both *Hell's Angels* and *Fear and Loathing in Las Vegas*. The dedication page thanks Geiger "for reasons that need not be explained here." This may have referred to some early advice the doctor had given Thompson. When he first began to ponder the notion of fusing fact and fiction, Geiger had told him, "Hunter, you are writing fiction. All writing is fiction. Experiences you experience, and words are words, so everything is fiction," which Thompson later interpreted as his own credo: "Fiction is a bridge to the truth that journalism can't reach."[23]

This brings us to one last question for this chapter: How much of *Fear and Loathing in Las Vegas* really happened? Already, I have mentioned some of the problems in establishing reliable biographical facts about Hunter S. Thompson and how this sometimes informs our interpretations of his work. In a sense, it is not hugely important what is real and what is imagined. This was precisely Thompson's point in blending fact and fiction. Yet it is obvious in this book as well as others that he *deliberately* hybridized truth and fiction, which makes it paradoxically worthwhile asking this seemingly pointless question.

Thompson grew to resent the question of whether this was a novel or a piece of journalism. He once said

---

23   The dedication could also have been thanks for help with his *Hell's Angels* book and the fact that Geiger allegedly first introduced Thompson to speed, the drug that made much of his writing possible. However, it is possible that he had been using speed since South America.

that "it should never be necessary for a writer to explain *how* his work should be read. In theory, all literature and even journalism should be taken on its own intrinsic worth."[24] When he tried to explain himself to reporters, he gave differing answers, but often these were exaggerated or distorted as much as any of his written works. In one instance, he said "I would classify it, in Truman Capote's words, as a 'nonfiction novel' in that almost all of it was true or did happen. I warped a few things, but it was a pretty accurate picture." To another interviewer, he claimed that "about 90 percent of it is true." Elsewhere, however, he was much more cautious, saying that it did not happen but subtly inferring that it did, probably as an ego trip. In short, he was never entirely candid about the realities of those two Vegas trips, and so an investigation into this matter involves some degree of speculation.

However, despite his suggestions that it was largely true, the drug use described in the book is undoubtedly exaggerated. While Thompson's actual drug use is well documented and some of what appears in the book seems plausible when compared to this, there is good reason to believe that there were hardly any drugs consumed at least during the first trip to Las Vegas, except for marijuana and Dexedrine, and that in the second trip their drug use may have been heavy but was obviously exaggerated for comic effect in the story.[25] During work on his book, Thompson wrote a letter to Jim Silberman in which he admits to having not consumed any hallucinogens during the first trip. He says that he later did drugs to experience "the same kind of bemused confusion [that] Raoul Duke & his attorney had to cope with in Vegas" and that the written version was just an "attempt to simulate drug freakout." He said that he "didn't really make up anything—but I did, at times, bring situations & feelings I remember from other scenes to the reality at hand." He then told Silberman to keep

---

24   In spite of this, he did in fact write a tongue-in-cheek guide called "Instructions for Reading Gonzo Journalism."
25   There are countless published accounts that testify to his prodigious capacity for illicit substances, but for a particularly informative account, see chapter four of Jay Cowan's *Hunter S. Thompson: An Insider's View of Deranged, Depraved, Drugged Out Brilliance.*

it to himself as the *Rolling Stone* people were "absolutely convinced [...] that I spent my expense money on drugs and went out to Las Vegas for a ranking freakout." There are some comments in tape recordings from the second trip that seem to confirm this, too, although they certainly had some drugs and were in pursuit of more.[26] As for the writing of the book, his wife claimed that it was just bourbon and Dexedrine that had sustained his long periods at the typewriter, and also the blues-jazz music of JJ Cale.[27]

In any case, to really understand the extent to which Thompson fictionalized *Fear and Loathing in Las Vegas*, we need to turn to verified facts, of which there are relatively few. We know for sure that the events described in the book did not in fact take place over the same timeline. The race and conference were a month apart but Thompson presented them as occurring just a few days apart in order to maintain a sense of "speedy madness." When *Rolling Stone*'s fact-checkers called Las Vegas to confirm a few details, they found that Thompson had made up the room number and that there was, in fact, no room 303 at his hotel. Thompson simply replied, "Don't worry about that. Let's move on." It was the same attitude he had taken with his *National Observer* editors when they called him out for making up Bible references.

As for what really happened, Thompson once claimed that "This is a tale of excess in many ways. And those details are hard to fake." But are they? He spent more than a thousand dollars on his Carte-Blanche card during the trip, in addition to a five-hundred-dollar retainer that he received from *Rolling Stone*, which he interpreted as being part of his expense budget. This suggests that he did not run out on two hotel bills but did run up vast room service bills. They did more or less destroy their white Cadillac and it does seem as though they smashed a coconut on its hood

---

26   In *The Gonzo Tapes*, we can hear Thompson and Acosta discussing drugs during the second trip. They have some marijuana, possibly mescaline, and a number of pills; however, there is no pharmacopoeia in the trunk of their vehicle. In a 1973 recording, Thompson also says he is trying cocaine for the first time, which means there was no "salt shaker half full of cocaine."
27   This was quite different from the Led Zeppelin records he listened to in Las Vegas. [*Gonzo Tapes*, CD 3, track 16]

using a hammer.[28] Thompson and Acosta also appear to have committed various transgressions that did not even make it into the book, such as ordering expensive food, then littering it with broken glass and condoms and sending it back, suggesting that their actions in the book were not entirely out of the realm of possibility. In explaining his terrible behavior, Thompson said that it was an important part of "Journalistic Science."

We can refer to Thompson's own audio tapes for some insight into how much of the story was true, and some of these have been published as *The Gonzo Tapes*. Aside from offering a fascinating insight into his journalistic procedures and frame of mind, a careful listening highlights some of the truth behind his Las Vegas story. For a start, the improbable Savage Lucy appears to have been based upon a real girl or woman that Acosta brought back to his hotel room. However, there is absolutely no mention of any of the unusual details of her life, suggesting that these were fabricated by Thompson later as he riffed upon reality.

The tapes tell the story of two men cutting loose in a strange city, but interestingly it is Acosta that pursues the idea of "the story" and covering the American Dream. Thompson seems more interested in finding ether, a drug it seems neither man has tried before. Both men appear quite in control of their faculties, yet also do and say humorous things. Thompson appears to have suffered from some minor paranoia but nothing quite like the ungodly fear felt by Raoul Duke. Acosta seems like a very, very toned-down version of Doctor Gonzo, quite frequently making proclamations and saying, "I advise you to..." Even Acosta's son acknowledged that Doctor Gonzo was a pretty accurate depiction of his father.

Amusingly, the tapes also attest to the music they listened to in their car, including "One Toke Over the Line," and they confirm that the conversation with the waitresses about the burnt-out nightclub really did happen. As for the DA convention, it appears that it was a bit boring and that the police were uninformed about drugs, but it was blown all out of proportion by Thompson in his book. He gives quite vivid descriptions of the damage

---

28   This was a scene that was cut from the novel but included in the 1998 movie adaptation.

they had done to their car and hotel room, describing vast quantities of vomit and grapefruit juice, as well as dozens of beer cans and liquor bottles. In short, it seems that Thompson's account of his visits to Las Vegas were somewhat exaggerated, with elements of fictionalization, yet heavily based upon reality. Though the book is often described as a novel, it fits quite nicely into Thompson's own definition of Gonzo journalism, which he later said was "essentially the 'art' (or compulsion) of imposing a novelistic form on journalistic content."

Still, as William Kennedy once said, "he claimed it was all true and that he could prove it with his notes, but that only makes his notes a transcript of his performance and his wild and fanciful imagination." Certainly, the cocktail napkins and tapes do exist but that does not prove that any of what he wrote really happened in any other sense than that he imagined some parts of the story while in Las Vegas. If this book were simply a novel, it would not matter, and if it were purely journalism, it would never have been published. The fact is that Thompson's most famous book was always intended to be somewhere in between this distinction, which he firmly believed was a hangover from a more ignorant time.

With the publication of *Fear and Loathing in Las Vegas*, one might think that Thompson had finally fulfilled his contract with Random House for a book on the Death of the American Dream. It certainly dealt with that subject, but it did so subtly, in the subtext. However, his editors thought it should be included as just a part of the American Dream book. Thompson strongly disagreed and pushed for it to be a separate book. Although he regarded it as a serious piece of writing, he was aware that the comic elements and the prevalence of drug abuse would detract from the tone of other pieces intended in the collection. "I can't see coming off a thing about Aspen politics (or the Murder of Ruben Salazar)," he said, "and sliding into a freakout in Las Vegas that was originally conceived in such madness that I didn't even want to sign it with my own name." He went further and explained, "I'd just as soon not be dismissed as a Drug Addled clown."

During the summer and fall of 1971, he argued with

his publishers about this, still trying to work out a way of fulfilling his Random House contract without sacrificing anything from his Vegas book. Besides, as time went by, he felt that the American Dream book was essentially a "political monster." At its heart were stories about Nixon, the Chicago Democratic Convention, gun control, and his own run for sheriff. He worried that "the style & tone of Vegas would fatally cripple any impact that" a serious political book might have.

In the end, Silberman acquiesced and the Death of the American Dream project remained on the back burner as they moved forward with something truly groundbreaking. It was a gambit that paid off, for when *Fear and Loathing in Las Vegas* was published in July 1972, perhaps surprisingly, reviewers grasped its humor and significance. In *The New York Times Book Review*, it was described as being "neither novel nor nonfiction" and lauded for its depiction of the sixties. It also called the book "the funniest piece of American prose since *Naked Lunch*." It was a rousing success, but Thompson's colleagues had a few words of caution for him: "Don't paint yourself into a corner."

Part Two
1972-2005

On the Campaign Trail

I like to think that I can still draw the line between savage humor and brute-serious journalism … but maybe not; and I suspect that when the final truth is known, if ever, there will be no real difference at all. Frankly, I've never seen one, myself.

Hunter S. Thompson

Hunter Thompson knew that he was lucky to have found *Rolling Stone* and Jann Wenner was delighted to have stumbled upon the outlaw writer with a wildly original voice. The magazine had given him the freedom to write about his own campaign for sheriff, to submit a nineteen-thousand-word essay about his friend's hunch that a reporter had been murdered in Los Angeles, and then they had published a fifty-five-thousand-word tale of drug-fueled mayhem in the desert. Here was a publication that would go out on a limb for him and put his weird words in front of a million readers. They still edited him, of course, but they allowed the drug references, the swear words, the sudden, violent digressions, and his endlessly self-indulgent misadventures. What he was writing had never been seen before, but *Rolling Stone* appreciated and encouraged it. "He taught me that different writers have different styles and that we shouldn't make them fit some mold that isn't theirs," said David Felton.

They knew from the start that Thompson was special and he was handled very delicately by the *Rolling Stone* staff. Many of them hated him for his temper, his ego, and his bad habits, but he was an untouchable. In a magazine about rock stars, this writer was fast becoming the literary equivalent—the Mick Jagger of journalism. His work elicited mountains of fan letters and even imitators. Before long, his name was on the masthead and he was earning a handsome salary on top of his ludicrous expenses. Finally, there was a home for Gonzo journalism that paid more than a hundred dollars an article. He could pretty much write what he wanted, and soon he wanted to write about politics.

When Thompson first wrote for *Rolling Stone*, Wenner was still cautious about including political content for fear of upsetting his advertisers but, by the early seventies, this was no longer a necessary or even profitable position. It had been easy for a rock and roll magazine targeted at young people to stay out of the realm of politics, but now the distinction was blurred. Elvis Presley had visited the White House in December 1970, and in July 1971 the voting age had been lowered from twenty-one to eighteen. With the peace and love hippie ethic fast becoming part of history and change very much in the air, Wenner allegedly quipped, politics "will be the rock and roll of the Seventies." Could politics be the next challenge for his star writer? Was it even possible to do Gonzo journalism in the context of a presidential campaign? It was a new era and there were no precedents to follow.

When Wenner arranged an editorial conference at Big Sur in September, few people expected the announcement that came on the final day. After four days that most attendees judged to be among the most boring of their lives, Wenner explained that a political campaign was, in many ways, just like a rock 'n' roll tour, and then informed the room that Hunter Thompson would be sent to Washington DC to cover the 1972 presidential campaign. It was an announcement that earned a huge outburst of laughter from nearly everyone in the room. To most of them, Thompson was a clown, a freak, and a novelty. Yes, he had substantial talent, but he was not a *serious* writer, was he? Only Wenner, Thompson, and a young writer called Timothy Crouse kept straight faces.

By the time "Fear and Loathing in Las Vegas" appeared on the pages of *Rolling Stone* in November 1971, Hunter S. Thompson was already on his next assignment. On November 1, he set off on the long journey from Woody Creek to Washington DC, traveling by car with his wife and child and Doberman. For most of 1971, he had been under the impression that he would go to Vietnam to report on the war, but his September 1 leaving date came and went. The sad truth was that the war would still be raging when the campaign ended.

Hunter arrived early in the morning and had to hit the ground running. He knew very little about politics aside from what he had learned during his own Aspen campaign, and what he had learned there only applied to Colorado laws and small-town elections. From the offset, he was swimming against the current. Not only did he have little knowledge of national politics, but he also lacked contacts and resources. He had been given the position of editor of the National Affairs Bureau but he had only one person working for him: a talented young journalist called Timothy Crouse.[1] Wenner was not willing to pay for Thompson to do the sort of research he wanted, and demanded that he write reports from the first moment he arrived.

But this was good. It provided the perfect Gonzo lens through which to view a presidential campaign. Even before Gonzo had earned its moniker, Thompson's schtick was being the outsider—the "frantic loser," to use Tom Wolfe's words. His best reporting looked at a story through the eyes of an incompetent journalist, struggling desperately to find out what was going on and usually failing. He was not a Washington insider and he never would be. This campaign would be covered like he would cover anything else—with lots of hard work, plenty of chaos, and total subjectivity. This was a one-off job, he thought, so he could afford to build bridges and then burn them down. His motto was: "Nothing is off the record."

Ahead of him was one whole year of messy campaigning, involving untold hours following various candidates. The Republican president, Richard Nixon, would be seeking re-election and so, for most of the year, he would be following the Democratic candidates as they vied for the right to challenge the incumbent. Thompson was vehemently anti-Republican, but at the same time he was far from being a Democrat. Ever since 1968, he had

---

1   Crouse had joined the magazine in 1970. Wenner despised him but Hunter was fond of him and so he was tolerated by the editor. [*Sticky Fingers*, p.204]

hoped the Democratic Party would tear itself apart and that out of its ashes new parties would form, returning America to its Jeffersonian roots rather than a crooked duopoly. He viewed the field of candidates largely with contempt and some of them were almost as abhorrent to him as Nixon. The only one that stood out as potentially decent was George McGovern, a senator from North Dakota, who had come out publicly against the war and in favor of amnesty for draft dodgers.

Throughout the campaign, Thompson struggled against deadlines that were far easier than those facing other journalists. *Rolling Stone* came out once every two weeks, giving him plenty of time to gather material, decide on his focus, and write an article. Somehow, though, each deadline saw a frantic struggle between Thompson and his editors as he attempted to lash together a manic report. The result was a series of articles that presented the campaign in a completely new light. Pretty soon, it was not just the usual readers of the magazine that were admiring Thompson's Gonzo reporting. Other members of the press were picking up copies of *Rolling Stone* and beginning to ask why they were confined to writing such boring reports.

For one whole year, Thompson zipped back and forth across the nation in search of stories, writing from hotel rooms or an office in his rented Washington home that he called "the Fear Room." He turned in articles to his editors at *Rolling Stone*, sending them via Mojo Wire, which was Hunter's name for the early, portable fax machine that *Rolling Stone* provided him for submitting his assignments. He wrote one article in January and February, two for March and April, one for May and June, two for July, and then one for each of the remaining months except July, when he wrote two pieces. His final campaign article appeared in November 1972, and after that he devoted his time to compiling the articles into a book—*Fear and Loathing on the Campaign Trail '72*. Follow-up articles were published in February and July of 1973.

Perhaps unsurprisingly, Thompson's first report from Washington begins more like a novel than a piece of political reporting. The article, published in January as "Fear and

Loathing in Washington: Is This Trip Necessary?" starts, "Outside my new front door the street is full of leaves. My lawn slopes down to the sidewalk; the grass is still green, but the life is going out of it." It is a description of his new home in Washington and it once again puts Hunter Thompson at the forefront of the story, rather than any piddling presidential campaign.

But if it sounds like the start to a traditional novel, this notion is soon quashed by the lines, "I burn a vicious amount of firewood these days [...] When a man gives up drugs he wants big fires in his life." On the next page, he tells us that he urinates off his front porch and then says that an "evil nigger" has thrown a newspaper through his window and that his Doberman has responded by savaging the poor man. The effect is an odd juxtaposition of tame reporting and unconventional, aggressive details.

He builds the story slowly, describing his surroundings and setting the scene. His prose is relatively conventional but there are certain quirks of style that make it very much a Hunter Thompson piece of writing, if not purely Gonzo like his most recent work. He often uses ampersands, such as in this piece of wisdom: "Life runs fast & mean." Certain words are capitalized against the rules of grammar in order to lend a certain importance to that word. Thompson had done both of these in his letters and a few published pieces of writing going back almost through his whole life, but they became much more common as time went by.

There are also, of course, references to drugs. He had told us in the second paragraph that he had given up drugs, possibly as a way of deflecting any unwanted attention after the publication of "Fear and Loathing in Las Vegas" in *Rolling Stone*. However, he was surely aware that the readers wanted and expected at least some drug references. In this first installment, he picks up two potheads whose car has broken down. These young men are used as a device for Thompson to relate his mission to the readers of the magazine, making them the equivalent of the hitchhiker Duke and Gonzo picked up on their way to Vegas. They are clearly intended as stand-ins for typical *Rolling Stone* readers, and Thompson explains to them that he has just arrived in Washington to cover the presidential campaign.[2]

This convenient setup allows Thompson to introduce himself to his readers. He had already talked about his home, but now in meeting these young men, we see that he is carrying a gun and a big bottle of Wild Turkey. Even after he begins to dig into politics for the first time, he comes back to himself, mentioning his habit for going off on tangents. He even states that *Fear and Loathing in Las Vegas* would be about two hundred pages of just tangents. This ends his first dispatch. He may have included the line "Welcome to Washington," but really he could have called this article, "Welcome to the World of Hunter S. Thompson."

Of course, as with all of his writing at this point, each installment of his campaign report was prefaced by a series of subheaders that offer fleeting summaries of the chapter, each part just a few words and separated by ellipses. For the first report, they read:

> Is This Trip Necessary?... Strategic Retreat into National Politics... Two Minutes & One Gram Before Midnight on the Pennsylvania Turnpike... Setting Up the National Affairs Desk... Can Georgetown Survive the Black Menace?... Fear and Loathing in Washington...

In his next report, "Fear and Loathing In Washington: The Million Pound Shithammer," Thompson comments on the state of journalism and the difficulty of his job, and tries to set himself apart from other journalists by saying that, in Washington, they all "dress like bank tellers." It was clear in the first piece that he wanted to set himself at or near the center of the story but as an outsider, unfamiliar with the territory yet oddly entitled to deliver authoritative statements. This was something he would continue to do throughout his reports from the campaign trail, often detailing his own misadventures alongside actual reporting on the candidates.

---

2   As their names are Lester and Jerry, it is not hard to imagine they were named for *Rolling Stone* writer, Lester Bangs, and Grateful Dead singer, Jerry Garcia.

He again informs his reader that he is here to cover the campaign, but this time he stresses that it will not be the usual political reporting. He makes clear that this is not an exercise in objective journalism while at the same time setting out his philosophy of reporting, explaining to his readers what to expect from these dispatches. He writes:

> Objective Journalism is a hard thing to come by these days. We all yearn for it, but who can point the way? The only man who comes to mind, right offhand, is my good friend and colleague on the Sports Desk, Raoul Duke. Most journalists only talk about objectivity, but Dr. Duke grabs it straight by the fucking throat. You will be hard-pressed to find any argument, among professionals, on the question of Dr. Duke's Objectivity.

This is one of his stranger comments on the idea of objectivity, as clearly Duke was about as far from objective as it was possible to be. Perhaps Thompson was trying to be funny, or perhaps he was implying that Duke was so upfront and open that his reporting could be viewed as objective. Thompson sets himself very much apart from this, saying, "As for mine... well, my doctor says it swole up and busted about ten years ago." He goes on to suggest that only a CCTV camera is capable of objective journalism and advises his reader: "Don't bother to look for it here." The implication is that traditional journalism is dull and Gonzo is exhilarating.

No one has ever accused Thompson of being objective when it comes to politics, and his campaign reports are considered a classic largely because of their uncompromising approach to describing the candidates. Indeed, shortly after explaining his lack of objectivity, he calls McGovern a "far-left radical bastard" and then descends into a weird fantasy about Hubert Humphrey that contains the phrase "million pound shithammer." *Fear and Loathing on the Campaign Trail '72* contains some of the most innovative and yet disgusting descriptions of political figures, including President Nixon, ever written, and these were printed alongside hideous illustrations by Ralph Steadman that added yet more grim darkness to the tale.

This second campaign story contains a lot more politics than the first but, even when attempting relatively straight political analysis, Thompson tends toward wild and unpredictable statements and ideas. He doesn't just say violent things, but instead takes off on crazy tangents to stories from the past in which he exhibits bad behavior, then tries to tie it to present thoughts, mixing in politics and sport. It is a bizarre combination and yet one that works for him. He ends the chapter by saying, "we're all fucked. [...] I feel The Fear coming on, and the only cure for that is to chew up a fat black wad of blood-opium [...] and get locked into serious pornography." Certainly, it was not the sort of campaign report that would grace the front page of the *New York Times*.

The following month, he pushed these themes further, admitting to using drugs, describing himself drunk driving, and calling himself an "egomaniac." The story follows his personal meanderings as he picks people up in his car and then discusses life, youth, and the sixties, while tying it coherently to a narrative of his own journalistic efforts, as well as the reality of national politics. It is, then, a more mature and complicated piece of writing than the first two, with all its different threads woven together carefully. There is a lot of his usual wisdom and he is now pushing his own political convictions.

Some critics have commented that the first few months of his reporting on the campaign trail resulted in weaker work than the rest of the book, but that is unfair. These were certainly different, and perhaps a little cautious, but they were not bad articles. In the framework of the book that contained all of his campaign writing, they function as an excellent introduction. If his aim in writing about the campaign was to involve the reader in the journalistic process, then it makes sense that we can see the writer establishing his first contacts and settling into the routine.

By late February, he was writing about how boring it was to cover a presidential campaign. When discussing the realities of trying to keep up with all the candidates, he complains that the public want "a man who can zap around the nation like a goddamn methedrine bat... sucking up the news and then spewing out the 'Five Ws.'"[3] The whole thing, he says, is "fucking dull." He explains, "With the truth so dull and depressing, the only working alternative is wild bursts of madness and filigree," which hints at the events to come. From this point on, Thompson moves constantly toward the center of the story and begins to interject more anger and humor.

In March, Thompson hit his stride with the articles "Fear and Loathing in New Hampshire" and "Fear and Loathing: The View from Key Biscayne." It is at this point that he seems to realize the real strength of his highly personal Gonzo journalism. By using all the devices at his disposal, he is able to make boring stories (or in the case of the Kentucky Derby, complete non-stories) into exhilarating, fast-paced tales of madcap adventure. One of the methods that he uses to succeed was communicating his present difficulties to the reader in order to emphasize the struggles he faced, thereby infusing the text with tension. After a long political passage, he suddenly stops and says, "it needs a bit more thought than I have time to give it now." It is a strange confession for a man ostensibly writing an article about politics; however, the narrative feels more immediate and relatable because of this.

Thompson frequently tells his readers about the process of writing. He is often up against a deadline or attempting to reach a certain word count. He writes this sort of thing frantically, stressing the importance of doing it before suddenly taking off on another tangent or returning to the main thread of the story. This commentary engages the reader and keeps them focused while the story meanders between different ideas. At one point, he says, "We seem to have wandered off again, and this time I can't afford the luxury of raving at great length about anything that slides into my head." He then tells the reader the deadline date and the remaining number of words he has to write. Elsewhere, he says, "It's almost dawn now... as soon as I finish this gibberish I can zoom off to Florida." The whole

---

3   This refers to the basic rule of journalism—reporting on what, where, why, when, and who. Thompson took this sentence, like many others in his book, from a letter he sent to Wenner. [*Fear and Loathing at Rolling Stone*, p.152] In both, he jokes that he cannot actually remember all five.

thing is an extension of the conspiratorial tone he had built within previous articles, bringing the reader into the story alongside him, foregoing the detachment offered by conventional political reporting. His first-person, stream-of-consciousness prose, with the minutiae of journalistic processes foregrounded, results in the same effect that Kerouac had achieved more than a decade before with his "spontaneous prose," creating a heightened sense of immediacy, removing the barriers between author, reader, and subject.

Throughout his career, Thompson was at his best when writing about impending doom. Douglas Brinkley once called him "a bull that carried his own china shop around with him" and Jim Silberman said "If there was *a worst way* to see something, Hunter saw it." He seemed determined to find a looming catastrophe, and he believed that this was what made it possible for him to produce great art. In interviews and letters, he often described the last-minute battle as an adrenaline rush and suggested often that he could not write well without it. After all, it was the *Scanlan's* deadline that had forced him into creating Gonzo. When his work lacked any real sense of drama or urgency, he could simply create it himself through paranoia or by bringing the reader into his own self-made apocalypse—a deadline that, if broken, could ruin his career. It was an extension of the Edge philosophy espoused in *Hell's Angels*. Sure, the reader knows how it ends, but somehow they are brought into the desperate frenzy that seems destined to lead to the author's doom.

This concept of bringing the reader into the process is taken to another level with the infamous Boohoo story that occurred in March. In a sudden Gonzo twist, Thompson becomes the protagonist and invokes a companion in the form of an unnamed *New York Times* reporter. He tells the story of his involvement in an incident on a train in Florida, but rather than present any sort of linear narrative, he goes into detective mode and tries to unravel the mystery.

First, he begins with the public story, which was that a strange man heckled Senator Ed Muskie as he delivered a campaign speech from his train. According to the story, that man was Hunter S. Thompson. As he relates this amusing tale, working backwards to find the truth, it becomes clear that he gave his press credentials to a man whom he calls "the Boohoo." He explains that the man, named Peter Sheridan, was down on his luck and in need of a free ride home. In fact, Jann Wenner explained in *Gonzo* that Sheridan was really Thompson's friend, Monty Chitty. The pair agreed for Chitty to cause a scene so that Thompson could write about it, hinting in the story that he had been responsible for the whole affair but never actually admitting it.[4]

When the story has gone on long enough, Thompson again brings the reader behind the scenes:

> I'd like to run this story all the way out, here, but it's deadline time again and the nuts & bolts people are starting to moan... demanding a fast finish and heavy on the *political stuff.*

The Boohoo story was Thompson's first really exciting report from the campaign trail. It was the first time his readers would have read the article and asked, "Can he *do* that?" or "Did that *really* happen?" Sure, there had been a few flights of fancy throughout his articles, but this was the first time that he appeared to intervene, quite possibly affecting the success of Ed Muskie's campaign. It was not, however, the last.

In April, Thompson included an excerpt from a monthly newsletter put out by Pharmchem Laboratories about a drug called Ibogaine. He went on to suggest that Muskie had been using Ibogaine, citing a rumor among the press. After the campaign, he would admit that he had started the rumor but that he had reported on it in such a way that he assumed no one would take him seriously. "I didn't realize until about halfway through the campaign that people believed this stuff," he said much later, explaining that he thought people went to the "traditional media" for information and read his work for fun. Of course, he did not lose much sleep over the matter: "Fuck 'em if they can't take a joke," he said. "[A]lmost everyone who read it

---

4   Thompson and Chitty were visited by the Secret Service and questioned before Thompson was given his press credentials back.

understood what was Gonzo and what wasn't. What the fuck. I can't be held responsible for the rest." He claimed that everything he wrote about Muskie that was untrue had been "*worded* as a fantasy," and therefore he was still writing the truth because he said there was a rumor—and this was *true*; it just conveniently omitted the part about him starting the rumor.

Certainly, in Thompson's mind there always seemed to be an obvious distinction between what he presented as true and what was included for satiric purposes. Jay Cowan explained: "When it came to important stories and political pieces, he tried to be very clear about what was obviously invention." Of course, that did not mean his readers understood exactly what he meant, but sometimes it was rather obvious, such as when he cited a *New York Times* report about Ed Muskie crying and beating his campaign manager, before an Asian woman attacked them. Thompson begins a new paragraph:

> Now that's good journalism. Totally objective; very active and straight to the point. But we need to know more. *Who* was that woman? *Why* did they fight? *Where* was Muskie taken? *What* was he saying when the microphone broke?

Thompson often referred to "the five Ws" of journalism with a mocking contempt, and in this case it should be clear to all but the most gullible readers that he was being bitingly sarcastic.

In addition to spreading humorous rumors, he was not afraid to say horrendous things about the candidates, from plain insults to including them in his violent fantasies. Of all the Democrats running for president, Hubert Humphrey was the one he loathed the most. He wrote that, "with the possible exception of Nixon, Hubert Humphrey is the purest and most disgusting example of a Political Animal in American politics today." He suggests that Muskie might revert to violence, calls him a "wiggy bastard," and claims that a presidential candidate is "like a beast in heat: a bull elk in the rut, crashing blindly through the timber in a fever for something to fuck." Meanwhile,

McGovern, whom Thompson considered the only decent candidate in the field, was doomed because of his "hard, almost masochistic kind of honesty."[5]

It is, of course, pure bias. Thompson is attacking those whom he dislikes and praising the man he likes. He felt empowered to insult candidates, spread rumors, and even give his press credentials to lunatics because the whole system for reporting on politics was deeply flawed in his mind, skewing the odds against the most decent candidates. He agreed with H.L. Mencken that "the only way a reporter should look at a politician is down," and thus was appalled when other reporters repeated candidates' claims even when they knew them to be completely false. In his mind, Gonzo political reporting leveled the playing field. It was more honest than regular reporting because it aimed to report truths creatively rather than repeat propaganda in plain language.

After a few months, the stress of the campaign trail was beginning to wear on Thompson. He was struggling to meet his deadlines and turning in writing that was inconsistent at best. "This is about the thirteenth lead I've written for this goddamn mess," he wrote, "and they are getting progressively worse." His writing had gotten better between January and April, but it started to dip in quality over the months that followed. It is clear from reading these sections that he had produced lots of short pieces of writing and then attempted to patch them together to make an article. It is something he had done many times before, but with such a high volume of material, it quickly became stale and repetitive.

For several years now, he had beguiled readers with his behind-the-scenes tales of journalistic derring-do but now he was just writing about writing. The constant references to deadline pressure work as a means of pulling the reader into the story, but when repeated too often they lose their power. Instead, there are long sections where he is just writing about needing to write and not being able to. It feels like a student's report on a book he has not actually read. He is killing time, eating up words, and giving his editors something—anything—to publish. There are

---

5   McGovern later said that "He was very perceptive. It was a very accurate portrayal of my character." [*Hunter*, p.154]

some excellent sentences or paragraphs, but these are disconnected and often repetitive.

In May, Thompson failed to report on the shooting of George Wallace, even though he was not far from the action, and so he inserted Crouse's article into his own. With nothing of his own to contribute, he again went back to the Kentucky Derby epiphany and used his notes. It had worked when walking around Churchill Downs, recording the things he saw and heard, but in a piece of political writing it is just tedious. These were merely notes about TV reports on the primaries. He had used a single line from a notebook in an earlier campaign report, but that was very much for effect. Here, it feels like a crutch.

The following month, he wrote, "Jesus! Another tangent, and right up front, this time – the whole *lead*, in fact, completely fucked." Then, later, after yet more commentary on his own lack of ability to write, he explains:

> My brain has slowed down to the point of almost helpless stupor… So this article is not going to end the way I thought it would… and looking back at the lead I see that it didn't even start that way, either. As for the middle, I can barely remember it.

Partly, he was playing the role of the helpless, incompetent journalist in order to give the reader a character to follow through this story, but it was also the truth of his situation. There had been a few missed deadlines or weak articles over the years, but now he was struggling to write. In the late sixties, he had excuses for missing assignments, but by 1972 he had everything he needed and it still wouldn't happen. Crouse often had to help him as a deadline loomed. He explained:

> One of Hunter's methods of composition was to write a bunch of ledes and then somehow fit them together. By lede, I mean the opening portion of a story, which is ordinarily designed to pack more of a virtuosic wallop than the sections that follow. Early on, I remember,

Hunter showed me a stack of ledes he'd accumulated, as if he were fanning a whole deck of aces. On a tight deadline, my job would sometimes be to stitch together the lede-like chunks that Hunter had generated. Ideally, the story would function like an internal-combustion engine, with a constant flow of explosions of more or less equal intensity all the way through.[6]

There was an entire team devoted to Thompson on deadline day and for the inevitable days that followed when they would still be waiting for his copy to arrive. "To edit Hunter Thompson was debilitating," Alan Rinzler, one of his editors, explained. He would send his story piece by piece. If Crouse had managed to string it together, it might be somewhat coherent, but usually it required the editors in San Francisco to pull together the cluster of leads he had sent, desperately attempting to make something from the mess of disconnected ideas. Thompson had a complex system for numbering pages, but to some of the editors it seemed like he was just making it up to screw with them.

Crouse observed that, when Thompson wrote, he would sit up and wait for inspiration, then write in sudden jolts of energy. He interpreted this as an attempt to bypass conventions and tap into some innate sense of what needed to be said. Despite references to drugs in his work, Crouse also claimed that Thompson wrote only on beer.[7] Rinzler commented that "In those days, he was very serious about his writing," and had not yet become "a babbling idiot." Thompson's own account of his writing process was that he would begin work at about 5:00 p.m. but only start writing at around midnight. "By that time, I'm pretty spaced out on booze and speed," he remarked. Looking back on this period, his wife, Sandy, recalled:

6   This quote is from *Gonzo*. In that book, "lead" is spelled in two different ways, and in this part it is spelled "lede." I have kept the original spelling.
7   Numerous people in Washington noted that Thompson appeared sober, even if he had a drink in his hand. They were surprised to know about his reputation for drug use.

He wanted to be read and thought of as a serious human being, a serious writer. And what happened was different. I mean, *Fear and Loathing in Las Vegas, Hell's Angels*— he rewrote and rewrote and rewrote and rewrote those. He had a lot of pride in those. With *Fear and Loathing on the Campaign Trail,* things were beginning to get harder for him.

Even though his political writing used vicious insults and involved bizarre fantasies, Thompson did not believe that should stop it from being factual. The *Rolling Stone* editors agreed, but Thompson typically submitted his work long after the deadline had passed and there was rarely enough time for anything to be fact-checked. When questioned about inaccuracies, he wrote a memo to Wenner:

> I still insist "objective journalism" is a contradiction in terms. But I want to draw a very hard line between the inevitable reality of "subjective journalism" and the idea that any honestly subjective journalist might feel free to estimate a crowd at a rally for some candidate the journalist happens to like personally at 2000 instead of 612... or to imply that a candidate the journalist views with gross contempt, personally, is a less effective campaigner than he actually is.

He went on to say that being subjective meant being brutally honest and reporting what you *feel* is the right thing to report. He explained that if he saw a candidate doing something unethical, he would not hesitate to present it in a way that would help the truth be known. "No doubt I would look around for any valid word or odd touches that might match the scene to my bias," he explained. His example is that if he saw a group of wealthy men making dubious campaign contributions, his reporting would draw attention to, for example, one of them wearing a monocle.

Later, in a memo reflecting upon the campaign, he wrote about arriving at an airport after McGovern's defeat to Nixon. Sander Berger was driving away from the airport when one of his passengers realized that they had left their suitcase behind. Berger pulled a U-turn across the median and drove back to get it, but in Thompson's versions of events, this became a metaphor for a sense of suicidal despair felt by McGovern's staffers. Berger later explained: "I think it's a good example of Hunter's technique, which was to take some event and then explode it into a story line that was compatible with the story already in his own mind."

In the memo, he did admit to getting some facts wrong and acknowledged that it was his fault. He offered a very rare apology, highlighting the importance he placed upon truth in political reporting. Frank Mankiewicz, McGovern's campaign manager, famously said that "It's the most accurate and least factual book about the campaign" and many would agree, but Thompson still felt that he had gotten most of the facts right, too. Even when he did get facts straight, his tendency to include the occasional run of pure fantasy distracted readers and earned him a reputation rather in opposition to the factually accurate reporter that he purported to be. He was aware of this and later lamented:

> I did all that craziness because I thought it was funny. But I think a lot of it was definitely harmful. It hurt my effectiveness. Like when I was denouncing Nixon in the terms that I did. That image took the edge off some of the fairly acute judgments that I made.

In July 1972, *Fear and Loathing in Las Vegas* was released and Thompson became even more of a celebrity in Washington. His articles in *Rolling Stone* had drawn people's attention, but now people were asking for his autograph. With the attention, of course, came trouble. He had worked long and hard to gain contacts and had become skilled at catching people off their guard. Now he was famous, however, it seemed everyone paid attention to him. He could not as easily speak with the people he needed to contact. As George McGovern's campaign started to take off, he became increasingly distanced from it. When he tried to go undercover at a Republican event, he was quickly recognized.

Even the press was reporting on Thompson's work. *Newsweek* called him "the counter-culture's most-listened-to voice during this election campaign," while *The Morning News*, out of Wilmington, Delaware, called him a "notorious [...] scourge of politicians [and] bane to mundane journalism" in their half-page profile. The writer went on:

> Thompson's free-wheeling style, devastating imagination and quick perception make his articles the most entertaining if irresponsible reading to come out of this election year.
>
> He may fabricate or exaggerate half his scenese [sic], but he captures a mood.

Although the quality of the writing did deteriorate at times, his coverage of the 1972 presidential campaign was generally groundbreaking. In spite of the digressions and some repetitiveness, it is always engaging and funny. He makes the campaign trail seem exciting, usually through his own flights of fancy, such as when he talks about "the Fixer." In describing the shady backroom dealings that occur throughout the political world, he descends into a sick fantasy in which a politician is drugged and forced to rape a child so that he can be blackmailed. Elsewhere, he imagines Frank Mankiewicz having his big toes cut off and envisages Nixon as a werewolf.[8]

As with previous works, these often-disturbing fantasy scenes are not just funny but serve other purposes. In the case of the "the Fixer," it is obviously a greatly exaggerated version of the truth. By "exploding" the truth into something even more horrendous, Thompson feels

---

[8]   For the Mankiewicz fantasy, he uses italics to make it clear that this is something purely fabricated, just as he had done in *Fear and Loathing in Las Vegas*.

that the reality is more visible. It is for the same reason that he goes into imagined scenes in the histories of England and the Deep South to explain the archaic—or, Thompson would say, *atavistic*—nature of George Wallace. If the regular press weren't conveying these ideas effectively with plain truth, Thompson could dress it up and get the message across more clearly.

He borrows another device from *Fear and Loathing in Las Vegas* when he includes a long, "98 percent verbatim transcript of" an interview with McGovern's "point man" Rick Stearns. Conducted on the beach and edited only to protect a source, the interview is the most extended on-topic political discussion of the book. Here, the reader gets to witness Thompson actually acting like a reporter, asking pertinent questions and maintaining a civil dialogue for an extended period.[9] It very much stands out from the rest of the writing he did on the campaign.

Like most of his writing, Thompson refers often to sports when discussing politics. He frequently draws a connection between the two fields. In one instance, he compares the meanness of politicians to tight ends in football, and elsewhere he compares political battles to boxing matches. After talking about politics, he moves on to discuss gambling in football. He says that "it gets harder to convince yourself, once you start thinking about it, that it could possibly make any real difference to you if the 49ers win or lose" before then explaining the problem of voting in a presidential election, which is that he could never find a candidate to vote for and instead was "always being faced with that old familiar choice between the lesser of two evils."

Thompson often brought sports into his writing, just like another of his favored topics: motorcycles. He had a natural affinity for both and was usually at or near the top of his form when writing about these subjects. At the beginning of his June article, "Fear and Loathing: Crank-Time on the Low Road," he explains, "I am growing extremely weary of writing constantly about politics" and then proceeds to review a new motorcycle. During this

9   Audio recordings of Thompson's interviews from the sixties and seventies show him to be an eloquent, intelligent interlocutor, constantly asking insightful questions.

review, he makes frequent digressions to politics. It is an odd reversal of what he had done thus far, ostensibly writing about politics and going off on tangents to other topics.

In August, he returned to the companion device in order to explain his theories about the political field with a character called Bobo the Pimp.[10] Thompson makes clear that he has to "compress about two hundred hours of work into sixty seconds" and then tries to explain what he thinks about Nixon and McGovern. When Bobo cannot understand it, Thompson explains what he means in simpler terms, and then Bobo repeats it back to him.

In earlier works, he had pranked people by telling them things that weren't true. Now, taking the place of Jimbo and the cop from Georgia are a group of young Republicans. Thompson tells them that an NBC reporter, John Chancellor, spiked his drink with acid, and then describes the trip: "It came up my spine like nine tarantulas." Again, it is an amusing image because it is so specific and weird. Not *a* tarantula; *nine* tarantulas. As for the gullible Republicans, Thompson presents them as about as intelligent as Jimbo and the cop. They are unfamiliar with the term "acid" but click when Thompson tells them that it means LSD. "Golly" is about all they can add to the conversation.

Toward the end of the book, the quality of the writing begins to pick up. In the final months, Thompson realized that McGovern's campaign was doomed and he became bitter about the whole thing. The anger brought out some of his best work. When he was mad, he could write brilliant but often violent descriptions. In September, when it was obvious that Nixon would win re-election, he wrote another of his great passages:

> This may be the year when we finally come
> face to face with ourselves; finally just lay
> back and say it — that we are really just
> a nation of 220 million used car salesmen

---

10   Thompson used the name "Bobo" occasionally when addressing Paul Semonin and also called Birney Jarvis, his first Hell's Angels contact, Preetam Bobo, in the book. In his second article for the *National Observer*, one of his contacts was a Dutchman named "Boeboe," who was likely invented.

with all the money we need to buy guns, and no qualms at all about killing anybody else in the world who tries to make us uncomfortable.

[…]

McGovern made some stupid mistakes, but in context they seem almost frivolous compared to the things Richard Nixon does every day of his life, on purpose, as a matter of policy and a perfect expression of everything he stands for.

Jesus! Where will it end? How low do you have to stoop in this country to be President?

This was followed by a short but brilliant chapter. Just three pages in the paperback edition of *Fear and Loathing on the Campaign Trail '72*, it is the writer at his sarcastic, vitriolic, creative best. In it, he describes Nixon as "a drooling, red-eyed beast with the legs of a man and a head of a giant hyena" as it leaves the White House one dark evening. It is his most devastating put-down yet of Richard Nixon, the man who was fast becoming his nemesis. It seems that Thompson's writing flourished when he had something to battle against, and particularly when it was something as heinous as Nixon.

The final weeks of the campaign were tough ones. Although they inspired some of Thompson's best writing, he was deeply unhappy and threatened to quit the magazine four times. *Rolling Stone* had taken issue with his expense claims, initiating a vicious battle of words between Thompson and Alan Rinzler. He wrote his editor:

I have never been much of a Christian, Alan, but I'm still Christian enough to warn you that if you come anywhere near me between Nov 8 and Jan 1, your hair will be cotton-white by groundhog day. A lot of people in publishing have knee-calluses, but not many can say what it's like to scrape scar-tissue off the bottom-side of their hip-bones—but your letter of Aug 1 indicates that you might be a pioneer of sorts, in that field.

To be fair, Rinzler had been quite patient and accommodating, offering to increase Thompson's payment for the book but stop paying expenses. He hoped that this would encourage his writer to be more reasonable with his expenditure, which had reached more than twenty thousand dollars by the middle of the summer. Battles of this nature would continue to plague his writing for the rest of his life, and sadly caused numerous promising books and articles to be aborted.

He spent those last weeks on the "Zoo Plane," which was the chaotic press plane that followed the candidates. When McGovern lost, Thompson flew to San Francisco and was put up at the Seal Rock Inn. The publishing arm of *Rolling Stone*, Straight Arrow Press, was going to print his campaign reports as a book and they had given him until January 1 to complete it. He needed to rewrite some of his articles and tie them all together, then pad out the final months with interviews because he had not written very much.

For the November section of the book, readers encountered another fake editor's note explaining that Thompson had been unable to finish his assignment, and so he had a conversation with Rinzler, which was recorded on a Nagra tape recorder. Thompson paced around the room, talking into a mic on the end of an eighteen-foot lead. Every few hours, people from *Rolling Stone* would come by and take the tapes to be transcribed, as Rinzler and Thompson talked for forty-eight consecutive hours. In the interview, Thompson is discursive and reflects well upon the now-finished campaign. He explains ideas better here than elsewhere. He is more coherent and focused, reviewing key points and not taking the sort of sudden digressions that he did in his writing.[11] This device is used again in his December article, along with an interview between Thompson and McGovern.

---

11   This coherence is perhaps due to Rinzler's line of questions, which they edited out of the final copy, making it seem as though Thompson was speaking more freely.

The book was finished several weeks later than planned because he wanted to include the Super Bowl as a conclusion. For this final chapter, Thompson gives a deranged description of the event, structured like a poem and filled with wild details. He then talks about sports writing and what he has learned from it, before saying "and here we go again, back on the same old trip: digressions, tangents, crude flashbacks… When the 72 presidential campaign ended I planned to give up this kind of thing…" It is not much of a conclusion and there is little in the way of reflection on the campaign. The book just ends.

Fear and Loathing on the Campaign Trail '72 contained excellent pieces of writing but it was largely stitched together. He had lost his ability to weave the threads and themes of a story or even write coherently for more than a thousand words, and so personal anecdotes are inserted into longer political passages to break them up or, when they are already disjointed, to link them. It is a good enough book due to the quality contained in those magnificent flourishes, but it was ultimately imperfect. However, that is what Thompson usually sought to achieve: a series of "high white notes." "I don't know about you," he told a friend, "but in my own mind I value peaks far more than continuity or sustained effort." He said that, when he read, he was more attracted to books that were dull for longer periods with sudden flashes of brilliance because the "high white notes" made it worthwhile.

Ultimately, the book succeeded because it was entirely different to anything anyone had written before it. Thompson had broken new ground by writing about the campaign in his Gonzo style—violent, rude, drugged-up, filled with fantasies, and "produced in a last-minute, teeth-grinding frenzy." It worked, he felt, as "more of a jangled campaign diary than … a reasoned analysis," with his role as "an eye in the eye of the hurricane." And that is perhaps as good a summary of the book as any.

In spite of the criticisms I have leveled at it in this chapter, *Fear and Loathing on the Campaign Trail '72* is a book about a political campaign from—at the time of writing—nearly a half century ago and yet it is still funny, relevant, and genuinely interesting. It was just like *Hell's Angels*, "The Kentucky Derby is Decadent and Depraved," and *Fear and*

Loathing in Las Vegas—Thompson had done something that no one else had ever done, and in the process created a timeless work of art. He had brought his own inimitable style to it and, even if it wasn't perfect, it was shocking, original, and hilarious. People loved it and, by 1973, Thompson was the author of three highly acclaimed and incredibly original books. He was famous enough that, in book reviews or articles about him, people would use his signature words and phrases. He didn't just have a famous name; his style of writing was so unique that it was known to readers across the country.

Gonzo Grows Stale

He couldn't write. I mean this is what he had always done. This was what he lived for. And all of a sudden he couldn't do it. He could go down in the basement. But it just wasn't happening. He was taking a lot of drugs. He was just getting really crazy, more violent.

Sandy Thompson

Throughout the 1960s, Hunter S. Thompson had developed his writing into something that, with the publication of "The Kentucky Derby is Decadent and Depraved," became known as Gonzo. He then worked with *Rolling Stone* to put his name in front of millions of people, earning praise for his unconventional genius. One journalist even explained to his readers that "Like Bob Dylan, Thompson is, to a small but fanatic following, a living legend, an authentic culture hero." But how many of his legions of fans really knew the difference between Hunter S. Thompson the writer and Raoul Duke the fictional character?

He had created a genre of writing so astoundingly original that only he could do it. As soon as *Fear and Loathing in Las Vegas* was published, others tried to imitate him, but no one could pull it off without sounding like a cheap facsimile. He had staked out his territory and created his own legend, but with this immense achievement came a problem that many had foreseen. Alan Rinzler had warned him not to become trapped in his gimmicks, but even by *Fear and Loathing on the Campaign Trail '72* it was obvious that he was struggling to avoid this fate.

When he first discovered Gonzo, he asked why he should bother trying to write any other way if he could "get away with" sending in torn-out pages of a notebook. It was an interesting innovation that earned him acclaim, but it could easily become a way of avoiding real work. For more than a decade, he had sweated over each word in his articles, desperately trying to find the right way to express an idea or capture an image, but it seemed he no longer cared. Rinzler observed that, "After [*Fear and Loathing in Las Vegas*] he was getting lazy, he didn't want to work that hard on each sentence." It was an observation many of the people around him made.

Gonzo was like a drug for Hunter. It was different, it was dangerous, and it was fun. But it was also addictive. He explained: "I'm pretty well hooked on my own style – for good or ill – and the chances of me changing now are pretty dim. A journalist into Gonzo is like a junkie or an egg-sucking dog; there is no known cure."[1] Of course, while it worked it was fine. With a defined style and a famous name, he could easily get writing assignments and command high fees for his work. But it was never enough, and there was another problem that had begun to plague him.

In Washington, Thompson sometimes acted out the role of Raoul Duke in public, but friends observed that he was comparatively normal in private. Through his books and articles, he had taken care to describe himself in ways that fit a larger narrative—that of the iconoclastic outlaw journalist, always dressed in a Hawaiian shirt and canvas sneakers, with a cigarette holder in one hand and a beverage in the other, often wearing aviator sunglasses, blundering his way awkwardly through his world, constantly enraged by the inconveniences and injustices around him. He made sure to live up to this image, as well as to the madcap prankster that he could be in his writing. There are countless tales from this era that attest to his eagerness to cause chaos and mayhem wherever he went, making sure that everyone knew they had crossed paths with the Doctor, but he lamented that he was becoming trapped in the character he had created. "I'm never sure which people expect me to be," he said. "Often they conflict." The wonderfully weird character that he had created for himself was rapidly becoming—to use one his favorite

---

1   Thompson repeatedly used the phrase "egg-sucking dog" throughout his writing. Like "swine," "atavistic," and many other unusual words and phrases, it entered the Gonzo lexicon.

literary allusions—his albatross. It was something he had keenly observed when reflecting upon Hemingway's suicide: "The strength of his youth became rigidity as he grew older."

When the campaign ended, Thompson sent Wenner his resignation but agreed to continue working for *Rolling Stone* on a freelance basis. After eighteen months of constant work, he was "physically and mentally & emotionally drained" and hoped to relax a little at Owl Farm. He was upset with Jann Wenner, too, for a number of reasons, but he knew that it would not be wise to burn this particular bridge. He had found a pretty tolerant group of people who would print just about anything he wrote and show it to a million or more people; however, he wanted more freedom and less pressure.

He was also keenly aware that he was under contract to Random House and owed them a book on the death of the American Dream. He had insisted upon *Fear and Loathing in Las Vegas* as a separate entity and so that had not fulfilled the contract, and *Fear and Loathing on the Campaign Trail '72* had been published by *Rolling Stone's* publishing arm, Straight Arrow Press. For five years now he had owed Silberman and Random House this elusive book and he was not enthusiastic about the prospect of paying back his advance.

He retired to Woody Creek and enjoyed life at home, away from the relentless action of the campaign, but he wrote and told Jim Silberman, "I want to get started on another book immediately." He had been working on another novel, one which he considered a "sequel" to *Vegas*. It was "a short, Vegas-type novel called 'Guts Ball,' a saga of madness & terror in the first-class compartment of a DC-10 on a midnight coast-to-coast flight from Washington to Los Angeles," but he noted that the story lacked realistic characters.[2]

The idea for *Guts Ball* came to Thompson whilst very high and lying in bed in the dark. He claims that the story appeared like a movie projected on a screen hovering

---

2   In 1974, still toying with the idea, he told Ralph Steadman that he expected him to illustrate it and called it "another *Vegas*." [*Gonzo Tapes*, CD 4, track 19]

in front of him. It is about Nixon's cronies returning to California, disgraced and ruined, after being forced to resign in April 1973.[3] With some Secret Service agents, they begin a game of football on the plane, forcing the other passengers to join in through intimidation, violence, and drugs. Predictably, the flight turns into a debauched orgy. "You have to imagine this movie unrolling," he told an interviewer. "I was hysterical with laughter." He described the process for getting the ideas out of his head and saved for posterity:

> I got a little tape recorder and laid it on my chest and kept describing the scene as I saw it. Just the opening scenes took about 45 minutes. I don't know how it's going to end, but I like it that way. If I knew how it ended, I'd lose interest in the story.

In 2008, this tape was released to the public and we certainly can hear Thompson laughing a lot, even though there is nothing obviously funny about what happens. However, we can reasonably assume from the situation he describes that the violence, chaos, and sheer absurdity would have been rendered in the same sort of dark comedy as *Fear and Loathing in Las Vegas*, squeezing humor from antics that would otherwise be appalling. As he talks and laughs into his tape recorder, Thompson describes the story in a surprising amount of detail, although the plot is no more complex than the short summaries he gave reporters. Indeed, that was the problem with this and other fictional stories that he attempted—it was an idea that was funny and had some outrageous elements that would shock its readers, but it was essentially just a single, extended scene. Thompson, however, believed that *Guts Ball* could be a novel, a movie, and even a Broadway play. Rather than fixating upon the story as a novel whose plot needed some serious development, he became obsessed with its financial value.

---

3   The original idea came to him in February but the events depicted occurred in April, showing that he had changed the details slightly. In interviews and letters, he suggested it came to him all at once but this is not possible.

Guts Ball was never written and so what is known about it is largely confined to a few interviews and the recordings he made. However, there is a lot that can be gleaned from his recorded ramblings. For one thing, he seemed to suggest that the theme was: "Nobody knows who's crazy; the lunatics appear to be saner than the others." Thompson's description of his planned novel sounds thematically quite similar to *One Flew Over the Cuckoo's Nest*, Ken Kesey's 1962 novel set in a psychiatric hospital, and of course the phrase "Guts Ball" was actually used several times in that book. Another theme that he appears to suggest is the conflict between East Coast and West Coast attitudes and values, which is something Kesey explored in his second novel, *Sometimes a Great Notion*.[4]

It is not clear to what extent Thompson would participate but he does use "we" a lot when talking about the passengers, so it is possible that he or Duke would have featured in the novel. It would also involve a great deal of madness, violence, and drugs, so it was hardly a departure from his recent efforts. He suggests that the people on the plane are heavily into Quaaludes, so it would likely be a reprisal of his drug adventures from Las Vegas, but it appeared to have more complexity, with extensive use of flashbacks to explore the characters' childhoods and backgrounds. Still, he was aware that his characters once again lacked depth, telling Jim Silberman, "the characters are still 2-dimensional, so I'll have to give it more thought." *Fear and Loathing in Las Vegas* had worked as a series of hysterical, insightful, and just plain weird scenes with two completely overblown characters, but his other efforts at fiction fell flat because he could not sufficiently bring them to life.

Although he talked about the book for several years, often weighing its potential against journalistic endeavors, it appears that he developed it little beyond his original audio recording. He had managed to sell the concept to a publisher on the basis of a rough outline, but throughout the 1970s he repeatedly put it aside in favor of other projects. In each case, the deciding factor was money. Five years after coming up with the concept, he explained to an interviewer: "I sold a novel called 'Guts-balls,' [sic] which I

---

4   The phrase "guts-ball" appears in this novel, too. [p.30]

never wrote. It's getting much more lucrative for me to sell ideas than it is to sell writing."

To Wenner, he wrote about his willingness to continue writing for the magazine, but without the tyranny of constant deadlines. Not only did he loathe the pressure, but he had grown embarrassed during the campaign about his inability to write. Every two weeks, he was pinned down by the editors and forced to produce something that he knew was not his best work. He explained: "I think it's about time I get back in the habit of writing at least a *second draft* of my gibberish, instead of lashing all this last-minute lunacy into print for no reason except to fill space or justify some ill-conceived headline in *RS*."

He also acknowledged that during the campaign he had been using a huge amount of amphetamines to keep himself going. This obviously came at a cost. "One of the central tenets of my concept of chemical 'speed,'" he said, "is that it is not energy in itself, but merely enables the brain & the body to tap *latent natural energy resources,* which amounts to willfully trading—on a two or three to one basis—time Now for time Later." This theory was quite possibly correct because, from the end of the 1972 presidential campaign onwards, Thompson always struggled with his writing. He had worked for a long time on this borrowed energy and that quite possibly accounts for the litany of failures that followed his meteoric rise to literary stardom.

Despite his fame and hard work, Thompson was not in a position to take a year off writing. He had earned good money working for *Rolling Stone,* and even after he quit they kept sending him a thousand dollars a month as a retainer. Yet he was terminally broke due to his profligate spending. Even worse, Straight Arrow had botched the printing of his new book, meaning that only five hundred copies were initially available for sale. It sold very well in the years that followed, but in 1973 he needed to line up more freelance work to pay the bills.

He had tried writing for *Playboy* several times in the past and, after too many bad experiences, swore that he was done with them. Likewise, the editors had promised that Thompson's name would never sully their magazine. However, now that he was a literary celebrity in need of some extra money, both parties suddenly became open to working together. In late March, they sent him to Cozumel to write about a deep-sea fishing competition. It took him an astonishing eighteen months to complete, but the story finally appeared as "The Great Shark Hunt" in December 1974, alongside writing by John Irving, Gene Wilder, and Arthur C. Clarke.

By now, there was virtually a Gonzo formula and "The Great Shark Hunt" would not stray far from the script. He was not going to Mexico to watch a fishing competition, then file a report that listed the winners and losers alongside the weight of their catches, with maybe a dash of philosophizing against the background of Latin American politics. It would be the story of Hunter Thompson *trying* to write about fishing—and encountering various problems. He took along a friend, Michael Solheim, to act as his sidekick, then proceeded to get inebriated and start lots of trouble in order to give him something to write about.

"The Great Shark Hunt" begins with a familiar scene: Thompson is in a hotel room, wondering how to flee from a massive bill and meet up with Solheim's character, Yail Bloor. He then sets up the story for his reader:

> This one had all the signs of a high-style bag job: Fly off to the Caribbean as a guest of the idle rich, hang around on their boats for a week or so, then crank out a lefthanded story to cover expenses and pay for a new motorcycle back in the Rockies. The story itself was a bit on the hazy side, but the editor at PLAYBOY said not to worry.

From there, it is largely just Hunter being Hunter, building his legend by telling stories from his past. He talks about drugs, getting fired from *Time*, and suffering from the bends after a scuba accident.[5]

As in the Kentucky Derby story, he is at the

---

5   This story was concocted from an unpublished fiction piece, which will be discussed later, but he repeated it often enough that it became a part of the Hunter Thompson legend.

competition to write about the people who are there rather than the event itself. In amidst the descriptions of his own craziness, he drops in snippets of other people's speech at a drunken party. Thompson and his friend take LSD and roam among the drunks, seeming relatively normal by comparison. It is also very much a repeat of *Fear and Loathing in Las Vegas*, as they hallucinate lizards and create comical chaos in their drug-addled state. Just as Doctor Gonzo had done in *Vegas*, Bloor acts as a vessel for the most outrageous statements and actions, telling some rich tourists that violence was about to break out on the island. Of course, it is hard to overlook the fact that Bloor's voice is suspiciously similar to Thompson's, a common theme throughout much of his writing.

There is not much of a plot and what story there is largely concerns Thompson and Bloor getting intoxicated, acting badly, and forgetting things, with the occasional mention of fishing. They do, however, manage to get aboard a boat, but quickly come to the conclusion that deep-sea fishing is "insanely fucking dull."

The story only really becomes interesting when it is time for the two men to return to the United States. Whilst flying home, the pair realize that they are loaded down with leftover drugs. They know that entering the US with their pockets filled with various illegal substances would result in decades of prison time, but they are not willing to flush it in the airplane toilets. Instead, they decide to take everything in such a way that they can pass themselves off as mere drunks. The only question is how to time their consumption for just the right effect.[6]

It is Thompson at his best—talking about drugs and being hysterically funny. However, the point of the story is essentially the same as in *Vegas*. Solheim and Thompson will take drugs but pretend to be drunk, knowing fine well that Customs will not trouble a drunken American tourist coming back into the country any more than a Vegas casino would turn away a blind-drunk customer.

---

6   According to Solheim, this story is largely true. He and Thompson did attempt to get back into the US and were forced to consume almost all of their stash. Thompson stored some in his shoe and the pills really did fall out as they walked through Customs, just as Thompson recounts in his story. [*Hunter*, p.172]

330

"Well. . ." he said finally, "what if we eat this stuff and go crazy – and they nail us?"

"Nothing," I said. "We'll drink heavily. If we're seized, the stewardesses will testify we were drunk."

He thought for a moment, then laughed. "Yeah. . . just a couple of good ole boys O.D.'d on booze. Nasty drunks, staggering back into the country after a shameful vacation in Mexico – totally fucked up."

In pretending to be "good ole boys" coming back from Mexico, it extends the critique of the wealthy, drunken tourists in Cozumel. When Thompson mentions the potential prison sentences they would receive for being caught in possession of narcotics, it also serves to critique the hypocrisy of a system that will gladly allow drunks to fly into the country, but will prosecute drug users even though there is no discernible difference in their behavior.

Alas, although the story is very funny at times, it was a little too similar to his previous work and showed the extent to which he had already become trapped in the Gonzo style and the Duke persona. Thompson was aware of this and not keen to have comparisons drawn. When David Felton said in an interview that "The Great Shark Hunt" was just a pale imitation of *Vegas*, he became defensive: "Let's not compare this stuff to the Las Vegas book. Vegas was like four or five drafts. Probably the further back you go in time, the more rewrites we get in each piece. The newer stuff, almost without exception, is essentially journalism, as it was written on the day, sent in for a deadline, not edited, either then or now, and published."

When he says this, it shows that he believes the lack of editing to be the optimal way of conducting Gonzo journalism, but given the astonishing decline in the quality of his work after *Fear and Loathing on the Campaign Trail '72*, it is perhaps easier to view it as an explanation for his downfall as a writer: He was no longer willing or able to do the hard work required to produce great writing. Tom Wolfe noted many years later that Thompson was not as funny in person because his writing was the product of careful revision: "You read Hunter and you think, 'Well, boy! This stuff is just pouring out of his head as fast as he can write it down!'—as if he were Jack Kerouac, who was supposedly doing automatic writing. But he worked at it. Those funny lines were not instantaneous."

While Thompson was in Mexico for the fishing competition, the Watergate story took on an entirely new dimension. It became clear that there was a massive cover-up leading to the highest office in the land, and so he met up with Oscar Zeta Acosta to discuss giving it the Gonzo treatment. The two men had fought bitterly over *Fear and Loathing in Las Vegas*, and would remain on acrimonious terms, but they put aside their differences to work on a story for *Rolling Stone* that Thompson called "Fear and Loathing in Acapulco." It was never published but Thompson worked on the story in Mexico and then back in Woody Creek in late April, aiming to submit it to Wenner by May 1.

In *The Gonzo Tapes*, we can hear Thompson and Acosta collaborating. Their story was about attempting to interview Henry Kissinger and in the available recordings we can hear them writing one of Thompson's fake editor's notes and also a fake telegram requesting money. They plan out ideas for the plot, which revolves around the exploits of Raoul Duke and Doctor Gonzo, but Thompson and Acosta often seem to mix up their real and fictional identities. To complicate matters, both Duke and Thompson are also characters in the story, with Duke assigned to care for Thompson, who has suffered a breakdown after his time on the campaign trail. It is obvious from the recordings that Acosta was an integral part of the writing process, constantly questioning Thompson and pushing him to improve the story, and also contributing his own ideas, such as taking Kissinger to a brothel. When doing so, it is not entirely clear where Acosta ends and Gonzo begins. "I got a couple of broads to go over there and start playing with his tits and his prick," he says, again suggesting that he could not separate himself from his alter ego.

Like "Fear and Loathing in Las Vegas," it would be credited to Raoul Duke rather than Hunter S. Thompson and would feature many "vicious subheads" to introduce the story. Although this was almost entirely a work of fiction, their imagined adventure results in failure and most of their conversations revolve around how to articulate their failures in comical ways, with them settling on a final, satisfactory concept: Thompson is taken scuba diving on a reef and surfaces too quickly, suffering the bends and having to be placed in a decompression chamber. The nearest one, he reasoned, was in Miami. This is the original version of the famous story that wormed its way into various other articles.

"Fear and Loathing in Acapulco" was intended as a sequel to *Fear and Loathing in Las Vegas*, with Duke and Gonzo back for more drug-fueled weirdness. Sadly, although it was extensively planned out, the story was never published. By June, Thompson had not turned his "loosely-constructed notes" into a full story and was "beginning to feel guilty" about having not done any real writing since the end of the campaign. It is not entirely clear why he did not write "Fear and Loathing in Acapulco," but it seems likely that it was due to another falling out with Acosta that occurred in the months after their Mexican reunion. Acosta believed that Thompson had sold the movie rights to the Vegas book and wanted to be compensated for his role in creating it. Perhaps Hunter knew that it would not be wise to once again profit from his friend's ideas and likeness.

The Watergate story appeared to be a godsend for a writer famous for his outspoken criticism of the president. There had been various attacks on Nixon in his work so far and, with the publication of his campaign articles and then the book that collected them all, he had become perhaps Nixon's most public of enemies. Now the president was in real trouble and millions of readers eagerly awaited a Gonzo interpretation of the unfolding scandal. Woodward and Bernstein had done the legwork, but they weren't gobbling tabs of acid or luring Kissinger into a brothel, and for all their meticulous research, they stopped short of describing the president as a slobbering werewolf.

Thompson had been in the Watergate Hotel during the burglary, using the swimming pool in the basement, but of course he could not have had any idea of the monumental event that was unfolding. Even when the story broke, he hadn't given much thought to it but, as the coverage developed in 1973, he was fixated upon his TV. "Watergate is about the only thing that interests me right now," he told Frank Mankiewicz in June. He had no plans to write about it, though, because he was in Colorado and limited by the news he could get through the TV or on the phone.

That was just fine for him. He explained to William Kennedy that he "couldn't live with the horror of" going to Washington again for work, adding "it's better on TV anyway." He was quite happy to enjoy the comforts of home, with the tedium of Washington confined to a TV screen. To the reporter, Hughes Rudd, he spoke of a "perverse refusal to cover Watergate." It was the story of the decade and it led to the end of his nemesis' presidency, but he could not get up the enthusiasm to report on it.

Eventually, after dragging his heels, he realized that he could not let this story go by without writing something, and he prepared for a return to Washington DC. There were two pieces of writing Thompson produced about Watergate—one from Owl Farm and the other when he was in the capital. The first was a memo under both the names Raoul Duke and Hunter S. Thompson, called "Memo from the Sports Desk & Rude Notes from a Decompression Chamber in Miami," which was published in August; the second was "Fear and Loathing at the Watergate: Mr. Nixon Has Cashed His Check," and this appeared in late September.

The memo largely talks about Thompson and his absence from public life. He mentions his trip to Mexico and again claims that he suffered from the bends after being involved in a serious scuba accident, reusing the idea he had developed with Acosta.[7] It is composed of several editor's notes, a letter from Duke, and a short article from Thompson. There is some talk about the Watergate scandal but mostly that is saved for the longer article in September. It is not a great piece of writing by any means, serving little purpose except to further build Thompson's personal mythology. William McKeen called it "mere treading water" and said it was "a strange and somewhat incoherent

---

7   He claims that the doctor treating him was called Dr. Squane. This, along with Bloor, was one of his favorite names for pranks and weird references in his writing.

story," which is an accurate assessment. When Thompson went back to Washington, everything had changed. His campaign book had been quickly released and positively reviewed. He was now a celebrity and even journalists asked him for his autograph. Whenever he attempted to get near the action, people watched him closely. *Was he on acid?* they wondered. *Was he going to do something crazy?* He looked around for a story and interviewed some people he knew from the '72 campaign but found nothing interesting, and certainly nothing that the traditional press hadn't already published. Instead of continuing to dig or stand around being asked for autographs at the trial, he met with Ralph Steadman and his wife and they conducted most of their "research" by the swimming pool at the Hilton.

There wasn't much action to get close to, anyway. The trials were dull and although he looked forward to Nixon's resignation, he couldn't get very excited about the whole process. There was no room for Gonzo reporting here; it was time for the traditional press to report the details of the trial. He had no inside information for his readers, so he had to present the trial from his perspective as a detached onlooker. As for madcap adventures, he devoted a lot of the article to a plan that involved kidnapping Charles Colson, Nixon's political saboteur, and dragging him behind a car down Pennsylvania Avenue. It can be inferred from the tapes of Acosta and Thompson planning "Fear and Loathing in Acapulco" that they kidnapped Kissinger, so this is another rehashed idea.

"Fear and Loathing at the Watergate" was another run-out of Thompson's recent literary playbook. There were fake editor's notes, fantasy dialogue, drugs, madness, and weird conversations. At the heart of it all was the reporter and his metajournalistic story. He discusses the state of the American press again, but this time concludes that they are finally doing their job. It is a rare compliment and a tacit acknowledgement that there were limitations to Gonzo.

Naturally, with this being a Gonzo story, Thompson felt the need to include some of his notes. These are prefaced:

> In any case, the bulk of what follows appears exactly as Dr. Thompson wrote it originally in his notebooks. Given the realities of our constant deadline pressure, there was no other way to get this section into print.

At one point in the story, he mentions his plans for kidnapping Colson and then calls it a "strange and violent reference." This structure (ADJECTIVE + AND + ADJECTIVE + NOUN) was another of his quirks, and often the first of those words was "strange," just like the subtitle for his first book, "A Strange and Terrible Saga." He liked to fill his writing with as many adjectives as possible and simply adding two before a noun was an easy way to do it. Ruth Prigozy observed that Fitzgerald's adjective use was also intensive and unusual. She explained that he used uncommon combinations of words to highlight the ambiguities of the era, such as describing Jordan's "charming, discontented face" or even assigning unlikely adjectives to inanimate objects, like "triumphant hat-boxes." Elsewhere, we have a character described as possessing a "tragic nose." Still, while Fitzgerald leaned on adjectives, Thompson took this to another level, and some passages of his work are loaded with these descriptive words, used with much less subtlety than Fitzgerald.

In this story, Thompson also introduces the word "Cazart!" Following a well-worn path, the word was tried out in his letters for about a year before being used in an article, and then it became a standard part of Gonzo vocabulary. He had heard this word in Brazil and hoped to import it into English and have Random House include it in their dictionary. He defined it as going beyond "mere shock & surprise; it also implies an almost doom-rooted acceptance of whatever grim situation has suddenly emerged." It was less "Oh shit!" and more "Oh shit! I should have known!"

The result was not his finest piece of writing. Biographer, Paul Perry, noted that the article "went on long after it had anything more to say" and quotes a *Rolling Stone* staffer who said, "Hunter always threw everything into his stories, including the kitchen sink. It was just that this time the kitchen sink was from K-Mart." Paul Scanlon said that Thompson's writing had become "screed without substance," and that is perhaps the best assessment of Gonzo journalism after 1972. Even Hunter himself noted in June 1973, after having reread some of his old work, that "I used to be a lot more coherent writer than I seem to be now."

Although he struggled to write both the Watergate story and "The Great Shark Hunt" at the same time, Thompson did manage to finish both pieces, which is sadly more than could be said for *Guts Ball*. After an enthusiastic start, the project petered out and the book was never written. In late 1974, he said that most of the story was on tape and not yet written, but by early 1976, he admitted that it was "in limbo" and after that it was referred to as just an idea he once had.

Later in 1973, the *Rolling Stone* editors sent him a reissued version of Sigmund Freud's *Cocaine Papers* to review. It would be dishonest, he felt, to talk about cocaine without trying it first. Strange as it may seem, until this point Thompson had avoided the drug because it seemed like a silly rich person's indulgence—"a drug for fruits," as he once put it. He binged on this new substance but remained thoroughly unimpressed, saying that it made him sound drunk and provided no obvious positive sensations. As the days went by, he continued his "experiment" but seemed at times uncertain of his purpose, suggesting that his aim was to "test [his] reactions against Freud's theory" perhaps in order to write an introduction to an excerpt. Speaking into his tape recorder, he said, "My name is Yail Bloor" and then simply reviewed the effects of cocaine. None of this, however, was published.

Cocaine, he quickly discovered, was not a good drug for productivity. It did not make him want to sit and write, and he had "no desire to read further in that fucking book." After five days of heavy use, he said it was at the "bottom of [his] list" in terms of drugs but noted several times that "the puzzling thing about coke is the desire for it despite any ability to explain why desire for it exists." This was a prophetic remark because, for the rest of his life, he would remain helplessly addicted. Before long, the drug's effects on his literary output would be highly detrimental. When he timed his bumps correctly, he could stay up for days on end, but despite having the time to work he struggled to put words on paper. Cocaine was fun but it came at an enormous price: it robbed him of his ability to write.

Douglas Brinkley observed that, after Hunter tried cocaine, his productivity nosedived. He is quoted in McKeen's biography as saying Thompson went from writing twenty good pages per day to just twenty per month. Timothy Denevi, in *Freak Kingdom*, noted that cocaine and fame marked a major turning point in his career, after which he was only capable of writing short pieces. After dabbling with coke, Denevi wrote, Thompson could "never again find the dedication and perspective to render the heart of the American condition – especially within a political context – in the way his more sustained work once had." Juan Thompson agreed, saying that his father's downfall came "almost certainly because of the cocaine and booze." David Felton went into more detail in *Gonzo*, emphasizing the burden that Thompson's addictions placed upon others:

> The problem was, when he was on cocaine, from my perspective, he really had a hard time concentrating on his writing. It would be very frustrating to him. He couldn't write more than one sentence that was about the same thing as the previous sentence. He'd be coked up, plus he'd be on uppers and all this other stuff, and he would mojo you, wire you three or four paragraphs, and then you would have to spend the next few hours trying to make the sentences deal with each other by adding some transition words or something like that. He'd be up for three or four straight days struggling with a piece, and you'd have to stay up for that length of time to take the morsels as they came in and work on it, so you didn't have any sleep either. Then he'd crash for a day or two, and you still had to stay up during that time and keep working on what he'd sent you. So basically, during a weeklong stretch you'd

gotten no sleep, he'd gotten some, and you were just frayed. The copy department and the art department and the printer would all be waiting for the story, and they'd start getting disgruntled and angry. Right around this time, Hunter would pull some sort of bullshit—he'd make some sort of serious threat or something, and you couldn't take it—and boom: breakdown.

The cocaine problem can be seen as a rapid acceleration of what was already a decline in his ability to write. Although he had grown as a writer throughout the sixties, developing his own inimitable voice, he struggled through the final years of the decade. Eventually, Gonzo was born out of a failure to write and he was lucky that what emerged could be used as another technique in his literary arsenal. But there was no escaping the fact that he tended to leave projects unfinished, jumping from one to the next and leaving old work incomplete. He had gotten distracted by drugs, politics, women, money, and friends. Anything, it seemed, but writing.

He had managed to make failure into an art form for a long time, presenting himself as the hapless reporter on a bungled assignment, bringing the reader into the process with his conspiratorial asides, and it worked because he was intelligent, talented, and witty. He intuitively grasped how to turn tragedy into comedy and present his failures in a way that readers loved. Failure was a huge part of Gonzo journalism, but now he was struggling to put together long pieces of coherent writing. Drugs may well have been an obstacle to writing in the past, but cocaine worsened the problem immeasurably.

If we look at his output as a writer, we can see a marked decline in the quantity and quality of his published writing as he achieved fame, cashed in on that success, and largely lost the motivation to invest serious time and effort into his work. Failures became common enough that editors had to seriously discuss whether it was worth risking a big chunk of their budget on a writer who was likely to miss his deadline or—worse—not bother submitting anything at all. As time went by, such failures became normal and they had to shoulder the serious burden of firstly getting anything from Hunter and then having to piece together pages of disconnected nonsense that may have contained, at best, a few clever sentences.

The people at *Rolling Stone* knew this and calculated that the financial risk was probably worth it in the long run, but often they would be disappointed in their star writer. In March 1973, Jann Wenner sent Thompson a list of five articles he was expected to write for the year, plus three features he was expected to look into for possible stories. None of these were ever written. It was just the beginning of a long trend in which the Gonzo journalist failed to write much of anything.

Thompson's celebrity now opened the door to *The New York Times*, who asked him to write the 1974 New Year's Day op-ed for the paper. "Fear and Loathing in the Bunker" is a grim and tedious outing in which an angry Thompson trots out what are now his catchphrases— "half-mad," "atavistic," "savage"—while lamenting the fact that Nixon's downfall appeared unlikely to result in the rise of any positive political prospects.

He begins by saying that he used to work for a milkman and much later attempts to connect this dull tale to Richard Nixon, who has been impeached but has not yet resigned. By way of a link between these two ideas, he simply says, "There is some kind of heavy connection between that memory and the way I feel right now about this stinking year that just ended." One gets the feeling that Thompson just began writing about something, attempted to tie this to a bigger issue, and then failed to lash it all together. It is more than a little incoherent and his usual blend of humor and pathos, which always resulted in a fine dark comedy, has deteriorated into disconnected fragments of bitterness.

It is not the sort of story that lent itself to Thompson's style of reporting. There is no event for him to cover and no companion for him to run around with, so there is no scope for Gonzo action. It is more of an essay than a fact-fiction hybrid piece, and while it is nice to read something other than the same rehashed tale, this is an essay that keeps going and going, seeming as though it will come to an end, but then picking up and continuing some more. It is the sort of story that a younger Hunter would have labored over for weeks and submitted as a concise, factual essay that slowly reeled his reader in with intriguing dialogue and teasing facts, but now he seemed incapable of such sustained efforts.

Later that month, Thompson went to the Super Bowl to watch the Miami Dolphins and the Minnesota Vikings compete in Houston, Texas. Had he been watching the game at home, he would have heard Bart Starr, whose discharge papers he had supposedly leaked at Eglin Air Force Base, commentating for CBS. The trip resulted in "Fear and Loathing at the Superbowl," which was published in *Rolling Stone* in February 1974.

It is a long and often rambling article, but surprisingly coherent given his recent output. Like so many of his stories, it begins in a hotel room—or, more specifically, on the balcony. Jann Wenner and others have described the process of getting Hunter to write, and often they noted that the hardest part was getting him started. To make this happen, they told him to write about his surroundings. Wenner said:

> He had to describe what the town looked like, what the motel looked like, if the rain was beating down, what the waves were doing. If he didn't get the geography and the weather established and get at least some chunk of the narrative going, you were in trouble.

For that reason, much of his work—particularly the pieces that saw major deadline battles—began in hotel rooms. The opening of the Super Bowl story sees him delivering a sermon from his balcony on the twentieth floor of the Hyatt Regency. He echoes the first line of *Fear and Loathing in Las Vegas* when he says, "It was just before dawn [...] when the urge to speak came on me."[8] His descriptions are vivid and he jumps back into the past logically, without the confusing leaps he had made in recent

---

8   He reused the "We were somewhere around *X* when *Y*" and "It was sometime around *X* when *Y*" structures occasionally throughout his later career.

pieces. Then, he breaks into comedy:

> Mother of Sweating Jesus! I thought. What
> is it—a leech? Are there leeches in this
> goddamn hotel, along with everything else?
> I jumped off the bed and began clawing
> at the small of my back with both hands.
> The thing felt huge, maybe eight or nine
> pounds, moving slowly up my spine toward
> the base of my neck.
>
> I'd been wondering, all week, why I
> was feeling so low and out of sorts ... but it
> never occurred to me that a giant leech had
> been sucking blood out of the base of my
> spine all that time; and now the goddamn
> thing was moving up toward the base of
> my brain, going straight for the medulla ...
> and as a professional sportswriter I knew
> that if the bugger ever reached my medulla
> I was done for.

Like William S. Burroughs, he could concoct almost
unimaginable scenes and present the grisliest details with a
dry, black humor. The image of a nine-pound leech on his
spine, quietly sucking blood until he thrashes about, trying
to get it off, is the sort of scene that Thompson was born
to write. His brain produced this sort of horrifying image,
and when he could manage to get them down in writing, it
was usually comic gold. The first of these two paragraphs
is completely over the top, with his initial outburst and
then the description of wild actions. The second, however,
goes for a more understated humor, with the amusing "it
never occurred to me that a giant leech…" and then the
final line about being a sportswriter. Such stark contrast
helped amplify the mischievous wit of his work.

Of course, the story is not about the Super Bowl—it
is about Hunter Thompson and his bizarre misadventures.
It could be viewed as him once again trotting out the old
Fear and Loathing in Las Vegas routine, and he certainly does
repeat a lot of the phrases, rhythms, and themes of that
book. The hotel motif is, of course, now familiar, and the
following line could hardly fail to ring a bell among readers

of his most famous book: "I filled the bathtub with hot water, plugged the tape recorder with both speakers into a socket right next to the tub." This time, however, it is Hunter listening to Rosalie Sorrels and Doug Sahm rather than Doctor Gonzo and Jefferson Airplane.

In part two, he talks about following the Oakland Raiders and the difficulty of getting the story. Here, it feels more like New Journalism than his usual brand of Gonzo. The reporting is much more conventional than in part one. Thompson walks around the Oakland training facilities and writes about what he sees, rather than giving sermons and wrestling with giant leeches. What he sees, of course, still concerns him. He uses some clearly fake quotes to report on people talking about him as the famous guy who wrote the book about Las Vegas. "Good god! I thought. That's it. ... If they read that book I'm finished."[9]

For part three, Mother Roberts, an old psychic, acts as the sounding board for his ranting, much like the hitchhiker at the beginning of the Vegas book. When Thompson speaks to her, he even paraphrases a line from Raoul Duke's spiel to the poor young man in the desert: "Yes, I am a white person, Mother Roberts, and we both know there's not a damn thing I can do about it. Are you prejudiced?"[10]

As usual, he squeezes in an attack on the mainstream press, complaining that journalists simply rewrite NFL press releases, and he again muses on the nature of truth as it pertains to reporting: "Absolute truth is a very rare and dangerous commodity in the context of professional journalism." This is said in spite of the fact that most of the "truth" he presents in this story is wild speculation rather than facts gained from serious research. He even admits to his own reticence to write with total honesty: "If I'd written all the truth I knew for the past ten years, about

---

9   This is possibly another reference to Fitzgerald, who in *The Beautiful and Damned* referred to his first novel: "Everywhere I go some silly girl asks me if I've read *This Side of Paradise*." [p.327]

10   In *Vegas*, Thompson had written: "He doesn't look like you or me, right? That's because he's a foreigner. I think he's probably Samoan. But it doesn't matter, does it? Are you prejudiced?" [p.6-8]

600 people — including me — would be rotting in prison cells from Rio to Seattle today." It was a point of pride for Thompson that he had reported over many decades without ever having one of his sources go to prison, and he credited that to his careful application of the truth in writing.

The article is one of Thompson's funniest pieces of work. It is not particularly original, but at least he had taken his Gonzo skills and used them in a coherent and thoroughly enjoyable piece of writing. The threads of the story work together and the various parts fit seamlessly, unlike most of his work from this period, and he even managed to finish it within a reasonable amount of time. Although there were some deadline day hijinks with the Mojo Wire to give him extra time, he submitted it in an uncharacteristically expeditious fashion, and "Fear and Loathing at the Super Bowl" was published in *Rolling Stone* just one month after the actual Super Bowl.

Unfortunately, his return to form was only too brief.

In his Super Bowl story, Thompson had finally veered away from politics after several years of focusing on Nixon and his cronies. His next idea for a book, however, would take him right back into the fray. After considering a run for the Senate, he decided to have *Rolling Stone* fund a Democratic conference that would bring together people that Thompson considered the main thinkers on the left side of the political spectrum. He wanted to heal the political wounds between the various liberal factions and avoid the "genuinely ominous power-vacuum" that he saw on the horizon. Ideally, they would emerge with a manifesto that would be adopted by the Democratic Party, but the plan was not only intended to steer his country in the right direction; Thompson hoped that these influential men would be able to contribute enough wisdom that, when the recordings were transcribed, it would form a book for which he only had to write the introduction. It was the perfect opportunity to grow his wealth and fame without researching and writing an article or a whole book.

Hoping to keep the conference a secret, Thompson pushed for it to be held in Elko, Nevada, and so political bigwigs from DC were flown into the remote desert town.

Despite encouraging the participants to use tire irons to settle their differences and reach some sort of consensus, Hunter could not force them into any kind of agreement. Petty rivalries ensured that the time was largely spent bickering instead of collaborating. He never understood why they could not put aside their differences and develop some sort of platform, but he also did not follow up on the idea when the conference ended. With no platform, there was no book, and *Fear and Loathing in Elko* went the way of *Guts Ball*.

But a larger failure loomed. The impeachment of Richard Nixon was a long and grueling process. The burglary at the Watergate had taken place on June 17, 1972, but it was only in 1974 that the impeachment trial formally began. More than two years after the Watergate fiasco had begun, Nixon resigned before he could be impeached. In those final months of the doomed presidency, Jann Wenner sensed that the end was near and decided that there should be a special issue of the magazine dedicated to this momentous event. He told the new editor, John Walsh, that Hunter Thompson needed to write the main story, which brought about groans from the staff, who were happy for him to stay as far away from the *Rolling Stone* offices as possible. Walsh thought it would be impossible to get him to write an article on time, but Wenner insisted.

Thompson was dispatched to Washington and, after a few weeks there, they brought him back to San Francisco and sat him down to write. He typed "The Quitter" at the top of a page and then just stared at it. He sat there all afternoon, all evening, and right through to the next morning. Whenever anybody checked in on him, he was still staring at the page with just those two words—and Hunter hadn't even come up with those; the title had been Wenner's idea. Walsh recalled him saying, "I can't find the drugs. I can't do this." His writer's block had now become debilitating.

Perhaps the problem was that Gonzo was essentially participatory journalism. In a story like Watergate and the subsequent resignation of the president, there was no space for his usual approach, and Thompson was unwilling or unable to try any other. He had political contacts but no real angle on the story, and he could not realistically ingratiate himself with the Nixon camp. Besides, running a drug freakout in the nation's capital did not seem like a wise idea.

In the end, the magazine ran a collection of Thompson's previous work, with Annie Leibovitz's photography as the main feature. There had been numerous articles he had failed to write in the past, but this one was the biggest disappointment. It was Nixon's resignation. His nemesis. So much of his writing had revolved around his relationship with the president that everyone expected one last article to resolve the story arc. Thompson had been calling for Nixon's impeachment for years. The story was practically written and it had the perfect ending. The million readers of *Rolling Stone*, who chomped at the bit for another Gonzo outing, must have been sorely disappointed that their hero could not rise to the occasion, but John Walsh was even more displeased. He was fired for failing to get an article out of Hunter.

Thompson did eventually produce an article about Nixon's impeachment, but as always it came late and did not live up to expectations. Nixon resigned from office on August 9, the resignation special was published on September 12, and his article appeared on October 10. In yet another nod to Hemingway, "Fear and Loathing in Limbo: The Scum Also Rises," Thompson explains that he had just finished writing an article about the impeachment when Gerald Ford unexpectedly called a press conference and gave Nixon a pardon for his crimes. Naturally, the story is not about Ford pardoning Nixon, nor about the psychological effect that this would have on the nation, but about Thompson's reaction and how it inconvenienced him:

> "Mother of babbling god!" I muttered. The word deadline caused my brain to seize up momentarily. Deadline? Yes. Tomorrow morning, about fifteen more hours ... With about 90 percent of my story already set in type, one of the threads that ran all the way through it was my belief that nothing short of a nuclear war could prevent Richard Nixon's conviction.

From this jangled beginning, the article soon digs into the resignation and pardon of Richard Nixon and it makes for a reasonably coherent article. Reality is blended with fantasy and there are plenty of references to people as "swine" and "fascist thugs." Thompson recounts going to Washington to witness Nixon leaving the White House because, he says, he needed to see it to believe it. However, Annie Leibovitz later pointed out that this was "concocted" and while "Every reporter on the planet was at the White House [...] Hunter was in the swimming pool at the Hilton with a battery-powered TV set." As for Thompson's attacks on the president, he is surprisingly reserved and almost seems to pity the man. When he does insult him, he merely offers tame, rehashed versions of brilliant put-downs he had delivered in previous years, such as this: "if it can be said that he resembled any other living animal in this world, it could only have been the hyena." It lacks the punch of his earlier description of Nixon as a hyena so demented that he did not realize that he had been killed and gutted.

As this is mostly a reaction piece, there is little for Thompson to do except offer his memories and opinions, as well as his made-up trip to the White House to watch Nixon depart. His wife, Sandy, makes a rare appearance because Thompson is at home at Owl Farm and needs a companion to bounce ideas off, but without his usual semi-fictionalized friends there is little in terms of wild action or dialogue. It relies more on phone calls to people than actual conversations, thereby reducing his ability to throw in weird actions and observations.

He goes off on a long tangent about his youth, confessing to several robberies. It is an odd thing to admit to, whether true or not. He eventually asks, "Ah ... mother of jabbering god, how in the hell did I get off on that tangent about teenage street crime?" and then ties it to Richard Nixon, whom he claims possesses a "street-punk mentality."[11] Then he goes off again: "Right ... and now we have gone off on a dangerous compound tangent. And it has mushroomed into something unmanageable ..." It is like his milkman story from "Fear and Loathing in the

---

11 Note the similarities between this and the earlier quote, "Mother of babbling god."

Bunker." It is not that there is no connection; it is just incredibly contrived and more than likely the result of his piecing together disconnected chunks of writing.

The article, again, is far from his finest work and by this point a little repetitive, but it is relatively amusing and, in places, quite intelligent. His involvement in the story as an incompetent reporter confounded by Ford's pardon, coupled with his experiences in Washington, allowed him to write from two different perspectives—the journalist who met Nixon and followed the presidential campaign and also the average person at home, who is hearing about this on the news. The rambling, personal style works in this instance but, with Nixon gone, Thompson had just lost his number one enemy—another of his reasons to write.

Failed Assignments

He didn't write anything after he came back from Zaire, he didn't write anything after he came back from New Orleans. He didn't write anything after he came back from Nixon's resignation. He refused to turn in the piece when he came back from Vietnam.

David Felton

The two years following the 1972 campaign were difficult ones as Hunter S. Thompson navigated the world of celebrity. He complained bitterly that being famous did not bring financial rewards and yet he avoided writing as much as possible. What he had once done for pleasure was now very much a source of pain, and almost every assignment he took descended into a battle with his own propensity to self-destruct and rebel against the matter at hand. Writing became harder and harder until even thinking about sitting at a typewriter was an unpleasant chore to be avoided at all costs. But, with the success of his three books and his rock star status at *Rolling Stone*, he found that there were ways to put off the writing process.

He learned quickly that he could make thousands of dollars by giving "lectures" at universities around the country, which was far easier than toiling over an article for weeks or months. For these speaking events, he would prepare nothing and simply go on stage to answer questions. A typical performance would see him arrive an hour late and stumble around drunkenly, mumbling so much that no one could understand him. Then he might get into an argument with a heckler and bark insults into the crowd. Sometimes they tossed him pills and joints, then cheered when he picked them up and took them. It was, in a sense, just Gonzo transposed onto a new form of expression, and it suffered from the same limitations. It certainly did little to convince people that there was any real division between Thompson and Duke, and it was a far cry from the man who had seemed "reserved, intellectual, and witty" to listeners during his 1970 campaign for sheriff.

By the end of 1974, Thompson had already become, in Ralph Steadman's words, "a prisoner of his own cult." This was, of course, entirely his own fault. Ever since his last book, he had done little but perpetuate the myths that he had built around himself. His writing had become repetitive and, even when it was funny or clever, he was still using the same ideas and the same language to tell the same stories. Most of these revolved around a drug-addled journalist, so that is what he became in public. Bill Dixon, one of George McGovern's campaign managers, toured the speaking circuit with Thompson, and noted that he stepped into character when he went on stage, changing from a relatively normal person into the drunken buffoon that the college kids loved. Thompson was very much aware of the repercussions of his actions, and he explained his situation in bleak terms:

> I've lost my perspective on what people believe any more. I mean, what kind of sane person is going to believe that I'm really the way I portray myself to be? Who's going to take that seriously? And yet they do. There's obviously a distinct line between writing a certain way, and being that way. If you start to believe in mythology, then you're in trouble. I don't go around announcing to people that I'm quite serious about my work, of course, but still some people actually expect me to be some drug-crazed rapist with a switchblade between my teeth.
>
> I'll tell you, there's a danger when a writer lets himself run wild into excess. A lot of stuff that I've written embarrasses me. As a matter of fact, that campaign stuff? The stuff on the '72 presidential election? I'm embarrassed about most of it.

He had worked hard to present an image of himself to the world that was grossly exaggerated, and in the end he felt he had to live up to it. Even when he tried to move on, he found he was trapped.

Perhaps Gonzo had worked initially because he was an outsider and no one paid much attention to him. His schtick was playing an inept loser, anonymous and perennially outside the fold. He put himself at the center of the story, but to most people he was still very much invisible. Gonzo was a shortcut to insightful, original writing, but as he became increasingly famous, he lost the ability to control his environment, and so the stories became sillier. He relied on old tropes, old phrases, and old plotlines. Without the sense of originality they once possessed, the wildness lost its edge and the articles lost any real meaning.

The situation worsened when he was used as the basis for Garry Trudeau's character, Uncle Duke, in *The Washington Post* comic, *Doonesbury*, in 1975. Trudeau had been working on his comic strip for more than five years by this point and it had grown incredibly popular, syndicated to countless newspapers throughout the country. That year, he became the first person to win a Pulitzer Prize for a comic strip, and soon after he introduced Duke—a character based on Hunter S. Thompson in every way. There could be no doubt that the Duke was an infringement of Thompson's intellectual property but, despite repeated threats, Thompson did not sue. He grumbled in public, but some people who knew him suspected that he was fine with being parodied because it further built his legend.[1]

Even though he claimed to be angry at Trudeau and trapped by his own celebrity, there was no denying that he had built his whole image very carefully, and even as he complained about it in the years to come he continued to maintain his Gonzo brand, both writing and acting out the lifestyle that millions of readers imagined. This naturally involved mind-bending substances, which Thompson not only enjoyed, but included as a significant element of his

1   A photograph from 1983 shows that he even had Trudeau's cartoon pinned up on his wall alongside photos of things he loved – his son, peacocks, naked women, and photos of himself. [*Outlaw Journalist*; 2nd photo segment]

writing. He had always admired Conrad's line from *Lord Jim*, "In the destructive element immerse!" It sat well with his personality and literary style, but pretty quickly he found himself in trouble.

Back home in Woody Creek, he was sleeping later and later. For most of his adult life, he rose in the middle of the afternoon and spent several hours consuming a complicated "breakfast" before starting work for the day. As time went by, the hour that he began writing was pushed further and further back. After he began using cocaine, he started sleeping until six in the evening, then going to the Jerome Bar and doing cocaine until four in the morning. There was little writing done after that. A natural nocturne, he had always enjoyed writing at night, but coke was a social drug and not the sort that made him want to lock himself in the War Room and write for days on end. Even when he did force himself to sit and write, he was blocked more often than not.

In 1974, *Rolling Stone* hired Joe Klein as their deputy Washington bureau chief. He quickly realized Thompson's problem with drugs, which he later articulated in the *New York Times*:

> He didn't want to become a dull parody of himself but feared he lacked the gumption to jump the gravy train. I asked if he'd ever thought about stowing the psychedelic pyrotechnics — his "gonzo" journalism — and sitting down and writing a serious, straight-ahead novel. Well, of course he had. But, he said, "Without that," and he glanced over at the satchel in which he carried his array of vegetation and chemicals, "I'd have the brain of a second-rate accountant."

Despite that moment of clarity, Thompson usually claimed that it was arguments with his employer, Jann Wenner, that were at the root of his difficulties. As we shall see in this chapter, although writing was becoming difficult for him and he often claimed to hate it and want out of journalism, there were still periods when he was producing good work. Alas, just as his war with the Scott Meredith Literary Agency had scuppered all his best work in 1967, petty fights with Wenner would make for fallow years in the mid-seventies.

Late in 1974, a former lawyer for *Scanlan's* convinced Thompson to fly to Zaire for the "Rumble in the Jungle" between George Foreman and Muhammed Ali. Considered to be one of the greatest sporting events of the twentieth century, the undefeated world heavyweight champion was knocked out by the challenger, Ali, who introduced his famous "rope-a-dope" technique during the fight. Norman Mailer and George Plimpton would be there, as well as every other self-respecting sportswriter on the planet. It was an opportunity for Thompson to break free from the curse of Raoul Duke and do something different—proving himself a serious and versatile artist—all the while rubbing shoulders with two of the writers he most respected. Instead, he called Ralph Steadman and told him it was time for more Gonzo hijinks.

"Gonzo, Gonzo, Gonzo," Steadman said. "How long do you think we can keep doing this kind of Gonzo thing?"

"I guess we can keep doing this kind of thing until one of us dies," Thompson replied.

Ralph relented and they both flew to Kinshasa. Thompson landed in Africa several weeks before Steadman and knew the terrain by the time his friend arrived, but he had not exactly been playing the role of a diligent reporter. He had been partying with his old friend, Bill Cardoso, and had found that drugs were not just readily available in Zaire, but *cheap*. For a dollar a pound, he had purchased a sack of marijuana that Steadman estimated weighed between forty and fifty pounds. Hunter doled it out to the other members of the press, delighting in his role as "medicine man."

It seemed to the other journalists in Kinshasa that Thompson viewed the Zaire trip purely as a vacation. He had not bothered to interview either of the boxers or even visit their training camps. While the rest of the press tried to learn the rules and techniques of boxing and studied the lives and styles of the fighters, Thompson continued to play the fool. When Ralph asked him about it, Hunter replied, "I didn't come all this way to watch a couple of niggers beat the shit out of each other." It was clear that he had no intention of actually writing about the fight, and whether he even intended on writing his usual Gonzo interpretation of events is debatable.

For the two weeks that Steadman spent with him in Zaire, Thompson mostly occupied himself looking for cocaine and partying with Cardoso. He spread rumors and suggested outrageous pranks, indicating that maybe he did intend on stirring up something he could write about, but he didn't even bring a notebook and never bothered to write anything down. He became even more obsessed with Martin Bormann and talked about finding him in Africa, which may have been another intended plot, but no story emerged. Thompson had said often that he had no interest in attending the fight but was unable to articulate *why* except that it would be no good and that he would have to "just sit there" for five hours. "All I want to do is lie down and listen to music," he complained.

Early in the morning of October 30, with the fight just about to start, Steadman frantically tried to find Thompson. He had held up his end of the contract, producing various illustrations, and was ready to watch the fight to get his final drawings, but Thompson was missing. He was swimming in the hotel pool, where he had dumped his huge bag of marijuana into the water, so that chunks of grass floated all over the surface. He was swimming lengths, a glass of fine scotch waiting for him at one end of the pool so that he could take a sip every few laps, quite happy in his own pointless indulgence. Steadman told him it was time to go or else they would miss it, but Thompson had sold their tickets. He had no intention of even watching the fight on TV.

Steadman, who had tolerated his unruly roommate throughout their stay, heroically enduring the binging, bitching, and raging, was understandably upset. He needed to *see* the fight to do his illustrations. At this point, he thought Thompson might still manage a last-minute, deadline-busting effort, with his own completely fabricated events. He knew his friend was capable of such feats when presented with the seemingly insurmountable obstacle of a looming deadline. But it just wasn't going to happen. Ralph reflected:

The newness had gone out of Gonzo. He couldn't do the same trick again, where he just pulls a story from his notes. I guess he didn't want to do that anyway. But in the end he couldn't have if he'd wanted to because he wasn't even taking notes.

Actually, Thompson had been taking notes, but only audio ones on his tape recorder, and these were more of a loose journal mixed with random conversations. In them, he sounds angry, confused, and deeply paranoid. During his first experiments with cocaine, he had noted that it made his speech badly slurred, and this is doubly true for the recordings from Zaire. Here, he acts sullen and moody, and is generally incoherent. He is argumentative and difficult with friends, and explosively violent toward strangers and anyone in the service industry, screaming "Punk!" "Asshole!" and "Loser!" at waiters and hotel staff. Sometimes he simply screams or makes pained noises into the recorder. His recorded notes also show a deeply contradictory stance toward the fight. He frequently says that he has no intention of watching it but at the same time rails against the government for supposedly commandeering several hundred press tickets. Thompson believed for a long time that they had lost their tickets and could not attend, which angered him, yet when they again had tickets he was adamant about not attending.

His aggressive, erratic behavior put a serious strain on his relationship with Ralph, who, struggling to keep his cool, repeatedly called Thompson "sick" and chided him, saying, "you got nothing!" But Thompson did not appear to care, telling his partner, "it's your article." Somehow, he had convinced himself that this whole thing was for Steadman's benefit and that anything he had written would have simply been an accompaniment to his friend's art. It was an excuse he would use later when struggling with collaborative projects, and which would allow him to move on from failures without much regret over the disappointed readers, exhausted editors, and vast sums of wasted money.

Norman Mailer, whose experiences in Zaire became *The Fight* (1975), believed that Thompson did intend to write something but that his plans just didn't work out how he wanted. He said that Thompson had been too lazy to learn about boxing but that he intended on watching the fight with Mobutu Sese Seko, the president of Zaire. Plimpton confirmed that Thompson had wanted this, explaining that "Hunter was always finding plots in Zaire." It differed from day to day, but he sometimes talked about watching the fight with the president and sometimes about going to find a missile in the Congo. Mailer thought that Thompson had taken a risk and that it hadn't paid off, but that he wasn't particularly affected by it. He was already a famous, successful author and his expenses were paid by someone else. What did it matter if there was no story?

Their journey back to the US would have made perfect fodder for another manic Gonzo tale. Paranoia gripped the journalists in Kinshasa as rumors spread that they would be arrested. Thompson, who was more paranoid than most, convinced Steadman to flee to America with him, even though he lacked a visa. They barely managed to survive four stops on the way to New York, where Thompson's ivory was confiscated from him by Customs. Or so it seemed. In fact, the Customs agents wanted an import fee of twenty-seven dollars, but Thompson's paranoia was raging. In his mind, he was smuggling illegal goods into the country and the Customs agents were stealing it from him. In a fit of paranoid rage, he stole back his ivory; however, a bill for the import tax was later delivered to Woody Creek.

During the Africa trip, he certainly went through the motions and lived out a classic Gonzo adventure, but he could not manage even a short caption to accompany his friend's artwork. *Rolling Stone*, having paid more than twenty-five thousand dollars in expenses and fees for the story, refused to run Steadman's illustrations, which they considered too dark to print without Thompson's writing. George Plimpton, who had become friends with Hunter on the flight into Zaire, said that Thompson could have written almost anything and his readers would have lapped it up, which was probably true. The fact that he had not seen the fight and had failed in almost every way as a journalist would simply have made it another typical Gonzo outing. "One of the troubles with Hunter," Plimpton said, "is he seems to constantly be afflicted with a type of writer's block."

Although others chastised him for his failings, it seems Hunter was happy to clown around for weeks while someone else paid the bills. Journalism was, after all, his entry pass to the sort of life he could not otherwise have lived. He said about the sixties and early seventies:

> I managed—by using almost any kind of valid or invalid journalistic credentials I could get my hands on—to get myself personally involved in just about everything that interested me: from Berkeley to Chicago, Las Vegas to the White House, shark-fishing, street-fighting, dope-smuggling, Hell's Angels, Super Bowls, local politics and a few things I'd prefer not to mention until various statutes of limitations expire.

It was true. Journalism had given him access to many of the most important or interesting events in that period of history, as well as allowing him the freedom to take drugs, work from home, and avoid the drudgery of regular working life that he had managed to shirk for almost two decades. But being a journalist usually involves reporting on an event, not just attending it.

Could it be that he had just stopped caring about writing? In July, he had written to a friend to say, "all I'm really sure of is that I'm getting out of journalism as soon as possible." It was an idea that he would toss around often in future, and he expanded further on this to another friend, saying, "I don't think I have anything else to say in my writing." Again, it was a sentiment that would often rear its head as he increasingly struggled to produce good work. Rather than make changes to his life that would allow him to write again, he talked about quitting altogether.

There are various possible reasons why he was now struggling to produce work, but the fact is that he was never the same again. Sandy Thompson put it the most succinctly when she said, "After Africa he just couldn't write. He couldn't piece it together."

***

Despite the Zaire farce, Wenner convinced Thompson that he should go back on the road for the 1976 presidential campaign. They agreed to a book deal that involved a seventy-five-thousand-dollar advance, but then Wenner sold Straight Arrow Press before it was paid. Thompson was furious and vowed never to speak to the publisher again. He even leaked the story to the news, telling journalists that Wenner was "a treacherous swine."

They maintained their distance for a while, but the silence was broken when Wenner called and asked Thompson to cover the fall of Saigon. Everyone knew that it was just a matter of time before the North finally ejected the US and united their country, and media outlets around the world were scrambling to get reports from inside the beleaguered capital city. Thompson had wanted to write about Vietnam for years, and in fact he had agreed to go there before signing his contract for the 1972 presidential campaign. It was the story of his generation. The war had been a part of his life for so many years now that he felt he had to cover its end, and this was something he could not just phone in from Woody Creek.

Thompson quickly forgot his vow and agreed to Wenner's offer, but as his departure date drew near, he became increasingly nervous. Wenner put him in touch with *New York Times* war correspondent, Gloria Emerson, who pressured him heavily, believing that "Fear and Loathing in the Final Days of Saigon" would be a Gonzo classic. Thompson was not so sure. Although he appears reticent to admit his fears in their recorded phone calls, he makes countless excuses for not doing the story. "I'm not sure I want to go and cover a long negotiation," he says at one point. Emerson explains to him that it will be "easy" and not in the least dangerous, and that he "can write the piece from *The New York Times* office." She even gives him the story, telling him places to visit and how to meet angry Vietnamese for good quotes, and says she will furnish him with facts and stories from the old days so that he can just compare it to the present by strolling around Saigon. She makes no attempt to hide the fact that he will undoubtedly exaggerate everything to bring a greater sense of paranoia and informs him of a "revolting" hospital that would add to the fear and loathing of it all. He says that he is worried

358

about being trapped behind enemy lines, but she tells him that he doesn't have to stay that long. It will be cakewalk: luxury hotels, good drugs, a little adventure, and nothing to worry about.

Before Thompson departed, the publisher and writer had another falling out, and so when Hunter arrived in Vietnam, he found that his company credit card had been canceled. Wenner, in one of his rages, had fired Thompson but his staff, familiar with his temper tantrums, waited a few days before filing the paperwork. Wenner calmed down, rescinded his decision, and so Thompson was never officially fired, but when he arrived in Vietnam, he believed that he was out of a job and lacking health insurance. He was furious again and for the rest of his life kept this grudge against Wenner.[2]

A year later, Thompson's friend and attorney, John Clancy, submitted what appears to be a co-written hatchet job called "Citizen Wenner" to *Hustler*. The article has neither man's name on it but refers often to Thompson and appears to have been written mostly by Clancy. It is attributed to "Deep Thrust," a nod to the Watergate story, but some of the ideas and phrasing have clearly come from Thompson, as well as almost all of the information. In the accompanying letter, Clancy calls it "the definitive slam of our friend Jann Wenner," and indeed it is a no-holds-barred assault on a man Thompson now passionately hated. Through detailed accounts of his compulsive hirings and firings, Wenner is portrayed as a greedy, dictatorial shyster and *Rolling Stone*'s success is laid solely at Thompson's feet. The article claims that Wenner only wanted to write about music, but that Hunter convinced him to expand into politics and culture, and is therefore responsible for the magazine's journalistic coups of the seventies. Claiming that Thompson "did more to put Rolling Stone on the map than any other person," it becomes bogged down in personal and financial quibbles like so many of his letters.

It is not hard to see why this article was never published.

---

2   Wenner claims that Hunter was always joking when he mentioned this incident, but it does appear he was serious. Thompson admitted that Wenner had tried and failed to fire him, but considered that to be more than enough to justify the grudge, and he spoke angrily about it for years.

Aside from the likelihood of legal action by Wenner, it did not have Thompson's name on it and was weaker than most of his post-1972 work. Clancy was a somewhat competent writer but he was asking for fifteen hundred dollars for the story, which failed as anything more than an extended piece of bitching, filled with cheap insults and industry gossip. Poorly written and impossible to fact-check, it is valuable only to people already interested in Thompson's life, and would have been rather confusing to most readers of *Hustler*.

When he arrived in Vietnam in April 1975, Thompson quickly made a name for himself among the press. He dressed just like they expected from Raoul Duke and paid boys to carry around a beer cooler so that he could always have a drink at hand. He took a lot of opium, became familiar with the local prostitutes, and did outrageous things like falling through a bamboo wall and destroying a restaurant's entire kitchen. The other journalists could see that he was not much different from his alter ego, Duke, but it wasn't as funny in real life—and especially not in a warzone. He was generally admired among the press, but this time many of the reporters were keen to stay away from him, leaving him feeling like "an intruder" among his fellow journalists. They knew him as the wild man of Gonzo and worried that he would get them killed. This was *war*; it was serious business. Recent estimates suggest that at least sixty journalists died while covering the conflict and few of them were running around high on drugs.

Socializing in the safety of the city, Thompson mingled with his peers, but found that not all of them appreciated his brand of journalism. Tape recordings show various journalists mocking him for his lack of knowledge about the war. He informs them that he has heard about a secret code word among the press and all of the journalists in the room laugh at him. They make fun of him, too, for having not gotten his press card from the government. When he opens up a little, telling them that this sort of journalist banter would be in his *Rolling Stone* story, one of the men replies, "What is all this 'Fear and Loathing' shit?" causing the rest of the journalists to laugh at him again. Cruelly, they tell him that he is not as talented as Norman Mailer, whose article on the Ali-Foreman fight had just come out in *Playboy*. The criticism must have stung Thompson, who was defensive: "I had no interest in the fight at all. For me boxing is… I just didn't write it." Later, when privately reflecting on the incident, he simply spat the words, "Fuck them," into his tape recorder.

When Hunter asked to be taken to the front lines, a fellow journalist warned him that he had better not pull any "Gonzo bullshit." The other reporters in the jeep were wearing flak jackets and helmets, but Thompson was wearing his usual Hawaiian shirt and had a cooler of beer with him. High on various substances, he screamed out suddenly during the journey to the front line, causing the driver to crash. Another journalist grabbed him by the throat and threatened him. Gonzo antics were funny back home, but here in Vietnam he was putting people's lives at risk. Thompson's only explanation for his outburst was: "There were four giant fucker pterodactyls that just went overhead," but that failed to elicit any laughter from the people around him. Later, the other journalists noticed that he was missing, and when they found him, he was wandering toward enemy lines, just a few hundred yards from a VC checkpoint. After seriously debating whether they should let him be killed, they chased after him, bundled him into the jeep, and took him back to Saigon.

Even the journalists who did like and respect Thompson found his actions in Vietnam baffling at best. Five days after arriving in the country, he suddenly fled to Hong Kong. *Newsweek* reporter Loren Jenkins, whom Thompson had known since 1963, was disappointed in him. "You're here to write *Fear and Loathing in Saigon*," he said, "not Hong Kong." Thompson claimed that he needed to sort out the situation with his insurance, but Jenkins felt that he was simply afraid. Years later, in *Kingdom of Fear*, Thompson wrote that he had gone to Hong Kong to pick up money and drugs for his journalist friends, but this was a lie. He had brought the money with him on his original flight and the opium he spoke of was available just about anywhere in the city, including the hotel's room service. Indeed, his audio recordings from a Hong Kong hotel room confirm that he left Saigon because "the cycle of panic and calm is so violent" that he could no longer stand it.

He remained in Hong Kong for six days, enjoying a stay at a luxurious hotel, where he attempted to write "a short piece" from the *Newsweek* offices and then cable it back to *Rolling Stone*—something he noted he hadn't done since Brazil. He quickly decided to return to Saigon, even though he considered the situation there "an extremely ugly thing." It was clear that he was feeling a great sense of shame over his recent failures and was willing to undertake a potentially deadly mission in order to redeem himself:

> I've come this far and it's my story and I blew the last one in Africa and I think I'll just run with this one, which means going right back into the eye of the storm […] a suicide orgy.

He ultimately convinced himself that it was worth the risk because he now had a new angle on his story. With the rest of the press supposedly fleeing in droves and the enemy expected to take the city in a matter of days, the story would now have a wild and unique element: "I'm gonna be the last man into Saigon," he said.

After those six peaceful days in Hong Kong, Thompson returned with a huge box of electronic equipment, which he distributed among the war correspondents, and then used an assortment of audio devices to record everything around him. What is clear from these, though, is just how much his speech had been impaired by drug use. In any audio recording prior to his 1973 "cocaine experiment," he had been easy to understand. Granted, his voice always had a peculiar, staccato quality, but now his words were often indistinguishable. This had been noticeable in his recordings from Zaire, but by Vietnam he had developed the trademark mumble ("mumblese," as Sheriff Bob Braudis called it) and for the rest of his life it became harder for people to understand what he was saying.

In total, Thompson stayed in Saigon for close to a month and, unlike his stay in Zaire, he did attempt to do real reporting. He conducted several interviews and stayed up for days on end in futile attempts to produce a lead, fueling his efforts with Dexedrine. His unique perspective morphed from being "the last man into Saigon" into being the only American journalist covering the story from the North Vietnamese side, and to make this happen he attempted to get in contact with Colonel Giang, spokesman for the Vietcong. People also recall him wandering around with a tape recorder, making verbal notes for his article, but unfortunately he was so out of it on opium that there was no tape in the machine. When he was taken along with other journalists to do an interview at American Legion Post 34, he was told to stay quiet and not embarrass them. One reporter told him that he could make up a bunch of fake, Gonzo stories for *Rolling Stone* but warned him "don't fuck up my interview."

Despite all this, Thompson's writing in Vietnam was largely limited to a few letters, and what reporting appeared in *Rolling Stone* mostly came from Laura Palmer, their other writer in Saigon. There was no grand article; only "Fear and Loathing in Saigon: Interdicted Dispatch from the Global Affairs Desk," a memo published in May 1975.[3] It is a good piece of writing that starts and ends in classic Thompson fashion but in the middle it is more informative, actually dealing with the end of the war. The article starts, though, with him describing his hotel room and the difficulty of getting ice. It was just like Wenner said: He needed to start by describing his surroundings or else nothing would be written. At the end, he includes a manic last paragraph that implies that Saigon will fall in the next few hours and that he is doomed. Clearly, he felt the need to insert a little of the paranoia that infused most of his writing.

Fearing how the evacuation would play out, Thompson left Saigon and flew to Laos, abandoning Palmer, who stayed behind and covered the fall of the city.[4] He claimed that he had enough material to write a good article without staying to see the end. From Hong Kong, he flew to Bangkok and then Vientiane, saying that he was in search of secret CIA prisons, which he thought would be his next big story.

---

3   He did, however, keep journals, an excerpt of which was included in *Fear and Loathing in America* several decades later.
4   Palmer's reporting was fantastic and Paul Scanlon attempted to include it in the 1977 book, *Reporting: Rolling Stone Style*. Wenner nixed it because it reminded him too much of Thompson's failure to cover the fall.

From there, he returned to Hong Kong to meet Sandy and then they traveled to Indonesia for a vacation. These drug-fueled adventures provided him with stories but mostly he was just describing his experiences with hotel rooms across Southeast Asia. Still, he was productive and wrote often throughout this trip. When Sandy arrived, she was stunned to see him actually sitting down and writing out of choice. It had been years since she had last seen him do that.

In *Fear and Loathing at Rolling Stone*, a collection of his work for the magazine, the editor claims that Thompson wrote nothing about Vietnam except for the memo, and elsewhere people have commented that his inability to cover the fall of Saigon was another in a string of failures, but this is not entirely true. In fact, he did write a long piece about the end of the war; he just refused to give it to *Rolling Stone* because of his anger at Wenner. It was only published in the ten-year anniversary of the end of the war. Titled "Dance of the Doomed," it finally appeared in *Rolling Stone* on May 9, 1985, and was reprinted in the similarly titled collection, *Songs of the Doomed*, in 1990.

Despite it being overlooked, "Dance of the Doomed" is a brilliant piece of writing, or rather, several brilliant pieces of writing. It is comprised of two stories, the first of which was written in Laos on May 5 and the second about a week earlier in Saigon. They are prefaced by the usual flurry of subheaders with ellipses, as well as a few quotations, including an AP report detailing the fall of the city.

The first part of "Dance of the Doomed" is called "Checking into the Lane Xang" and it is simply the story of Hunter checking into a hotel with that name in Vientiane. In typical Thompson fashion, this is more complicated than it should be. He has to bribe the night clerk to get a room, but the clerk wants to sell him his daughter. Thompson then describes his hotel in great detail before getting to the issue at hand: the fall of Saigon. By this time, the city has fallen, but Thompson's descriptions make it seem as though he was there during the evacuation. He does not claim to have witnessed the city being overrun, but he plays up the danger that surrounded him and the imminent nature of the invasion so much that readers would have assumed he was present.

There are some of the usual Gonzo tropes, of course. He references Martin Bormann and describes what he is wearing—LL Bean shorts. The final sentence in particular is a typical Thompson effort:

> In its last hours, [Saigon] became a desperate, overcrowded nightmare full of thieves, losers, pimps, conmen, war junkies and many, many victims. Including me, although I am just beginning to understand this.

The list of nouns describing outsiders and losers contains standard images for Thompson and these words were often repeated throughout his writing.

The second story is called "Whooping it up with the War Junkies" and begins with the lyrics of Don McLean's "American Pie," which is referenced a few times in the article. The effect is to contrast the quaint, folksy song with the violence of his surroundings. As the article begins, Thompson describes himself and some journalists watching the bombs fall just a few miles away. These journalist friends are interviewed later, before Graham Greene's novel, *The Quiet American*, is excerpted.[5]

He also talks about his attempts to reach Colonel Giang and his impressions of the charismatic Vietcong man. Later, he includes a letter that he wrote to Giang, in which he states his case for letting him cross the line and cover the Vietcong advance.[6] The collage of stories, letters, and excerpts brings an extra dimension to "Dance of the Doomed," allowing for the reader's immersion in the chaos of competing ideas and highlighting the eerie juxtaposition of Americana and American military might. He had been doing this since at least *Hell's Angels* and had

---

5   Thompson stayed at the Continental Hotel, which Greene was fond of and which appeared in his novel.

6   Thompson had also suggested to Gloria Emerson, in a brief departure from his worry over matters of safety, that he might attempt to embed himself in the Vietcong and cover the story from the perspective of the North. She quickly convinced him that it was not only a bad idea but totally impossible. [*Gonzo Tapes*, CD 5, track 4]

quite possibly borrowed it from John Dos Passos.

Again, Thompson describes himself and this time goes into so much detail that one wonders whether he was receiving kickbacks from the companies mentioned: Converse, LL Bean, Ray-Ban, Arnold Palmer… He had been doing this for years, making sure that the reader could picture him in their mind since he was always at the center of the story.

The message at the end of these stories is implied rather than stated. Thompson is happy to see the end of the Western influence in Southeast Asia. The French colonialists and American occupiers have been unceremoniously booted out, and Vietnam is free to be united as one under its own rule for the first time in nearly a century. He does not say whether or not this will work out, but he seems glad that it is in the hands of the local people rather than cruel, wealthy imperialists.

Although the articles do not exactly fit together and should perhaps have been published separately, they are individually fantastic pieces of writing, and collectively it somehow works as a bizarre, endearing assemblage of fragments. McKeen called it "one of the best examples of pure Gonzo journalism, assembled as much as written," which is perhaps true. Thompson seems to have stumbled upon a new path in Gonzo, pushing his innovation in a more post-modern direction. Reading his work chronologically, they make for a tremendously refreshing change of pace. They include some of the features of his usual writing (and also a nod to the dwarf from *Fear and Loathing in Las Vegas*), but they are straightforward, concise, and engaging. He talks about himself and describes his hotel room, but these are just features of otherwise varied writing. There are no stupid antics and no attempts at over-the-top humor or unrealistic dialogue.

From his letters to Wenner around this time, we can see him playing with different ideas in his writing, then going through several drafts in order to come to the best possible version. "Dance of the Doomed" may have been a good example of Gonzo writing but, like *Fear and Loathing in Las Vegas*, it was clearly the result of several drafts rather than a spontaneous prose sketch. This was something sorely lacking in much of his work after 1971. The result was a polished, mature version of Gonzo. In June, when back home at Owl Farm, he wrote Wenner to say that he had one hundred pages of writing from Southeast Asia. However, their rocky relationship and Hunter's generally difficult disposition meant that these great stories were buried away. What is even more disappointing is that they are a glimpse of what could have been. Whilst Thompson was struggling to write during the mid-seventies, these articles show that he was capable—at least in short pieces—of writing coherent and informative journalism that retained his subjective perspective and personal flair. Despite this being listed as perhaps his greatest failure, the truth is that his Saigon reporting, though printed ten years too late, was among his finest work and stands as a shining example of what Gonzo could be when its creator invested the necessary time and effort.

While it is perhaps unfair that his attempt to cover the fall of Saigon is commonly labeled as a failure and proof of his rapid downfall as a writer, it is admittedly true that 1975 was a poor year in terms of his written output—just like 1973 and 1974. In fact, for the entire year he claims to have earned no money from journalism. His only published writing had been a relatively short memo in *Rolling Stone*. Even Garry Trudeau's Uncle Duke character had been more prominent in the magazine, as Wenner had given him the August 28, 1975 cover to spite Thompson.

When he returned from Vietnam, Thompson decided to try reporting on the 1976 presidential campaign. He discussed writing it for *Playboy*, but the deal fell through and he was forced to go with *Rolling Stone* again even though he was livid about his lost advance. His relationship with Wenner was now permanently strained, but both men thought that it would be a good idea for him to repeat his '72 success with a follow-up. Wenner wanted him to write shorter articles than in 1972, but Thompson knew he was being paid a thousand dollars per page and wanted to write longer articles again. He was also keen to focus on the book rather than individual pieces of writing, viewing any submissions to *Rolling Stone* as excerpts from his book rather than having a book comprised of different pieces of writing. This, he felt, would be more profitable.

It was a reasonable idea, but of course there was no *Fear and Loathing on the Campaign Trail '76*. He went to Washington in the summer and wrote fifteen pages of something called "Fear and Loathing on Embassy Row," but refused to give it to Wenner and never published it anywhere. Later, he flew out to cover the first primaries but before long he was sick of the old routine and quit, heading home to Owl Farm. He complained that he could not work because everyone was looking at him and asking him for autographs, but it is also likely that his drinking and drug use had increased so much that he was simply no longer capable of doing the work that he had done in 1972.

The closest thing readers got to that proposed book was a long article called "Fear and Loathing on the Campaign Trail '76: Third-Rate Romance, Low-Rent Rendezvous." Published in *Rolling Stone* on June 3, 1976, it begins with an unusual, made-up story about a rogue, Floridian dog castrator called Castrato. It is an amusing, disturbing, and thoroughly creative tale, which uses Thompson's late friend, Lionel Olay, as the source for some funny remarks. Of course, the story has absolutely nothing to do with politics, and so when it draws to an end, Thompson starts a new section and begins talking about his efforts to cover the campaign and his lack of enthusiasm for it. Then, he attempts to once again bring the reader into the story by commenting on the process of writing it: "I just reread that Castrato business, and it strikes me that I am probably just one or two twisted tangents away from terminal fusing of the brain circuits." It is pure stream-of-consciousness rambling. Even when he is writing about something, he will still make comments on the writing process within the narrative.

After that odd beginning, Thompson moves into fairly straight political analysis, peppered with a number of quotations from newspapers and an excerpt from a legal definition of sodomy. There are, of course, various long digressions, such as a tract on his philosophy of breakfast. He comments upon this in the next paragraph:

> It is not going to be easy for those poor
> bastards out in San Francisco who have
> been waiting all day in a condition of
> extreme fear and anxiety for my long and
> finely reasoned analysis of "The Meaning
> of Jimmy Carter" to come roaring out
> of my faithful mojo wire and across 2000
> miles of telephone line to understand
> why I am sitting here in a Texas motel full
> of hookers and writing at length on The
> Meaning of Breakfast. . .

As it had done in 1972, Thompson's conspiratorial tone, seemingly subversive admissions, and in-the-moment rambling serve to bring the reader closer to the story, increasing the sense of immediacy felt. His words seem directed at the reader—bypassing the editors altogether—and so by throwing what seem like pointless asides into the text, he is addressing his audience more directly. It is an article about Jimmy Carter in the same way that *Fear and Loathing in Las Vegas* was a novel about that desert city of sin. In other words, the subject is often the subtext and the main event is the writer and his personal journey to record the story. Once again, Thompson puts himself at the center of the story and includes lots of his conversations, ultimately producing an article about Carter that no one else could have written.

The main purpose of this article, though, is not to write about his failures in covering the campaign trail, but to describe a speech that he had heard Jimmy Carter give at Georgia Law School in May 1974. Thompson had been genuinely moved by Carter's impromptu speech, in which he excoriated lawyers in front of a room full of them. It didn't hurt that he referred to Bob Dylan, either. It wasn't often that Thompson was impressed by a politician, but this was one of the very few times. Carter seemed honest, principled, and driven. When Thompson writes about his speech, he drops his sarcasm, vitriol, and fantasies. He is sincere and straight and applies liberal doses of his patented wisdom.

"Fear and Loathing on the Campaign Trail '76" is another good article, but it was his only published work that year. Wenner had put a banner on the front of the magazine claiming that the story was an endorsement of the presidential candidate, but Thompson did not believe that any journalist should endorse a candidate. This, coupled with Wenner's refusal to pay Hunter's exorbitant expenses, set off another row between the two men, and he sent no more of his writing to *Rolling Stone* that year. For the second consecutive year, he had just written a single article.

There were, of course, more attempts to write. Through all of the fallow years, he had various projects—perhaps too many. In the sixties, he had juggled different articles and managed to usually make one of them work but, by the mid-seventies, he was unable to focus and, when he did write, it was hit or miss. Clearly, he still had the talent, but he was too distracted or disinterested to use it.

During the 1976 Democratic Convention, Wenner threw a big party in New York and Thompson went along, aiming to write about the convention. He enjoyed the week-long party, with plenty of women and drugs and whiskey, but he wrote nothing and did not make as much as a single note. His only writing related to this event was an excellent stream-of-consciousness journal entry, which was published in his letter collection, *Fear and Loathing in America*. This was written just two hours before leaving for the convention.

Aside from that, Thompson claimed to be at work on a book about gun-running in Texas. It was a tale of "Violence, Texas, and drugs," he told one interviewer in spring, but said that he didn't know much more than that. By the end of 1976, he had added into the mix that it was about the American Dream. This was because he had decided to pitch it to Jim Silberman at Random House in order to fulfil a contract that was now nearly ten years old. In a letter to Silberman, he explained that he had considered a book about Texas for two years, but it was only when faced with the choice between reporting on Jimmy Carter or writing his novel that he had seen the light—the Texas book, which he now called *Galveston*, would be a novel.

He explained to his editor that *Galveston* would be a "journalistic novel" rather than pure fiction and it would, of course, be told from the first-person perspective.

However, he still didn't seem to know much more about it than that. Writing it, he felt, would have required him to move to Texas for several years, which he was not ready for, and, besides, "the sudden millstone of personal notoriety" was weighing heavily on him, making it harder to focus on anything.

It was an interesting idea for a book but after two years of thinking about it, there is no evidence that he had written anything more than a few ideas. He shaped the plot (when he finally developed one) into a screenplay but it eventually fizzled out. It was just one more addition to a growing pile of projects that were sadly never completed.

This mentality unfortunately became a pattern and, over the next three decades, he would often come up with ideas for books (or movies) and then abandon them without writing much. He was famous enough that he could command good money for his ideas and it was a hell of a lot easier than writing. He also found that he could profit from his old writing again by gathering and publishing his collected works. In December 1976, he wrote an introduction to *The Gonzo Papers*, a proposed collection of his work to date that was published three years later as *The Gonzo Papers Volume I: The Great Shark Hunt* under Jim Silberman's Summit Books, an imprint of Simon & Schuster.

The book is an incredibly valuable collection in that it gathered work from all through his life, including his fake news release from Eglin Air Force Base and some of his reporting from South America. A lot of this had previously been impossible to come by for the fans who knew him from *Rolling Stone*, so it was viewed as a treasure chest of Hunter Thompson's best work. The only downside was that, to borrow a description from David Felton, it was "the worst-edited and most self-indulgent book since the Bible." There was no order to it at all, frustrating fans and scholars for the past forty years by jumping around pointlessly in time.

Various reviewers commented on the horrible arrangement of material and the fact that the mixture highlighted weaknesses in his later work rather than pointing to development. One particularly perceptive reviewer noted the flaws as follows:

> The most recent work contained in the anthology is also the weakest. Thompson thrives in that gray zone between telling the story, and telling the storyteller's story. [...] Thompson, it seems, has fallen victim to his own success. He no longer has to strain the borders of accepted journalistic practice. Rolling Stone appears to allow him to write anything he wants, any way he wants to write it. The edge is gone.
>
> The Great Shark Hunt is a symptom of Thompson's present troubles. It contains virtually nothing that was written especially for the anthology. His page-and-a-half introduction is full of flat Thompson phrasing, meaningless and enervated.

Although he was as popular as ever, critics and editors were aware of his failings. Thompson, too, knew that it was time to redeem himself. Perhaps it was time for a rebrand. By this point, he was thoroughly sick of his Gonzo image, complaining that "All the humor has gone out of that 'fear & loathing' logo." In the note, he says that he is in a hotel room and imagines jumping out of the window, killing himself. It would be a symbolic act; the end of the first part of his career. He signed the note, "HST #I, R.I.P."

Would this be the end of Raoul Duke and Gonzo Journalism?

Attempts to Quit Gonzo

I don't like to write. I don't care what happens after I write. Once I've gotten the story in my mind, the rest is just pain.

Hunter S. Thompson

By 1977, Hunter Thompson was reaching new lows in terms of his productivity. The man who had once written compulsively in order to understand himself and his world could now barely sit still long enough to write a thousand words, and when he could he lacked the focus to stay on any one topic or even link together his sentences and paragraphs. He had published just one memo in 1975 and a single article in 1976, and his plans for new books constantly fell apart as he jumped around from one idea to the next. He was addicted to cocaine, struggling with fame, and he had become thoroughly trapped in his Gonzo persona. Grover Lewis, another *Rolling Stone* editor, said, "It made him wealthy and made him very famous, but I think it hurt him. I think it ruined him as an artist, frankly."

By now, his marriage was also crumbling. Sandy, who had kept him fed, shielded him from visitors, typed his work, and generally done everything possible to let Hunter live his dream, was now growing tired of the physical and verbal abuse, and of Hunter's frequent infidelity. He had always been handsome and charismatic, but now that he was famous, too, women threw themselves at him wherever he went, and he was not the sort of man who said no to fun, regardless of the consequences. They would remain married for another few years, but it was clear to most of their friends that the end was drawing near.

In February 1977, Thompson flew to New Orleans to write about Mardi Gras for *Rolling Stone*. The story was slated to have a predictable title ("Fear and Loathing at Mardi Gras") but the most predictable outcome of all was that Thompson simply did not write it. Wenner had proposed the article and so Thompson decide to abuse his expense account, taking various friends to Louisiana for an all-expenses-paid party. Whilst there, he met Dan Aykroyd and John Belushi, who were in town filming the Saturday Night Live Mardi Gras special. Over the years, he would make numerous famous friends and their wild, Hollywood parties presented him with another distraction from the exhausting realities of writing.

When the event was over, Thompson's friends all disappeared. They liked to party, but they still had lives to live and jobs to do. Hunter, however, floundered. "You gotta stay with me," he told Bill Dixon. "Someone's gotta stay with me now while I try and write." He had been struggling for several years to sit down and write without someone forcing him to do so, but of course the presence of friends also made it easy for him to goof around. In the end, the Mardi Gras story was never written.

It was just another in a long series of failures to produce articles. In the early sixties, he would take an assignment and do whatever was necessary to report on it as well as he could but, after he had made his name, he was content to take the money, have fun, and not even turn in an article at the end. *Rolling Stone* put up with it because he had become a rock star. They knew that if he did turn in an article, it would make them a fortune because his name now guaranteed high sales. As for Thompson, he knew that they would print things no one else would, so he continued to write for them even though he was constantly disappointed by Wenner.

When *Rolling Stone* moved from San Francisco to New York that year, Wenner told the *Chronicle* that the city had become "a provincial backwater," but many felt that what he really meant was, "we can make a lot more money in New York." Already unhappy with the magazine and its owner, Thompson was further convinced by their flight to New York that they had lost their way. New York was the home of the Establishment, of major publishers and media companies. Once a voice for the youth, *Rolling Stone* was now just another glossy magazine like all the others. At the beginning of the decade, it had put cutting-edge countercultural characters on its cover, but by 1977 rock icons had made way for pop stars and Hollywood heartthrobs. Wenner had always been careful to position his magazine so that it could appeal to a broad range of people and earn good money from its advertisers, but now that it was in New York, Thompson felt that it had sold out entirely. Although he loved hanging out with famous people, he had no respect for this sort of vapid journalism.

Joe Hagan, author of *Sticky Fingers: The Life and Times of Jann Wenner and Rolling Stone*, ties Hunter and Jann together as participating in the downfall of the magazine and the wider American press' descent into shallow, celebrity-obsessed reporting:

> At its base, *Rolling Stone* was an expression of Wenner's pursuit of fame and power. He reinvented celebrity around youth culture, which equated confession and frank sexuality with integrity and authenticity. The post-1960s vision of celebrity meant that every printed word of John Lennon's unhappiness and anything Bob Dylan said or did now had the news primacy of a State of the Union address. It meant that Hunter Thompson could make every story he ever wrote, in essence, about himself. It also meant that climbing into bed with Mick Jagger was only worth doing if you had a Nikon handy. Self-image was the new aphrodisiac.

Despite the continual animosity, there were constant overtures to get him back into the magazine. Various editors tried with varying degrees of success, and several people lost their jobs because Hunter simply wouldn't or couldn't write. In 1977, Harriet Fier, *Rolling Stone*'s latest managing editor, stepped up efforts to get Hunter Thompson back. She ran through the usual playbook of compliments and threats, and then finally put a note in the magazine:

> Attention all you readers who are constantly on our back about where the hell Dr. Hunter S. Thompson is. Please write to him yourself and tell him to get off his ass and start writing again: c/o Woody Creek, Colorado 81656.

Her tactics worked, and in December, one and a half years since his last published work, *Rolling Stone* printed one of Thompson's best pieces of writing, "The Banshee Screams for Buffalo Meat."

Ever since he had written *Fear and Loathing in Las Vegas*, Hunter's relationship with Oscar Zeta Acosta had been on a steep downward trajectory. Acosta's attempts to derail the book's publication had enraged Thompson and their letters to one another had grown inflammatory. While Thompson's career had taken off, Acosta's life had become miserable. He grew resentful of his famous friend and in 1973 he wrote to *Playboy* to angrily refute their claim that Thompson was the progenitor of Gonzo. He explained that the story and the method of reporting were created through the combined efforts of both men, "hand in hand."

As we saw in the last chapter, they briefly reconciled in Mexico to work on an ill-fated story, but it is not easy for two paranoid and aggressive people to stay on good terms, and by late 1973 they were at each other's throats once again. In what was likely his last letter to Hunter, Acosta complained that he was forced to use food stamps and shoplift in order to feed himself. He pleaded for help, but none came. Instead, Thompson wrote back with a callous, vicious letter that rebuked his desperate friend, then signed it, "Whitey." Less than six months later, Acosta was missing and presumed dead. He is believed to have been murdered at sea while smuggling drugs off the coast of Mazatlán in May 1974.[1]

---

1   His son, Marco, who was probably the last person to hear from his father, and who spoke with people that were with Acosta in Mexico, believes he was murdered while at sea with drug dealers, attempting to smuggle something (probably cocaine) from Mazatlán to San Francisco. He said, "The body was never found, but we surmise that probably, knowing the people

When Acosta's sister wrote Thompson in October 1974 to say that Oscar had been missing for many months and was presumed dead, he began to think about writing something for *Rolling Stone*, but it was only in 1977, when prompted by Harriet Fier, that he began to take the idea seriously. Fier and the other women at the magazine had discussed Thompson's work and thought that maybe he should write something different from the usual Gonzo stories. "Wouldn't it be great," she said, "to see Hunter write about sex, or relationships, or people, or just himself rather than his monolithic paranoia."

From his reaction to her suggestion, Fier felt that he had never even considered it before. They discussed ideas that involved him taking a gentler approach and then decided upon an article about Acosta, which Thompson called "Requiem for a Crazed Heavyweight." It would be printed in the tenth-anniversary issue of *Rolling Stone* on December 15, 1977.

Although Fier and Thompson had discussed a softer approach to writing, the resulting article was surprisingly brutal, even by Thompson's standards. He laid into his deceased friend, hurling vile insults at him—many of which were racial or deeply personal—including "rotten fat spic" and "a stupid, vicious quack with no morals at all and the soul of a hammerhead shark." Readers must have been mystified. Many of them would not have known the full backstory of Hunter and Oscar's relationship, and few would be aware that Thompson treated his friends to awful insults as a form of kindness. It was a point of honor among many to keep those offensive, creative, late-night faxes and letters filled with his favorite harsh words and phrases. As Ralph Steadman once said, "He berated most of his friends a lot, but somehow it was funny. His way of expressing love for people was to be both angry

---

he was involved with, he ended up mouthing off, getting into a fight, and getting killed." [http://gettingit.com/article/603] Other theories suggest he had suffered a mental breakdown, and indeed he had been hospitalized not long before his death and had revised his will several times during his final months. Marco said, "I think he knew that eventually something was going to happen to him, that he was going to be assassinated or [...] it was gonna be foul play somehow." https://youtu.be/-S6fYUi1c-0

and insulting. I always thought that when he was the most rude to me was when he loved me the most."

Yet there was another reason for the cruelty. Years later, he told an interviewer that he had deliberately insulted Acosta in the worst ways in the hope that, if he had been in hiding somewhere, he would have made contact. He did not, and Thompson had known that he wouldn't. Oscar had led a life on the Edge, like Hunter, but he had pushed too far. Both men had believed they would die young, but only Acosta went so far that it became an inevitability. While Thompson wrote about the outlaw life, Acosta had lived it. Thompson used words; Acosta relied upon actions.

The article begins, as is normal now, with the usual flurry of subheaders. This is followed by a fake editor's note that gives some background, although more space is given to details about his agreement with *Rolling Stone* than Acosta's life. Strangely, the editor's note says that Acosta "disappeared under mean and mysterious circumstances in the late months of 1974, or perhaps the early months of 1975." In fact, he disappeared in May 1974, which Thompson knew. After that, there are two quotations, one of which comes from Acosta's *Autobiography of a Brown Buffalo*.

The article begins with the narrative directed at Oscar: "One of the great regrets of my life is that I was never able to introduce you to my old football buddy, Richard Nixon." Thompson addresses his dead friend for two paragraphs before turning to his reader and continuing. He describes Acosta's downfall with sad and intelligent commentary, painting a picture of a man of great character, who had walked a difficult path in life and then fallen hard from grace. The narrative is colorful, personal, and informative. It has been carefully written and drafted, yet it retains a conversational, informal tone.

The second part of the story appears to go off-topic as Thompson recounts being at home one night, when two of his peacocks are killed by an owl. The tone has switched from sober to something more akin to Thompson's version of manic normality. It is personal as he describes his home and mentions his wife (just giving her first name; no explanation). He then makes an odd remark to the reader. After saying that Tom Benton had arrived at Owl Farm, he adds in parentheses: "you know Tom, with that fine artist's eye that he has." There is some typically bizarre dialogue between Thompson and Benton that seems to serve no real purpose in the story, and then he is given a message that says Acosta is still alive. Thompson recounts, in vivid detail impossible for anyone to know without having been there, a story about Acosta smuggling drugs in Florida. It is a fantasy sequence but there is no such indication in the text. Again, he is pressing his reader to ask questions and avoid assumptions.

In the third part of the story, he launches into a barrage of insults. It is vicious, but at the same time tempered by the occasional word of admiration:

> There was more mercy, madness, dignity and generosity in that overweight, overworked and always overindulged brown cannonball of a body than most of us will meet in any human package even three times Oscar's size for the rest of our lives.

Even when Thompson descends into harsh words against his friend, he does so in a way that gives Acosta the greatest compliment—it builds his legend. For Thompson, the appearance of being an outlaw was just about the most important thing in life, and here he heaps praise upon Acosta for being violently opposed to the establishment. In his own mind, he is adding Acosta to the outlaw pantheon. He alludes several times to Acosta's supposed firebombing activities and depicts him as a crusader for justice who was not in the least afraid of going to jail or dying for his beliefs. He is a maverick, a true individual. Thompson describes his hunger for LSD, saying that Acosta took it like other lawyers took Valium. In a sense, despite the insults, Acosta emerges from this story a kind of outlaw hero.

When Thompson is writing passionately about his friend, he is on fine form. His writing is sublime, much like when he was attacking Richard Nixon or describing an acid trip in Las Vegas:

Oscar was not into serious street-fighting, but he was hell on wheels in a bar brawl. Any combination of a 250-pound Mexican and LSD-25 is a potentially terminal menace for anything it can reach – but when the alleged Mexican is in fact a profoundly angry Chicano lawyer with no fear at all of anything that walks on less than three legs and a de facto suicidal conviction that he will die at the age of thirty-three – just like Jesus Christ – you have a serious piece of work on your hands. Specially if the bastard is already thirty-three and a half years old with a head full of Sandoz acid, a loaded .357 Magnum in his belt, a hatchet-wielding Chicano bodyguard on his elbow at all times, and a disconcerting habit of projectile-vomiting geysers of pure red blood off the front porch every thirty or forty minutes, or whenever his malignant ulcer can't handle any more raw tequila.

In this paragraph, we can see Thompson's use of long sentences, punctuated with em dashes, layering image upon image by prefacing most nouns with at least one strong adjective in order to make his point, creating an eruption of ideas that bombards the reader. Like his "wave passage," the punctuation here is intended to dictate breath and this is clearly meant to be read aloud. The rhythm in his language has returned. There is one short sentence and two extremely long ones, building a steady pace in the text that sweeps the reader along into increasingly vivid imagery. In the next paragraph, the structure is exactly the same. This leads into the final lines of the third part of the story. Thompson is like an expert orator, building his audience into a frenzy with the cadence of his prose.

In part four, Thompson tells the story of his troubles with Acosta during the publication of *Fear and Loathing in Las Vegas*, and in the final section, he goes back into attack mode, but this time leaves a few clues as to his purpose:

> We should have castrated that brain-damaged thief! That shyster! That blasphemous freak! He was ugly and greasy and he still owes me thousands of dollars!
>
> The truth was not in him, goddamnit! He was put on this earth for no reason at all except to shit in every nest he could con his way into – but only after robbing them first, and selling the babies to sand-niggers. If that treacherous fist-fucker ever comes back to life, he'll wish we'd had the good sense to nail him up on a frozen telephone pole for his thirty-third birthday present.
>
> DO NOT COME BACK OSCAR! Wherever you are – stay there! There's no room for you here anymore. Not after all this maudlin gibberish I've written about you. . .

Clearly, this was intended as a message to Oscar. *If you are still alive, please let me know.* The message is so over the top that it is odd even by Hunter Thompson's standards. The exclamation marks set this apart as the sort of hyperbolic vitriol that he reserved for close friends for the purpose of amusement, and the reference to his own writing as "maudlin" is an attempt to bring the reader into the joke.

"The Banshee Screams for Buffalo Meat" is an astonishing piece of writing. In it, Thompson has written one of the most bizarre eulogies imaginable, hurling insults at the dead but somehow letting a tone of admiration and love shine through. It is a stoic's lament, not bogged down in emotion but dealing aggressively with the issues at heart. His writing is polished, organized, original, and gripping.

The following year, Thompson was visited by a team from the BBC, who wanted to shoot a documentary about his life and work. "Fear and Loathing in Gonzovision" saw him meeting with Steadman near Owl Farm, then traveling through Las Vegas to Hollywood. In the film, he speaks candidly about being trapped in the persona of Raoul Duke, saying "most people are impressed I walk on two legs." He talks at length about fans expecting him to act a certain way and never being sure whether he should act as Duke or just be himself. In one scene, we can see him hiding from autograph-seeking crowds despite being dressed up to look like Duke. He says that he feels great pressure to play a certain role, and that even on camera for this documentary he has been pushed into acting as Duke.

The interviewer points out what almost every viewer must have thought: Hunter S. Thompson the writer was not all that different from Raoul Duke the character. He was openly taking drugs and shooting guns, mumbling and barking strange things, and dressed just like in his books. But although he was still very much acting a role in the documentary, Thompson was sincere about changing. He felt that Duke had become a millstone and worried about its effect on his writing. He tells the viewers, "I've started to repeat myself" and says he wants to "kill off" Duke and create "a new identity." At the end, two pieces of film are cut together to make it appear as though Thompson is shooting Duke off a motorbike. It was time for a change.

Thompson's greatest failure at this point had been his expensive trip to Zaire to watch Muhammad Ali fight in one of history's great sporting events. Four years later, he accepted *Rolling Stone's* offer to cover Ali's 1978 fight against Leon Spinks. The idea had been George Plimpton's. He suggested that he and Thompson cover the fight together and take it in turns to write paragraphs, but alas, when the fight began, the seat next to Plimpton's was empty and he had to write the article by himself. Still, Thompson was eager to meet one of his true heroes and he arranged an interview with Ali. It began with an agreement to write a short article, but it soon spiraled into another twenty-thousand-word metajournalistic epic.

In "Last Tango in Vegas," published in the May 4 and May 18 issues of *Rolling Stone*, Thompson offered a slow-building, two-part story about interviewing Ali. In the first part, we see a different approach that shows Thompson moving away from the Duke persona and some elements of Gonzo style. Like his mid-sixties writing, it is mature and methodical, as he very slowly unwinds the story of trying to meet Muhammad Ali. The frantic chaos of Gonzo is gone and he is more interested in telling the reader a story than presenting himself in any particular light. His is more observer than participant, more Thompson than Duke.

Duke appears, but only in a memo in the first part; otherwise, the text is quite conventional and informative, with little intrusion by the narrator. There is one random burst of fantasy in which he imagines beating Leon Spinks, and a few more Gonzo elements intrude: he comments on his journalistic process, uses some of his favorite words and phrases ("atavistic," "savage," "swine," "the fat was in the fire"), and refers to Fitzgerald's "high white note" when he talks about Ali's entourage "working that high white vein." He even claims that Ali's famous quote, "My way of joking is to tell the truth; that's the funniest joke in the world," is a good definition for Gonzo journalism.

While the first part started with the narrative focused on boxing, the second is more personal. Thompson receives the message that he has been rejected by Ali and explodes with rage, using words like "pigfucker." He transitions smoothly into talking about Ali and then discusses how difficult it is for reporters to get past his "moats"—by which he means layers of fake personality. He believes there are nine and aims to reach level seven or eight, which is an unusually candid remark for a journalist to make.

When Thompson is with Ali, he knows he is basking in the presence of greatness, but he still acts more or less like himself. He drinks and smokes in front of the champ, an unthinkable transgression among his followers, but Ali is amused and Thompson reports several times that his actions and comments earn applause from the whole room. Although he puts Ali at center stage, he also seems to boast about these things by mentioning them. When he speaks rudely of Ali, it is a very mild version of Thompson's usual reporting of his own outbursts, but still it seems shocking because it is Muhammad Ali whom he calls "bastard" and "giggling yoyo." He is still a wild man, even if he is toned down:

> But I was mercifully and obviously ignorant of what I was doing. Smoking and drinking and tossing off crude bursts of language are not *second* nature to me, but *first*—and my mood, at that point, was still so mean

and jangled that it took me about ten minutes of foul-mouthed raving before I began to get a grip on myself.

This is followed by a "99 percent verbatim transcript" of his two-hour interview with Ali—a repetition of his language from *Fear and Loathing on the Campaign Trail '72*. He had managed to disarm Ali, who had little patience with interviewers. He had made him laugh several times and so Ali was open and honest, giving what a member of his entourage called "one of the best [interviews] I've ever seen." Thompson was a good interviewer and it was evident from his *Campaign Trail* book that he knew what sort of questions to ask and how to get people talking. He was also quite perceptive, able to read Ali well and describe him in ways that other journalists could not:

> He has a very lonely sense of humor, and a sense of himself so firmly entrenched that it seems to hover, at times, in that nervous limbo between Egomania and genuine Invulnerability.

The article ends with another reference to Fitzgerald, this time with Thompson calling Ali the "brown Jay Gatsby." He had compared many people to Gatsby but it is in this article that he makes his strongest case and offers the most admiration. There are few people whom Thompson described that really earned his total respect, and Ali was one. At the very end, he writes, "He came, he saw, and if he didn't entirely conquer—he came as close as anybody we are likely to see in the lifetime of this doomed generation." Then, he signs off with a new phrase—"Res ipsa loquitur." It is a Latin phrase used in legal systems around the world to mean "the thing speaks for itself." However, Thompson seemed to imply "let the good times roll" when he used it.[2] From the late seventies until the end of his life, it was a common feature of his writing.

---

2   David Felton claims, perhaps jokingly, that Thompson defined it as, "Don't fuck with this," because it was usually written at the end of an article that was handed in too late to edit properly. [*Hunter*, p.189]

Altogether, the story is coherent and entertaining. He seems knowledgeable on the subject of boxing and guides us through the players in the Ali camp and the standings in the world of boxing as of 1978. When he enters the story with any crazy antics, these act as comic interludes and it is much more effective than when he tries to dominate a whole story with such drama. This, then, can be viewed as partially redeeming his failure in Zaire and also as a genuine effort to move forward with Gonzo.

A few months after it was published in *Rolling Stone*, "The Banshee Screams for Buffalo Meat" was purchased by the filmmaker, Art Linson. Few people thought that the movie would ever be made as it was such an odd idea, but those who did warned Thompson that it would just compound his problems with fame. It had been three years since Uncle Duke had first appeared in *Doonesbury* and the last thing he needed was yet another frivolous caricature shaping public perception. But the rights to the idea came with a check for one hundred thousand dollars, and so it was a risk he was willing to take.

While Thompson could be incredibly high-minded about art, sometimes he was quite honest about his greed, openly admitting, "Shit, I did it for the money," as though it would be foolish to refuse. When Steadman accused him of selling out, he said he didn't see anything wrong with it, and when other friends cautioned him about cheapening his image, he replied that he had earned the right to capitalize on his fame. He had done this, of course, with the farcical speaking tours, but it was even more lucrative to allow filmmakers to try to adapt his books. He often sold the rights to *Fear and Loathing in Las Vegas*, confident that no one would ever make the movie because it was so difficult to transfer to film. He could earn ten thousand dollars just optioning it for six months, so it provided him with a handsome income.

When production started to move along, he quickly realized that the movie—called *Where the Buffalo Roam*—would be no good, but he did not worry too much about it. It was just another way of gaining more fame and wealth, and he was resolute in his belief that neither of these could justifiably be used to criticize him. If a movie about his life was terrible, it was no reflection on him; the filmmakers were at fault. In public, he sometimes referred to it as a "piece of shit" but mostly he did not seem to care.

When it was released in April 1980, *Where the Buffalo Roam* was panned by critics, including David Felton at *Rolling Stone*, who called it an "embarrassing piece of hogwash utterly devoid of plot, form, movement, tension, humor, insight, logic or purpose" and called Thompson "a drug-crazed greedhead," borrowing the writer's own language. Others criticized it for being little more than a series of ridiculous scenes with nothing resembling a coherent plotline, and film critic Leonard Maltin said that it "will baffle those who aren't familiar with Hunter S. Thompson's work and insult those who are." To be fair to the director, these were all criticisms equally leveled at Thompson's own later writing.

Perhaps it was a doomed project from the start. It was the director's first movie and the script had been rewritten so often that, by the time they were ready to film, Bill Murray, who played Thompson, was worried that it made no sense. In the end, the only saving grace was that Murray made an excellent Hunter, having managed to adopt his mannerisms throughout their time together.[3] Thompson, who was brought in as a consultant, was paid an additional twenty-five thousand dollars to write a speech for the end of the movie. Just like his usual writing, he put it off for weeks and only sat down to write at the very last moment.

Thompson was delighted with their work on the speech, which they naturally did in the wee hours. It was handwritten and no one was allowed to see it except the two Hunters. When it came time to record it, Murray delivered the lines exactly as Thompson had written them, with no editorial interference. The audio recording was then transferred immediately onto the film. Thompson felt

---

3   Murray was a big fan of Thompson's work and had already met him in Aspen. They spent a lot of time together in Los Angeles during filming, and by the end Murray had a lot of trouble getting out of character again. (This is apparent from the 1981 movie, *Stripes,* as well as his SNL performances.) They remained friends and Thompson's last published writing, written a few days before his suicide, was about a phone call he made to Murray at 03:33 one morning.

it was an amazing breakthrough in Gonzo filmmaking. "We finally found a way to cut through all the editors, printers, even the typewriter," he said. Still, the material was not great. The short speech was repetitive and, like the rest of the movie, cartoonish. It sounded more like a high school student's impression of Hunter Thompson than the real thing.

Where the Buffalo Roam was released just a few months after *The Great Shark Hunt*, which was discussed in the previous chapter. The movie created a new phenomenon—scores of Gonzo fans who had never actually read one of Thompson's books, but who worshipped at the altar of meaningless excess. The book provided his more literate fans with a vast amount of writing going back to his *National Observer* days, but it seemed to have been collected almost at random. Between the movie and the book, one could get the impression that he was happy to let his bank account and fame grow and was no longer concerned about his literary reputation.

Although he felt no shame about *Where the Buffalo Roam*, Thompson was somewhat worried when a theater in London put on an adaptation of *Fear and Loathing in Las Vegas*. He told the director, "I'm coming out to see it. If I don't like what you've done with the book, I'm going to tear your theatre apart." Hunter flew to England to watch it, and while there he was commissioned by *Time Out* to write a cover story. They paid his exorbitant expense bill as he tore up London for a fortnight, but when his deadline came and went, there was no story submitted. Finally, just before the magazine went to press, they received a cassette tape with a "largely inaudible" account of his trip. They were unable to salvage anything usable and had to write off their losses.[4] It was the risk that now came with hiring Hunter S. Thompson.

After nearly two decades of abuse, Thompson's long-suffering wife picked up and left him in 1980. The police had to come and escort her from the property as Hunter threatened her and threw all of her writing onto a fire. He was distraught, but the sadness soon turned to pettiness and he had a new reason not to write—he did not want

4   Two years later, they were able to print excerpts from his next book, *The Curse of Lono*.

Sandy to get her hands on any more of his money. He told the courts that he was "reluctant to undertake any new literary works in which the Respondent wife may declare a marital interest" and that he hoped the divorce would be granted so that it "would allow him to freely create new literary properties without fear."

Despite claiming that his lack of productivity was due to his unwillingness to work for money that would go to Sandy and her lawyers, in a 1980 interview he also expressed a complete disinterest in writing, except as a way of making money. He said that he only wrote when he was broke and that he could make more money by answering the phone than by actually putting together a serious article. "I don't like to write," he said. "I don't care what happens after I write. Once I've gotten the story in my mind, the rest is just pain."

Beyond the petty squabbles over money, the divorce affected him a great deal. Thompson's writing often put him at the center of a story, but he only ever wrote about a version of himself that he wanted to portray to the public—whether wise, strong, or comically incompetent. He almost never wrote about serious, personal matters, including his relationship with Sandy. More than a decade later, he even threatened to murder a journalist who asked him about it. There were countless events that marked him deeply, including his father's death, the Democratic Convention in 1968, the death of his daughter, his divorce, or his failing health in later years.[5] In all of these moments, there was a tremendous sense of pain and a feeling of weakness within him that he was clearly not comfortable sharing with the wider world. He could write about drug frenzies, crimes, violence, and paranoia, but he could not or would not write about emotions. This is likely another reason why he became trapped writing the same tired old stories in the eighties and beyond.

The seventies had started with a bang for Hunter Thompson—the advent of a new literary genre followed by two highly successful books. However, it had turned

5   Sandy had given birth to a baby girl called Sara in July 1969, but she died soon after being born. Thompson never spoke or wrote about this.

sour as he failed to complete his assignments or offered up relatively weak and derivative efforts. There had been some good pieces, but not many, and certainly no more than one per year. At the start of a new decade, he knew that he had to reinvent himself and put an end to the Raoul Duke character that had defined and finally trapped him. Although outwardly he did not appear to care, on the inside he believed himself to be a serious writer and he hoped for a return to his late-sixties/early-seventies form.

When Sandy left, Hunter nailed the door shut at Owl Farm and went into a period of self-imposed isolation. But he was a social person by nature and so it didn't last long. With Owl Farm painfully empty, he took off for Florida. His friend, Jimmy Buffett, owned a house in Key West that he rarely used, so he lent it to Hunter. Key West was once the playground of Ernest Hemingway, so it is perhaps little surprise that Thompson's days there were among the happiest of his life. McKeen noted, in Mile Marker Zero, that it allowed "a man with a serious Hemingway fixation" to live out his "literary he-man dream." After this first visit, he would return almost every year to escape the cruel Aspen winters. The weather was great, he could drink and smoke pot on the beach, and there were beautiful women everywhere. The island still had a reputation for drawing literary types, and Thompson made plenty of good friends, including the author, Jim Harrison, and a young writer called Tom Corcoran. The former had recently learned how to write screenplays and Thompson was eager to learn from him. Unperturbed about the failure of *Where the Buffalo Roam*, he decided that maybe he should write a script. It seemed easier and more profitable than another book.

As luck would have it, Jann Wenner was looking to push *Rolling Stone* into film production and asked Thompson if he would write a screenplay. He had learned a lot from the people around him in Key West, but it was Corcoran that Thompson relied on most. The young writer knew the technical details that Thompson didn't, and together they began working on a script called *Cigarette Key*. The subject of the film would be drug smuggling—something that had always fascinated Thompson—and, like *The Rum Diary*, it would be set on a tropical island. In fact, for a while he considered "cannibalizing" his old novel, but eventually decided that *The Rum Diary* was a complete work and should remain that way. Jay Cowan explained that "he wasn't sure how well its more realistic and character-based plot would mesh with a *Cigarette Key* story line that variously involved everything from smugglers with submarines to Cuban gangsters chopping up cops." His research for the novel involved going out in the mangroves on his new boat and then studying the newspapers for stories about drug busts, clipping and pinning what he found to a large bulletin board.

The two men worked on the screenplay and wrote a treatment, which Wenner was able to sell to Paramount Pictures, but the film was never made. The screenplay was largely written by Corcoran, with Thompson primarily providing ideas. Laila Nabulsi, Thompson's assistant and girlfriend, called him Hunter's ghostwriter. Corcoran explained:

> When we started writing the script, his work habits were going down the tubes and his relationship with Laila was building, fast. He was head over heels in love with her and not caring at all about work. And so the work fell to me. I started writing and okaying things with him, and not okaying things with him.

This was just one of Thompson's ideas for a movie. He began plotting out movies that had lots of ideas but absolutely no character development, then he would become bored and think of a new movie. There was one called *The Day the Blood Ran Out* and another called *The Magician*. All of his ideas tended to involve "lots of drugs and madness" but little substance, according to Cowan. It hardly mattered. He knew that a single good idea could earn more money than a year or more of writing, so he kept pitching movies to contacts in Hollywood. He sold so many, in fact, that it became hard for him to keep track. After Corcoran wrote almost all of *Cigarette Key* alone, Thompson squandered their payment so he gave him a story called *The Mole* to sell, but Corcoran later discovered that Thompson had already sold it to another studio.

While he was in Key West, the Mariel boatlift began, which saw the mass migration of ten thousand Cubans to the United States. It was a huge news story and Corcoran realized that, with the action so close, he needed to cover it. He found his way onto a boat and took off to join the boatlift, intending to photograph the immigrants for *Newsweek*. When the boat pulled out to sea, he saw Hunter standing on the pier. It struck Corcoran as incredible that any journalist would not want to be part of it, but Thompson was not interested. He would watch it on TV in a bar.

Instead of covering the boatlift as a journalist, Thompson decided to write a novel about it. He later said that he knew it was a good story and that he had been interested in writing about it as a journalist but felt "there was not enough room in a journalistic format for the characters I wanted. So I finally decided to write the story as a novel." He began work on a book called *The Silk Road* but never finished it. Several chapters were published in *Songs of the Doomed*, and it is not impressive. There is a flurry of action, but in the middle of it Thompson takes off on his standard political digressions. It lacks focus, is repetitive, and the narrative often becomes disjointed, including when Thompson tackles a luggage thief and the perspective switches from Thompson to the thief. It is tempting to think that this may have been deliberate but given the problems in his writing at this time, it does seem rather unlikely.

The lack of focus goes beyond just the action and into the characters and the narrative. The novel seems to be about Thompson and another man, Gene Skinner—a new persona he had invented to replace Raoul Duke. It is not exactly clear who Skinner is and, just as he had done with Duke, Thompson changes his background and personality in other stories. All that is clear is that Skinner is the new persona—a character entered into the text for fundamentally the same reasons that Duke had been invented in the sixties. He said that Skinner was "the freak for the 80s," implying that Duke was a relic of the sixties, and claimed that Skinner was more suitable for the "anti-humanist" era of Reagan. "I've given up Duke," Thompson explained.

"He's funny. Skinner is not so funny." Still, as with his other fictional creations, it is unclear where Thompson ends and Skinner begins. The two men seem to switch personalities, and it possible to view Skinner as Thompson's alter ego—a means of bringing the contents of his own mind out into the open as a conversation between two people.

A clue to his intentions for Skinner come in the form of a hand-written outline. Thompson describes *The Silk Road* as "A fast, strange & occasionally violent story" that he believes will end up around eighty to ninety thousand words, and which will fuse the "narrative precision" of *The Great Gatsby* with the "high humor" of *Fear and Loathing in Las Vegas*. At its core, the novel was intended to answer the question, "Is Skinner a good guy or a bad guy?" He goes on to ask himself whether Gatsby was good or bad and says, "Skinner should fit the 80's like Gatsby fit the 20's." So much of his writing was an attempt to compete with Fitzgerald that this is hardly a surprising claim. He often looked at stories and asked himself: *Where is the green light? Who is Gatsby here? Could there be a Daisy?* Perhaps this was another reason for the repetitious nature of his work.

In *Songs of the Doomed*, Thompson includes further details about how the book would proceed. He explains that he viewed himself as Nick Carraway and Skinner as Jay Gatsby, and that the plot would involve Thompson going to Key West to scuba dive with his friend before the chaos of the boatlift began. He goes on to say, "The raw elements of the story are (in no special order): sex, violence, greed, treachery, big money, fast boats, blue water" and the list goes on. He said "in no special order" but there certainly was a reason for putting "sex" first. He had been criticized several times for not including sex in his writing, most notably in a review of *The Great Shark Hunt* by William F. Buckley.[6] He had attempted to explain this carnal omission a few times but now intended to give readers what they were missing—lots of orgies.

Thompson often composed stories out of order, writing the final pages early so that he knew where he was going, and he wrote the end of *The Silk Road* in the form of

---

6   Buckley claimed: "Hunter Thompson has no apparent interest in sex." [https://www.nytimes.com/1979/08/05/archives/blunt-instruments-thompson.html]

a passage called "The Murder of Colonel Evans," in which a man called Evans attempts to kill Skinner and is then shot dead by an unseen person. It is a strange section that makes little sense without the rest of the book, but strangest of all is the choice of name. Colonel Evans was the man at the Eglin Air Force Base Office of Information Services who wrote the recommendation letter that Thompson often included in his books, saying, "this Airman, although talented, will not be guided by policy or personal advice and guidance."

The descriptions that Thompson gave for this book show how little he was able to keep ideas in order at this point in his life, which possibly explains his deterioration as a writer. The ideas he presents are unclear and it is uncertain how much of the book was ever actually written, but it was certainly never brought close to publication. Once again, Thompson had become fixated on an idea but was unable to invest enough effort to see it through. What writing did survive—and was evidently distinguished enough to make it into his collected works—was shockingly poor in quality. It was a lazy, badly written, and uninteresting piece of fiction.

When Thompson was offered fifteen thousand dollars by *Esquire* to cover the boatlift, he took the money and ran up a further fifteen thousand dollars of expenses. Unsurprisingly, he did not bother to write anything, and instead offered them an excerpt of *The Silk Road*, which they declined. Even though they had paid thirty thousand dollars for it, the editors could not bring themselves to publish such an embarrassing effort.

In early 1980, Paul Perry, then the editor of a Nike-owned magazine called *Running*, wrote to Thompson and asked him to cover the Honolulu marathon. It was an odd pitch. For Thompson, anyone who ran was a masochistic idiot and one can only imagine what the average runner thought of Thompson's lifestyle. Still, Perry had faith that a Gonzo approach to running might bring in new readers. In May, he wrote back and agreed, provided that the magazine pay his huge fees. He recommended that they contact Ralph Steadman, too, to give the piece an extra Gonzo dimension. When Perry called Steadman, Ralph warned him that

Thompson had not written anything good in eight years and had developed the habit of starting but not finishing projects, all the while running up huge expense tabs. He offered a five-point plan for getting Thompson to write, which could be summarized thusly:

1. Pay him in advance.
2. Keep hassling him for the article.
3. Keep him locked in a hotel room—do NOT let him go home.
4. Provide all required drink and drugs.
5. Do not compete with him in terms of drink and drugs.

For a bonus, Steadman added: "The most surefire way of getting him to produce a story is to send me along. We're right the right chemistry and I'll make him work." He had apparently forgotten Zaire.

Together with his assistant, Laila Nabulsi, Thompson flew to Hawaii. He had planned to jump in near the end of the race and run the last few miles but was persuaded instead to watch it from the back of a van, where he could drink and smoke and hurl insults at the competitors. Once the race was over, he and Ralph relocated to the Kona Coast in order to do some marlin fishing, but the weather turned bad and the seas grew angry.

As usual, Steadman did his work first, attempting to get inside the mind of a runner and explore the psychology of this bizarre habit. When his illustrations were done, they were hung up around Thompson's typewriter and it was his turn to work. Incredibly, he produced a draft inside a week. He acknowledged that, as usual, it was a bit disorganized, but said, "The jumps and breaks need work, but it's a fucking monster article. A monster."

The article needed more work because certain parts were disconnected and most needed various degrees of rewriting, so Thompson and Perry locked themselves in a hotel room in Eugene, Oregon for five days until the piece was finished. Perry recalled him listening to music on repeat, then loading up with drinks, joints, and pills until he was ready to start. He explained:

Output on that first night wasn't great. He stayed with it, gazing at white paper until inspiration arrived and then exploding with a couple of "hot damns" or "fucking A's" that were followed on the page by a torrent of words. Sometimes he ripped the page out of the typewriter, wadded it up, and threw it in the direction of the wastebasket a few feet away. Other times he praised his effort with a "yes" or "now you're golden" and set the page on the typing stand's pull-out shelf.

After he had produced his ten-thousand-word article on the Honolulu marathon, Thompson explained why he had been successful this time and not in the past:

> The difference between this gig and some of the ones that didn't work out is that you stayed with me and kept me on track. That's the problem with New York publishers, they just want to give me assignments and then leave me alone. They don't realize that I require special attention.

He swore that, going forward, he would no longer deal with big publishers, and would only sell his work to independent companies. He even offered to go on a world tour of marathons for *Running*. Of course, he had overlooked the fact that such outlets could not afford his huge fees and expense bills. The *Running* article only worked because it was funded by Nike.

When "The Charge of the Weird Brigade" was published in 1981, it was Hunter Thompson's first piece of journalism in three years. Billed as "Adventures in Paradox," the article shows its author crashing into the Honolulu marathon to insult the runners. He attempts to find out why people would endure such a horrendous experience and concludes that it is the latest or last avenue of the liberal mind, driven away from protest and art and into pointless, masochistic endeavors such as this. In a sense, he is attempting to explain how the sixties transformed into the eighties, asking "What would the hippies and protesters be doing now?" The answer: Running. It was illustrated magnificently by Steadman, who took advantage of the glossy form to produce colorful, detailed drawings that depicted, among other things, the winners of the race as zombies, distended freaks berating the runners, and a male runner kicking a female runner in the crotch.

Although he was pleased with his work, Thompson took issue with some initial edits to the story. Paul Perry explained:

> A "politically correct" editor at the magazine was upset about some of Hunter's language and changed several of his expressions to ones she found more benign. She changed "goddamn race" to "beastly race," and the exclamation "Jesus" to "geeze." "Shit," as in "kicking the shit" out of someone, became "tar." "Bastard," as in "look at that bastard run," was now "guy."
>
> At one point in the story, Hunter is talking to his fictional friend Gene Skinner about a black man who pushes a stewardess off a cliff. He wrote, "All of a sudden this crazy nigger just runs up behind her and gives a big shove." She changed "nigger" to "guy." At another point, she completely eliminated a sentence in which Hunter describes a black marathoner as "the fastest crazy nigger in the world."

When he received the galleys, Thompson angrily explained that he did not say "geeze." Perry apologized and said he would return his "fucks" to the article, but that maybe they should remove the more racist language. Thompson explained:

> I am a bigot. I'm what they called a "multi-bigot." [...] A unibigot is a racist. A multibigot is just a prick. I don't necessarily like any group or type or identifiable race,

creed, or color. They all deserve mockery
and shame and humiliation.

It was a reasonable argument but the article still
contained some troubling elements. Certain groups of
people (like Koreans and Samoans) are depicted in roving
gangs, with no interest in anything except violence. His
use of "nigger" was obviously questionable, too. While he
sometimes used such language in his writing as a means of
satirizing racist attitudes, at other times it seemed like he
was using them just for shock value.

In any case, his swears were returned and, when the
magazine was printed, the first paragraph contained the
word "ratbastard." His racial slurs were kept, too, and there
are various references to hard drugs. About fifty of the
magazine's readers threatened to cancel their subscriptions
in response.

It was an excellent story with some strong writing
in both conventional and Gonzo forms. There are his
usual flights of fancy, random outbursts, violent images,
and other assorted madness. Throughout the article, he
manages to create a sense of impending doom and looming
violence, even though not much happens. It begins with a
flurry of headlines and a quote from Tennyson, and from
there Thompson starts by describing the weather, before
bringing the plot in later—which is, once again, the story
of getting the story.

Jann Wenner seethed with jealousy, and a number of
other editors who had worked with Thompson wondered
how the hell Perry had gotten a story out of him—and
a *good one*, at that.[7] How had this magazine about *running*
managed to do what no one else could? They hoped that
this was the beginning of a fertile new period in his career.
Maybe the seventies had just been a difficult time for him.

With the success of his latest article, Thompson
decided that the sensible thing to do was turn it into a
book-length project. In 1980, he had gone to Washington
DC to write a book about Ronald Reagan, but after
running up the usual ludicrous expenses, nothing came of

7   Wenner, seeing that Thompson was back on form,
asked him to write about John Lennon's murder, but Thompson
refused and called him morbid. [*Fear and Loathing*, p.212]

it. He had realized in the seventies that books were more profitable than journalism, and so much of his planning for journalism projects revolved around whether or not it could be spun off into a book. Besides, Hawaii had been fun and writing a book would be a good excuse for another trip. A few months later, he returned to Hawaii and began work on *The Curse of Lono*.

While the article had been a surprisingly painless experience, the book would be very different. The writing for *Lono* took three years and required Thompson to visit Hawaii three times and Washington DC once. It was a nightmare process that relied heavily on the efforts of friends and editors to bring it to completion. Thompson moved his base of operations from the downstairs War Room to the kitchen, where he would attempt to write while conversing with the various people that passed through. Without Sandy shielding him from visitors, he became easily distracted. After his death, his son Juan noted:

> The War Room was the creative heart of the house up until my parents separated. It was Hunter's hideout. More than an office, it was his sanctum, with its own giant fireplace, no windows, significant books along one wall, and the typewriter. It was the place where he would not be disturbed, where he could be alone and thrash out the words, battle with his writer's block, or drift in a drug- or alcohol-induced stupor.
>
> After 1980 or so, the kitchen became the creative and social heart. With satellite television and no wife and child to distract him, it was natural that he would take up residence there, and that friends and visitors would find him there. With football, basketball, CNN, or the Playboy Channel in the background, he wrote, talked on the phone, entertained guests, screamed, ate, threw things, read the newspaper, did his drugs, and told stories for the next twenty-five years.

He struggled so badly, in fact, that various people had to visit Owl Farm just to help him write. Steadman flew in from the UK and Alan Rinzler, now working at Bantam Books, made frequent visits. Rinzler, who had worked with Thompson on *Fear and Loathing on the Campaign Trail '72*, was again in the unenviable position of being his editor. He noticed that, ten years later, Hunter had become far more preoccupied with drugs and cared much less about his work. His writing had also grown more "tangential," and there was little order to the material that he wrote. It would be Rinzler's job to fit together a few good paragraphs, a lot of filler, and no story.

Early versions of the book had been so bad, in fact, that after reading sections of it, the editors at Bantam had called in Ian Ballantine, Thompson's publisher for *Hell's Angels* almost twenty years earlier. It was an act of desperation. Maybe this was what it would take to get Hunter writing properly again. When Ballantine came to look at the book, however, he found that there was hardly any writing and nothing that was worth keeping was connected to anything else. Only Steadman's art possessed any value. He had checked into a nearby motel and produced numerous illustrations, which had been pinned up around Thompson's workspace for inspiration.

Ballantine flew to Woody Creek four times to help get the book in shape, and while he was there he set down strict rules about Hunter's drink and drug intake, refusing to work with him while he was out of his mind. Even so, it could take days to get him in the mood to write, and then when he started he could only concentrate for a few minutes at a time. Whenever he wrote a paragraph, he would get up and start pacing, but when he sat down again he could hardly remember what he had written or where it was going. Ballantine believed that he had given himself brain damage from his years of drug and alcohol abuse.

Thompson was embarrassed about his inability to write well and engaged in what Ballantine called "evasive behavior." When Rinzler attempted to contact him to push forward with publishing the book, Thompson made every attempt to keep him away. In the end, he waited until Thompson fell asleep and then stole the book, some of which was written on bits of brown paper bags, and then took it back to New York with him. Back at Bantam, he did his best to salvage the story, but the results were nonetheless appalling. With no plot and hardly any good writing, the book was centered around Steadman's art, filled with quotes from Richard Hough's *The Last Voyage of Captain James Cook* and a few excerpts from Twain, and then printed on extra heavy paper in order to make it seem bigger. All of this just made Hunter feel worse. He was bitter that Steadman's art was so central to the book and he came to resent the fact that Ralph could produce work freely while he struggled. This caused a major rift between them and Thompson stopped asking for Steadman's illustrations to accompany his work.[8]

The Curse of Lono was published in 1983 by Bantam books. Rinzler admitted that it was a failure of a project, saying, "It was a patchwork, a cut-and-paste job. It doesn't quite make sense." Elsewhere, he called it "disorganized and incoherent in places." Thompson's writing here is generally acknowledged as poor and *Lono* sounds like a college student's lame attempt to imitate Gonzo journalism. Aside from the parts that had been cannibalized from the magazine version, it is just uninspired and sophomoric.

There are only a few positive things that can be said about it. No matter how weak his writing became, he was always able to put together at least a few words of wisdom and could occasionally write a paragraph that might generously be described as a "high white note." *The Curse of Lono* has several of these. Near the beginning of the book, there is a letter to Steadman that is very funny. It uses good sports language to make running sound exciting, saying that champion runners "come out of the blocks like human torpedoes" and "race like whorehounds." His absurd imagination also possesses some value. He says that Ralph has been entered into a surfing competition and that Hunter will fight a rooster, and then suggests that they enter and win the marathon. It is an amusing, deadpan piece of comedy. He also manages to mix completely absurd fantasy with comic understatement. In one line, he

---

8   On his own handwritten front page for the manuscript, Thompson scored out Ralph's name from beside his and included it only in small font at the very bottom of the page, underneath Laila's name.

talks about Ralph, who is sick: "This was his first trip to the tropics, a thing he'd been waiting to do all his life… and now he was going to die from it." Elsewhere, he blends boring fact with outrageous fantasy: "We spent so many hours talking to runners that I finally lost track of what it all meant and began setting people on fire." There are some Burroughsian moments that possess some comedic value, but mostly they are now predictable and stale. At times, the book feels like little more than a vehicle for amusing anecdotes that he had heard in Hawaiian bars.

Unfortunately, the problems vastly outweigh any merit that the book possesses through its twisted stories and occasionally witty lines. Once again, his inability to create believable or even vaguely complex characters was a major problem. There are several characters in the story, with Thompson acting as the protagonist, narrating in the first person. Others include Gene Skinner and a man named Mr. Ackerman. Ackerman is a character that Thompson meets on the plane to Hawaii, who has turned one of his arms completely blue by reaching down into the airplane's toilet. Thompson describes him:

> He had the look of a man who had once been a tennis pro in Hong Kong, then gone on to bigger things. The gold Rolex, the white linen bush jacket, the Thai Bhat chain around his neck, the heavy leather briefcase with combination locks on every zipper. . .

Later on, he introduces Skinner:

> He was wearing a white linen reef jacket with at least thirteen custom-built pockets to fit everything from a phosphorous grenade to a waterproof pen. His blue silk slacks were sharply creased and he wore no socks, only cheap rubber sandals that slapped on the tile as he paced. He was a head taller than anyone else in the airport and his eyes were hidden behind blue-black Saigon-mirror sunglasses. The heavy,

square-linked gold Bhat chain around his neck could only have been bought in some midnight jewelry store on a back street in Bangkok, and the watch on his wrist was a gold Rolex with a stainless steel band.

With their white jackets, Rolexes, and Thai Baht chains, they are obviously the same person, and probably both based upon Hunter himself.[9] These two characters just seem like vehicles for Thompson to do and say more outrageous things than he could do himself, and by the end of the novel it appears Thompson and Ackerman have swapped personalities. At one point, Ackerman remarks that someone is "so crooked that he has to screw his pants on every morning," which was one of Thompson's favorite lines and had appeared in his writing numerous times.

His failure to delineate these two characters stemmed not just from his inability to keep track of simple information but also the loss of his creative capacity. These descriptions were borrowed from a 1976 letter, describing an unnamed person at the New Hampshire primaries:

> … some wild-eyed fucker wearing a Hong Kong tailor-made jacket with only two buttons and a $2000 gold Cambodian chain bouncing on his chest & a gold Rolex on his wrist […]

Still, it is important to note that there is no mention of Raoul Duke. Even if Gene Skinner is basically the same character, it shows that Thompson was consciously attempting to distance himself from, if nothing else, the name Duke. It was the beginning of a new decade and he was keen to reinvent himself and his writing.

In addition to this strange conflation of two separate characters, Thompson also repeats himself, forgetting that he had already said something. He mentions the fact that Japanese runners are going past Pearl Harbor three times, for example. There are other problems, too. Through

---

9 Hunter bought a gold Thai Baht chain from his friend and neighbor, Jay Cowan, and had of course been to both Saigon and Hong Kong.

the opening sections of the book, he describes his flight to and arrival in Hawaii, including his experiences with various people along the way. It is much later that we are told he is traveling with his fiancée. Clearly, she has been with him the whole time but was never introduced until it was convenient. As well as demonstrating a startling level of self-absorption, this also shows that he struggled badly with the fundamentals of narration.

There are other inconsistencies and problems in the text. At one point, Ralph is lying on a bed getting a massage but, when Thompson gives him some bad news, he suddenly collapses onto the bed. It is a lazy error from an author who is struggling to maintain any degree of focus, and also a sign that his editors were so sick of dealing with the book that they let these mistakes slip into the printed version.

The book moves at a frenetic pace but nothing really happens. It is a boring story that is livened up by outrageous comments and silly tales that Thompson had heard. Surprisingly, he does cover the race, even giving a little description and stating the winner's name, but his digressions in this book seem irrelevant, repetitive, and dull. When the marathon finishes, suddenly he complains about the press but there is little to connect these things. In a sense, he has once again attempted to take the Kentucky Derby/Las Vegas story template and apply it to a new setting. He seems to have again attempted to become the thing he criticized—a greedy, boastful man of the eighties, representing yet another decade of decline in the United States. If one were being kind, it could be said to be a critique of US neo-colonialism and a satire of the cult of celebrity, but the weak, disjointed prose obscures any coherent theme. Instead, there is a skeletal story supported by random chunks of writing that deal with themes as disparate as the Hawaiian god Lono, imperialism, Captain Cook, health freaks, weather forecasts, land development, and fishermen. It was like William Kennedy had told him at the beginning of his career: "You raise questions, then trail off into foolishness."

His usual rhythm is gone and there is no music to the language like there was in his best writing. He had always been good at describing action, but here it was weird and oddly mild. Some of the dialogue is funny but everyone sounds like Thompson, so it is unconvincing. Again, he has put a transcript in the text—this time it is a phone call to the police about the waves outside his rented house. It adds no real value to the story except to pad out the book by a few more pages.

About halfway through, he enters into a weird, nonsensical stream-of-consciousness passage that appears to be another excerpt from a notebook. In this case, Thompson has simply lost the thread of the story and was filling in space. Elsewhere, there are other clues that suggest he had intended to write something but simply had forgotten or been unable to finish it. Some of the chapter titles, for example, clearly refer to things that do not appear within those chapters, but which Thompson likely intended to include.

There is also plenty of wisdom; however, here it is obvious that everything he has learned about running, Hawaii, and fishing has basically come from drunken conversations with barflies. His knowledge is limited and his descriptions sloppy. Compared with the meticulous research that he had done for *Fear and Loathing on the Campaign Trail '72*, this is embarrassing. Even for the Ali interview, just five years before, he had been willing to ask questions, read books and articles, and learn everything needed to educate his readers. Jay Cowan explained that, at a certain point, he began to write what he *felt* was true rather than what he *knew*: "Once he began believing his own press, he got lazier and tended to rely less on well-placed sources and more on his own instincts."

Of course, there are fantasies and elements of fiction. Some refer to *Lono* as a novel but like his other works it simply defies categorization. While Thompson did go to Hawaii several times, the book makes it feel as though it is one trip, and some elements have definitely been fabricated. Thompson did not, for example, have a Ferrari and there was no man on the plane with a blue arm. Still, some of it was real, at least. The scenes on Captain Steve's boat more or less happened and, incredibly, Captain Steve himself was a real person called Steve Kaiser. Ralph Steadman went as far as to claim, "Most of it actually really did happen."

There are places in the text where it is clear that

Thompson started something and then just gave up. At one point, he describes a wild car ride. It is a chance for more of his favorite action words, but instead the description is dull. Thompson and Ackerman are in a car that is flying downhill at a hundred miles per hour, but then he goes on a digression and just ends the section. The story is never picked up again and they never do reach the bottom. From this point on, there is hardly any narrative from Thompson. The rest of the book is comprised of silly, disconnected letters to Ralph and quotes from other writers. The author had given up and the publishers had decided to patch it together and publish it to mitigate their financial loss.

The grand finale to the book is recounted second-hand. At the end, Thompson realizes that he is a reincarnation of the god Lono. This is told through a letter to Steadman rather than as an epiphany that comes to his character organically as part of the book's rather tenuous plot. Ironically, Thompson then comments:

> And besides, this *is* the story. I don't know music, but I have a good ear for the high white sound. . . and when this Lono gig flashed in front of my eyes about 33 hours ago, I knew it for what it was.
> Suddenly the whole thing made sense. It was like seeing The Green Light for the first time.

In all of his writing prior to this, he had sought those goals and believed that, with *Fear and Loathing in Las Vegas*, he had managed to rival Fitzgerald's great American novel. Undoubtedly, most of his writing was a string of "high white notes" with a bit of filler, but the notes were pitch perfect and the filler made sense. With *The Curse of Lono*, however, the notes were all off key. A good novel with great moments is an entirely different thing to a terrible novel with some half-decent ones.

With this final notion that he was Lono, Thompson seems to have mistaken a strange idea for a burst of genius. He had struggled to find the thread that tied the elements of the book together, and this seemed to be it. But it was just an idea and one mentioned in a letter. He had not written it into the narrative because that would have been too much work.

When Rob Fleder, a huge fan of Thompson's work, was working at *Playboy* in 1983, he convinced them to buy the rights to excerpt part of *The Curse of Lono*, but when he received the book he was dismayed by how weak it was. The only good parts, he thought, were the ones already published by *Running* in 1980. "The rest of the book," he said, "was mostly a series of false starts and half-baked ideas. I was surprised by the degree of degeneration in Hunter's work." Fleder and Thompson holed up for three miserable days in an attempt to cull something usable and, in the end, *Playboy* published a vaguely intelligible section of the book in their December edition.

Ultimately, *The Curse of Lono* is an incomplete book. Its composition had been a farce, exposing its author's total lack of interest in writing and his lack of responsibility to his readers. After its publication, Hunter Thompson and Bantam Books went their separate ways. He had somehow been aggrieved at what he perceived as their unfair treatment of him. He believed that Steadman had been given more page space and that the final theft of the manuscript was a cheap trick. Bantam was giving up one of the biggest names in literature, but they knew fine well that there was little chance of another great book. It had been ten years since the last one.

Rather than a mature, developed book, Thompson's readers received a collection of quotes, some wonderful artwork, a few amusing letters to Ralph, and a small amount of pitiful writing. It is true that there are some good sentences throughout the book and some of the fishing sections were mildly entertaining, but it was otherwise disappointing. Few books have been more cynically foisted upon the public than *The Curse of Lono*.

To absolutely no one's surprise, it was poorly reviewed and sales were weak. It was only reprinted in 2005 as a signed, limited edition publication by Taschen before being more widely released in 2014, by which time Thompson's name was enough to ensure some measure of success.[10]

---

10   The Taschen edition was published a month after Thompson's death.

Many years after its publication, he reflected that it has been "a noble effort, although flawed in many ways" and toward the end of his life he became even more positive about it, but it was the first book he had published that fell massively short of his reputation as an author. If he had wanted to quell the suggestions that he had lost his skills as a writer somewhere between 1972 and 1983, this was not the book to do it.

Brief Returns to Form

It took me a long, long time to give up. For so long it had been, "That would be perfect for Hunter. Let's try it." Finally I had to understand that it was not worth making the phone call. It was frustrating and upsetting. So I stopped.

Jann Wenner

By the mid-eighties, Hunter S. Thompson was living off the royalties earned by his first three books, all of which had been published more than a decade earlier, coupled with the occasional speaking fee, movie option, or idea that he pitched to someone. As we saw in the previous chapter, he was still capable of excellent writing but tended to produce it only occasionally. By 1983, when *The Curse of Lono* was published, he had not written for *Rolling Stone* for five years and he had little other work on the side. His inability to meet deadlines and the consistency of the work he did submit, coupled with his notorious attitude toward expenses, tended to give other editors the willies.

Terry McDonell was the managing editor of *Rolling Stone* at this point and when he told Jann Wenner that he was going to approach Thompson with an idea for a story, Wenner just laughed and said that it would never happen. The story was the divorce trial of Palm Beach millionaire, Herbert Pulitzer Jr., and his younger wife, Roxanne. The trial had captured the media's attention with its lurid tales of cocaine and orgies, and McDonell felt as though the scene was perfect for Thompson's journalism.

McDonell spent a long time on the phone, trying to persuade the writer to come around. In the end, he asked Thompson if he could even remember what it felt like to sit down and really write. "And that struck him," McDonell said, "and over the next twenty years or so, he would bring that up. […] he wanted to work, and he wanted his work to be great." It didn't hurt that Thompson was in love with Florida and that this story gave him the chance to escape the harsh Colorado winter.

He agreed to McDonell's offer and set off for Palm Beach, where he began covering a story that he would later title, "A Dog Took My Place." According to Roxanne Pulitzer, he was in the front row for twenty-one consecutive days, but others have suggested that he might have just shown up once or twice. In any case, he managed to get to court and did so *in the morning*, which was almost unheard of for him. But still, fame often got in the way of reporting. On day one, the judge blurted out, "I'm so honored to meet you, Mr. Thompson." Hunter cringed.

He was not just attracted to the story because he wanted a free trip to Florida or because he felt he owed his readers something new. Despite his often cruel, egotistical behavior, Thompson had a strong sense of justice, an attachment to the underdog, and a burning contempt for the wealthy establishment. Here in Florida, the media was having a field day reporting on the lewd and lascivious details of the lives of the Pulitzer family, with Roxanne being publicly shamed for her alleged drug use and sexual proclivities. Her husband's lawyers hammered her in court, and of course the media—both tabloid and traditional—picked up on it and repeated the accusations across the nation. It seemed deeply unfair.

Thompson realized that he could use his writing as a weapon against three of his favorite targets—the press, the courts, and the wealthy. In the Pulitzer divorce trial, he attacked the rich and did not hold back. His friend, Pat Caddell, talked about Thompson's interest in exposing corruption and called "A Dog Took My Place" "the greatest attack on the Gatsby class since *Gatsby*," a description that would no doubt have pleased Thompson. Paul Scanlon thought that it was "Hunter at his best, exploring the sex-and-drugs culture of well-heeled Palm Beach denizens in wide-eyed amazement and disdain."

From the very beginning of the article, it is clear how he feels about the wealthy and the poor. He talks about rich people as though they are another species entirely:

"The stomping of the rich is not a noise to be ignored in troubled times. It usually means they are feeling anxious or confused about something, and when the rich feel anxious and confused, they act like wild animals." It is a place, he says, where "naked millionaires gnaw brassieres off the chests of their own daughters in public."

He portrays Palm Beach as an alien location, where weird people do depraved things with no consequences because they have the money to make any problem go away. Despite this, he notes, "scandals pass like winter storms in Palm Beach." For this first section, Thompson is relatively absent, commenting on Palm Beach society and the divorce trial rather than inserting himself into the text in a participatory sense, but he does mention that he is not welcome there now that he is reporting on the trial. He is making it clear that he is an outsider reporting on a tight-knit, secretive society.

Thompson's role as reporter moves to the fore as he writes, "I arrived in Palm Beach on a rainy night…" He focuses on the hearing room for the divorce trial and his own efforts to get one of the few available press seats, then recounts some of the details of the trial by paraphrasing Mr. Pulitzer and his lawyers, calling Roxanne "an incorrigible coke slut." While the rest of the media were gleefully repeating the intimate details of the Pulitzers' lives, Thompson simply reported what he felt lay between the lines and it highlights the contempt the wealthy felt for outsiders in their ranks.

The writing in this article has a far greater clarity than in many of his other works, particularly of the eighties. His language is slightly toned down and he has thrown out some of the more cartoonish quirks of his style in favor of more direct descriptions. As for his behavior, he is not playing the Gonzo fool but rather watching and observing, then commenting viciously upon the behavior of the rich. The story is coherent and when it appears that Thompson is going to go off on a tangent, he usually takes the narrative somewhere that it should go instead. He draws the reader seamlessly through the history, the landscape, the characters, and the details of the case.

Of course, there are metajournalistic elements, though here these show more useful aspects of the journalistic process than in previous efforts, highlighting parts of the story that he felt deserved attention. He brings the reader into the evidence room at the courthouse, where under Florida laws the public are permitted to examine the evidence pertaining to the case, then grabs a few beers and guides his reader through some of the more interesting finds. It is a searing indictment of the wealthy class, who pay their nanny one hundred and fifty dollars per week but have listed four hundred and forty-one thousand dollars for "miscellaneous" expenditure, which presumably meant cocaine.

In this story, Thompson uses italics for his fantasy scenes. He had done this before on occasion, including *Fear and Loathing in Las Vegas*, but in this instance it was very much a form of legal protection. The editing process normally involved disputes with lawyers, and when they could not persuade him to drop something, the fantasy section would be italicized to provide plausible deniability in the case that someone suggested it was being presented as fact. However, the problem here is that sometimes the italicized fantasy scenes do not mesh naturally with the rest of the prose. They are sometimes logically and grammatically disconnected, making these scenes jarring but pointless, and ultimately detracting from more subtle satire elsewhere. When using fantasy without italics, he was more likely to let it arise organically from the text.

His narrative is intelligent, hilarious, and aggressive, and his voice clear and confident, filled with witty put-downs and wisdom. When talking about the rich, he compares them with dolphins and Nazis, and, in one italicized fantasy scene, asks, "And what's wrong with incest anyway? It takes two hundred years of careful inbreeding to produce a line of beautiful daughters." Similarly, he offers a defense for the unusual hobbies of the ultra-rich:

> If a woman worth $40 million wants to swim naked in the pool with her billy goat at four in the morning, it's nobody's business but hers. There are laws in Florida against sexual congress with beasts, but not everybody feels it is wrong.

The article, of course, is not about the divorce of two people, nor is it a vicious attack on the upper classes. It is an excoriating put-down of the press, which has simply invaded these people's lives in order to serve up sensational stories to the masses. When the trial is going on, Thompson is watching the press, and in court he seems concerned with how the law and media conspire to make justice unlikely. He claims that there were so many scandalous stories told about Roxanne that no charges needed to be proved when it came to adultery because it seemed to everyone that she was guilty. This surely resonated with a man who had as a teenager been locked up for alleged past crimes rather than the one for which he was supposedly being charged. Thompson's assessment is that the judge had no interest in fairness, and that Roxanne had been dragged through an ordeal with no hope of justice. He illuminates the unfairness of laws that expose people's private lives and of the system that guaranteed a poor settlement for Roxanne.[1] The judge's lack of interest in fairness is also exemplified by Thompson's observation that he smoked constantly even though no one else in the room was allowed to. The trial is meaningless, he thinks, and only carried out to shame this poor woman and entertain the baying masses.

The Hunter Thompson who wrote this article is nearly unrecognizable from the one who had phoned in the ghastly *Curse of Lono*. "A Dog Took My Place" was a staggering return to form, in which the writer has produced a genuinely brilliant article that has traces of Gonzo without being completely overwhelmed. Like *Hell's Angels*, this is a methodical and logical piece of writing that smashes conventional wisdom through straightforward, intelligent analysis. In addition to a few strong adjectives, some made-up HST words ("suckfish," "swinesucker"), and some frank references to sex and drugs, there is a section where Thompson compares the settlement Roxanne received to expenses the Pulitzers had recorded previously. He points out that they spent more money on boat maintenance in a single year than he gave Roxanne.

---

1   One can hardly fail to note the irony in Thompson's criticisms, though. He had done everything in his power to limit Sandy's claims to their shared property and wealth during his own divorce trial.

Toward the end of the story, Thompson goes back into a more traditional mode and brings us into his hotel, where he heads to the bar for a drink. Here, the bartender speaks just like Thompson because this whole section was made up. The bartender tells him:

> I look at this scum and I look at the way
> they live and I see those shit-eating grins
> on their faces *and I feel like a dog took my place.*

When Thompson asks for clarification, the bartender tells him "It's a term of art." It is a bizarre scene that does not make much sense and is the only real intrusion of Thompson's literary persona on the story. He demands to see the dog and the bartender tells him that he should be on trial. "These Pulitzers are *nothing* compared to monsters like you," he says. It descends into more violence as Thompson maces the man and threatens to rip his testicles off.

The scene with the bartender was entered into the story because of a fight Thompson got into with the magazine's lawyers. Jay Cowan explained:

> [The title] became the object of a pitched
> battle when the lawyers immediately
> quashed it for fear of lawsuits from the
> Pulitzers over intimations of bestiality.
> "Intimations?" he fumed to me. "That's
> all anyone down there talks about, is
> fucking their pets!" Eventually, he created
> a fictional scenario for the title's derivation
> that pleased everyone, but he didn't forget
> or forgive the lawyers for their numerous
> transgressions.

Thompson was forced to write this section into the article in order to justify his weird title. Avid readers of his work would have picked up on this, though. "A Dog Took My Place" was the name of a chapter in *The Curse of Lono*. Again, Thompson had latched onto a phrase he liked and was eager to get good mileage from it.

The problem is that, in an unusually coherent story, there is now a completely random and pointless section that functions as little more than comic relief. It is followed by another odd section in which he attempts to find meaning in the trial, but then describes himself driving to an orgy with a car full of champagne, marijuana, and lesbians. Perhaps he has become one of the Palm Beach elite and no longer cares—or perhaps there is no meaning to the trial. It is just the bickering of rich folk—a habit that has now become a spectator sport for the poor. He ends with an amusing statement about feeling a bond with the rich because of bestiality: "I have always loved animals," he says. "Animals don't hire lawyers." It was a story that began conventionally and ended about as unconventionally as it gets.

Cowan recalls him taking "practice runs" at this article before beginning properly. He would sit and type out a few thousand words of the story just to get the feel for it, then start again. Once he managed to write a good paragraph, he would carefully rework it until he had found just the right combination of words to convey his meaning effectively. Cowan details several examples of descriptive addition, bringing concrete details to passages by replacing nouns and adding adjectives, resulting in phrases like "berserk sleaziness," that have a peculiarly Gonzo feel. Clearly, this was not something that he did for every story, though. The Pulitzer article was, according to some, his "last great piece of reporting." Thompson certainly felt proud of it, although he liked the weird parts more than the conventional ones. "There is some genuinely sick stuff in it," he said, highlighting the value he placed upon shock tactics in writing.

The Pulitzer trial had taken place between September and November 1982 and Thompson's article appeared in *Rolling Stone* in July 1983. It was not exactly expedient journalism, but at least he had written something. Between 1978 and 1985, his *Running* magazine story, *The Curse of Lono*, and "A Dog Took My Place" were his only new works. Fans and editors alike were growing worried.

In 1975, in the midst of attempting to cover the fall of Saigon, Thompson noted the almost unbearable paranoia that came with the assignment and said, "this is maybe the last war I'll ever fool with." Eight years later, however,

415

Rolling Stone sent him on another war assignment. This time, he headed for Grenada to cover the US-led invasion of the island nation. Once again, with the other reporters in flak jackets and helmets, Thompson appeared in a Hawaiian shirt and his friend, Loren Jenkins, had even brought a date with him. Jenkins had invited Thompson after spending a little time covering the invasion and realizing that there was no real danger there for journalists. Hunter flew over but somehow became lost *en route* for three days and refused to explain to anyone what had happened. When he arrived, Jenkins told him that he was only the second most famous writer in their hotel. V.S. Naipaul was staying there. Thompson claimed to have never heard of him, but the two writers met soon after and became good friends.

Thompson's time in Grenada was filled with pranks and other shenanigans, and there was even a little Gonzo chaos when Jenkins was arrested and violently restrained by US soldiers. But, of course, no story emerged. Wenner recalled:

> I thought it was certain we were going to get the Grenada piece, but the editor who I delegated to hand-hold that one made the mistake of letting Hunter come to New York to write, and then also went along with Hunter's work-avoiding notion that a transcript of this interview he had had with a fucking taxi driver in Grenada was going to be the larger part of the piece. It was another broken play.
>
> It took me a long, long time to give up. For so long it had been, "That would be perfect for Hunter. Let's try it." Finally I had to understand that it was not worth making the phone call. It was frustrating and upsetting. So I stopped.

Thompson goofed around for the duration of his stay but did not file a story. What little writing he did do was included in *Kingdom of Fear*, some twenty years later. This was made up primarily of immediate observations in a fairly pure Gonzo style, and the focus on a taxi driver actually makes it quite engaging.

The following year, *Playboy* paid him to write about feminist pornography, so he went to San Francisco to work at the O'Farrell Theater, which he called "the Carnegie Hall of public sex in America." Once again, he quickly decided that this was an article that could be spun off into a book, and he sold the idea to Random House. For a year, he conducted research into the project and wrote letters to the editors at *Playboy* that made it seem like the story was coming together, but it quickly evolved from what the editor termed "a tightly focused magazine story" into one that was too political, trying to encompass too many ideas. Rob Fleder traveled to Woody Creek and spent five days with Thompson, trying to work out what the story was about, but they made no progress. Thompson was constantly making distractions for himself. In the end, neither project came to fruition and the book, which he called *The Night Manager*, died on the line.[2]

That same year, Paul Perry suggested to Thompson that he write a book called *The Rise of the Body Nazis*, which would follow on from the article he had written for *Running*. Together, they had formulated the idea of liberals morphing from the free-love hippies of the sixties into the militant, joyless "body nazis" of the eighties. It was essentially one of the many themes from *Lono*, brought into clearer focus. "Any book with Nazi in the title is my kind of book," Thompson replied, gleefully speculating that it might earn him a quarter-million-dollar advance.

He confided in Perry that this book would need to be sold without telling his agent or Jim Silberman, as he owed them a novel he had sold ten years earlier. It is not exactly clear what novel that would be, as Thompson sold a great many ideas, but it may have been *Guts Ball*. When Perry sent the pitch for *The Rise of the Body Nazis* to Simon & Schuster, it was handed over to a committee of editors that included Silberman and the idea was shot down. Silberman was furious because Thompson had been avoiding him since receiving half of another quarter-million-dollar

---

2   A reporter who visited him around this time claims that the novel was "completed" but not sold. [*Last Interview*, p.74]

advance.[3]

The idea died. *The Rise of the Body Nazis* was never written, nor was *Guts Ball, Galveston, The Silk Road,* or *The Night Manager.*

In 1985, Hunter Thompson began writing a column for the *San Francisco Examiner.* He had resisted attempts by *Rolling Stone* to coax him into becoming a columnist, but the *Examiner* paid twelve hundred dollars per column, making it easy and profitable work. It was a strange choice, though. Thompson had joked before that the *Examiner*'s readers "fear King George III might still be alive in Argentina," and he had given no reason to suggest he could meet a weekly deadline. The paper's owner, William Randolph Heart III, told *Boston Globe* reporter, Curtis Wilkie, that it was in keeping with the "libertarian" tradition of the publication, which had previously printed work by Mark Twain and Ambrose Bierce. Amazingly, his four-year stint was quite successful. There were, of course, constant deadline battles, with one editor fired partially because of Thompson's refusal to adhere to his Friday deadlines, but he turned in an article almost every week. Perhaps because he only had to write about a thousand words, he managed to write a successful column and, in 1988, he allowed Silberman to publish them as *Generation of Swine: Gonzo Papers Vol. 2: Tales of Shame and Degradation in the '80s.*

Since he first began writing for *Rolling Stone* in 1970, Thompson had been given a great deal of freedom with his prose, but now that he was going to write for a mainstream publication again, his writing would have to be drug-free and there could be no "pigfuckers" or any other strong profanity. Still, he was allowed to write about whatever story or non-story he wanted and to exhibit his trademark anger and weird behavior. These columns had no real focus and mainly concerned the daily dramas of an angry man who saw greed, corruption, and incompetence wherever he looked. They mark another phase in his move

---

3   Thompson had failed to deliver several books he had sold to Silberman, including the Death of the American Dream title that he had agreed to in 1967. According to Margaret Harrell, this contract was never directly fulfilled but Random House may have let it go later in exchange for another book.

away from Raoul Duke but are not exactly free of Gonzo prose. They are still a mix of stories largely focused on his own life, with plenty of references to Nixon, a blend of fact and fantasy, and much of his usual language. Gene Skinner appears, there are many nods to Fitzgerald, and various attacks on the press.

The first article included in *Generation of Swine* is a perfect example of Thompson's approach to reporting on reporting.[4] In it, he takes his assistant, Maria, to get a tattoo. Her getting the tattoo is going to be the story and he mentions the fact that they "need the story" three times. Suddenly, he is back in his hotel, remembering a time he rode a motorcycle, and then they are returning from the tattoo, satisfied that they somehow got the story. Thompson ends with one of his favorite lines: "we are, after all, professionals." Readers of that column may well have wondered, "Who is Maria?" and "Why is she getting a tattoo?" as this was never explained in the text. A *New York Times* reviewer made much the same point, warning prospective readers, "Many of the names in these columns are obscure and require a knowledge of Mr. Thompson's friends and previous books." Readers were no doubt baffled by aspects of this and other columns that he wrote as he seemed to expect the world to already know about his personal life and so did not bother to explain anything.

The story did not make much sense, nor did it serve any real function whatsoever. There were mutterings among the *Examiner* staff that hiring Thompson had been some kind of joke or publicity stunt. Fortunately, his work got better, but it was often very disconnected. He frequently just wrote about a conversation he had, mixed with some political commentary or his reaction to something that appeared on TV. Often the jumps between scenes are jarring, and it is likely that these were random fragments of writing that Thompson had done that week and were on hand at deadline time when he had no other ideas. He most likely cobbled them together without transitions. In one

---

4   This was not the first column he wrote for the newspaper and the book does not present his articles in chronological order. This story was published in December and Thompson had been writing for the *Examiner* since September 23.

such case, he writes about Richard Nixon having a Chinese mistress and also about an insane, dying whale, and then he cuts to a parking lot where people are talking about prostitution. There is no connection and no explanation offered.

One of the better stories in the collection is the titular "A Generation of Swine." In it, Thompson is watching *Rocky IV* at the drive-in and then goes to test his health at a machine in the snack bar. He beats up a pack of dogs, forces spectators to use the machine, and then finally takes the test and registers "no pulse." The story is short, focused, and uproarious. He had always been good with shocking action and weird comedy, and this sort of fantasy allowed him to do just that, bashing dogs against cars and making people cry when they take his health test. His fantastic imagination is on display, and when it comes to unexpected actions, his passion for sportswriters' verbs allows him to make his descriptions vivid and exciting. It was one of the rare columns when he focused on a single story, taking the reader from start to finish, and even giving them an amusing ending.

It is true that there was no real point to it and it did not tackle any political or philosophical matter. It was fun, pure and simple. Often, that was when Thompson was at his best, but he had a tendency to cram short action scenes into places that they did not belong. In his columns, he was able to present fictional (or heavily fictionalized) stories simply for the sake of it. This gave him a greater freedom to experiment with humor, leaving the wisdom to the subtext.

His articles were wildly inconsistent, with some of them brilliant for their powerful language, humorous imagery, or astute observations, and others just too repetitive or fragmented to work. Sometimes there are almost two distinct pieces of writing within one column and they are not always of equal value. Mostly, though, Thompson appears still to be grasping for that "high white note" and throughout his columns there are plenty of brilliant lines but few examples of him keeping focus and remaining eloquent for a full thousand words.

In "Full-time Scrambling," he opens with a paragraph

that has since become famous thanks to the internet.[5] In it, he offers some examples of why his writing was so brilliant:

> The TV business is uglier than most things. It is normally perceived as some kind of cruel and shallow money trench through the heart of the journalism industry, a long plastic hallway where thieves and pimps run free and good men die like dogs, for no good reason.

We can see a repeat of an old form of paragraph structure in which he begins with a short sentence that gives a non-specific idea, and then a much longer sentence that lays image upon image to clarify the meaning implied in the first sentence. We can also see his use of strong adjectives doubled up in "cruel and shallow money trench" and his preferred nouns, "thieves and pimps," which always grab and focus the reader's attention. There is also the violent end, "good men die like dogs," and the tragic postscript, "for no good reason." It is an emotive, unsubtle paragraph that succinctly puts across the author's feelings about TV news, which will soon be elaborated upon. In the next paragraph, he focuses our attention with the sentence fragment, "Which is more or less true," before he tells us about the exceptions to the rule, in which case he compares "the twisted Rev. Gene Scott" to "a sleepless ferret." It is the sort of wildly specific, completely unconventional imagery that made Thompson so unique and brilliant.

This article also features a character called "Cromwell," Thompson's next attempt at replacing Raoul Duke. In these columns, he mentions Skinner but occasionally brings in the new persona. Cromwell appeared a few times in his mid-eighties writing but was killed off in 1989, when his son shot him dead in front of Thompson. The character was resurrected in 2001 as Thompson's neighbor for his ESPN column.

Just like his earlier, longer stories, Thompson often talks about hotels, expenses, and weird activities. There

---

5   The internet being what it is, the quote is typically butchered and the subject often changes from the TV business to showbusiness, the music industry, or just about anything else.

are many references to his own life and to writers that he admired, like Fitzgerald, Hemingway, Poe, and Coleridge. A great deal of the column is devoted to upholding the legend that he had built around himself, even as he seeks to move away from the Duke persona. When he needs to put forth some wild political speculation, he trots out Gene Skinner, who can converse with Thompson to make claims he would have made himself.

Some of the stories are entirely fictionalized versions of his own life, like one in which he is offered a thousand dollars per day to "exterminate a herd of 'killer crocodiles'" in Tanzania. It is a wild distortion of the real story, which was that he had been offered a travel writing job. In Thompson's mind, of course, the fantasy was so absurd that it could be presented as true and no one would misunderstand. Elsewhere, he writes about his friends or things that he had heard or read. In one story, he talks about Skinner being gored by a buffalo. This idea came from a flyer that Jay Cowan had given him after a visit to Yellowstone National Park. It is pure fiction, with Skinner's character padded out with attributes of Cowan's.

His most effective columns are ones where Thompson has seen something in the news and decided to comment upon it in his own unique way. As always, his imagination kicked into gear best when thinking about dark things and he was able to create more powerful, musical language when angry. About a trash barge stuck at sea, he wrote, "It's like a death ship, a stinking hulk full of shame and disease… with a crew on the verge of mutiny and a captain going crazy with fear." Again, he starts with a simple image and adds more and more details, presenting the most repugnant possible idea. As in previous works, he is able to conjure musical language for great effect, as in the following lines:

> Lt. Col. Oliver North (USMC) did not hear any high lonesome music when the white van came for him last week, and neither did Gary Hart. They died like dogs, for no good reason at all – or at least no real reason except craziness.
>
> There was no way to explain it. Oliver North apparently moved into the White

House basement about five years ago and turned himself into something worse than the mad Dr. Frankenstein... He was given control of everything he could reach, from the president of Israel and secret U.S. Army bank accounts in Switzerland to the CIA and George Bush and the home phone number of the Chinese defense minister... until he finally hooked up with a truly savage little criminal named Carl "Spitz" Channel, who used him for years as a sort of billion-dollar Judas goat and then finally turned him in.

Again, punctuation is used to lead the breath as the reader verbalizes the words. The result is a distinct cadence like some of Thompson's best work. It is a familiar pattern that made him so adept at powerful writing. When he wanted to, he could create real emotion with his words. But again, we see weakness too. The line "They died like dogs, for no good reason at all" appeared in another of his articles, which was quoted earlier in this chapter.[6] His propensity for reusing words and ideas made his writing quite repetitive, especially in collected editions of his work.

The columns are incredibly uneven in terms of quality. While there is plenty of good writing, there is a lot that is lazy and uninteresting. Various people, including Cowan, have noted that Thompson struggled so badly to write even these short columns that he allowed others to write parts for him. He had no objections to stealing ideas and quotes from his friends, or even using them as characters, but he felt a great deal of guilt about turning in other people's writing as his own.[7]

---

6   This phrase was also used in his tape recordings for the plot of *Guts Ball*, suggesting that it had been in his vocabulary since at least the early seventies. [*Gonzo Tapes*, CD 4, track 1] In 2012, *For No Good Reason* was used as the title of a documentary about Ralph Steadman.

7   Despite this, it appears that Thompson had let other people write for him even since his days at the *National Observer*. In *Gonzo*, Bob Geiger mentions having written some of his *Observer* pieces. [p.83]

Cowan also wrote about Thompson's tendency to get so completely blitzed on alcohol and drugs that he would be unable to speak or type, and that this sometimes affected his ability to meet that week's deadline. In one particularly bad case, he was handed the opportunity for a huge story but was borderline unconscious and unable to write it. The presidential candidate, Gary Hart, had decided to drop out of the race and Bill Dixon, Thompson's friend, had quit as Hart's campaign manager. He headed straight for Woody Creek to talk with Thompson, who would have been the first journalist in America to know about it. Cowan writes:

> He was sitting upright in front of his typewriter, he could open his eyes, roll his head around and utter noises, but that was it. By the time Bill [Dixon] arrived [...] Hunter was still gargling unintelligibly about the unfinished column, trying to read what he'd already written and remember what he'd been thinking when he started.

Dixon wanted to speak with Thompson privately, but found him surrounded by friends and unable even to reply. He was furious. He had traveled a long way at a difficult time to speak with his friend. By the time Hunter was able to communicate, Hart had dropped out of the race and the story had broken.

In some places, the columns begin very much like his old *National Observer* articles. He presents an opening line that is intended to grab the reader by hinting at something sensational to come and often they share a rhythm with an old style of newspaper reporting. Three such openings are: "The Saga of Martin Fitzwater is a tragic one," "There was blood in the water in Washington last week," and "Big George bit the bullet Sunday night, and it was a powerful thing to see." They are mere teasers for what is to come, and often a little over-dramatic.

These opening lines would then be expanded upon in the first paragraph, creating an intriguing idea that would be explored later. Thompson told Cowan during the writing of these columns that the beginning was the most important part:

> It's all about the lead, especially in something as short as a column. But even in a magazine story, you want to make sure you have them by the short hairs from the start. […] That's all I really care about. I want to do something they won't read anywhere else. Get a couple of graphs like that in, and you don't have to worry so much about the rest.

Editors often complained about this in his writing. David Felton said, "There was no beginning and no end. Everything he wrote was a lead." Sometimes he just modified opening sentences from old stories that he had written, including *Fear and Loathing in Las Vegas*: "We were somewhere on the freeway near the San Diego Zoo when I mentioned to my friend…" When he wanted to end an article, he would do so by bringing it to a witty or poignant ending. Even when he wandered off topic and descended into pointless digressions, he could still bring the story to a close with some sort of wisdom or punchline.

Thompson's writing had gained certain quirks, which have been discussed many times in this book. With articles published once every year or so, it was not obvious how repetitive he had gotten, but in his columns he started to repeat himself badly. The weaknesses in his writing also become more noticeable, such as the fact that most of his characters sound exactly the same or that they lack any sort of depth. In some cases, he just invents a character and offers no description whatsoever, then repeats his *Vegas* line by simply referring to "my attorney." One man even has his nationality changed in the middle of an article. In another, otherwise strong story about a man buying a motorcycle and then being hit by lightning, he starts by saying that the events took place "last week" but by the end of the article he suggests that years have passed by. He had demonstrated in *The Curse of Lono* that he could not keep track of his narrative, but in such short columns it was even more obvious.

In one of his articles, he asked, "Where are the sons of Woodward and Bernstein, the great new wave of investigative journalist?" One cannot fail to wonder where

Thompson saw his own position relative to that question. He was in the same place that he had been when Woodward and Bernstein brought down a president—goofing around at home, watching the news. Even in some of his best political columns, it is clear that he has the language and instincts to talk about these issues, but he is just providing commentary as he watches TV. It is funny and informative, but ultimately just an echo of his 1972 political reporting.

By the time *Generation of Swine* was published in 1988, Thompson's writing was as stale as it had ever been. There were good turns of phrase, a few decent paragraphs, and some wisdom, but he had begun to rely too heavily on catchphrases. He had introduced Skinner and Cromwell, but he had done nothing to de-emphasize the Duke side to his own personality or move away from the same tired themes.

The column wound to an end shortly after the publication of *Generation of Swine*. Between 1984 and 1988, he had managed to write an almost weekly column but in 1989 he began writing less frequently, leaving a month or more between installments. The final one was printed on November 5, 1990. In 1988, he had begun writing a column for *The Boston Globe*, with more or less the same content—politics, sport, and the adventures of Gene Skinner—but he only wrote five pieces, which ran between January and May. He also worked on a column called "Year of the Wolf" for *Esquire* in 1991, but he only managed three installments between February and April.

The book sold well among his extensive fanbase but it was notably weaker than his first collection, *The Great Shark Hunt*. While the first book showed years of development and a range of writing styles, this was more repetitive and tedious. There was more anger and name-calling, but less intelligence and flair. These were thousand-word articles stitched together and often written by friends, while the first volume had been comprised of a variety of works that without a doubt had witnessed a far greater investment of time and effort.

The author's note for *Generation of Swine* is littered with now-famous quotes like, "It's a strange world. Some people get rich and others eat shit and die." In places, it is lyrical and profound, or at least it seems that way on first reading. The more one reads, the more one gets the feeling that these are sentences that sound good but which have little meaning and lack cohesion. In fact, the author's note appears to be three distinct pieces of writing, which were quite possibly stitched together into a single piece of writing with no transitions to join them. They sound good, but they say little. It is funny and dark, extending the author's view that the eighties were the decade when sex and rain became potential harbingers of death, but ultimately it is just more rambling tangents with nothing to hold them together.

Only two years after *Generation of Swine*, Thompson published the third volume of his collected works—*Songs of the Doomed: Gonzo Papers, Vol. 3: More Notes on the Death of the American Dream*.[8] Unlike the first two collections, this one was intelligently edited to follow a chronological path through his career, with work arranged by decade. Each section is broken down into events, with Saigon, for example, making up one such event. For these, Thompson recorded short overviews, which were then transcribed and used to introduce the writing from each period. What a wonderful book *The Great Shark Hunt* would have been if only this approach had been taken.

The result was an important addition to his legacy, featuring excerpts from his unpublished novels, *Prince Jellyfish*, *The Rum Diary*, and *The Silk Road*. There were also rare pieces of writing from throughout the five decades covered, which added up to a pretty comprehensive summary of his career, minus the work that had been included in the first two volumes. Whilst he was compiling the book, Thompson was arrested and involved in a much-publicized court case that he considered a political trial. He won and the case found its way into the book, too. There was not much new writing in this book, nor was there much published elsewhere in the late eighties. Indeed, between 1985 and 1988, he had no new writing published anywhere except in his *Examiner* columns. Even by 1990, there had only been a handful of other pieces, most of which were spun off from the columns. Indeed, the nineties section of

8   The collection was accepted by Jim Silberman in lieu of a novel for which Thompson had long since been paid a large advance.

the book is comprised of articles written by other people alongside fake editor's notes, memos, and other pieces of insubstantial writing.

By the late 1980s, Hunter Thompson was in a continual slide in terms of literary output. He was more interested in selling ideas than doing real writing, and he had moved on from ideas about books and movies to inventing products, such as Gonzo t-shirts and bikinis. He took to writing a newsletter that promoted his merchandise, wrote advertising copy for J. Peterman's catalog, and by the turn of the next decade, he had gotten into art—shooting cans of spray paint over posters of people like J. Edgar Hoover. He even shot a pilot episode of a TV show he intended to host called *Breakfast with Hunter*, but he could not be roused before noon and so the idea fizzled out.[9] Part of this came from an ever-present desire to have more money and part was just that these ideas tended to be weird and fun. But there was little serious writing. When Terry Sabonis-Chafee, another of his assistant/fiancées, talked with him about doing important work, he said that he could no longer do it. "He had all these stories," she said, "but they were fragmented and very personal, and he felt that he had to write something that was big, that really told why it was important, and he couldn't do it."

He still began projects and grew excited about them, but as they had done ever since *Hell's Angels*, most of these ideas just fizzled away as he grew bored, distracted, or simply failed to put the words on paper. Still, he was not yet ready to retire. In *Songs of the Doomed*, he teased his readers with the promise of two forthcoming books. He said he was "currently at work on *99 Days: The Trial of Hunter S. Thompson* and a long-awaited sex book, *Polo Is My Life*." Of course, neither of them was ever written. He also failed to deliver a repeat of "A Dog Took My Place" in 1991, when he attempted to cover the William Kennedy Smith rape trial in Palm Beach.

That same year, Thompson was approached by his friend and neighbor, Don Henley of the Eagles, to write

9   The name and some of the footage was later used by director, Wayne Ewing for his 2004 documentary on Thompson. [https://www.ewingfilms.com/product/breakfast-with-hunter/]

a thousand words about conservation for a forthcoming book that would raise awareness about the proposed destruction of Walden Pond. Thompson, passionately opposed to aggressive land development, sent along an unusual story with a note saying, "Here is the essay I wrote for yr. Walden Environmental book. It came together real easy, once you aimed me in the right direction." What he sent, however, was an article he had written for the *Examiner* almost five years earlier, about torturing a red fox. Thompson had often sold two or more versions of the same story, sometimes copying a few lines or even paragraphs, but this time he had taken an entire article and attempted to reuse it. It was not even for money; he was supposedly helping out a friend and supporting a good cause. Once again, he had sunk to a new low.

1991 also saw the release of *Screwjack*, a collection of short stories. Thompson had written dozens of these in the fifties and sixties and had played with the form a few times since then; however, fans were enraged that the book was published only as a leather-bound, limited edition of just three hundred copies... and that it sold for three hundred dollars each... *and* that it only contained three stories. It had been almost two decades since he had released a good book and his scores of loyal fans would not even have the chance to find out if he had magically returned to form.

The first story in *Screwjack* was "Mescalito," written in 1969 and already published in *Songs of the Doomed*. It told the story of Thompson's first time taking mescaline. If you are inclined to believe his claims, Thompson did not generally write under the influence of anything other than alcohol, tobacco, and speed; however, he had tried the drug while staying in Los Angeles and had decided to write as its effects took hold. It is an interesting piece of experimental writing that he had never intended for publication. It appears to be several excerpts of a journal leading up to a February 18/19 trip, and from there is pure stream-of-consciousness reporting as the drug took hold. Reading it does feel very much like the thoughts are just pouring out of the author's head, fast-paced and jumbled.

The second story is "Death of a Poet," a darker and altogether different tale. It is short, funny, and disturbing. In it, Thompson goes to meet FX Leach, his newest persona.

If Duke was for the sixties and seventies and Skinner was for the eighties, then the nineties had Leach. This story sees Leach explain to Thompson that he has overcome a wife-beating problem by buying sex dolls and thrashing them viciously, sometimes two at a time. At the end, the police come to the door and Leach shoots himself. It is a focused piece of writing that allows Thompson to utilize his talent for dark humor without tangents and philosophizing.

Raoul Duke returns in the third and final story, "Screwjack." Thompson had invented him in order to do the sorts of things that even a madman wouldn't dare, and in this short story about a man's sexual relationship with his cat, it is clear that Duke had served that purpose. It was a legendary tale that Thompson had shared among his closest friends for years before putting out into the public and even by his standards it was pretty shocking:

> I lifted him up to my face and kissed him deeply on the lips. I forced my tongue between his fangs and rolled it around the ridges on the top of his mouth. I gripped him around his strong young shoulders and pulled him closer to me. His purring was so loud and strong that it made us both tremble.

It is a shocking image, but it gets worse. Thompson imagines that "the next time we met he would weigh 200 pounds and flip me over on my stomach and fuck me from behind like a panther."

Fans and critics had been asking for years for a little sex to be added to the Gonzo mix, but this was presumably not what they had anticipated.[10] Perhaps it was a "fuck you" to the people who had complained, but it is more likely that Thompson just enjoyed shocking people. By the nineties, that was harder to do, but bestiality was still a sure-fire way to get a rise out of readers. Cowan wondered if perhaps it was an homage to Burroughs: "The influences for such a piece are many," he said, "ranging from the ever-pressing

---

10   "They wanted a book on politics, they wanted a book on drugs, they want a book on sex, I figure I'd give them one," Thompson says in the film, *Breakfast with Hunter.*

need to be original and bold to his on-going fascination with the life and work of William S. Burroughs."

From this weird love scene between man and tomcat, Thompson then switches into a more conventional scene. The first part was ostensibly written by Raoul Duke but the second is by Hunter Thompson, who is contemplating whether or not his cat will bite him. He grabs the animal by the throat but then it frees itself and watches him from the corner.

It is a strange story, of course. Thompson's depictions of animals could often be shocking in that way. He was known to torture his mynah bird, Edward, and play tape recordings of the distressed animal to visitors in order to make them uncomfortable. For him, it was hilarious, but few others ever saw comedy in it. In the aforementioned 1986 *Examiner* article about torturing a red fox, he describes trapping the animal and then gluing feathers to it and macing it. As it runs back into the wild, he shoots it with buckshot, leaving it bloodied and waiting for the birds to eat it. A few months later, after many complaints, he claimed that it "was a *political allegory*. The fox was Pat Buchanan."

Thompson may well have upset his fans by publishing a limited-edition book that few could afford, but at least it was good writing and two of the three stories were new to readers. It was provocative, weird, and hilarious, which was largely what people wanted from Gonzo journalism.

In 1992, he was asked by *The Observer*, a British Sunday newspaper, to write about the royal family for their relaunched magazine. Word had reached the editors that the legendary bad boy of literary journalism had calmed in recent years and was becoming more reliable with deadlines. He even managed to be polite in his correspondence as they negotiated the terms of the assignment. Of course, taking Hunter Thompson anywhere was a stressful and astonishingly expensive affair, filled with destruction and hurt feelings. In this case, within four hours of arriving in London he was so inebriated that his minder, *The Observer* journalist, Robert Chalmers, said he "sounds like William Burroughs reading *Finnegan's Wake*." By midday, he was blind drunk and furious about being in England, having evidently forgotten his assignment. The rest of the trip

431

was typically farcical, with Thompson barricading himself in his room for the duration, refusing to fly to Scotland, where he was scheduled to attend the Braemar Games. After staying in his room for two whole days, he fled the country without telling anyone, leaving just one written word on a room service menu: "Dorthe."

Thompson did in fact produce an article, but it came through a flurry of faxes from Woody Creek. "Fear and Loathing at the Palace" was not a classic and is quite difficult to find as it was never collected anywhere. Thompson begins with a clearly fabricated version of his own childhood, before he turns to the matter at hand, saying, "I was not born to write about the Royal Family and I was not born to visit peacefully in England, either. This trip to London was one of the worst experiences of my life." It is made up of several short sections, strung together with headings and transitions written by *The Observer's* staff. It actually functions very well in this sense, making for a readable story. Other parts, which jump around more freely, are connected by editorial commentary in italics. Thompson's own inability to connect the pieces of his writing had been overcome by the editors' smart choices.

The article does not actually discuss the royal family all that much and Thompson of course never met with any royals during the two days he spent locked in a hotel room. He rambles from topic to topic and talks about disliking the United Kingdom, while most of the space is taken up by photos of him, an illustration and short reflection written by Ralph Steadman, and even one of Hunter's poems, which laments, "London is/ the worst town/ in the world." When he does talk about them, he writes, "the British Royal Family is a bloodless, pan-sexual tribe." Despite the editors giving carte blanche to insult the royals, Thompson's last fax to *The Observer* said only, "I am tired of your shit-eating censorship. Fuck you. HST."

It is not a well-known article because it is not brilliant, but the fact that it was not terrible by 1992 makes it noteworthy. At this point, it was very rare for him to do any sort of journalism, and whatever writing he did was totally unfocused and weighed down with clichés. Perhaps the editors were responsible for the former being fixed, but he has written a decent article that does not get totally overwhelmed by Gonzo lunacy and his odd stylistic quirks. Still, there were a few of his usual hallmarks. One new addition to the list of quirks is the word "Bubba," which would dominate much of his writing in the nineties, and which he overused to the point of irritating even his most ardent fans.

For Hunter Thompson, the 1990s had started well. Two new books and an article in a major newspaper was a good output—even if the writing was mostly old or had been held together with editorial commentary. It had been twenty years since he was this productive.

In 1991, he was back on speaking terms with Jann Wenner and, when the publisher sent his writer a copy of Kitty Kelley's *Nancy Reagan: The Unauthorized Biography*, Thompson wrote an amusing letter that acted as a sort of review ("a squalid tale from a squalid time") and then wandered off on tangents about politics and pornography. It was his first new, original writing for *Rolling Stone* since "A Dog Took My Place" in 1983.[11] Wenner published it as "The Taming of the Shrew" in May, and thus began a resurgence in their relationship. During the final decade of the century, he wrote more than a dozen pieces for the magazine. Soon, he began faxing pages of strange fiction to the *Rolling Stone* office.

During the confirmation hearings for Clarence Thomas' appointment to the Supreme Court, Thompson began writing a story about a car crash in the Nevada desert. In it, he approaches the vehicle and discovers that it contains Thomas and two prostitutes.[12] The four of them flee and tension develops between the men as they hide out in Elko, the small Nevada town where Thompson had arranged his 1973 Democratic conference.

---

11   In November 1990, they also published parts of the 1990s section of *Songs of the Doomed*, and they had printed articles about him or interviews with him by other writers. 1985 had also seen the publication of "Dance of the Doomed," but this had been written ten years earlier.

12   Thomas is not actually named in the short story part, but he is named in the preceding letter. That was probably enough for the *Rolling Stone* lawyers, for there is nothing that explicitly says that the judge in the story is Thomas.

Thus begins "Fear and Loathing in Elko," which was published in January 1992. Wenner said that it was Thompson's best comic writing—a "dark, sustained masterpiece of violence and madness." Told in four parts, it is a messy story, albeit a funny one. The first part is a letter to Wenner introducing a memo by Raoul Duke, and the second begins the actual story about Thompson and Thomas in Elko. It ends directed at Wenner again. In a sense, it is a continuation of his collage approach to narrative form that had been trialed in efforts like "The Banshee Screams for Buffalo Meat" and which switches switch back and forth between perspectives and themes and styles over many thousands of words, further hybridizing journalism and fiction.

The writing in part one is atrocious, just like Thompson's letters from this period. He had a habit of capitalizing words for effect as a young man, but from the late eighties onwards he had begun capitalizing more arbitrarily. This was just one of many crude, repetitive features that made their way into his published work. He printed some words entirely in capital letters and overused italics, giving the text a cheap, messy appearance, such as in the following example:

> Okay. Congress *is* a sinkhole of Whores. We *all* know that. Shit. Sexual Harassment is what Congress is *all about*. It was the *Way of Our Forefathers*, and it is Right!
> Hot damn: *I feel good about Myself* today, Doc. I feel *Innocent*, for a change… and I guess you feel the Same Way, eh?

It sounds more like the unwanted ramblings of an incoherent, semi-literate Twitter troll than published writing from a literary giant.

Thankfully, this was just the preamble and the story itself is written more carefully (or perhaps edited more extensively). He describes driving fast on a dark road and suddenly seeing a herd of sheep in front of him. His description of hydroplaning toward the animals goes on for one thousand words before he actually collides with them because he keeps expanding upon each image and idea that he mentions. Each paragraph becomes a tangent, taking him to some new alley of thought, returning to the sheep with the same sort of sentence fragment he had learned to use in the sixties: "Which was probably true."

When he hits the sheep, he breaks the news to his reader as though it were a surprise, saying, "Just a sickening *thud*, like running over a body, a corpse — or, ye fucking gods, a crippled 200-pound *sheep* thrashing around in the road." He seems to have forgotten that he already told us this in the first sentence of part two. A similar confusion occurs later, when he finds out that the man in his car is a judge. He is shocked and breaks the news to the reader— but he had already told us this earlier, when it would have been impossible for him to have known. Thompson had never been good with plots and characters; he was better at observing or participating in real events and then recording or distorting them in his personal, manic style.

The two men and the prostitutes take off for Elko, but paranoia quickly sets in. Thompson assumes that the judge will murder him. Indeed, Thomas soon shows himself to be borderline psychotic, rather like Doctor Gonzo in *Fear and Loathing in Las Vegas*. As they frantically travel around Elko at night, he instigates all sorts of trouble and then tells Thompson that they are going to meet FX Leach. "I'm *afraid*, Doc," he says. "Leach is a monster, a criminal hermit who understands nothing in life except point spreads. He should be locked up and castrated."

When Leach appears, he is basically another version of Hunter, appearing with a half-gallon of Wild Turkey and saying things like, "I'm doomed." He is described as a poet and lives in a trailer park.[13] Thompson introduces him:

> We pulled into a seedy trailer court behind the stockyards. Leach met us at the door with red eyes and trembling hands, wearing a soiled cowhide bathrobe and carrying a half-gallon of Wild Turkey.

---

13   Thompson mentions seeing a poem about pigs lying on a table. The poem, entitled "I TOLD HIM IT WAS WRONG" was included in this story. In late 1994, it was published in a very limited run under the name FX Leach.

It is very similar to the second story from *Screwjack*, "Death of a Poet," which contains the line:

> The address he had given me turned out to be a trailer court behind the stockyards. He met me at the door with red eyes and trembling hands, wearing a soiled cowhide bathrobe and carrying a half-gallon of Wild Turkey.

This section of the book is largely the same as the short story from his 1991 collection, with a few small changes to the narrative. Some sections, however, are identical. When Thompson finds the first sex doll and then Leach throws it at him, it is word-for-word the same passage as in "Death of a Poet." The short story had ended with Leach killing himself; however, in the longer version, Thompson flees with the judge amidst a frenzy of shooting from the police. They escape to an airstrip, where Thompson unloads the judge onto a small, private plane.

Part four of the story is a sudden departure to Thompson's memories of Christmas in New York, filled with random acts of destruction. From there, he moves into seemingly random political digressions, but the theme is clear—times have changed, and not for the better. One of his headings from this section was "Nation of Jailers" and, in the eighth paragraph, he complains, "Everybody you see these days might have the power to get you locked up...." These were the first days of the age of political correctness, and Thompson was bemoaning the sterile and oppressive new era that lay ahead. The eighties had seen the conservatives wage war on drugs, sex, fun, and free speech, and now the liberals would have their turn.

Much of Thompson's oeuvre had concerned this theme. The best-known example was, of course, *Fear and Loathing in Las Vegas*, which was a lament for the lost ideals of the sixties. Some have argued that he was happily hammering the nails into the hippies' coffin, but he was certainly sad that some of the values they embodied had died away and been replaced by Nixonian politics. His writing during the seventies and eighties had decried the depressing turns taken by his country and its move toward soulless, corporate greedheadism and this would be a theme that continued for the remainder of his life.

He would also, of course, continue to wage war on those he perceived as corrupt or hypocritical. The judge in his story is a powerful symbol—a man who has broken all the rules and survived, but whose job it now is to punish others for doing the same. As with many of his stories, this one also spoke to the hypocrisy inherent in power. When Thompson gave it to Wenner, he told him to reread *Fear and Loathing in Las Vegas* to compare how dark they were. "'Elko' makes *Vegas* look like a tale of innocence," Wenner admitted.

The story ends with "To Be Continued" but it never was and it never looked like it would be. Unlike some of his work, "Fear and Loathing in Elko" was fairly self-contained and came to a satisfying ending. The fourth section was a continuation of the original letter to Jann, and in it Thompson strikes a defiant tone. The forces of oppression—left and right—are closing in, and there is nothing left to do but remain the same. Call it old-fashioned or atavistic, Thompson was keen to live out his remaining years with the values he had picked up in the fifties and sixties.

As we have seen many times in this book, fact and fiction often merged in the writings of Hunter S. Thompson and it is not particularly useful to attempt to look at his books in traditional terminology such as "novel," but here we do in fact have a story that is purely fictional. Despite this, there are a handful of references to real life, with Thompson acknowledging his work at the O'Farrell Theater and observing a sign in Elko that says, "Studebaker society." This was the name that he had given for the Democratic conference he had hosted there in 1974.

Jann Wenner was delighted when Thompson produced this long, funny, and often brilliant story after so many years of shockingly diminished output. He maintained that Elko was the best thing Hunter had written in years, but he also admired another story that came soon after.

Throughout much of his adult life, Thompson had considered Richard Nixon to be his mortal enemy.

Although he sometimes talked about Ronald Reagan and George H. Bush being worse, there was never the same energy and creativity in his writing about other politicians as there was about Nixon. In the sixties, he had offered witty, brutal commentary until Nixon's election in 1968, after which his journalism morphed into a form of guerilla warfare against the president and his cronies.

Nixon's fall from grace came suddenly and publicly, like Thompson's own declining literary powers. Both men were undone by egotism and stubbornness. By the time Nixon was impeached, Thompson was already struggling badly to complete assignments, and although his insults against Nixon were the finest ever put forth, he was not there to adequately chart his nemesis' downfall. Yet through the seventies and eighties, Thompson's writing repeatedly made reference to his own boogeyman—the impossibly evil former president who still represented everything wrong in the world. He was, in a warped way, Hunter's muse. Thompson sometimes acknowledged this, once saying, "That's why I've done so well with Nixon. Because the majesty of his evil challenged my talent."

When Nixon died in April 1994, Thompson was in New Orleans. He celebrated by getting drunk, but soon realized that he had to write something, and he worried that he may not be able to do it justice. He often spoke of H.L. Mencken's obituary for William Jennings Bryan, a three-time Democratic presidential candidate who had attacked the teaching of evolution in American classrooms during the 1925 Scopes Trial. Mencken's satirical journalism had greatly influenced Thompson's own writing, and his dictum, "The only way a reporter should look at a politician is down," guided the Gonzo approach to political engagement.

When Bryan died shortly after the Scopes Trial, Mencken launched a vicious attack on him in *The Baltimore Sun*. In a savage and yet deeply humorous obituary, Mencken lampoons his opponent, not remotely ashamed to be kicking a man who can no longer kick back:

> Bryan lived too long, and descended too
> deeply into the mud, to be taken seriously
> hereafter by fully literate men, even of the

kind who write schoolbooks. There was a scattering of sweet words in his funeral notices, but it was no more than a response to conventional sentimentality. The best verdict the most romantic editorial writer could dredge up, save in the humorless South, was to the general effect that his imbecilities were excused by his earnestness – that under his clowning, as under that of the juggler of Notre Dame, there was the zeal of a steadfast soul.

Of course, Thompson had no intentions of "conventional sentimentality" and told Douglas Brinkley, "I have to out-Mencken Mencken."

A little over a week after Nixon's death, Thompson wrote a memo called "He was a Crook" for *Rolling Stone*. It began with a subject line that informed his reader that he would not be copping out and taking the high road: "The Death of Richard Nixon: Notes on the Passing of an American Monster ... He was a liar and a quitter, and he should have been buried at sea ... but he was, after all, the President." It begins fittingly:

> Richard Nixon is gone now, and I am poorer for it. He was the real thing—a political monster straight out of Grendel and a very dangerous enemy. He could shake your hand and stab you in the back at the same time. He lied to his friends and betrayed the trust of his family.

He goes on to describe how hatred for Nixon had defined his life and brought him closer to other people. He does indeed try to "out-Mencken Mencken" with brilliant lines like, "Nixon had the unique ability to make his enemies seem honorable." He calls him an "evil bastard," compares him to Hitler and Rasputin, and then comes to this:

> If the right people had been in charge of Nixon's funeral, his casket would have been launched into one of those open-sewage

> canals that empty into the ocean just south of Los Angeles. He was a swine of a man and a jabbering dupe of a president. Nixon was so crooked that he needed servants to help him screw his pants on every morning. Even his funeral was illegal. He was queer in the deepest way. His body should have been burned in a trash bin.

It is utterly, unrepentantly vicious, pulling no punches and not even hiding behind a thin veil of sarcasm. In uncharacteristically short sentences, Thompson adds detail after detail, finally presenting the shocking image of Nixon's corpse burned in a bin. One of the problems with Gonzo is that it relied heavily upon shocking the reader, and after a while it becomes harder to shock those same people. Finally, with this vile image of a former president's corpse, he had managed to say something memorable again.

Of course, the writing is comparatively weak when viewed against his sixties and seventies attacks. There is little in the way of lyricism and the sentences bump awkwardly against one another, lacking the intuitive rhythm of his best work. It is even contradictory. Should Nixon's body have been launched into a sewage canal or burned in a trash bin? Within just six sentences, he has evidently changed his mind. As for the line about screwing on his pants, it was simply rehashed from earlier writings on the disgraced former president, whilst words like "swine" and "dupe" and "queer" are similarly repetitions of more potent insults from earlier writings.

These attacks on the dead president are juxtaposed against several acknowledgements that Nixon had been important in Thompson's life. From the first line about "being poorer for" his death to his admission of being a "self-stigmatized patriot," it is in places surprisingly self-reflective. He normally hid behind his overblown personae, but in this article he bares more of his soul than usual. Nixon has died and Thompson has been forced to look back at his life and ask difficult questions.

There are many more hideous insults littered throughout the obituary, with words like "scum" tossed in, but in one section Thompson uses Nixon to expound upon his theories of literary journalism:

> Some people will say that words like *scum* and *rotten* are wrong for Objective Journalism—which is true, but they miss the point. It was the built-in blind spots of the Objective rules and dogma that allowed Nixon to slither into the White House in the first place. He looked so good on paper that you could almost vote for him sight unseen. He seemed so all-American, so much like Horatio Alger, that he was able to slip through the cracks of Objective Journalism. You had to get Subjective to see Nixon clearly, and the shock of recognition was often painful.

It is for this reason that Thompson has compared him to a cornered badger or a drooling hyena, much the same as Mencken wrote of Bryan:

> Thus he fought his last fight, thirsting savagely for blood. All sense departed from him. He bit right and left, like a dog with rabies.

It is not objective but instills in the reader a more accurate representation of the true character of the subject than any "conventional sentimentality" could have done, or even an "Objective" obituary that touched upon the facts and attempted to provide balance.

When Nixon died, Thompson may have lost his muse, but he gained the ending to his latest book, *Better Than Sex: Gonzo Papers Vol 4: Confessions of a Political Junkie: Trapped Like a Junkie in Mr. Bill's Neighborhood*. Published in 1994, "He was a Crook" slotted nicely into the end of the newest volume of his writing as "Chapter 666." However, whilst the obituary was well received, the book itself was abysmal. William McKeen said that *"Better Than Sex* was Hunter's most inconsistent book; much of it was made up of faxes and photocopies," and that it read "like an unedited diary."

It was another political book, but as he was no longer capable of going on the campaign trail, he just sat at home watching it on TV and noting his reactions.

The first volume of Thompson's writing had covered more than a decade of his work, the second had included a hundred collected columns from the eighties, and the third had filled in the gaps from the other two and then continued gathering his work until 1990, but this fourth collection is incredibly poor. Like *The Curse of Lono*, it is a thin, insubstantial book and the writing is appalling. It is largely a collection of random, political-themed notes with little focus, and it leans heavily on his more annoying quirks, such as overusing the word "Bubba" and inserting variants on the phrase "Ho ho."[14] There are references to his personae, FX Leach and Cromwell, and Raoul Duke returns several times, including as the author of a fake news story about the assassination of Ross Perot.

At its core are the 1992 presidential campaign and Thompson's own run for sheriff, but the bulk of the book is made up of faxes, pictures, and other random and uninteresting items, all arranged to take up as much space as possible so that the actual writing would appear more substantial. Visually, it is an interesting book but it is not well written and there are few redeeming qualities. In some of the collected writings, there is humor and wisdom, and occasionally it is lyrical, but essentially it is a collection of scraps, as though someone had swept under his writing desk and jammed the various pieces of paper into a binder, regardless of content or quality. In an interview, he freely admitted having a lack of enthusiasm for the project:

> I didn't want to do the book. They said it will be easy, but there's no such thing as a free lunch, as they say. I had all these faxes. It never occurred to me I was going to have to write an ending. This is my last book on politics.

Still, although *Better Than Sex* was a terrible book, it sold well. Thompson was also writing regularly for *Rolling*

---

14   Bubba is said an astonishing and irritating sixty times and "ho, ho," is repeated twenty-nine times.

Stone, contributing more to the magazine in the first few years of the nineties than he had between 1976 and 1990—even if most of it was low-quality, repetitive work. He was also working on another novel—and this time it seemed like he might actually get it done.

At some point in the late eighties, Thompson found himself in love with a beautiful, rich woman called Paula Baxt, who was a part of the Aspen polo scene. He suggested that they run away together and she replied, "You don't understand. Polo is my life. I can't run away with you. Who would take care of my ponies?" Just as he had done with "A dog took my place," Thompson fell in love with the phrase and, even years later, would break into laughter thinking about it. Finally, he had his Daisy Buchanan and what seemed like a novel that could rival *Gatsby*.

For years, he worked on *Polo is my Life*, a story about a man who leaves his job at a sex theater and flees to the mountains, but like so many of his book projects, it was never finished. In 1994, however, *Rolling Stone* published "Polo Is My Life: Fear and Loathing in Horse Country," about Thompson's trip to the US Polo Open on Long Island. He went to gather material for his book and at the same time write a two-part story for *Rolling Stone*, illustrated by Steadman. Alas, only one part was written due to Thompson running up a forty-thousand-dollar expense bill.

"Polo is my Life" is not the story of Thompson and Paula Baxt. It is instead a long, winding tale of Hunter and horses and rich people. Unlike other, similar outings, he does talk at length about horses and polo and even attends and writes about a match. However, he is more interested in reprising the theme of "A Dog Took My Place" (or, going back further, "The Kentucky Derby is Decadent and Depraved") by skewering the rich once again. There are countless references to *The Great Gatsby*, some subtle but most rather obvious, as Thompson repeatedly points to his surroundings and tells the reader: *This is it – these are those people, straight out of Fitzgerald!* A similar theme is raised with the introduction of a Swiss character called Hugo, presumably named for Victor Hugo, whose work raised this sort of social commentary.

In places, this is a very mature piece of writing that shows where Gonzo could have gone if Thompson had put the effort in. For all the clowning and silliness that obscures parts of it, the prose is quite impressive in places. He is able to present genuinely picturesque representations of the scenery but then juxtapose them with his typically aggressive prose. He briefly describes driving through the scenic countryside and then suddenly interjects, "Only animals, filthy stupid animals. And the rotten blazing sun. The thirst, the anger, the crippling sense of helpless bovine dumbness when you pass the same deserted barn for the third time in forty minutes and then suddenly run out of gas on a rutted uphill grade overlooking nothing . . ." He tells us how much he hates horses, which are "dangerously stupid beasts," and recalls a time when he was almost trampled by one. Apparently, his Uncle Lawless killed it with a shotgun and the vet declared it a suicide.

Obviously, it is another comic outing. Whether or not Thompson intended his novel to be serious or romantic (and that is unlikely), the article was savage and comical. One horse is referred to as "an all-knowing, dissolute slut horse, insanely rapacious yet very inviting and maternal," and the article was accompanied by various illustrations by Ralph Steadman, one of which is of a four-eyed horse with large breasts. Horse sports are all about cheating and degeneracy, he says, because of "the legacy of Genghis Khan," whom Thompson speculates invented the game. Polo, he believes, is the "natural sport for the '90s in America" because of the greedy, vapid people who are attracted to it, a crowd that is "dangerously hagridden with narcissism and treachery."

There are various characters that come and go throughout the story, including Tobias Perse, who worked as an editorial assistant at *Rolling Stone* that year. Perse had accompanied Thompson throughout the Open as he researched his story, then visited him twice at Owl Farm. He suffered through Thompson's rages for months and was repaid by Hunter's inclusion of him in the story as a simple-minded creep. Perse recalls that it could have been worse:

He had been writing me into the "Polo" story as a character, and that character went from being kind of fierce—beating people with golf clubs and that sort of thing—to being introduced like this: "The magazine sent me an assistant, a tall, jittery young man. He said, 'My name is Tobias, but my friends call me Queerbait.'" Over four months, I cut "Queerbait" every time I sent it back to him, and every time he'd change it back. I finally had it cut in the copy department just before we closed the issue.

He repeats a theme that had cropped up throughout his work since the late sixties—that Jay Gatsby's world is gone now. In *Generation of Swine*, he had noted that *The Great Gatsby* would have been a very different book "if Daisy had been a carrier of AIDS, or if Gatsby's lonely swimming pool took on a crust of poison water every time it rained." In "Polo is my Life," he again describes a world that has been utterly changed, and not for the better:

It was Fitzgerald's valley of ashes seventy years later and fifty times uglier. I felt an overwhelming sense of doom as we drove through it with the windows rolled up to keep out the poison gas. A brownish cloud seemed to hang over everything as far as the eye could see. Even inside the car the air smelled of deadly carbon monoxide, and a strange chemical film was forming on the windshield.

This sense of loss permeates much of Thompson's writing, stemming at least from his time in South America, if not before then. It became a more common theme after the events of 1968, leading to his "wave passage" in *Fear and Loathing in Las Vegas*, and in the eighties and nineties his work often lamented the triumph of darker elements in the national character as well as noting the ecological devastation that had diminished the beauty of the planet, turning it into this poisonous, inhospitable landscape. At the end of the story, he morphs into the characters that he has encountered in Horse Country, declaring:

> I am a polo person now, and I know the Polo Attitude. I smoke the finest opium, and I drive a Ducati 916. Birds sing where I walk, and my home is a magnet for children.

It is a repetition of a device used in *Hell's Angels*, "The Kentucky Derby is Decadent and Depraved," and *Fear and Loathing in Las Vegas*. He has become the thing that he has been studying and criticizing. He is no longer Hunter S. Thompson; he is a wealthy, horse-loving, amoral pedophile.

Although getting the story written and edited had been unpleasant as always, the result was another relatively strong article. Paul Scanlon called it "his last great piece of lyrical, expansive writing" and Wenner considered it one of the highpoints of his career.

It is a great shame that *Polo is my Life* was never published as a book. In all of Thompson's writing, there are few realistic, strong characters, and this is doubly true for the female ones. Women are just stand-ins where they are strictly necessary, with little, if any, backstory given. There are only a handful of women in his fiction and most of them are not particularly believable and given little depth, and in his articles he tends to ignore the women around him in favor of his male counterparts. When female companions do appear in his work, they are often just mentioned by name, with no explanation and no apparent personality. They appear and disappear as needed. *Polo is my Life*, however, would have had a woman at the center of it, and would have dealt with love, another concept largely absent from his work. Thompson often fell in love and had a deep affection for his friends and family, but he was unwilling or unable to write about these. *The Rum Diary* was as close as he came to writing honestly about matters of the heart, but in 1998, when pressed about the real Chenault, he was awkward and evasive, saying, "It's too mushy."

This all presupposes the inclusion of sentimentality, which has been suggested by people that talked with him

[""]

when he planned his novel. However, when Thompson himself described it, he tended to present it more like the stories from *Screwjack*:

> It's what's called a sex book – you know, sex, drugs and rock and roll. It's about the manager of a sex theatre who's forced to leave and flee to the mountains. He falls in love and gets in even more trouble than he was in the sex theatre in San Francisco. Most of my stories are tales of anguish, stress and grief.

Elsewhere, he claimed that his novel would solve the murder of John F. Kennedy, but the book was never published, even though he worked on it for between twelve and fifteen years. Kevin T. McEneaney speculates that he gave up following the publication of Norman Mailer's *Oswald's Tale* in 1995. Thompson had been interested in the Kennedy murder as a journalist and often stated in interviews that the press' failure to definitively solve it was unforgivable, but perhaps now he felt that Mailer had come closer than he ever could. McEneaney argues that there was precedent for this: He believes that Thompson had decided not to write about the 1968 Democratic Convention after Mailer's *Miami and the Siege of Chicago* and he had given up writing about the "Rumble in the Jungle" after Mailer published *The Fight*.

When he needed to keep Jim Silberman happy, Hunter sent him a massive storyboard that he had built at Owl Farm. A photo of the board shows the various elements that were intended to make up the plot of the novel, including peacock feathers, bullets, polo mallets, and a photo of Kennedy. There is also the picture of Jilly used in the Aspen Wallposter and the panther that Maria had as a tattoo in one of his *Examiner* columns.[15] Beneath this are various pages of writing assigned to different sections of the book. The board does not tell us much about the novel, but it was how Thompson had planned most of his written

---

15   Jilly is the name of a character in several of his *Examiner* columns. These appear to have been intended as sections of the book.

work since the seventies. He required the visual stimulus to begin writing and then to help him later connect different threads.

Polo is my Life was the closest that any of his nearly-published books ever came to seeing the light of day, even being assigned a release date and an ISBN by Simon & Schuster. Whether or not McEneaney's theory was correct, there were various other factors contributing to his not writing it, including angry disagreements with his agent and publisher over the contract, but in the end it was another Hunter S. Thompson book that was never published. His friend and neighbor, Wayne Ewing, who helped him work on the story, said that his "biggest frustration was not being able to get Hunter to finish that book," and explained:

> Hunter struggled to turn that sports article into a book because he keep trying to make it another *Gatsby* and he was not good at creating true narrative fiction. I urged him to just tell his own story of a poor boy from Kentucky with a doomed love for a gorgeous woman in the rich world of polo, but he had no interest.

Two more reasonable pieces of Gonzo writing emerged in the mid to late nineties. In 1995, Thompson reviewed the Ducati 900SS for *Cycle World*. In the oddly titled "Song of the Sausage Creature," the writer shares his wisdom on motorcycles and especially the fast ones. Luckily for him, the Ducati 900SS was about as fast as they came, and his descriptions of riding it are enthralling. He was always good at describing motorcycles and cars, and he had not lost that ability. There are weaknesses to the article (too many "ho hos" and "Bubbas" again) but the actual parts describing the machine are wonderful.

The titular "sausage creature" is mentioned several times and refers to the state one finds oneself in after an horrendous crash—no skin, no teeth; just a palpitating bag of flesh. It is a gruesome image, but the article is largely about riding that fine line between exhilarating fun and gory death. It is another incarnation of his Edge philosophy from *Hell's Angels*. The Hell's Angels are mentioned a few times, of course, and Thompson is keen to relate the story of his BSA Lightning as a means of comparing it to the Ducati. He is of the opinion that the Ducati, although much faster, is a lot safer than the BSA.

Although it is a relatively strong piece of writing, at times it feels like his interest is primarily in cementing his legend through casual boasting and name-dropping:

> I have been a connoisseur of fast motorcycles all my life. I bought a brand-new 650 BSA Lightning when it was billed as "the fastest motorcycle ever tested by *Hot Rod* magazine." I have ridden a 500-pound Vincent through traffic on the Ventura Freeway with burning oil on my legs and run the Kawa 750 Triple through Beverly Hills at night with a head full of acid... I have ridden with Sonny Barger and smoked weed in biker bars with Jack Nicholson, Grace Slick, Ron Zigler and my infamous old friend, Ken Kesey, a legendary Café Racer.

The same could be said of "Doomed Love at the Taco Stand," an odd story from 1997. Thompson finally returned to his old employer, *Time*, for this tale of fast, expensive cars and late-night adventures. The events depicted allegedly occurred during the filming of *Fear and Loathing in Las Vegas*, and so Johnny Depp is mentioned frequently and Thompson has a bizarre phone conversation with Benicio del Toro, who played Doctor Gonzo.

"Doomed Love at the Taco Stand" is set amidst the degenerate Hollywood elite. Thompson assaults an astrologer and pretends to be Johnny Depp, before driving north to Big Sur with a beautiful woman he has rescued from a pack of vicious dogs. *En route*, they stop at a taco stand, where the threat of violence looms but never descends. They finally skid off the road and crash into a waterfall, where they sit and talk and the story fizzles out with the words "To be continued..."

Like most of Thompson's stories, there was not much

of a plot but along the way there were some amusing lines and a little wisdom. Here, the story appears to lead up to the revelation that Thompson has the "soul of a teenage girl in the body of an elderly dope fiend." He says this three times near the end of the story, with the idea first raised by the girl he has rescued, Heidi:

> "It's because you have the soul of a teenage girl in the body of an elderly dope fiend," she whispered. "That is why you have problems." She patted me on the knee. "Yes. That is why people giggle with fear every time you come into a room. That is why you rescued me from those dogs in Venice."

Throughout this story, like his others, Thompson's characters are shallow and unconvincing, but Heidi was in fact a real person and did give Thompson this bizarre insight. The idea of him as a teenage girl trapped in an old drug addict's body is one that he often quoted in interviews because he found it funny, and in his 2003 memoir, *Kingdom of Fear*, he repeats it four times. Thompson states there (and elsewhere) that these were his second wife, Anita's, words, and Anita claims they were Hunter's "favorite self-description," but Wayne Ewing, who helped edit *Kingdom of Fear*, confirms that Heidi had indeed given him the insight, and that Thompson simply changed her name for the 2003 book.

Though the dialogue was unconvincing and there was little in the way of plot, it was nonetheless an amusing tale. It was short, simple, and relatively focused. The absurdity of the conversations and the ridiculous action scenes, such as hitting an astrologer in the testicles or stabbing a dog in the ribs with a fork, are weird enough to be funny. Thompson excelled at presenting these moments of understated but bizarre comedy. Wayne Ewing reflected upon these bursts of creativity as the genius of his Gonzo writing. At this point, he was typing as Hunter dictated stories, and was frustrated by how slowly Thompson put together his sentences. When working together on a eulogy, Ewing and Thompson's assistant, Deborah, kept pushing him to "Get to the point!"

> But Hunter had other things in mind for the
> Eulogy, and in the end he was right. The
> description of the crowd in the bar became
> elaborate – drunken women dancing on
> the bar drinking liquid MDA from brandy
> snifters – was one of his inventions. And
> that's what took the time: the inventions,
> the elaborations on reality. As I typed his
> halting twists on reality, I realized that this
> was the essence of Hunter's style, the nature
> of Gonzo Journalism – his contribution to
> Literature.

Indeed, throughout his whole career, from the best
writing to the worst, there were a great many instances
of his "elaborations on reality." For Thompson, these
stemmed from a lifelong passion for weird comedy and
confusion of reality and fiction that had grown out of his
childhood pranking.

After his 1994 story, "Polo is my Life," Thompson's
work for *Rolling Stone* dropped off once again, and what
he did write was pretty short. In 1995, he ran up a bill
of more than thirty thousand dollars for a story that he
never wrote, but Wenner kept pushing to get him back in
the magazine. He offered almost sixty thousand dollars for
Thompson to write a story called "The Wilderness Sisters"
but Thompson just replied, "Fuck you. […] Do not repeat
NOT publish anything by me or attached to my name in
any way without my written Approval and a signed contract
inre: Money for my services." In 1998, Wenner practically
begged him to write about Clinton's impeachment,
employing plenty of flattery. Thompson replied, "Well...
for $10K Quick I'll give it a quick whirl." He wrote a
short memo for the magazine in March, commenting on
Clinton's popularity. "Most historians," he writes, "now
agree that Clinton's lasting image will be as the president
who Legalized Sodomy and set millions of Americans free
from the chains of prudery and hopeless Ignorance." It is
an amusing but unremarkable piece of writing.

A better effort came fourteen months later, with

"Hey Rube! I Love You: Eerie Reflections on Fuel, Madness & Music." Immediately, the reader is struck by a completely different Hunter S. Thompson. Where are the arbitrary capitals?[16] Where are the catchphrases? Where are the dashes and ellipses? Where are the long elegiac sentences punctuated by short, terse sentence fragments and interjections? Instead of that, Thompson writes an incredibly fast-paced, straight narrative that offers a lucid series of events and reflections that almost tackle emotions. He deals with love and talks fondly of his childhood.

In almost all of Thompson's writing, there is a familiar cadence as well as the usual Gonzo lexis that I have so often mentioned in this book. You can pick up almost anything that he has written and, if you are familiar with his style, you will immediately recognize it the same way you would recognize a van Gogh painting—the violent, improbable, utterly unique styles setting them apart entirely from their peers. Here, however, the narrative seems far more conventional:

> It was a LaSalle sedan, as I recall, a slick-looking brute with a powerful straight-eight engine and a floor-mounted gearshift, maybe a 1939 model. We never got it started, because the battery was dead and gasoline was scarce. There was a war on. You had to have special coupons to buy five gallons of gas, and the coupons were tightly rationed. People hoarded and coveted them, but nobody complained, because we were fighting the Nazis and our tanks needed all the gasoline for when they hit the beaches of Normandy.

It is a strange, reflective, but—in places—quite beautiful piece of writing. Its stream-of-consciousness narrative takes us from the present day to the past, and from his grandma to William S. Burroughs. He wanders,

16   These do, unfortunately, make an occasional appearance and so does the word "bubba," but all of this is restrained and does not interfere with one's enjoyment of the text.

452

seemingly with no place to go, but the article begins and ends on the subject of music as fuel. In the final paragraphs, he writes about how music inspired him:

> It happens over and over, and sooner or later you get hooked on it, you get addicted. Every time I hear "White Rabbit," I am back on the greasy midnight streets of San Francisco, looking for music, riding a fast red motorcycle downhill into the Presidio, leaning desperately into the curves through the eucalyptus trees, trying to get to the Matrix in time to hear Grace Slick play the flute.
>
> There was no piped-in music on those nights, no headphones or Walkmans or even a plastic windscreen to keep off the rain. But I could hear the music anyway, even when it was five miles away. Once you heard the music done right, you could pack it into your brain and take it anywhere, forever.

The overall tone in this article is one of nostalgia, as we can see in these paragraphs. It is a surprisingly open, honest, and very nearly real Hunter S. Thompson that appears, with his ego and bravado temporarily caged. Though a little uneven in places, "Hey Rube!" serves as a welcome sign that Thompson was willing and able to write differently from his usual style.

Final Words

I do not think he was a great writer. I think he clearly had great potential, both as a writer and a leader. However, he fell, dramatically, and a very, very long time ago. Hunter wanted to be a great writer and he had the genius, the talent, and, early on, the will and the means. He was horrified by whom he had become and ashamed – or I really should say tortured. He knew he had failed. He knew that his writing was absolutely not great. This was part of the torture. [...] he never became the great American writer he had wanted to be. Nowhere close. And he knew it.

Sandy Thompson

On the dust jacket for *Better Than Sex*, published in 1994, it said that Hunter S. Thompson would "be gone by the year 2000." When asked about this in an interview later that year, he explained that he was sick of writing and that the process of putting together even that flimsy book had been too painful to repeat. He was cagey as to whether he meant he would be dead by the millennium or whether that would be the beginning of his retirement. The interviewer appeared to think the former but Thompson seemed to be suggesting the latter.

It had been a running theme throughout much of Thompson's life that both he and his friends expected him to die young, and he often remarked that he had expected to be dead by thirty. He was a strong and quite athletic man, whose body stood up well to decades of abuse, but by the mid-nineties his health was declining rapidly. According to Ralph Steadman, he had suffered from arthritis for most of his life, and in his final decade he experienced terrible problems with his hip and spine. His once sturdy frame could no longer cope with his clumsiness and intoxication, and he had several bad falls that resulted in various broken bones. These resulted in difficult hospital stays and arduous recuperation periods that sapped his energy. He continued drinking heavily and taking vast quantities of drugs, including powerful painkillers that eased his pain slightly but drastically increased the mental fogging that made his writing so weak. Bob Bone, his friend from Middletown, Puerto Rico, and Brazil, saw Thompson in 2001 and later commented: "He seemed not much more than a shell of the vigorous and vital friend that I knew nearly a half-century ago."

As the millennium drew closer, he did not do much new writing but certainly found ways to make money from his archives. The obvious choice was to publish a collection of his letters. He had been saving them ever since he had gotten into journalism at Eglin and had even joked as a young man that they were so brilliant that he might be the first author to sell his correspondence *before* becoming famous. As it turned out, he had so many letters piled up that three volumes of them were scheduled for publication.

The first was *The Proud Highway: Saga of a Desperate Southern Gentleman 1955–1967*, published in 1998 and providing insight into the mind of an angry young man bent on literary success, with absolutely no doubts about his own talent. These letters show the development of his mind into something approaching the warped genius that created *Fear and Loathing in Las Vegas*. They make for wonderful reading and the book sold well. The second volume, *Fear and Loathing in America: The Brutal Odyssey of an Outlaw Journalist 1968–1976*, which was published in 2000, looked at the difficult years during which the author achieved tremendous fame but hit a creative wall and began to become trapped in the style that he had created. Together, these two volumes show the creation of a revolutionary literary and journalistic fusion against the turbulent backdrop of 1960s and '70s America.

To date, there has been no third volume, but *The Mutineer: Rants, Ravings, and Missives from the Mountaintop 1977–2005* has been awaited for two decades. With no explanation for the long delay, it has been suggested that perhaps his vastly diminished writing ability made the third volume a difficult publication. The rambling brilliance of the early letters may contrast unflatteringly with the crude, angry gibberish that he produced during the last two decades or more of his life, perhaps sullying his reputation. In 1996, X-Ray Book Company released Thompson's second chapbook, *Mistah Leary, He Dead: a eulogy for Dr. Timothy Leary*. Like *Screwjack*, it was another limited-edition book, with a hand-printed run of only three hundred numbered and twenty-six lettered copies. It consisted of a single sheet of folded paper, with a total of around two hundred and fifty words Thompson had written for *Rolling Stone*. In addition to this, it featured a sheet of simulated blotter acid with Leary's face printed on it. It sold for twenty-five dollars and quickly became a collector's item.

Thompson had never liked Timothy Leary and had made various disparaging remarks about him in his work, but by the nineties he was ready to bury the hatchet and recognize a man who had lived through some of the same experiences and survived. They had taken different roads, but on some level they were fighting the same fight. Thompson's short eulogy offers rare praise and even a little tenderness that suggests regret for lost years.

There were several other eulogies to write in the late nineties as his literary and cultural peers began to pass away. The eulogies he wrote for Allen Ginsberg and William S. Burroughs show his determination to remain offensive and humorous, but at the same time offered genuinely kind words. These show a mellowing in his attitude and a desire to be seen in his rightful place among the countercultural giants of his era.

In 1998, he finally became a published novelist. *The Rum Diary*, billed as "The Long Lost Novel," was released to eager fans. It had never been lost, of course. The novel was simply not good enough for publication in the sixties and by the time he had invented Gonzo, he viewed it as juvenile and poorly written. However, with the ever-pressing need for money, he dusted it off and edited it down for release.[1] Sixty percent of the original book was cut, and the result

---

1   Publishing the book was Douglas Brinkley's suggestion. In video shot by Wayne Ewing, he says that he told Thompson, "Why don't we have this count as one of your book advances, 'cause it was done already." [https://www.ewingfilms.com/2-17/]

High White Notes

was a surprisingly focused story with minimal intrusion of pointless tangents. Video footage of Thompson's editing work shows him removing extraneous and confusing imagery, making his language more concise. Journalist Curtis Robinson remarked that the intention of the editing process was "to edit it without changing anything," which was a problem because the book pre-dated Thompson's obsession with words like "brutal" and "doomed," which Robinson calls his "old friends." Thompson struggled to accept the beautiful, lyrical passages he had written forty years earlier, and felt the urge to Gonzo-fy them, but with the prompting of friends and editors, he agreed to preserve his youthful voice.

The book proved to be a big hit among his fans, just like the two volumes of letters.[2] It not only sold well but showed fans and critics alike that he was capable of an entirely different style of writing to the one that had made him famous. But it only confirmed what he must have known deep down—that readers connected much better with the things he had written decades before.

When the millennium came, Thompson knew that he had become a modern literary legend, but he was also plagued by the undeniable fact that he had not fulfilled his potential. As a young man, he had been a magnificent writer and threw every ounce of energy he had into his work, but after achieving fame he had become lazy and distracted. For the first half of his life, he dedicated himself to his craft, and for the second half he had simply attempted to recapture some of the brilliance he had once possessed. It had not worked and his loss of talent was an open secret.

Worst of all was his failure to produce great fiction. He had only gotten into journalism as a means of becoming a great writer and he had always thought that if Hemingway had done it, it was good enough for him. But Hemingway had gotten out of journalism and written some of the greatest novels of the twentieth century. Thompson had fused fact and fiction in three of the most brilliant books

---

2   Still, he was unhappy, complaining to his publisher that they had not printed enough copies to get him farther up the bestseller list than twenty-second. He called it "the sloppiest job of Book Publishing I've ever seen." [*Gonzo Personas*]

458

of his era, but he had not managed to produce a genuinely good work of pure fiction to rival his best journalism. He could not craft a plot or present characters with any real depth, and the action and dialogue that he wrote were funny but not believable.

As his close friend, William Kennedy, said, "He had put in the time as an apprentice in fiction, but then he stopped and did other things." Ralph Steadman added, "All his heroes like Joseph Conrad, Ernest Hemingway and William Faulkner wrote proper stories and then there was Hunter, this magnificent outlaw [...] whose prose style was peerless, but whose ability to write a novel eluded him to the end." Whether it was the drugs, the fame, or—as he insisted—he was just a "lazy hillbilly," his career can easily be divided into two parts—trying hard and then hardly trying. In the end, his only true novel was *The Rum Diary*, and whilst it is an enjoyable tale, it is no masterpiece. Had it been published shortly after it was written, it would surely have been overlooked as a minor work. Thompson's agent, Lynn Nesbit, said, "*The Rum Diary* came out when it did because he needed money, absolutely. He never would've published that twenty years before."

The two volumes of his correspondence secured his place in American letters, casting off any doubts about his ability to produce fiercely intelligent work, but the last letter had been written in 1976. Terry Gilliam's adaptation of *Fear and Loathing in Las Vegas* brought more attention to his best novel, spiking sales and introducing a new generation to Gonzo. It made Thompson into a popular Halloween costume, but that didn't help him write again. Many of his fans had not yet been born when he last wrote something truly original. This is partly because, ever since the early seventies, he had struggled with chronic writer's block. As time went by, the problem worsened. His son, Juan, explained:

> Hunter gradually lost the ability to sustain the necessary concentration to write, almost certainly because of the cocaine and booze. He wasn't a binge cokehead. Hunter snorted a little bit all day, probably to balance the whiskey, but I'm sure it impaired his ability to concentrate.

As with almost any author, this inability to write affected him greatly. It became common for his friends and assistants to find him alone, crying. He told Douglas Brinkley, "I don't think I can take it anymore. I'm making a fool out of myself." He had always acted tough, but he could not cope with this failure, and he wept from frustration and regret. Laila Nabulsi recalled walking in on him staring at his typewriter, completely unable to put words on paper, and speaking aloud to himself: "I used to know how to do this. I used to know how to do this. Why can't I do this?"

It was time to go back to basics. In mid-2000, Hunter Thompson, still using a typewriter rather than a computer, became a blogger for ESPN's *Page 2* website. He had begun as a sportswriter and here he was in his old age, writing about sports again. It was John Walsh who offered him the job. In 1974, Thompson's failure to write an article about the Nixon impeachment trial had gotten Walsh fired from *Rolling Stone*, but the two men respected and liked each other, and they sensed that this could be a fruitful relationship.

It was fruitful and Thompson managed to turn in columns on a regular schedule. Despite painful deadline sessions, he contributed dozens of articles each year for four years. His new assistant (and later, his wife), Anita, was on hand to help him. She recalled:

> There was screaming sometimes. He would get upset when there were too many cooks in the kitchen. He worked best with one, no more than two people around. He needed a group of people around at the beginning of the night to help him organize. But then he liked it calm, so his mind could work. We'd keep his drink filled and have a snack around him, so he wouldn't be distracted, so he could stay at the typewriter.

Walsh knew from the beginning that it was not going to be a great column, but he was happy to have Thompson's name on it and the occasional funny line or word of wisdom. He later acknowledged that "Hunter was in pretty good decline physically and intellectually" when they began working together. He continued:

> It was clear that he didn't have his A game, and especially on a weekly basis, he couldn't focus enough to pay enough attention. We would give him stories and tips and clues, but it rarely registered. He would frequently be distracted and go in another direction—a direction that sometimes led to not such a good place. The story didn't hang together. There wasn't enough there to make a piece out of it. Sometimes it would take days.

It began as a sports column but of course Thompson could never focus on one single thing and so it quickly evolved to tackle other issues like politics. He began writing for ESPN on November 6, 2000, but after a column pushing for a rule change in baseball and another about football, he switched to include more politics. Gambling was a near-life-long interest that he had written about occasionally, including in his *Command Courier* and *Examiner* columns, and this aspect of sport would dominate *Hey Rube*, the name given to his column.[3] Later, he covered a wider range of topics, including the case of Lisl Auman, who had been imprisoned for the murder of a police officer despite having been under arrest when the actual killer shot the officer.

The ESPN blog forced Thompson to sit down and write something each week. The columns were very short and he had a huge amount of freedom in what he could write, but sadly the results were once again poor. Jann Wenner said that by this point "his writing consisted of disjointed fragments of larger thoughts and fairly lifeless repetitions of his brilliant phrasemaking and descriptions of people and places." He was partially referring to the fact that Thompson's repetitiveness had grown to ludicrous

---

3   *Hey Rube* was one of the names he proposed for his death of the American Dream book in the late sixties, and when these columns were compiled in 2004, it was the name he used for that collection.

proportions. In *Hey Rube: Blood Sport, the Bush Doctrine, and the Downward Spiral of Dumbness*, a collection of eighty-three of his ESPN blog posts, it is obvious just how much he leant on these catchphrases. He said "ho ho" thirty-six times, "doomed" thirty-five times, "swine" twenty-five times, "Bubba" fifteen times, "mahalo" sixteen times, and "whoops!" twenty-two times. He also used the phrases, "How long, O Lord" and "The fat is in the fire" repeatedly. The text is littered with ampersands and arbitrarily capitalized words. He often showed inconsistency by capitalizing a phrase one way and then another, such as writing "Pro football" and "Pro Football" within the same article.

By this point, the music was long gone from his once lyrical language. There is little sense of rhythm and often there are careless repetitions, with certain words appearing far too often, even in the same sentence. If we take a look at two paragraphs from his third column, we can see just how bad his writing had become:

> We have seen weird Times in this country before, but the year 2000 is beginning to look super weird. This time there really is nobody flying the plane…. We are living in dangerously weird times now. Smart people just shrug and admit they're dazed and confused. The only ones left with any confidence at all are the New Dumb. It is the beginning of the end of our world as we knew it. Doom is the operative ethic.
>
> The autumn months are never a calm time in America. Back to Work, Back to Football Practice, etc…. Autumn is a very Traditional period, a time of strong Rituals and the celebrating of strange annual holidays like Halloween and Satanism and the fateful Harvest Moon, which can have ominous implications for some people.

Pieces of his writing like this highlight the fact that he was either unwilling or unable to read and correct his own work, and hints at a genuinely startling degree of cognitive decline and the sort of inability to process language that plagued Hemingway prior to his suicide. The repetition of "weird" in the first paragraph is lazy and it seems in both paragraphs as though he said something, tried to move on, and then said it again.[4] The capitalization is careless and in the second paragraph he refers to "Satanism" as a holiday. He tried to redeem himself in the next paragraph with shock value by referring to pedophiles kidnapping children and swapping them as Christmas presents, but there is little point to it. Shock value worked in warped masterpieces like *Fear and Loathing in Las Vegas*, but in a poorly-written blog post it is just embarrassing.

In his early career, he had learned that, once you knew the rules of grammar, you could begin to bend and break them for effect. He had realized that he could use sentence fragments to refocus the reader's attention after a digression, for example, or that the rules of punctuation could be bent to produce a rhythm that echoed the content. Much of his writing involved breaking the rules but it worked because it was done deliberately to achieve a particular effect. In *Hey Rube*, however, there are countless sloppy mistakes and they appear accidental. A month after his first blog post went online, he used the phrase, "loyal lifetime rabid fans." It is sometimes hard to believe that these blogs were written by a native speaker of English.

For his *Examiner* column, he had begun a section called "Swine of the Week" but had not been focused enough to issue the award on a weekly basis. He attempted to resurrect it for the ESPN blog but his one and only effort was too poor even for a blog post. He wrote, "Swine of the Week is always a difficult choice, but this first one is an obvious No-Brainer." How can something "always" be hard but at the same time a "No-Brainer"? This section was cut from the blog by his editors but he chose to include it in the book. He also wrote the following: "We can Relax and get back to sports. So let's get back to Al Gore for a minute." It makes absolutely no sense and in fact his editors caught and corrected this, but it was still printed in

---

4   Jay Cowan noted that he had done this in the 1990s. He would write something twice and often relied upon editors to take out one of the versions because he could not choose which was better. [*Hunter S. Thompson*, p.89]

the book version.[5] Wayne Ewing explained:

> It is not that Hunter made a point of
> changing them back, but rather the fact
> that we worked from Hunter's final drafts
> which were sent to ESPN, not by pulling
> down the final published versions from the
> ESPN website.

Just a few months before his death, Thompson told
an interviewer, "You don't have to be a sports fan to read
this. It is a really brutal political book." Sadly, the first part
is not really true. In 1972, Thompson had written a dense
guide to American politics, yet nearly a half century later,
it is still a genuinely wonderful book that people continue
to enjoy. You do not have to know, like, or even care about
American politics of the seventies to read it, but *Hey Rube*
is so horribly written that one would need to have a strong
interest in sports and gambling in order to get any sort of
value out of it. His best work captured an era so well that
it was frozen in time, but no such praise could be offered
for *Hey Rube*.

By the new millennium, those "high white notes"—be
they wisdom or musical prose—were few and far between.
The articles are a crude mix of uninteresting information,
half-formed ideas gleaned from watching too much TV,
and dubious statistics. It is shallow and dull, with no
involvement because he is now stuck at Owl Farm rather
than going out to investigate a story. Even though most
of the columns are very short, they are poorly organized
and when he jumps from idea to idea, it is not done as
energetically and comedically as he had done in *Fear and
Loathing on the Campaign Trail '72*. At ESPN, people were
having serious doubts about his work. "Should we keep
paying Hunter?" they asked. John Walsh felt embarrassed
for him and was forced to intervene. "You know, Hunter,"
he said, "you've got to get these better."

Jann Wenner saw this, too. He had tried several times

---

5   In the December 18, 2000 blog post, it said, "Everybody
can Relax and get back to sports ... unless you happen to
live in Tennessee." [https://proxy.espn.com/espn/page2/
story?id=957395]

over the years to get Thompson to commit to a column, but he was not willing to tolerate the sort of poor-quality material that ESPN accepted. He said:

> I made several serious attempts to get him to write a 1,500-word column once a month. I offered him quite a bit of money to do it—anything to get Hunter back in the paper—even if for purely mercenary purposes on my part, just to have that byline back and some of that energy. How difficult can that have fucking been? Fifteen hundred words for $10,000. Write that once a month. Just sit there and closely consider any subject. Watch television and write about some outrage you saw. But he couldn't do it.

In 2004, Thompson gathered his columns and collected them into *Hey Rube*, the book. He had published several collections in the past and each time he had written an author's note to accompany them, but this time he was unable even to write an introduction. He just copied some text from one of the blog posts and used that instead, alongside a few rambling sentences about George Bush and Bob Dylan. His fans were getting less and less for their money. He stuck the Eglin Air Force Base report from Colonel Evans in alongside it, presumably to remind his readers of his rebellious past.

The most famous blog post from this collection was the one that appeared on September 12, 2001. It is indeed very different from his other posts and almost seems as though it were written by another author. As he writes about the tragic events of 9/11, the random capitalization is gone, along with most other features of laziness and self-imitation, but it is remembered more for its prophesy than its literary merit, as he predicted with some accuracy the horrors of our post-9/11 world. Still, it is a reasonable piece of writing. Even a brief look at this blog tells the reader that its author had spent far more time on it than the ones that came before. Thompson most likely knew that this was a major world event and did not just wait until deadline time to turn in his ill-formed, half-written notes as he would normally do.

The articles that follow are better. The next features a brief phone conversation with Johnny Depp, before Thompson runs outside and begins shooting into the darkness, expecting to kill a terrorist. It is a clever parody of America's hysterical reaction and prophesied the needless violence that followed the atrocities in New York and Washington DC. For several articles, his ideas are clear and flow from one to the next. His language is better and there are fewer pointlessly capitalized words. It seems that crisis had again brought out the best in him.

Sports and politics were blended throughout these columns as they were throughout much of his work, oftentimes with the same sort of language used. Note the similar, violent language used in these two very different sentences: "the preternaturally arrogant Los Angeles Lakers stomped the 76ers into quivering blood sausage" and "The White House was blindsided and fatally paralyzed by the horrible news." In each case, he has relied upon his sportswriters' verbs, mixed with a few strong adverbs and adjectives.

Through the sports and politics, he weaves a bizarre story about two of his supposed neighbors—Prince Omar and Princess Omin. It is a completely fictional story intended to speak for the atmosphere of political insanity and racism that had gripped his country. Omar loses a bet to Thompson and leaves his sister as payment. Later, the sister is arrested so that a cop can yell, "We have a lot of New Laws these days. You Have No Rights." It is a strange tale that he tried to continue throughout several weeks of his blog, but eventually he lost interest and dropped it.

He also brings in his friends and various celebrities, but it is notable that most characters speak through Hunter's voice. He simply made up what people said and that usually resulted in their voice sounding like his own. This was a problem for serious fiction but worked in comedic circumstances because the overblown language just made the story funnier. In *Hey Rube*, he reports Sean Penn as shouting, "You fool!" and Princess Omin as saying, "Don't touch me, you Swine!" Both are clearly fabrications.

Both Cromwell and Leach appear in these columns:

Cromwell as Thompson's neighbor and Leach as the author of a short poem. However, in the very next line after the poem, Thompson writes, "That is a poem I wrote last week…" Again, he was struggling to keep his facts straight.

Read individually, Thompson's ESPN columns are mostly dull and badly written, with a few possessing some small degree of merit. As a book, however, it is far worse. The repetition and mistakes build up into a truly frustrating text that shows a once-great writer struggling even to put together a few hundred words of anything but terrible prose. Cowan observed that "*Hey Rube* would often lurch back into old, trackless meanders that echoed his personal confusion and confirmed an inability to complete anything longer than a thousand words."

While writing his ESPN column, Thompson began work on what was a sort of autobiography, *Kingdom of Fear: Loathsome Secrets of a Star-Crossed Child In the Final Days of the American Century.* It was not a conventional autobiography, of course, but Thompson did not do many conventional things. He knew, however, that he had led an interesting life and that a memoir of sorts would go over well with his fans. What's more, it would be easy to look back through his past, tell a few stories, and embellish them with a little Gonzo flair.

He was interviewed many times during the process of publicizing *Kingdom of Fear* and he occasionally discussed whether the book was a memoir or not. Certainly, it was not clear because the book was a mix of old and new work, much of which was autobiographical but with various other pieces of writing interspersed. What biographical details exist are also dubious. He was unsure about it himself and claimed to have the definition of "memoir" taped up next to his typewriter. In one interview, in language that highlights his confusion about the project, he suggested that it had begun as a memoir and evolved into something else:

> It started off—it's supposed to be a memoir; I think it started off as memoirs. You know, it just sort of—a very quick and

active story about how I got to be what I am today, at different key adventures in my life.

Although he claimed in interviews that all the writing in it was "totally new," much of it was collected material from previous decades. This is abundantly clear when old and new writing are presented side by side, as the writing he was doing in the 2000s was simply atrocious. It is messy and hastily compiled, with some genuinely awful pieces mixed in with other, much better ones. This just further highlighted how badly he had fallen as a writer.

Wayne Ewing reflected on the process of helping Thompson compile this book, recalling that Hunter originally sat and wrote nine pages of quite funny material, but then could not write anything more for several months. As had happened with the ending of *Fear and Loathing on the Campaign Trail '72*, he was interviewed by a friend and his answers were subsequently edited. This time, it was Ewing, Anita Thompson, and an assistant called Jennifer Stroup who "edited and massaged" the transcripts into useable form.

The book starts as though it is a normal memoir, taking us back to Louisville and Hunter's childhood. However, the stories he tells from the past are probably fictional interpretations of real events. At the beginning of the book, he recounts being questioned by the FBI at the age of nine and learning the valuable life lesson of not blabbing to the authorities. This story has been repeated several times by biographers and others who take it at face value, but appears to have been made up, distorted, or otherwise exaggerated. For one thing, although tampering with a mailbox is, as Thompson claimed, a federal offense, it is investigated by the US Postal Inspection Service rather than the FBI. At the time of his alleged questioning, the postal inspectors were commonly known as "special agents" and the Service as "the Bureau" so it is possible that he genuinely misremembered rather than simply fabricated this part of his past. Through various exaggerated tales, he presents a picture of his own childhood with him an almost Byronic hero. Some of the stories from his teenage years contradict versions he had given elsewhere or things that

468

eyewitnesses and evidence had proven. This "memoir," then, appears to be another example of fact and fiction coming together, the truth brushed aside in favor of a good story.

If these exaggerations and fabrications were deliberate, then at least it is a valid literary technique. He had made his living from distorted versions of reality and, in most cases, he assumed that the reader knew what he was doing. It is quite possible that he assumed the reader interpreted his life story as perhaps allegorical rather than literal truth. However, there are countless mistakes and problems throughout the book that frustrate anyone unlucky enough to have purchased it. He begins stories but does not finish them, moving on to other sections in the book, leaving the reader wondering what happened. In one instance, Hunter and Anita drive up a hill but before they reach the top, a new section of the book begins. We are never taken back; it is utterly pointless.

Memoirs are mixed with present day musings and pieces of writing from different periods in a patchwork of unfinished, unpolished, and disconnected stories. Some of the worst sections drag on the longest, such as the parts about his 1990 "lifestyle bust." As with most of his bad writing, there are moments of true wisdom and some good lines, but the jumps between his old writing and the new are jarring and highlight his deterioration as a writer.

The best writing in the book is from the seventies, with an hilarious account of George McGovern shooting sharks from his hotel balcony. There is also some of his work from Saigon and Grenada, as well as "Song of the Sausage Creature." For Thompson scholars, there is a lot of material that had not appeared elsewhere and is valuable for research purposes, but it is badly organized and the casual reader would hardly be aware of why they were being presented with these disjointed fragments of writing. Parts of the book are padded out with letters and excerpts, suggesting that he was too lazy to write new material for those sections.

Just like the *Hey Rube* column and book, *Kingdom of Fear* features irritating and inconsistent quirks of style. In addition to the arbitrary capitalization and overuse of italics, he had grossly stepped up his use of the ampersand.

Throughout the decades, he had sprinkled these into his work, usually between two nouns, such as "Fear & Loathing." However, by 2000 he had begun using them randomly to replace the word "and." Not all *ands* were replaced and there was no consistency to how it was done. He had also begun writing numbers in both numerical and written form, but again this was arbitrarily applied. He simply lacked the mental acuity to track such decisions and thus would write things like, "I almost went crazy—drunk & AWOL for two (2) months…" and then elsewhere write "two months earlier."

The New York Times called Thompson out for being incoherent and for padding the book with old material that served no real function. In a review titled "Bedtime for Gonzo," they offered a brutally accurate critique:

> The silly approach/avoidance game Thompson plays with his life story proves he isn't the fearless exhibitionist he plays on the page. Whenever "Kingdom of Fear" brushes up against the aching interior spaces that feed genuine autobiography – family, lost friends, regrets – he recoils and hides in bad gonzo clichés. You'd think that at this point in his life – Thompson is 65 – he'd be more interested in exorcising his demons than in making cartoons out of them.

But a cartoon was precisely what he had become. Ever since his sudden rush to infamy in the late sixties and early seventies, he had become trapped in this ridiculous Gonzo persona. Douglas Brinkley called "the Hunter Figure" (referring to his various literary personae) "one of the great artistic creations of the 20th century," but there can be little doubt that Thompson soon became trapped and stifled by it. In his writing as in his life, he was limited by these creations and the associated literary devices and vocabulary that he had invented. Even when he had the chance to redeem himself, he descended into the clownish. It was almost as though he had forgotten how to do serious writing.

Final Words

***

Hunter S. Thompson's last major publication came in June, 2004. "Prisoner of Denver," printed in *Vanity Fair*, looks at the case of Lisl Auman, a twenty-two-year-old woman found guilty of the murder of a police officer despite the fact that she was in police custody at another location when the murder took place. Thompson had been horrified by the injustice in her prison sentence and attempted to rally public support in various ways.

"Prisoner of Denver" is a good article but alas it was mostly written by another journalist, Mark Seal. Only the beginning and end of it are by Thompson and these are predictably repetitive and unfocused. He leans too heavily on old tropes, even repeating this joke for what feels like the millionth time: "Ho ho ho. Richard Nixon was so crooked that he needed servants to screw his pants on every morning." He also ventures into a story about his own childhood and touches upon his most common theme—the loss of the innocence of the past: "But that was a long time ago in a very different country. Now I know different."

Thompson's contribution to "Prisoner of Denver" is extremely thin but it is interesting just how easy it is to distinguish between the parts of the article written by Thompson and the parts written by Seal. Without any names assigned to their respective sections, one can still look and see the common words and even the cadence of the language used and know, "This is Hunter S. Thompson":

> I know that police are the Enemy, cruel and stupid and greedy and dishonest in a way that would shame the Hell's Angels. At least the Angels get Respect. [...] Denver has never pretended to be a civilized place. When you think of Denver, you think of cowshit and gunfights, small brains and big guns, dumb brutes and wild whores with hearts of cheap gold. Yes, sir, that is Denver in a nutshell—a cowboy town with cowboy rules and cowboy justice. When

you come to Denver, Bubba, you'd better be ready to fight. Kick ass or die is what the Denver Police Department is all about. It is kill or be killed in this town. The D.P.D. has never been anything but a dangerous gang of vengeful, half-bright cowboys with a vicious reputation for brutality and what the Hell's Angels used to call "massive retaliation."

This passage features many of the trappings of Thompson's writing. There are words capitalized for significance, combinations of adjectives for increased impact, lists of nouns with strong adjectives before them, the word "Bubba," the phrase "hearts of cheap gold," which he had begun using frequently in the last decade of his life, the word "half-bright," which he'd used throughout his whole life, and of course the mention of the Hell's Angels. It is no longer fresh or interesting, but it is his own. He had created his own literary genre and gotten trapped within its rigid confines, but at least he had marked out his territory and had sole ownership over it.

Kingdom of Fear was published in 2003 and *Hey Rube* came out the following year. One of his old short stories was published as *Fire in the Nuts* in 2004—another limited edition, small press publication featuring artwork by Ralph Steadman.[6] Though more substantial than *Mistah Leary, He Dead*, it was another book that bypassed most regular fans and went directly into collectors' vaults.

In November 2004, Thompson wrote his final article for *Rolling Stone*. "The Fun-Hogs in the Passing Lane" was the first article he had written for the magazine in five years and it was about the 2004 presidential election. Thompson's friend, John Kerry, was running against George W. Bush, a man that Thompson loathed; however, he was not able to deal with Bush the way that he had dealt with Nixon. He even relies on his old nemesis to explain the malignant evil that is Republicanism in the twenty-first century:

---

6   The title was reused from his 1983 *Rolling Stone* article, "A Dog Took My Place." "Fire in the Nuts" was the heading of one section.

> Richard Nixon looks like a flaming liberal today compared to a golem like George Bush. Indeed. Where is Richard Nixon now that we finally need him?
>
> If Nixon were running for president today, he would be seen as a "liberal" candidate, and he would probably win. He was a crook and a bungler, but what the hell? Nixon was a barrel of laughs compared to this gang of thugs from the Halliburton petroleum organization who are running the White House today [...] I despised everything he stood for—but if he were running for president this year against the evil Bush-Cheney gang, I would happily vote for him.

Thompson continues to take shots at Nixon and his criticisms are funnier, fairer, and more insightful than anything he ever said about Bush or Karl Rove. Could it be that he needed his old nemesis in order to write the sort of searing, hysterical tracts that he had once churned out so easily? In this book, I have looked at cocaine and fame as the main culprits in Hunter S. Thompson's agonizing downfall as a writer, but it is worth noting that his decline began around the end of Nixon's presidency and that often the best lines in his work were knives in Nixon's back. In his obituary, he provided a fantastic assault on Nixon's legacy, but even though he claimed Bush Sr. and Bush Jr. were far worse, he could never convincingly take them apart like he could with Nixon. It just didn't work. Maybe it was because, by 2004, people were not afraid to insult their president. Thompson was proud to have savaged Nixon in an era when such things were uncommon, and he had publicly made statements that would have been viewed as treasonous in an earlier era or other countries. By the time Nixon was gone, though, the world was changing and insulting a president was perfectly normal. When Thompson wrote, "Bush is a natural-born loser with a filthy rich daddy who pimped his son out to rich oilmongers," he was just saying the same thing as millions of others. It was not bad writing by any means, but it was hardly an original thought.

At the end of the article, Thompson appears in high spirits. Despite having previously claimed that a reporter should never endorse a candidate, he endorses John Kerry and reflects on their shared battle to end the war in 1972. He then ties it to the effort to unseat George W. Bush and put America back on track. He writes:

> We were angry and righteous in those days, and there were millions of us. We kicked two chief executives out of the White House because they were stupid warmongers. We conquered Lyndon Johnson and we stomped on Richard Nixon—which wise people said was impossible, but so what? It was fun. We were warriors then, and our tribe was strong like a river.
>
> That river is still running. All we have to do is get out and vote, while it's still legal, and we will wash those crooked warmongers out of the White House.

A few days after the article was published, Bush was re-elected. Thompson became increasingly depressed and four months later, on February 20, 2005, he put a gun in his mouth and ended his own life.

There is seldom one single reason why a person chooses this drastic course of action and in the case of Hunter S. Thompson, there were various contributing factors. Few of his family and friends were surprised when he killed himself because he had spoken often of it during his lifetime. In the end, a strong, active, and energetic man was no longer able to look after himself or live the life he wanted. A brilliant mind had been reduced to near-permanent confusion; a great writer had lost the ability to put words together in any meaningful sense. It had been a long, slow decline but, by 2005, there was simply no way he was going to become fit and healthy, suddenly learn to write again, and then put his country back on track.

As a young man, he had asked himself whether he was a writer of action or of thought. He came to the rather obvious conclusion—he was more Hemingway than

Faulkner. He was a physical presence in his books, looming over his subjects. Gonzo was about participation—getting into the story and giving it a shove to see what happens, then following it until its conclusion. But those days were not just past, they were ancient history. There could not have been another *Hell's Angels*, another *Fear and Loathing in Las Vegas*, or another *Fear and Loathing on the Campaign Trail '72*. He was about as likely to write another great book as he was to become a professional athlete.

When Thompson ended his life in his kitchen at Owl Farm, he left behind an extraordinary legacy, having changed literature, journalism, and politics with his larger-than-life personality and his manic writing. He will be best remembered for offering the definitive epitaph for the sixties, a decade for which he was ideally suited. Perhaps his greatest achievement was successfully fusing the high-brow and low-brow, the disparate experiments and philosophies of that turbulent era, presenting serious social commentary through his hilarious stories. It was an updating of Burroughs' achievement in *Naked Lunch*, except far more accessible. He thrived amidst chaos and needed something to fight for, preferably among other energetic, passionate activists and artists, but the reality of life in subsequent decades gave him little hope. "In the '60s, we may have been foolish," he once said, "but we thought we could change the world." By 2005, there was little left that inspired optimism.

Never mind the publication of books like *Better Than Sex*, *Kingdom of Fear*, and *Hey Rube*; Thompson had secured his place in the annals of history with his brilliant tale of two men's drug-fueled exploits in Las Vegas, his own creative interpretation of a charged presidential campaign, and his ballsy reporting on a vicious motorcycle gang. All of those books were published in a six-year period some three decades before his death, but they are all classics now and mark an important and confusing time when journalism and fiction were brought together as a new form of art. Of the countercultural movements of the twentieth century, we recall the Beat Generation, the hippies, the punks, but also Gonzo—a term used to describe the work of just one man. It was work so brilliant that after fifty years of shameless attempts, no one has been able to copy it successfully—not even its own creator.

Regardless of the terminal decline into which his literary skills entered after the campaign book, Thompson's contributions to literature remain of tremendous importance. The litany of failures that followed will not erase the elegance and importance of his three best books and the articles that marked the high white notes of an exhilarating career.

Thompson talked often of his desire to compete with F. Scott Fitzgerald and in particular he yearned for his own interpretation of that mysterious phrase. If he could just have a few good lines or paragraphs in an article, that was enough, he felt, to hold the whole thing together. When those singular moments were of pure enough quality, they could overcome any number of dull sentences and result in a truly great story. Hunter managed to produce three books that were not just brilliantly written, but wholly original. Then there were his collections of letters, which are as fine as any in the English language. He had hit those high white notes not just in a few *bon mots*, but in whole books and articles that have changed lives and permanently altered our world. For this, he should be considered one of the finest writers of the twentieth century… a man whose work was so fiercely original that it required the creation of its own literary genre.

Notes

The following books were cited in *High White Notes*:

Anson, Robert Sam, Gone Crazy and Back Again: The Rise and Fall
    of the Rolling Stone Generation (Doubleday: New York, 1981)
Barger, Sonny, Hell's Angel: The Life and Times of Sonny Barger and
    the Hell's Angels Motorcycle Club (Perennial: New York, 2001)
Baughman, Judith (ed.), F. Scott Fitzgerald on Authorship (University
    of South Carolina Press: 1996)
Bloom, Harold (ed.), Ernest Hemingway's A Farewell to Arms
    (Bloom's Literary Criticism: New York, 2009)
-    Ernest Hemingway (Chelsea House Publishers: Philadelphia,
    2005)
Bone, Robert W., Fire Bone! A Maverick Guide to a Life in
    Journalism (Peripety Press: Walnut Creek, 2017)
Conrad, Joseph, The Nigger of The Narcissus: A Tale of the
    Forecastle (Pinnacle Press, 2017)
Cowan, Jay, Hunter S. Thompson: An Insider's View of Deranged,
    Depraved, Drugged Out Brilliance (The Lyons Press: Guilford,
    2009)
Denevi, Timothy, Freak Kingdom: Hunter S. Thompson's Manic,
    Ten-Year Crusade Against American Fascism (PublicAffairs:
    New York, 2018)
Feehan, Rory Patrick, The Genesis of the Hunter Figure: A study of
    the Dialectic between the Biographical and the Aesthetic in the
    Early Writings of Hunter S. Thompson (PhD thesis)
Fitzgerald, F. Scott, The Basil and Josephine Stories (Scribner: New
    York, 2003)
-    Tender is the Night (Penguin: London, 1970
-    The Beautiful and Damned (Warbler Classics Edition: 2019)
-    The Great Gatsby (Scribner: New York, 2018)
Hagan, Joe, Sticky Fingers: The Life and Times of Jann Wenner and
    Rolling Stone Magazine (Canongate Books: Edinburgh, 2017)
Harrell, Margaret A., The Hell's Angels Letters (Norfolk Press: San
    Francisco, 2020)
-    Keep this Quiet (Saeculum University Press: Raleigh, 2011)
Hellman, John. Fables of Fact: The New Journalism's New Fiction
    (University of Illinois Press, 1981)

Hemingway, Ernest, Death in the Afternoon (Scribner's: New York, 1932)
- Men at War (Bramhall House: New York, 1955)
Kerrane, Kevin, and Yagoda, Ben (eds), The Art of Fact: A Historical Anthology of Literary Journalism (Touchstone: New York, 1998)
Kesey, Ken, Sometimes a Great Notion (Bantam Books: New York, 1965)
López, Ian F. Haney, Racism on Trial: The Chicano Fight for Justice (Harvard University Press, 2004)
McEneaney, Kevin T., Fear, Loathing, and the Birth of Gonzo (Rowman & Littlefield: London, 2016)
McKeen, William, Outlaw Journalist (W.W. Norton: New York, 2008)
- Mile Marker Zero (University Press of Florida: Gainesville, 2016)
Meyers, Jeffrey, Hemingway: A Biography (Da Capo: New York, 1999)
- Orwell: Life and Art (University of Illinois: Chicago, 2010)
Miller, Henry, Big Sur and the Oranges of Hieronymus Bosch (New Directions: New York, 1957)
Perry, Paul, Fear and Loathing (Plexus: London, 2009)
Poe, Edgar Allan, The Tell-Tale Heart and Other Stories (Dover: Mineola, 2020)
Rodgers, Marion Elizabeth, Mencken: The American Iconoclast (Oxford University Press: New York, 2005)
Stavans, Ilans, Oscar "Zeta" Acosta: The Uncollected Works (Arte Público Press: Houston, 1996)
Stephenson, William, Gonzo Republic: Hunter S. Thompson's America (Continuum: London, 2012)
Streitfeld, David, The Last Interview (Melville House Publishing: New York, 2018)
Thompson, Anita, Ancient Gonzo Wisdom: Interviews with Hunter S. Thompson (Da Capo: Cambridge, 2009)
- The Gonzo Way: A Celebration of Dr. Hunter S. Thompson (Fulcrum: Golden, 2007)
Thompson, Juan F., Stories I Tell Myself: Growing up with Hunter S. Thompson (Alfred A. Knopf: New York, 2016)
Thompson, Hunter S., Fear and Loathing in America: The Brutal Odyssey of an Outlaw Journalist 1968–1976 (Simon & Schuster: New York, 2006)
- Fear and Loathing in Las Vegas: A Savage Journey to the Heart of the American Dream (Vintage: New York, 1998)
- Fear and Loathing on the Campaign Trail '72 (Harper Perennial: London, 2005)
- Generation of Swine (Vintage: New York, 1989)
- Great Shark Hunt: Strange Tales from a Strange Time (Simon

& Schuster: New York, 2003)
- Hell's Angels: A Strange and Terrible Saga (Ballantine: New York, 1995)
- Hey Rube: Blood Sport, the Bush Doctrine, and the Downward Spiral of Dumbness (Simon & Schuster: New York, 2004)
- Kingdom of Fear: Loathsome Secrets of a Star-Crossed Child In the Final Days of the American Century (Simon & Schuster: New York, 2003)
- Proud Highway: Saga of a Desperate Southern Gentleman 1955–1967 (Ballantine: New York, 1998)
- Screwjack: Kindle Edition (Simon & Schuster: New York, 2004)
- Songs of the Doomed: More Notes on the Death of the American Dream (Simon & Schuster: New York, 1990)
- The Curse of Lono (Taschen: Cologne, 2005)
- The Rum Diary (Bloomsbury: London, 2004)
Watkins, Daniel, J., Freak Power: Hunter S. Thompson's Campaign for Sheriff (Meat Possum Press: Aspen, 2015)
Wagner-Martin, Linda (ed.), New Essays on The Sun Also Rises (Cambridge University Press: New York, 1987)
Wenner, Jann, Gonzo (Little, Brown, and Company: New York, 2007)
White, William (ed.), By-Line: Ernest Hemingway: Selected Articles and Dispatches of Four Decades (Charles Scribner's Sons: New York, 1967)
Whitmer, Peter O., When the Going Gets Weird (Hyperion: New York, 1993)
Wildfang, Frederic, Gonzo Personas (unpublished manuscript)
Wolfe, Tom, The New Journalism (Harper and Row: New York, 1973)

Other Media

Breakfast with Hunter (2003)
Fear and Loathing in Gonzovision (1978)
Freak Power (2020)
Gonzo Tapes: The Life and Work of Dr. Hunter S. Thompson (2008)
Gonzo: The Life and Work of Dr. Hunter S. Thompson (2008)
TotallyGonzo.org

Part One

The Birth of a Writer

The Great Puerto Rican Novel

75   **"I was beginning to get the fear"** The Rum Diary, p.109
75   **"I'm a journalist myself, you know"** The Rum Diary, p.61
75   **"savage rush"** The Rum Diary, p.86
76   **"A few big freighters stood at anchor"** The Rum Diary, p.95
76   **"but Nelson Otto was a man"** The Rum Diary, p.2
76   **"And he shuffled off down the street"** The Rum Diary, p.95
76-77 **"I was feeling smart, but reading"** The Rum Diary, p.201
77   **"I had just reread Conrad's preface"** F. Scott Fitzgerald on Authorship, 140
77   **"A work that aspires, however humbly"** Nigger of the Narcissus, p.3
77   **"Art is long and life is short"** Nigger of the Narcissus, p.6
77   **"considered it dogma for writers"** The Hell's Angels Letters, p.231
77-78 **"There was a flurry of premature snow"** The Basil and Josephine Stories, p.222
78   **"high white FUSION in [his] brain"** Gonzo Personas, no page number
79   **"Five good pages in a 15-page story"** Proud Highway, p.292
80   **"San Juan is rotten"** Proud Highway, p.215
80   **"a boat called Fat City"** When the Going Gets Weird, p.106
80   **"Sandy's mother's friend owned a motel"** When the Going Gets Weird, p.106
81   **"almost a hundred painters"** Big Sur and the Oranges of Hieronymus Bosch, p.12
81   **"soak up the 'essence'" of a place"** When the Going Gets Weird, p.115
82   **"He leaned on her for criticism of his work"** Fear and Loathing, p.58
83   **"He worked every night and every day"** Outlaw Journalist, p.63
83   **"his income was nine hundred and seventy"** Fear and Loathing, p.63
83   **"personal journalism"** Proud Highway, p.406
83-84 **"He had taken it apart sentence by sentence"** When the Going Gets Weird, p.115
84-85 **"At 11 o'clock on Saturday morning"** Louisville Courier-Journal, 23rd April, 1961, p.10
85   **"A percussion corps of drunkards was"** The Rum Diary, p.153
85   **"We hurried off down a side street"** The Rum Diary, p.154

Literary Journalism

Outsiders and Outlaws

111   "Today, the Indian is as sad and hopeless" National
        Observer, 10th June, 1963
112   "A fine old Indian tradition" National Observer, 10th
        June, 1963
112   "'Ah, senor,' he said, 'this is a wonderful'" National
        Observer, 10th June, 1963
113   "At age 22 I set what I insist is the all-time" The
        Vancouver Sun, 29th July, 1963, p.5
113   "it's hard to argue with the rumor" http://ralphehanson.
        com/west/HST/hstnews.htm
114   "to make journalism the great literature" Proud
        Highway, p.404
115   "about the best magazine in the country" Proud
        Highway, p.414
115   "All this is true" Great Shark Hunt, p.39
116   "Negro executive with adequate funds" Great Shark
        Hunt, p.44
116   "there is no human being within 500 miles" Proud
        Highway, p.420
116-117 "Hunter used to claim that the phrase" Gonzo, p.126
117   "Fiction is dead" Proud Highway, p.421
117   "every man with balls" Proud Highway, p.420
117   "I feel ready for a dirty game" Proud Highway, p.420
117   "He is like a hyena that you shoot" Proud Highway,
        p.424
118   "a sort of Okie shack" Proud Highway, p.439
118   "the Brazil of America" Proud Highway, p.439
118   "named for the president who had been shot" Gonzo,
        p.66
118   "shooting gophers at four" Gonzo, p.70
119   "more out of habit than amusement" Cavalier, August,
        1960, p.80
119   "one can reasonably expect to find" Cavalier, August,
        1960, p.83
119-120 "The next time I want to see" Cavalier, August, 1960, p.81
120   "The 1890s atmosphere is badly addled" Cavalier,
        August, 1960, p.83
121   "The San Francisco Examiner also suggested" San
        Francisco Examiner, 3rd August, 1967, p. 49
121   "I am deep in the grip of a professional" Proud
        Highway, p.449
122   "I have turned into a fuck-off" Proud Highway, p.436
123   "That power of conviction is a hard thing" Great Shark
        Hunt, p.372
123   "The function of art is to bring order" Great Shark
        Hunt, p.372

Hell's Angels

154   **"They rode with a fine, unwashed arrogance"** Hell's Angels, p.5

154   **"tender young blondes with lobotomy eyes"** Hell's Angels, p.5

154   **"the wary expression of half-bright souls"** Hell's Angels, p.9

155   **"I have long admired Ron Whitehead"** The Hell's Angels Letters, p.iix

155   **"loon"** Gonzo Tapes, CD 1, track 15

156   **"In a prosperous democracy"** Hell's Angels, p.80

157   **"flagrant libel"** Hell's Angels, p.25

158   **"For some reason it was impossible"** Hell's Angels, p.222

158   **"The bike was going sideways"** Hell's Angels, p.96

160   **"and then, Sweet Jesus"** Hell's Angels, p.116

160   **"It sounds like the creation of"** Hell's Angels, p.168

160   **"This sparks a long section"** Hell's Angels, p.191

161   **"Together they looked like figures"** Hell's Angels, p.178

161   **"an hysterical woman screaming"** Hell's Angels, p.180

161-162 **"If the News had put two and two"** Hell's Angels, p.216

162   **"an inspired piece of film journalism"** Hell's Angels, p.66

162   **"not in the realm of"** Hell's Angels, p.243

163   **"For nearly a year I had lived"** Hell's Angels, p.254

164   **"psychic masturbation"** Hell's Angels, p.262

164   **"Midnight on the Coast Highway"** Songs of the Doomed, p.116

164   **"You can barely see at a hundred"** Hell's Angels, p.271

165   **"I sat and wrote the whole thing"** Songs of the Doomed, p.115

165   **"until the Angels I had always"** Songs of the Doomed, p.115

165   **"stomped"** Hell's Angels, p.272

166   **"I tried to compose a fitting epitaph"** Hell's Angels, p.273

166   **"a minor disagreement"** Hell's Angels, p.272

166   **"He sometimes said that Thompson"** Hell's Angel, p.127; Gonzo, p.82

166   **"it was his contention that Thompson"** Outlaw Journalist, p.111

166   **"The problem I have is that it just"** Outlaw Journalist, p.111

167   **"egomaniac"** Ancient Gonzo Wisdom, p.138

167   **"In a nation of frightened dullards"** Hell's Angels, p.259

168   **"a grab-bag of word-photos"** Proud Highway, p.547

168   **"unless I get on one wild blasting"** Gonzo Tapes, CD 1, track 20

Origins of Gonzo

496

Gonzo is Born

209   **"I could tell from his notes"** Fear and Loathing, p.127

209   **"innocent abroad"** He has used this line in countless interviews, including this: https://www.sfweekly.com/topstories/splat-the-art-of-ralph-steadman/

209   **"filled countless pages"** Fear and Loathing, p.126

209-210 **"I arrived in NY in a state of"** Fear and Loathing in America, p.296

210   **"According to his wife, Sandy"** Gonzo, p.121

211   **"I got off the plane"** Great Shark Hunt, p.24

211   **"Don't they respect anything?"** Great Shark Hunt, p.26

211   **"get [his] act together"** Great Shark Hunt, p.26

211-212 **"He was back to settle"** Gonzo, p.121

212   **"I think that that was a moment"** Gonzo, p.122

212   **"If a man is making a story"** Ernest Hemingway's A Farewell to Arms, p.75

212   **"If I'm going to go"** Ancient Gonzo Wisdom, p.153

213   **"He had done a few good sketches"** Great Shark Hunt, p.31

213   **"Fuck England"** Great Shark Hunt, p.32

213   **"Creeping Jesus"** Great Shark Hunt, p.29

213-214 **"Thousands of raving, stumbling drunks"** Great Shark Hunt, p.31

214-215 **"But now, looking at the big red"** Great Shark Hunt, p.33

215   **"Rain all nite until dawn"** Great Shark Hunt, p.33

215   **"After you learn to write"** By-Line, p.216

215   **"pink faces with a stylish"** Great Shark Hunt, p.34

216   **"banshees on the lawn"** Great Shark Hunt, p.34

216   **"The rest of that day"** Great Shark Hunt, p.36

216   **"I think the instant/verbal"** Fear and Loathing in America, p.143

216   **"the writer's eye as"** Fear and Loathing in America, p.178

216   **"Total chaos, no way"** Great Shark Hunt, p.35

217   **"There he was, by God"** Great Shark Hunt, p.37

217   **"Inside, people hugged"** Great Shark Hunt, p.24

218   **"Goddam, did you hear"** Great Shark Hunt, p.31

218   **"The journalist rams the big car"** Great Shark Hunt, p.38

220   **"It's a shitty article"** Fear and Loathing in America, p.295

220   **"I wish there'd been time"** Fear and Loathing in America, p.296

220   **"Editing Hunter was like"** https://grantland.com/features/looking-back-hunter-s-thompson-classic-story-kentucky-derby/

220-221 **"When he wrote the Kentucky Derby"** Gonzo, p.121

221   **"The legendary New Orleans"** Gonzo, p.124

222   **"the writing is lame bullshit"** Fear and Loathing in America, p.304

Freak Power and Brown Power

Fact and Fiction in Las Vegas

504

288   "Let's keep in mind" Fear and Loathing at Rolling Stone, p.78-79
289   "only seven sentences" Gonzo Way, p.17
289   "Hunter has stolen my soul" When the Going Gets Weird, p.183
290   "some fucking native" Fear and Loathing in America, p.447
290   "useless" Gonzo Tapes, CD 3, track 6
290   "became the kind of monster" Gonzo Tapes, CD 3, track 10
290   "I can sink the whole publishing house" Fear and Loathing at Rolling Stone, p.398
291   "Hunter, you are writing fiction" Gonzo, p.69
291   "Fiction is a bridge to the truth" Proud Highway, p.529
291-292 "it should never be necessary" Fear and Loathing in America, p.420
292   "I would classify it" Ancient Gonzo Wisdom, p.176
292   "about 90 percent" Ancient Gonzo Wisdom, p.151
292   "the same kind of bemused" Fear and Loathing in America, p.405
292   "didn't really make up anything" Fear and Loathing in America, p.406
292   "I spent my expense money on drugs" Fear and Loathing in America, p.406
293   "just bourbon and Dexedrine" Hunter, p.143
293   "Don't worry about that" Gonzo, p.128
293   "This is a tale of excess" Fear and Loathing in America, p.383
294   "Journalistic Science" Fear and Loathing in America, p.383
294   "there is absolutely no mention" Gonzo Tapes, CD 2, track 3
294   "I advise you to" Gonzo Tapes, CD 2, track 15
294   "Even Acosta's son" When the Going Gets Weird, p.184
295   "essentially the 'art' (or compulsion) of" Fear and Loathing in America, p.722
295   "he claimed it was all true" Gonzo, p.139
295   "I can't see coming off" Fear and Loathing in America, p.406
296   "political monster" Fear and Loathing in America, p.430
296   "the style & tone of Vegas" Fear and Loathing in America, p.428
296   "neither novel nor nonfiction" https://www.nytimes.com/2005/02/21/books/hunter-s-thompson.html
296   "Don't paint yourself into a corner" Fear and Loathing, p.170

Part Two
On the Campaign Trail

310   **"When it came to important stories"** Hunter S.
       Thompson, p.48
310   **"Now that's good journalism"** Campaign Trail '72, p.87
310   **"with the possible exception of"** Campaign Trail '72,
       p.195
310   **"wiggy bastard"** Campaign Trail '72, p.128
310   **"like a beast in heat"** Campaign Trail '72, p.359
311   **"hard, almost masochistic"** Campaign Trail '72, p.79
311   **"the only way a reporter"** Campaign Trail '72, p.94
311   **"This is about the thirteenth lead"** Campaign Trail '72,
       p.175
312   **"Jesus! Another tangent"** Campaign Trail '72, p.210
312   **"My brain has slowed down"** Campaign Trail '72, p.235
312-313 **"One of Hunter's methods"** Gonzo, p.156
313   **"To edit Hunter Thompson"** When the Going Gets
       Weird, p.200
313   **"sudden jolts of energy"** Gonzo, p.156
313   **"In those days, he was very"** When the Going Gets
       Weird, p.200
313   **"By that time, I'm pretty spaced"** When the Going Gets
       Weird, p.203
314   **"He wanted to be read"** Gonzo, p.172
314   **"Thompson typically submitted his work"** Gonzo, p.164
314   **"I still insist 'objective journalism'"** Fear and Loathing at
       Rolling Stone, p.107
314   **"No doubt I would look around"** Fear and Loathing at
       Rolling Stone, p.107
315   **"I think it's a good example"** Gonzo, p.169
315   **"It's the most accurate"** Gonzo, p.171
315   **"I did all that craziness because"** Bob Greene, "Hunter
       Thompson Glad to be Free of Rolling Stone," in The
       Miami News, 4 June 1975, p.6B
316   **"the counter-culture's most-listened-to voice"**
       Newsweek article reprinted here: http://www.gonzo.org/
       books/ct/ct162f.html
316   **"notorious [...] scourge of politicians"** Curtis Wilkie
       "Counter-culture Dissects Politics," in The Morning News,
       15 May, 1972
316   **"descends into a sick fantasy"** Campaign Trail '72, p.248-
       250
316   **"he imagines Frank Mankiewicz"** Campaign Trail '72,
       p.210
316   **"envisages Nixon as a werewolf"** Campaign Trail '72,
       p.391
317   **"98 percent verbatim"** Campaign Trail '72, p.271
317   **"it gets harder to convince"** Campaign Trail '72, p.48

Gonzo Grows Stale

327   "Nobody knows who's crazy" Gonzo Tapes, CD 4, track
         4
327   "the characters are still 2-dimensional" Fear and
         Loathing in America, p.512
327-328 "I sold a novel called 'Guts-balls'" Ancient Gonzo
         Wisdom, p.111
328   "I think it's about time" Fear and Loathing in America,
         p.514
328   "One of the central tenets" Fear and Loathing in
         America, p.514
328   "a thousand dollars a month" Fear and Loathing in
         America, p.513
328   "only five hundred copies" Fear and Loathing in America,
         p.515
329   "This one had all the signs" Great Shark Hunt, p.423
330   "insanely fucking dull" Great Shark Hunt, p.433
331   "'Well. . .' he said finally" Great Shark Hunt, p.440
331   "Let's not compare this" Ancient Gonzo Wisdom, p.141
332   "You read Hunter and you think" Gonzo, p.380
332   "submit it to Wenner by May 1" Fear and Loathing in
         America, p.513
332   "I got a couple of broads" Gonzo Tapes, CD 4, track 8
332   "vicious subheads" Gonzo Tapes, CD 4, track 6
333   "loosely-constructed notes" Fear and Loathing in
         America, p.527
334   "Watergate is about the only thing" Fear and Loathing in
         America, p.520
334   "couldn't live with the horror" Fear and Loathing in
         America, p.524
334   "perverse refusal to cover Watergate" Fear and Loathing
         in America, p.525
334-335 "mere treading water" Outlaw Journalist, p.207
335   "he met with Ralph Steadman" Outlaw Journalist, p.208
336   "In any case, the bulk of" Great Shark Hunt, p.261
336   "strange and violent reference" Great Shark Hunt, p.254
336   "charming, discontented face" The Great Gatbsy, p.xxxi
336   "Cazart!" Great Shark Hunt, p.266
336   "He had heard this word in Brazil" Fear and Loathing in
         America, p.523
336   "mere shock & surprise" Fear and Loathing in America,
         p.523
336-337 "Hunter always threw everything" Fear and Loathing,
         p.172
337   "screed without substance" Fear and Loathing, p.172
337   "I used to be a lot more coherent" Fear and Loathing in
         America, p.526
510

337 **"a drug for fruits"** Fear and Loathing, p.175
337 **"test [his] reactions against"** Gonzo Tapes, CD 4, track 12
337 **"My name is Yail Bloor"** Gonzo Tapes, CD 4, track 17
337 **"no desire to read further"** Gonzo Tapes, CD 4, track 14
337 **"bottom of [his] list"** Gonzo Tapes, CD 4, track 17
338 **"He is quoted in McKeen's biography"** Outlaw Journalist, p.211
338 **"never again find the dedication"** Freak Kingdom, p.262
338 **"almost certainly because of"** Stories I Tell Myself, p. 237
338-339 **"The problem was, when he was"** Gonzo, p.208-209
340 **"There is some kind of heavy"** Great Shark Hunt, p.19
341 **"He had to describe what the town"** Gonzo, p.173
341 **"It was just before dawn"** Great Shark Hunt, p.46
342 **"Mother of Sweating Jesus!"** Great Shark Hunt, p.48
343 **"I filled the bathtub"** Great Shark Hunt, p.52
343 **"Good god! I thought."** Great Shark Hunt, p.57
343 **"Yes, I am a white person"** Great Shark Hunt, p.61
343 **"Absolute truth is a very rare"** Great Shark Hunt, p.71
343-344 **"If I'd written all the truth"** Great Shark Hunt, p.71
344 **"genuinely ominous power-vacuum"** Fear and Loathing in America, p.586
345 **"Walsh thought it would be"** Fear and Loathing, p.172
345 **"the title had been Wenner's"** Fear and Loathing, p.173
345 **"I can't find the drugs"** Gonzo, p.183
346 **"Mother of babbling god!"** Great Shark Hunt, p.301
347 **"concocted"** Freak Kingdom, p.370
347 **"if it can be said that he resembled"** Great Shark Hunt, p.318
347 **"Ah ... mother of jabbering god"** Great Shark Hunt, p.327
347 **"Right ... and now we have gone"** Great Shark Hunt, p.327

Failed Assignments

349 **"He didn't write anything after"** Hunter, p.174
350 **"reserved, intellectual, and witty"** Freak Power, p.124
350 **"a prisoner of his own cult"** Outlaw Journalist, p.232
350 **"he stepped into character"** Outlaw Journalist, p.225
350 **"I've lost my perspective"** Bob Greene, "Hunter Thompson Glad to be Free of Rolling Stone," in The Miami News, 4 June 1975, p.6B
352 **"He didn't want to become"** Joe Klein, "Forever Weird," https://www.nytimes.com/2007/11/18/books/review/Klein-t.html

353   "convinced Thompson to fly" Fear and Loathing, p.178
353   "Gonzo, Gonzo, Gonzo" Fear and Loathing, p.178
353   "a sack of marijuana" Fear and Loathing, p.180
353   "medicine man" Fear and Loathing, p.180
353-354 "I didn't come all this way" Fear and Loathing, p.182
354   "obsessed with Martin Bormann" Fear and Loathing, p.181
354   "just sit there" Gonzo Tapes, CD 4, track 21
354   "just sit there" Gonzo Tapes, CD 4, track 23
354   "dumped his huge bag of marijuana" The Joke's Over, p.129
355   "The newness had gone out of Gonzo" Fear and Loathing, p.182
355   "explosively violent" Gonzo Tapes, CD 4, track 20
355   "Sometimes he simply screams" Gonzo Tapes, CD 4, track 20
355   "you got nothing" Gonzo Tapes, CD 4, track 27
355   "it's your article" Gonzo Tapes, CD 4, track 27
356   "He said that Thompson" Gonzo, p.189
356   "Hunter was always finding" Hunter, p.174
356   "the Customs agents wanted" Fear and Loathing, p.184
356   "too dark to print" Fear and Loathing, p.184
356   "One of the troubles with Hunter" Hunter, p.174
357   "I managed—by using almost" Fear and Loathing in America, p.720
357   "all I'm really sure of is" Fear and Loathing in America, p.640
357   "I don't think I have anything" Fear and Loathing, p.192
357   "After Africa he just couldn't write" Gonzo movie
358   "a treacherous swine" Bob Greene, "Hunter Thompson Glad to be Free of Rolling Stone," in The Miami News, 4 June 1975, p.6B
358   "Wenner put him in touch" Gonzo Tapes, CD 5, track 3
358   "I'm not sure I want to" Gonzo Tapes, CD 5, track 3
358   "can write the piece" Gonzo Tapes, CD 5, track 3
358   "She even gives him the story" Gonzo Tapes, CD 5, track 5
358   "revolting" Gonzo Tapes, CD 5, track 5
359   "the definitive slam of our friend" Gonzo Personas, no page number
359   "did more to put Rolling Stone" Gonzo Personas, no page number
360   "falling through a bamboo wall" Kitchen Readings, p.46
360   "an intruder" Gonzo Tapes, CD 5, track 14
360   "at least sixty journalists died" https://www.britannica.com/topic/The-Vietnam-War-and-the-media-2051426

Attempts to Quit Gonzo

p.437
385   **"Shit, I did it for the money"** Fear and Loathing, p.189
386   **"piece of shit"** Fear and Loathing, p.190
386   **"embarrassing piece of hogwash"** Fear and Loathing, p.191
386   **"will baffle those who"** https://en.wikipedia.org/wiki/Where_the_Buffalo_Roam
386   **"twenty-five thousand dollars"** When the Going Gets Weird, p.252
387   **"We finally found a way"** When the Going Gets Weird, p.252
387   **"I'm coming out to see it"** https://www.prospectmagazine.co.uk/arts-and-books/my-time-with-hunter-s-thompson-fear-and-loathing-in-las-vegas
387   **"largely inaudible"** https://www.prospectmagazine.co.uk/arts-and-books/my-time-with-hunter-s-thompson-fear-and-loathing-in-las-vegas
388   **"reluctant to undertake"** When the Going Gets Weird, p.256
388   **"I don't like to write"** Ancient Gonzo Wisdom, p.142
389   **"His friend, Jimmy Buffett"** Gonzo, p.223
389   **"a man with a serious Hemingway"** Mile Marker Zero, p.75
389   **"Thompson was eager to learn"** Hunter S. Thompson, p.177
390   **"cannibalizing"** Hunter S. Thompson, p.178
390   **"he wasn't sure how well"** Hunter S. Thompson, p.178
390   **"His research for the novel"** Outlaw Journalist, p.268
390   **"When we started writing the script"** Outlaw Journalist p.269
390   **"lots of drugs and madness"** Hunter S. Thompson, p.178
390   **"a story called The Mole"** Outlaw Journalist p.270
391   **"It struck Corcoran as"** Outlaw Journalist p.271
391   **"there was not enough room"** Songs of the Doomed, p.242
391   **"the freak for the 80s"** When the Going Gets Weird, p.270
391   **"anti-humanist"** Outlaw Journalist, p.275
391-392 **"I've given up Duke"** When the Going Gets Weird, p.266
392   **"A fast, strange & occasionally"** From Gonzo, Ammo Books, p.187
392   **"Is Skinner a good guy"** From Gonzo, Ammo Books, p.187
392   **"Skinner should fit the 80's"** From Gonzo, Ammo Books, p.187
392   **"The raw elements of"** Songs of the Doomed, p.242
393   **"When Thompson was offered"** Fear and Loathing, p.199

515

Brief Returns to Form

439   "Nixon had the unique ability" Fear and Loathing at
        Rolling Stone, p.506-507
439-440 "If the right people had been" Fear and Loathing at
        Rolling Stone, p.508
440   "self-stigmatized patriot" Fear and Loathing at Rolling
        Stone, p.508
441   "Some people will say that" Fear and Loathing at Rolling
        Stone, p.510
441   "Thus he fought his last fight" https://history.msu.edu/
        hst203/files/2011/02/Mencken-In-Memoriam-WJB.pdf
441   "Better Than Sex was Hunter's" Outlaw Journalist, p.321
442   "I didn't want to do the book" The Last Interview, p.109
443   "You don't understand" https://charlierose.com/
        videos/7995
443   "it was never finished" Gonzo, p.273
443   "a forty-thousand-dollar" Fear and Loathing at Rolling
        Stone, p.513
444   "Only animals, filthy" Fear and Loathing at Rolling Stone,
        p.519
444   "dangerously stupid beasts" Fear and Loathing at Rolling
        Stone, p.517
444   "an all-knowing, dissolute slut" Fear and Loathing at
        Rolling Stone, p.521
444   "the legacy of Genghis Khan" Fear and Loathing at
        Rolling Stone, p.521
444   "natural sport for the '90s" Fear and Loathing at Rolling
        Stone, p.521-522
445   "He had been writing me" Gonzo, p.324
445   "if Daisy had been a carrier" Generation of Swine, p.259
445   "It was Fitzgerald's valley" Fear and Loathing at Rolling
        Stone, p.534
446   "I am a polo person now" Fear and Loathing at Rolling
        Stone, p.544
446   "his last great piece of lyrical" Fear and Loathing at
        Rolling Stone, p.8
446   "It's too mushy" https://www.ewingfilms.com/2-17/
447   "It's what's called a sex book" http://www.
        fargonebooks.com/hunter.html
447   "Kevin T. McEneaney speculates" McEneaney, p.230
447   "McEneaney argues" McEneaney, p.230-231
448   "angry disagreements with his agent" Gonzo Personas,
        no page number
448   "biggest frustration was not" E-mail to author
449   "I have been a connoisseur" Kingdom of Fear, p.173
449   "To be continued" http://content.time.com/time/
        magazine/article/0,9171,136844,00.html

Final Words

461   "his writing consisted of disjointed" Gonzo, p.384
462   "We have seen weird Times" Hey Rube, p.3
463   "loyal lifetime rabid fans" Hey Rube, p.8
463   "Swine of the Week" Hey Rube, p.10
463   "We can Relax and get back" Hey Rube, p.18
464   "It is not that Hunter made" E-mail to author
464   "You don't have to be a sports fan" The Last Interview,
        p,160
464   "Should we keep paying Hunter" Gonzo, p.383
464   "You know, Hunter" Gonzo, p.383
465   "I made several serious attempts" Gonzo, p.382
466   "he preternaturally arrogant" Hey Rube, p.80
466   "We have a lot of New Laws" Hey Rube, p.119
466   "You fool!" Hey Rube, p.114
466   "Don't touch me" Hey Rube, p.115
467   "That is a poem I wrote" Hey Rube, p.214
467   "Hey Rube would often lurch" Hunter S. Thompson, p.69
467   "claimed to have the definition" Ancient Gonzo Wisdom,
        p.311
467-468 "It started off—it's supposed" Ancient Gonzo Wisdom,
        p.298
468   "totally new" Ancient Gonzo Wisdom, p.311
468   "sat and wrote nine pages" https://www.ewingfilms.
        com/2-11/
468   "edited and massaged" https://www.ewingfilms.com/2-
        11/
469   "lifestyle bust" Songs of the Doomed, jacket copy
470   "I almost went crazy" Kingdom of Fear, p.44
470   "two months earlier" Kingdom of Fear, p.83
470   "The silly approach/avoidance" https://www.nytimes.
        com/2003/02/23/books/bedtime-for-gonzo.html
470   "one of the great artistic" The Genesis of the Hunter
        Figure, p.71
471   "Ho ho ho" https://www.vanityfair.com/news/2004/06/
        innocent-murderer-200406
471   "But that was a long time ago" https://www.vanityfair.
        com/news/2004/06/innocent-murderer-200406
471-472 "I know that police" https://www.vanityfair.com/
        news/2004/06/innocent-murderer-200406
472-473 "Richard Nixon looks like" Fear and Loathing at Rolling
        Stone, p.567
473   "Bush is a natural-born loser" Fear and Loathing at Rolling
        Stone, p.568
474   "We were angry and righteous" Fear and Loathing at
        Rolling Stone, p.570
475   "In the '60s, we may" When the Going Gets Weird, p.12

Hunter S. Thompson Bibliography

Year	Date	Publication	Title
1947-49		Southern Star	Various articles
1954		The Spectator	Open Letter to the Youth of Our Nation
1995		The Spectator	Security
1956-57		Command Courier	Several articles and one column per issue from 6th Sept '56-15th Aug '57
1957		Playground News	Sports articles and column
1960	29-May	Louisville Courier-Journal	Munoz Skilfully Keeps Foes Off-Balance
	26-Jun	Louisville Courier-Journal	A Louisvillian in Voodoo Country
	10-Jul	The Royal Gazette Weekly	They Hoped to Reach Spain but are Stranded in Bermuda
1961	26-Mar	Chicago Tribune	California's Big Sur Lures Tourists with its Solitude
	23-Apr	Louisville Courier-Journal	Carnival Time in St. Thomas
	08-Oct	Chicago Tribune	Baja California Has Honky-Tonks, Solitude
	October	Rogue	Big Sur, The Tropic of Henry Miller
	Dec	Rogue	Burial at Sea
1962	18-Feb	Chicago Tribune	Renfro Valley
	24-Jun	National Observer	'Leery Optimism' at Home for Kennedy Visitor
	16-Jul	National Observer	Nobody Is Neutral Under Aruba's Hot Sun
	06-Aug	National Observer	A Footloose American in a Smugglers' Den
	27-Aug	National Observer	Democracy Dies in Peru, But Few Seem to Mourn Its Passing
	17-Sep	National Observer	How Democracy is Nudged Ahead in Ecuador

523

| | 01-Oct | National Observer | Ballots in Brazil Will Measure the Allure of Leftist Nationalism |

01-Oct   National Observer   Ballots in Brazil Will
                                     Measure the Allure of Leftist
                                     Nationalism
15-Oct   National Observer   Operation Triangular:
                                     Bolivia's Fate Rides With It
11-Nov   Louisville Courier-Journal Beer Boat Blues
19-Nov   National Observer   Uruguay Goes to Polls, With
                                     Economy Sagging
31-Dec   National Observer   Chatty Letters During a
                                     Journey from Aruba to Rio
1963   07-Jan   National Observer Troubled Brazil Holds Key
                                     Vote
         28-Jan   National Observer It's a Dictatorship, but Few
                                     Seem to Care Enough to
                                     Stay and Fight
         11-Feb   National Observer Daybreak at the Domino:
                                     Brazilian Soldiers Stage a
                                     Raid in Revenge
         11-Mar   National Observer Leftist Trend and Empty
                                     Treasury Plague the Latin
                                     American Giant
         15-Apr   National Observer A Never-Never Land High
                                     Above the Sea
         20-May   National Observer Election Watched as
                                     Barometer of Continent's
                                     Anti-Democratic Trend
         03-Jun   National Observer A Time for Sittin', Listenin',
                                     and Reverie
         10-Jun   National Observer He Haunts the Ruins of His
                                     Once-Great Empire
         15-Jul   National Observer Kelso Looks Just Like Any
                                     $1,307,000 Horse. . . A Day
                                     With a Champion
         22-Jul   National Observer When the Thumb Was a
                                     Ticket to Adventures on the
                                     Highway. . . The Extinct
                                     Hitchhiker
         05-Aug   National Observer Where Are the Writing
                                     Talents of Yesteryear?
         19-Aug   National Observer Why Anti-Gringo Winds
                                     Often Blow South of the
                                     Border

	02-Sep	National Observer	An Aussie Paul Bunyan Shows Our Loggers How
	09-Sep	National Observer	Executives Crank Open Philosophy's Windows
	07-Oct	National Observer	One of the Darkest Documents Ever Put Down is 'The Red Lances,'
	28-Oct	National Observer	Can Brazil Hold Out Until the Next Election?
	11-Nov	National Observer	Donleavy Proves His Lunatic Humor Is Original
	02-Dec	National Observer	The Crow, a Novelist, and a Hunt; Man in Search of His Primitive Self
	16-Dec	National Observer	What Miners Lost in Taking an Irishman
	16-Dec	National Observer	When Buck Fever Hits Larkspur's Slopes
	19-Dec	The Reporter	A Southern City With Northern Problems
1964	10-Feb	National Observer	And Now a Proletariat on Aspen's Ski Slopes
	09-Mar	National Observer	The Catch is Limited in Indians' 'Fish-In,'
	09-Mar	National Observer	Dr. Pflaum Looks at the Latins, But His View is Tired and Foggy
	20-Apr	National Observer	When The Beatniks Were Social Lions
	20-Apr	National Observer	Brazilian's Fable of a Phony Carries the Touch of Mark Twain
	27-Apr	National Observer	Golding Tries 'Lord of the Flies' Formula Again, But It Falls Short
	25-May	National Observer	What Lured Hemingway to Ketchum?
	01-Jun	National Observer	Whither the Old Copper Capital of the West? To Boom or Bust?
	15-Jun	National Observer	The Atmosphere Has Never Been Quite the Same

	22-Jun	National Observer	Why Montana's 'Shanty Irishman' Corrals Votes Year After Year
	13-Jul	National Observer	Living in the Time of Alger, Greeley, Debs
	14-Sep	National Observer	Bagpipes Wail, Cabers Fly as the Clans Gather
	28-Sep	National Observer	You'd Be Fried Like a Piece of Lean Bacon
	02-Nov	National Observer	People Want Bad Taste. . . In Everything
	21-Dec	National Observer	A Surgeon's Fingers Fashion a Literary Career
1965	17-May	The Nation	Motorcycle Gangs: Losers and Outsiders
	27-Sep	The Nation	Nonstudent Left
	Sep	Pageant	It Ain't Hardly That Way No More
	13-Oct	Spider Magazine	Collect Telegram from a Mad Dog
	Dec	Pageant	The 450-Square Mile Parking Lot
1966	Jan	Esquire	Life Styles: the Cyclist (excerpt of H.A.)
1967	26-Feb	L.A. Times	A Man's Best Friend is his Hog (excerpt of H.A.)
	26-Feb	Louisville Courier-Journal	The Motorcycle Gangs
	14-May	New York Times	The 'Hashbury' Is the Capital of the Hippies
	Aug	Pageant	Why Boys Will Be Girls
	Aug	Cavalier	Nights in the Rustic
	Nov	The Distant Drummer	The Ultimate Freelancer
1968		Collier's Encyclopedia Yearbook	The Hippies
	July	Pageant	Presenting: The Richard Nixon Doll
1969	23-Feb	Boston Globe	Memoirs of a Wretched Weekend in Washington
	Sept	Pageant	Those Daring Young Men in Their Flying Machines
1970	January	Other Scenes	How the Freaks Almost Took the Town

	Mar	Scanlan's Monthly	The Temptations of Jean-Claude Killy
	Mar-Oct	Aspen Wallposter	Various Writings
	June	Stag Annual	The "Angel" Wreckers of Bass Lake
	June	Scanlan's Monthly	The Kentucky Derby Is Decadent and Depraved
	Sept	Scanlan's Monthly	Police Chief: The Indispensable Magazine of Law Enforcement
	01-Oct	Rolling Stone	The Battle of Aspen
	08-Oct	Aspen Times	Only Serious People Can Laugh
1971	29-Apr	Rolling Stone	Strange Rumblings in Aztlan
	02-Sep	Rolling Stone	Memo From the Sports Desk: The So-Called 'Jesus-Freak' Scare
	11-Nov	Rolling Stone	Fear and Loathing in Las Vegas: A Savage Journey to the Heart of the American Dream (Part I)
	25-Nov	Rolling Stone	Fear and Loathing in Las Vegas: A Savage Journey to the Heart of the American Dream (Part II)
1972	06-Jan	Rolling Stone	Fear and Loathing in Washington: Is This Trip Necessary?
	03-Feb	Rolling Stone	Fear and Loathing In Washington: The Million Pound Shithammer
	02-Mar	Rolling Stone	Fear and Loathing in New Hampshire
	16-Mar	Rolling Stone	Fear and Loathing: The View from Key Biscayne
	13-Apr	Rolling Stone	Fear and Loathing: The Banshee Screams in Florida
	27-Apr	Rolling Stone	Fear and Loathing in Wisconsin
	11-May	Rolling Stone	Fear and Loathing: Late News from Bleak House
	08-Jun	Rolling Stone	Fear and Loathing: Crank-

			Time on the Low Road
	06-Jul	Rolling Stone	Fear and Loathing in California: Traditional Politics with a Vengeance
	20-Jul	Rolling Stone	Fear and Loathing: In the Eye of the Hurricane
	17-Aug	Rolling Stone	Fear and Loathing in Miami: Old Bulls Meet the Butcher
	28-Sep	Rolling Stone	Fear and Loathing in Miami: Nixon Bites the Bomb
	26-Oct	Rolling Stone	Fear and Loathing: The Fat City Blues
	09-Nov	Rolling Stone	Ask Not For Whom the Bell Tolls ...
1973	15-Feb	Rolling Stone	Fear and Loathing at the Superbowl: No Rest for the Wretched. . .
	05-Jul	Rolling Stone	Time Warp: Campaign 72
	02-Aug	Rolling Stone	Memo from the Sports Desk & Rude Notes from a Decompression Chamber in Miami
	27-Sep	Rolling Stone	Fear and Loathing at the Watergate: Mr. Nixon Has Cashed His Check
1974	01-Jan	New York Times	Fear and Loathing in the Bunker
	28-Feb	Rolling Stone	Fear and Loathing at the Super Bowl
	04-Jul	Rolling Stone	Fear and Loathing in Washington: It was a Nice Place. They Were Principled People, Generally
	10-Oct	Rolling Stone	Fear and Loathing in Limbo: The Scum also Rises
	Dec	Playboy	The Great Shark Hunt
1975	22-May	Rolling Stone	Fear and Loathing in Saigon: Interdicted Dispatch from the Global Affairs Desk
1976	03-Jun	Rolling Stone	Fear and Loathing on the Campaign Trail '76: Third Rate Romance, Low Rent

528

			Rendezvous
1977	15-Dec	Rolling Stone	The Banshee Screams for Buffalo Meat: Fear and Loathing in the Graveyard of the Weird
1978	04-May	Rolling Stone	Last Tango in Vegas: Fear and Loathing in the Near Room
	18-May	Rolling Stone	Last Tango in Vegas: Fear and Loathing in the Far Room
	15-Sep	Louisville Courier-Journal	Ali-Spinks (reprint of Last Tango in Vegas)
1981	April	Running	The Charge of the Weird Brigade
1983	21-Jul	Rolling Stone	A Dog Took my Place
	Dec	Playboy	The Curse of Lono (excerpt)
1984	April	Penthouse (Australia only)	The Curse of Lono (excerpt)
	24-May	Time Out Magazine	The Curse of Lono (excerpt)
	30-Aug	Rolling Stone	The Sequins were Michael's Idea (excerpt of FLLV)
1985	09-May	Rolling Stone	Dance of the Doomed
	23-Sep	San Francisco Examiner	Buffalo Gores a Visitor
	30-Sep	San Francisco Examiner	The Geek from Coral Gables
	04-Oct	San Francisco Examiner	Death to the Weird
	07-Oct	San Francisco Examiner	666 Pennsylvania Avenue
	21-Oct	San Francisco Examiner	Nixon and the Whale Woman
	28-Oct	San Francisco Examiner	Bad Nerves in Fat City
	04-Nov	San Francisco Examiner	Full-time Scrambling
	11-Nov	San Francisco Examiner	Making Travel Plans
	18-Nov	San Francisco Examiner	The Beast with Three Backs
	25-Nov	San Francisco Examiner	The Doctor will See you Now
	03-Dec	San Francisco Examiner	Revenge of the Fish Heads
	09-Dec	San Francisco Examiner	Saturday Night in the City
	16-Dec	San Francisco Examiner	A Generation of Swine
	23-Dec	San Francisco Examiner	Apres Moi, La Deluge
	30-Dec	San Francisco Examiner	The Dim and Dirty Road
1986	16-Jan	San Francisco Examiner	Off with their Heads
	13-Jan	San Francisco Examiner	How do you Spell Hitler?
	20-Jan	San Francisco Examiner	Crank Time in Tripoli

26-Jan	San Francisco Examiner	Nothing's Moving on Lincoln Avenue
27-Jan	San Francisco Examiner	Meat Sickness
03-Feb	San Francisco Examiner	Last Train from Chicago
10-Feb	San Francisco Examiner	Kill them Before they Eat
17-Feb	San Francisco Examiner	Four Million Thugs
24-Feb	San Francisco Examiner	Memo from the War Room
03-Mar	San Francisco Examiner	The Gonzo Salvage Co
10-Mar	San Francisco Examiner	Salvage is not Looting
17-Mar	San Francisco Examiner	Down at the Boca Chica
24-Mar	San Francisco Examiner	Let the Cheap Dogs Eat
31-Mar	San Francisco Examiner	Ox Butchered in Tripoli
07-Apr	San Francisco Examiner	Never get off the Boat
14-Apr	San Francisco Examiner	They Called him Deep Throat
21-Apr	San Francisco Examiner	The Pro-Flogging View
28-Apr	San Francisco Examiner	Just Another Terrorist
05-May	San Francisco Examiner	The Woman from Kiev
12-May	San Francisco Examiner	Two More Years
19-May	San Francisco Examiner	They all Drowned
26-May	San Francisco Examiner	Four More Games
02-Jun	San Francisco Examiner	Last Dance in Dumb Town
09-Jun	San Francisco Examiner	Rise of the TV Preachers
16-Jun	San Francisco Examiner	Dealing with Pigs
23-Jun	San Francisco Examiner	Deported to Malaysia
30-Jun	San Francisco Examiner	A Clean, Ill-Lighted Place
07-Jul	San Francisco Examiner	Slow Day at the Airport
14-Jul	San Francisco Examiner	Lester Maddox Lives
21-Jul	San Francisco Examiner	Sex, Drugs and Rock and Roll
04-Aug	San Francisco Examiner	Dr. Thompson's Odds for '88 Race; Campaign '88: The Early Line
11-Aug	San Francisco Examiner	Welcome to the Tunnel
18-Aug	San Francisco Examiner	Strictly Business
25-Aug	San Francisco Examiner	Midnight in the Desert
01-Sep	San Francisco Examiner	Showdown in the Pig Palace
08-Sep	San Francisco Examiner	Down to a Sunless Sea
15-Sep	San Francisco Examiner	The Turk Comes to TV News
22-Sep	San Francisco Examiner	Bull Market on the Strip
29-Sep	San Francisco Examiner	The South African Problem

	08-Oct	San Francisco Examiner	Loose Cannon on the Deck
	13-Oct	San Francisco Examiner	Let the Good Times Roll
	20-Oct	San Francisco Examiner	A Death in the Family
	03-Nov	San Francisco Examiner	The Garden of Agony
	05-Nov	San Francisco Examiner	Back to Ormsby House
	10-Nov	San Francisco Examiner	The White Helicopter
	17-Nov	San Francisco Examiner	White Trash with Money
	24-Nov	San Francisco Examiner	A Night at the Track
	30-Nov	San Francisco Examiner	The Lord and a Good Lawyer
	08-Dec	San Francisco Examiner	Ronald Reagan is Doomed
	15-Dec	San Francisco Examiner	God Bless Colonel North
	22-Dec	San Francisco Examiner	Orgy of the Dead
	29-Dec	San Francisco Examiner	The Year of the Pig
1987	05-Jan	San Francisco Examiner	Mixup at the Hospital
	12-Jan	San Francisco Examiner	The Gizzard of Darkness
	19-Jan	San Francisco Examiner	Crazy Patrick and Big Al
	26-Jan	San Francisco Examiner	Trapped in Harding Park
	02-Feb	San Francisco Examiner	The Great White Hope
	09-Feb	San Francisco Examiner	Expelled from the System
	16-Feb	San Francisco Examiner	Gone with the Wind
	23-Feb	San Francisco Examiner	New Blood on the Tracks
	03-Mar	San Francisco Examiner	The Lake of Fire
	23-Mar	San Francisco Examiner	Doomed Love in the Rockies
	30-Mar	San Francisco Examiner	The Scum of the Earth
	06-Apr	San Francisco Examiner	The Losers' Club
	13-Apr	San Francisco Examiner	Hagler Lacked Buoyancy
	20-Apr	San Francisco Examiner	The Loved Ones
	27-Apr	San Francisco Examiner	The Death Ship
	04-May	San Francisco Examiner	The American Dream
	11-May	San Francisco Examiner	Calligula & the 7 Dwarfs
	18-May	San Francisco Examiner	Memo to my Editor
	25-May	San Francisco Examiner	The Time of the Geek
	01-Jun	San Francisco Examiner	A Wild and Crazy Guy
	15-Jun	San Francisco Examiner	Ollie's Choice
	23-Jun	San Francisco Examiner	The Trickle-Down Theory
	29-Jun	San Francisco Examiner	Four More Years
	06-Jul	San Francisco Examiner	Dance of the Seven Dwarfs
	13-Jul	San Francisco Examiner	It was you, Charlie
	20-Jul	San Francisco Examiner	Fat Men on Horseback
	27-Jul	San Francisco Examiner	Cowboys at Sea
	03-Aug	San Francisco Examiner	The Honor of the Dead Bill

17-Aug	San Francisco Examiner	The Last Taxi to Scotland
09-Sep	San Francisco Examiner	Gary Hart Talks Politics
14-Sep	San Francisco Examiner	Swine of the Week
21-Sep	San Francisco Examiner	Here Come de Judge
28-Sep	San Francisco Examiner	Wooing the Degenerate Vote
05-Oct	San Francisco Examiner	The Weak and the Weird
12-Oct	San Francisco Examiner	The Time has Come
26-Oct	San Francisco Examiner	The Worm Turns
02-Nov	San Francisco Examiner	Never Apologize, Never Explain
16-Nov	San Francisco Examiner	The End of an Era
23-Nov	San Francisco Examiner	The Continental Op
30-Nov	San Francisco Examiner	The Waiver Wire
14-Dec	San Francisco Examiner	Pigs in the Wilderness
16-Dec	San Francisco Examiner	They Laughed at Thomas Edison
22-Dec	San Francisco Examiner	Back in the Saddle Again
28-Dec	San Francisco Examiner	Remembering Oscar
1988 11-Jan	San Francisco Examiner	Just Say Yes
18-Jan	San Francisco Examiner	Acid Flashback No. 327
25-Jan	San Francisco Examiner	The Hangman Cometh
27-Jan	Boston Globe	No Paranoia for Mecham; Fears are Justified
08-Feb	San Francisco Examiner	The Wimp Croaks in Iowa
15-Feb	San Francisco Examiner	The Fat is in the Fire
17-Feb	San Francisco Examiner	Miracle in N.H.: Resurrection of George Bush
17-Feb	Boston Globe	Robertson May Put Fat in the Fire
22-Feb	San Francisco Examiner	The Hellfire Club
29-Feb	San Francisco Examiner	High Man on a Seesaw
09-Mar	San Francisco Examiner	It's all Over Now, Baby Blue
14-Mar	San Francisco Examiner	Darkness at Noon
21-Mar	San Francisco Examiner	The Other George Bush
24-Mar	Boston Globe	A Blaze of Gibberish on Bush
28-Mar	San Francisco Examiner	Guess Who's Coming to Dinner?
30-Mar	Boston Globe	Wearing the McGovern Tattoo
04-Apr	San Francisco Examiner	There Go the Foundations
16-Apr	San Francisco Examiner	If it Rains, You Lose

25-Apr	San Francisco Examiner	A Sickness Unto Death
09-May	San Francisco Examiner	Underground Journalism
23-May	San Francisco Examiner	Doctor Baker Will See You Now
25-May	Boston Globe	Sorting Out the Weird Ones
30-May	San Francisco Examiner	The Drug War at Waterloo
06-Jun	San Francisco Examiner	Apartment in Borneo
13-Jun	San Francisco Examiner	Static Detonates the Gel
20-Jun	San Francisco Examiner	I Told you it was Wrong
27-Jun	San Francisco Examiner	The Student Prince
11-Jul	San Francisco Examiner	The Whole World is Watching
20-Jul	San Francisco Examiner	800-lb Gorilla
22-Jul	San Francisco Examiner	The Family Doctor
25-Jul	San Francisco Examiner	Why is this Man Whining?
21-Aug	San Francisco Examiner	The Seas of Politics Often Lead to Silliness
22-Aug	San Francisco Examiner	President Quayle?
12-Sep	San Francisco Examiner	Weird Today, Gone Tomorrow
19-Sep	San Francisco Examiner	Post-Hypnotic Transgressions
27-Sep	San Francisco Examiner	Bush's Big Deal: Just a Slip of the Tongue?
Fall	Smart	The Man Without a Country
03-Oct	San Francisco Examiner	There is no Pulse
06-Oct	San Francisco Examiner	When Quayle Wrapped Himself in JFK's Mantle
10-Oct	San Francisco Examiner	The Meaning of Life in 250 Words
14-Oct	San Francisco Examiner	No Hits, No Errors in Debate
07-Nov	San Francisco Examiner	Last Train from Camelot / I Slit My Own Eyeballs
22-Nov	San Francisco Examiner	The New Dumb
06-Dec	San Francisco Examiner	They Also Serve, Who Only Stand and Feed
13-Dec	San Francisco Examiner	Love in the Age of Greed
21-Dec	San Francisco Examiner	Year of the Alligator
1989 09-Jan	San Francisco Examiner	Let's You and Him Fight
30-Jan	San Francisco Examiner	Fear & Loathing in Sacramento

	06-Feb	San Francisco Examiner	Strange Ride to Reno
	13-Feb	San Francisco Examiner	Omnia Vincit Amor
	27-Feb	San Francisco Examiner	The Death of Russell Chatham
	06-Mar	San Francisco Examiner	Whiskey Business
	13-Mar	San Francisco Examiner	I Knew her When She Used to Rock & Roll
	03-Apr	San Francisco Examiner	Another Vicious Attack
	10-Apr	San Francisco Examiner	No More Semper Fi
	22-May	San Francisco Examiner	Don't Tread on Me
	29-May	San Francisco Examiner	Let the Hundred Flowers Bloom
	26-Jun	San Francisco Examiner	[Title in Chinese Characters]
	31-Jul	San Francisco Examiner	The Bull Market
	07 Aug	San Francisco Examiner	Welcome to the Abyssal Zone
	30-Aug	San Francisco Examiner	Nightmare on Thunder Road
	26-Sep	San Francisco Examiner	The Rich are Still Hungry
	20-Nov	San Francisco Examiner	The German Decade
1990	05-Feb	San Francisco Examiner	Medical Bulletin #666 - We Think
	May	Northwest Extra	Community of Whores
1990	01-Nov	Rolling Stone	Welcome to the Nineties: Gunfight at the Gonzo Corral
1991	Feb	Esquire	Year of the Wolf
	March	Esquire	Where Were You When the Fun Stopped?
	02-Mar	War News	Untitled Fax
	April	Esquire	Death of a Sportsman
	30-May	Rolling Stone	Memo: The Taming of the Shrew
1992	23-Jan	Rolling Stone	Fear and Loathing in Elko
	11-Jun	Rolling Stone	Fear and Loathing in Las Vegas: A Savage Return to the Heart of the American Dream
	17-Sep	Rolling Stone	Bill Clinton: The Rolling Stone Interview; Dr. Thompson on Mr. Bill's Neighborhood
	October	Playboy	The Unmaking of the President
	04-Oct	Observer Magazine	Fear and Loathing at the

			Palace
1994	16-Jun	Rolling Stone	He was a Crook
	15-Dec	Rolling Stone	Polo Is My Life: Fear and Loathing in Horse Country
1996	08-Aug	Rolling Stone	Mistah Leary, He Dead
1997	12-Jun	Rolling Stone	Proud Highway (excerpt)
	18-Sep	Rolling Stone	The Shootist
	10-Nov	Cycle World	Song of the Sausage Creature
1998	19-Mar	Rolling Stone	Memo from the National Affairs Desk
	Nov	Esquire	The Rum Diary (excerpt)
1999	13-Mar	Rolling Stone	Hey Rube! I Love You: Eerie Reflections on Fuel, Madness & Music
2000	06-Nov	ESPN Page 2	Baseball Has Become Unruly
	13-Nov	ESPN Page 2	Just Binge, Baby!
	20-Nov	ESPN Page 2	Prepare for the Weirdness
	27-Nov	ESPN Page 2	The Fix is in
	Dec	Vanity Fair	Postal Disturbances (excerpts from Fear and Loathing in America)
	04-Dec	ESPN Page 2	The FNL, Election & Generation Z
	11-Dec	ESPN Page 2	State of Disgrace
	18-Dec	ESPN Page 2	Ready for Sainthood
	25-Dec	ESPN Page 2	Gambling Fever
2001	02-Jan	ESPN Page 2	The Curse of Musburger
	08-Jan	ESPN Page 2	Watch the Economy Shrink While Breasts Expand
	15-Jan	ESPN Page 2	Fear & Loathing on Super Sunday
	22-Jan	ESPN Page 2	Abandon All Hope Ye in Tampa… and Washington
	29-Jan	ESPN Page 2	Giants, Gamblers Go Down in a Ball of Fire
	05-Feb	ESPN Page 2	Several Grave Injustices
	12-Feb	ESPN Page 2	Mad Cows and Sick Sports
	19-Feb	ESPN Page 2	Death in the Afternoon
	21-Feb	ESPN Page 2	XFL, RIP
	Mar	Men's Health	Total, Utter Confusion
	Mar-Ap	Mountain Gazette	Politics & the F-word

05-Mar	ESPN Page 2	A Crime Against Nature
12-Mar	ESPN Page 2	Warning to Gamblers: Beware the Ides of March
19-Mar	ESPN Page 2	Cat Scratch Fever
26-Mar	ESPN Page 2	Memo from a Gambling Victim
30-Mar	ESPN Page 2	Where Were You When the Fun Stopped?
09-Apr	ESPN Page 2	Notes on the Wrong Way to Gamble
16-Apr	ESPN Page 2	NBA and the Downward Spiral of Dumbness
23-Apr	ESPN Page 2	Bad Craziness at Owl Farm
30-Apr	ESPN Page 2	Can the Three Stooges Save the NBA?
May	Harper's	Hunter Goes to Hollywood
07-May	ESPN Page 2	Kentucky Derby and Other Gambling Disasters
14-May	ESPN Page 2	Going to War for Justice
21-May	ESPN Page 2	How 'bout that Patrick Roy
28-May	ESPN Page 2	Patrick Roy and Warren Zevon - Two Champions at the Top of their Game
04-Jun	ESPN Page 2	Jack Kerouac and the Football Hall of Fame
11-Jun	ESPN Page 2	Wild Days at the Sports Desk
14-Jun	ESPN Page 2	Cockfighting - a Savage & Noble Sport
20-Jun	ESPN Page 2	Eerie Lull Rattles the Sports World
25-Jun	ESPN Page 2	Olympic Disaster in Utah
02-Jul	ESPN Page 2	Hey Rube' Goes to Hollywood
10-Sep	ESPN Page 2	The Wisdom of Nashville and Violence of Jack Nicholson: A Football Story
12-Sep	ESPN Page 2	Fear & Loathing in America
18-Sep	ESPN Page 2	When War Drums Roll
25-Sep	ESPN Page 2	Will Sports Survive Bin Laden?
02-Oct	ESPN Page 2	Stadium Living in New Age
10-Oct	ESPN Page 2	Football in the Kingdom of Fear

	17-Oct	ESPN Page 2	Banish Cowboys, 'Skins - Forever
	23-Oct	ESPN Page 2	Foul Balls and Rash Predictions
	31-Oct	ESPN Page 2	Getting Weird for Devil's Day
	06-Nov	ESPN Page 2	The Yankees are Dead; Long Live the Yankees
	12-Nov	ESPN Page 2	The Man who Loved Sports too Much
	20-Nov	ESPN Page 2	The Shame of Indianapolis
	27-Nov	ESPN Page 2	Revenge of the 49ers
	06-Dec	ESPN Page 2	Failure, Football & Violence on the Strip
	11-Dec	ESPN Page 2	Madness in Honolulu
	18-Dec	ESPN Page 2	Skunks Like Me
2002	14-Jan	ESPN Page 2	Break up the Ravens
	21-Jan	ESPN Page 2	Pay up or Get Whpped
	29-Jan	ESPN Page 2	Braced for the Last Football Game
	14-Feb	ESPN Page 2	Domestic Terrorism at the Super Bowl
	25-Feb	ESPN Page 2	Ed Bradley & the Stigma of Bull Worship
	05-Mar	ESPN Page 2	For What it's Worth
	19-Mar	ESPN Page 2	Be Like George - Bet on Kentucky
	28-Mar	ESPN Page 2	Slow Dance in Rap Town
	30-Apr	ESPN Page 2	Dr. Thompson in Beirut
	24-Sep	ESPN Page 2	Dr. Thompson is Back from Beirut
	09-Oct	ESPN Page 2	Walking Tall in the Sport of Swine
	14-Oct	ESPN Page 2	The NFL Uber Alles
	28-Oct	ESPN Page 2	Blood on the Walls of Hollywood
	05-Nov	ESPN Page 2	My 49er Habit
	11-Nov	ESPN Page 2	Don't Let This Happen to You
	25-Nov	ESPN Page 2	White Death in the Rockies
	03-Dec	ESPN Page 2	Grantland Rice Haunts the Honolulu Marathon

537

	16-Dec	ESPN Page 2	The Honolulu Marathon is Decadent and Depraved
2003	02-Jan	ESPN Page 2	The Death of the 49ers
	07-Jan	ESPN Page 2	Public Shame and Private Victory
	13-Jan	ESPN Page 2	Oakland Uber Alles
	20-Jan	ESPN Page 2	The Last Super Bowl
	27-Jan	ESPN Page 2	Super Bowl Fool
	29-Jan	ESPN Page 2	Braced for the Last Football Game
	03-Feb	ESPN Page 2	Extreme Behavior
	19-Feb	ESPN Page 2	A World of Pain
	03-Mar	ESPN Page 2	Saturday Night at the Fights
	11-Mar	ESPN Page 2	Kentucky Uber Alles
	26-Mar	ESPN Page 2	Love Blooms in the Rockies
	31-Mar	ESPN Page 2	Love in the Time of War
	Apr-May	Relix	Jesus Hated Bald Pussy (excerpt from Kingdom of Fear)
	10-Apr	ESPN Page 2	A Sad Week in America
	18-Apr	ESPN Page 2	Back in the Day
	21-Apr	ESPN Page 2	The Tragedy of Naked Bowling
	01-May	ESPN Page 2	The Royal Wedding
	06-May	ESPN Page 2	Seventh Heaven
	10-May	Daily Telegraph	Night of the Hunter (excerpt from Kingdom of Fear)
	12-May	ESPN Page 2	The Sport of Kings
	21-May	ESPN Page 2	The Good, The Bad and the Vicious
	27-May	ESPN Page 2	Rewarding the Ugly
	02-Jun	ESPN Page 2	Killed by a Speeding Hummer
	10-Jun	ESPN Page 2	Thoroughbred Conspiracy Theory
	Jul-Aug	Adbusters	Untitled essay
	22-Jul	ESPN Page 2	Welcome to the Big Darkness
	28-Jul	ESPN Page 2	The Nation's Capital
	12-Aug	ESPN Page 2	On in a Million
	19-Aug	ESPN Page 2	Not so Sweet Dreams
	25-Aug	ESPN Page 2	Speed will Rule the NFL
	08-Sep	ESPN Page 2	Death of an American Poet
	09-Sep	ESPN Page 2	Bush League

	15-Sep	ESPN Page 2	Soured on the Sweet Science
	29-Sep	ESPN Page 2	George Plimpton Uber Alles
	08-Oct	ESPN Page 2	A Bad Bet
	14-Oct	ESPN Page 2	Fast and Furious
	28-Oct	ESPN Page 2	Submitting to Sports
	04-Nov	ESPN Page 2	Wild Monday Night in Denver
	18-Nov	ESPN Page 2	Am I Turning into a Pervert?
	25-Nov	ESPN Page 2	In your Dreams, Buddy
	09-Dec	ESPN Page 2	Running Wild
2004	January	Playboy	Fear and Justice in the Kingdom of Sex
	13-Jan	ESPN Page 2	Being a Betting Man
	19-Jan	ESPN Page 2	Note to Self
	28-Jan	ESPN Page 2	Mr. Brady Goes to Washington
	03-Feb	ESPN Page 2	The Final Score
	11-Feb	ESPN Page 2	Goose Bumps
	18-Feb	ESPN Page 2	Presidential No-No
	18-Mar	ESPN Page 2	Tournament Time
	23-Mar	ESPN Page 2	Kentucky's Disgrace
	30-Mar	ESPN Page 2	Duke's a Hazzard
	06-Apr	ESPN Page 2	No Contest
	13-Apr	ESPN Page 2	Strange Days
	18-May	ESPN Page 2	Let's Go to the Olympics!
	25-May	ESPN Page 2	Let's Get Physical
	June	Vanity Fair	Prison of Denver
	06-Jul	ESPN Page 2	Security Blanket
	14-Jul	ESPN Page 2	Buy My Book!
	27-Jul	ESPN Page 2	Don't You Dare
	10-Aug	ESPN Page 2	Opening Bet
	25-Aug	ESPN Page 2	Stirring the Pot
	15-Sep	ESPN Page 2	Just Pay Up
	02-Nov	ESPN Page 2	D-Day
	09-Nov	ESPN Page 2	End of Days
	11-Nov	Rolling Stone	The Fun-Hogs in the Passing Lane
	30-Nov	ESPN Page 2	State of Emergency
	16-Dec	ESPN Page 2	Monday Night Fools
	21-Dec	ESPN Page 2	A Monster Weekend
2005	15-Feb	ESPN Page 2	Shotgun Golf with Bill Murray

Index

544

Printed in Great Britain
by Amazon

70814836R00315